Becoming Hindus and Muslims

Reading the Cultural Encounter in Bengal 1342–1905

Saumya Dey

Munshiram Manoharlal Publishers Pvt. Ltd.

इति सज्जनः परार्थघटकाः स्वार्थे परित्यज्य ये

ISBN 978-81-215-1290-9
First published 2015

PRINTED IN INDIA
Published by Vikram Jain *for*
Munshiram Manoharlal Publishers Pvt. Ltd.
PO Box 5715, 54 Rani Jhansi Road, New Delhi 110 055, INDIA

www.mrmlbooks.com

Contents

Acknowledgements

THIS BOOK ORIGINATED AS A PHD THESIS written under the supervision of Prof. Bhagwan Josh at the Centre for Historical Studies, Jawaharlal Nehru University. I am grateful for all the help, support and encouragement I received from Prof. Josh while under his tutelage.

I owe some special thanks to Mr B.R. Das who taught me Hisotry in school. Mr Das patiently listened to the febrile ramblings of my sixteen year old self and lent order and direction to my thoughts and readings. Thank you Sir, for providing me guidance when I needed it most.

I am grateful to the staff of National Library, Asiatic Society Library and Bangiya Sahitya Parishad, Kolkata, for their help and cooperation. I owe a special mention to Mr Subhash Behera at the Asiatic Society Library for helping me locate the *Bibidhārtha-Saṅgraha* in its musty basement.

I am grateful to Prof. Momin Chaudhary and Prof. Mohammad Aksadul-'Ālam at the Department of History, University of Dhaka, for making my trip to Dhaka possible. Besides, I owe my most earnest thanks to Mr Mohammad Moizuddin Khan, Deputy Librarian, Dhaka University Library, and all the library staff. Their efficiency and readiness to help made my trip a most fruitful one. I must also thank all those numerous people who showered me with warmth, kindness and affection during my stay in Bangladesh. I do not know their names but do know for sure that they make me want to return to that beautiful country of kind, warm-hearted people.

Thanks are due to Saswata, Manas, and Maheep without

whose help at crucial stages this book would not have seen the light of the day.

Finally, I am grateful to Ma and Baba, my twin lodestars. Thank you, for you inspired me to wonder how far away are the stars and how deep the oceans. Thank you, for never scolding me for all the toys and gadgets I took apart as a child and did not manage to put back together. Thank you, for never losing faith in me and always standing by me, even when I let you down. This modest effort of mine has emerged from the curiosity and sense of wonderment you instilled and encouraged in me as a child.

SAUMYA DEY

New Delhi
26 January 2015

Introduction

[This book has a clumsy title, but it is one which meets the purpose. *Making*, because it is a study in an active process, which owes as much to agency as to conditioning. The working class did not rise like the sun at an appointed time. It was present at its own making.]

—E.P. Thompson, *The Making of the English Working Class*[1]

[What we have in mind with the term "history" is not so much 'the past' in the sense of that which is past, but rather *derivation [Herkunft]* from such a past. Anything that 'has a history' stands in the context of a becoming. In such becoming, 'development' is sometimes a rise, sometimes a fall. What 'has a history' in this way can, at the same time, 'make' such history. As 'epoch making,' it determines 'a future' 'in the present.' Here "history" signifies a 'context' of events and 'effects,' which draws on through 'the past,' the 'present,' and the 'future.']

—Martin Heidegger, *Being and Time*[2]

WRITING HALF A CENTURY AGO, E.P. Thompson demonstrated that the working class did not explode upon history, fully formed and with an innate revolutionary consciousness, with the emergence of industrial civilisation. Thus, his masterpiece traced what things shaped the working class and, more importantly, how it shaped itself, how "it was present at its own making." Like Thompson, we too wish to study an "active process" and establish that Hindus and Muslims did not "rise like the sun" at the appointed moment—the coming of colonialism to the Indian subcontinent. Instead, they "became" through a great diversity of consciously made choices. The word "becoming," as a result, and the process implied by it, will form the core of our methodology. Because, like Heidegger, we too believe that history is derivation from a past and "stands in the context of a becoming." We find it implausible that the immense numbers of the subcontinent discovered their passionately contested religious allegiances suddenly in the nineteenth century upon being prodded by the white man. For long this has been the narrative, the result of a "primacy attributed to colonialism in forming contemporary Indian identities."[3] An example of this primacy is Sandria Freitag's argument that the "process of forging group identities" was "part prompted by the efforts of an alien British administration to identify the constituent units in Indian society." As a result, she says, "drawing on European historical experience, the administrators applied the collective labels 'Hindu' and 'Muslim' to groups who were far from homogeneous communities."[4] An understanding as Freitag assumes that before the arrival of colonialism Indians were either not aware of or not using the group labels "Hindu" and "Muslim." Her kind of analysis is also completely oblivious of cultural encounters which began with the arrival of Islamic ideas and modes of worship in India. Hence, a narrative like the one presented by Freitag fails to explain the perceptions of, or prejudices for, each other we find individuals or groups calling themselves "Hindus" and "Muslims" holding and expressing long before an alien administration arrived on the Indian scene. Though it ought to, if these group labels were, after all, fabricated by colonialism. We do not deny, however, that the colonial state's interventions and the vocabulary used by it to describe the community signifiers *helped* the process of consolidation of individuals under collective labels. Freitag's narrative also does not explain the coexistence of multiple codes of consciousness, of conflict and concord, friction and accommodation which always marked, and still marks, the interaction of Hindus and Muslims. Nor can we gather from it as to why, from the very beginnings of political agitation in colonial India, the language employed by the protagonists was one of cultural exclusivity. Our tale will take an amble down the long centuries and look for answers to these questions in leaves of verse and prose etched in a corner of the pre-colonial subcontinent—Bengal. We will observe the becoming of the "Hindus" and "Muslims" and witness how our protagonists were consciously at work to become what they did. We will deal at length with their cultural encounters long before the colonial official strode in with the census register. Like Thompson's workers, we will find them present at their own becoming.

Today, Bengali speaking Muslims form one of the largest Muslim communities in the world. The result is Bangladesh, located thousands of miles away from the desert peninsula where Islam had its beginnings, being the third largest Muslim country in absolute demographic terms. Legend has it that the region fell to Turkish cavalrymen on a fateful day in the year 1204. The ensuing centuries saw the rule of the Ilyas Shahis[5] and the Husain Shahis.[6] They were followed by the Mughals who established their sway over Bengal in the final decades of the sixteenth century.[7] These centuries saw the expansion of Islam in this easternmost margin of the subcontinent. Apparently, the diffusion of Islam in Bengal was gradual. Richard M. Eaton locates its final spurt in the decades following the establishment of Mughal rule. As understood by him, the process was driven by the promotion and expansion of the agrarian economy in the region by the new state.[8]

Islam, planted in the fertile deltaic soil of Bengal, became of it. This belief system, as also the cultural complex surrounding it, expressed itself in the language of the soil. Alongside, Bengali grew in refinement and firmly established itself as a literary language under the rule of the Muslim dynasties. Fourteenth century onwards, the language cast forth a prolific *kāvya* tradition. *Maṅgala kāvyas* and *vijaya kāvyas* were the two main strands that twined to make this luxuriant vine. The former were mainly devotional odes to the various demigods and goddesses while the latter sang their triumph or of the Prophet of Islam. Enduring till the eighteenth century, the tradition was authored and nurtured by both non-Muslim and Muslim hands. The *kāvyas* form a voluble repository of the universe of emotions and experience of the age and reveal its constant becoming. They, thus, provide the ideal material with which to illustrate the process of the becoming of "Hindus" and "Muslims." A substantial part of this book is based on the material available in these texts.

Eaton posits Islam as contriving itself into a web of beliefs which were yet indeterminate and unself-conscious. As seen by him, the Islamic deity was first identified with the existing deities and in the course of time supplanted them. As he claims, "one readily sees local cosmologies expanding in order to accommodate new superhuman beings introduced by foreign Muslims"[9] in the corpus of the pre-modern literature produced in Bengali. He, however, cites no concrete evidence or source to cast light on the complex mechanisms of this process. All Eaton does to substantiate his thesis is to provide us with a scrap from an East Bengal ballad.[10] What aided this process of accommodation was also the fact that, as he avers, there were groups of people in Eastern Bengal who had not yet been incorporated in the Hindu social order. This was the case, for example, in Chittagong.[11] We will, thus, begin by trying to form an idea of the social organisation and religious beliefs of the region from a set of contemporary texts. Then, we will attempt to get a measure of the perception of Islam from the *kāvyas* of non-Muslim authorship. We will note that they yield a weave of emotions, sentiments and anxieties which makes for a cogent religious cosmos. This cosmos has sharply defined deities enshrined within its bounds and yields evidence that religious identities had had their beginnings. Beginning with the fourteenth century, Bengal saw the emergence of the cult of numerous folk deities. Mostly strong willed and irascible goddesses, it does not appear to us that they were very amenable to identification with any deity from without the bounds of their cosmos. The *kāvyas* of non-Muslim authorship, thus, evince a cultural vocabulary which is very conscious of its distinctiveness, though, as we will see, it was sometimes permeated with ambiguities and ambivalences. Most importantly, we have their authors calling themselves and their audience "Hindu" in a denominational sense. They also, apparently, are cognizant of Islam forming a distinct complex of culture and belief. These description of the practices and professions of the Muslims are borne out very well by Kavi Kankan Mukunda in the *Chandimangal* (চণ্ডিমঙ্গল) *kāvya.* The *kāvyas* of non-Muslim authorship also often associate Islam with peoples of foreign provenance, such as Mughals and Pathans, and sometimes with state-power represented in the form of some zealot *qāzī.* In the end, they betray anxieties, as done by the authors of *Manasā Mangal* (মনসা মঙ্গল) and *Śrī Chaitanya Bhāgbat* (শ্রীচৈতন্যভাগবত) when they put in their tales the archetypal zealot *qāzī* bent on effacing what he terms *Hinduāni.* It seems obvious that in some form the presence of Islam was contributing to the becoming of the "Hindu." One study, for example, notes the Vaishnavas calling themselves "Hindu" only when engaging with the Muslims.[12]

The poets of the age who strove to be "Muslim" also perceive a cultural cosmos which is parallel and different. This is what someone like Alaol, a poet in the far off court of Arakan, apparently does when he mentions *Hinduāni* as being one of the several things that his guru was versed in.[13] Unlike what is claimed by Eaton, the verses of these poets too reveal no perceptible sign that any process of conflation of deities across cosmogonies was on. True, we have one Daulat Qazi referring to *Allāh* with the Sanskritic sobriquet of *niranjan.*[14] But Qazi is also unflinchingly sure that it is *sharī'ah* alone that can lead to this deity. It is as though the poets of the age are speaking with the aid of two very distinctive cultural thesauri and are acutely aware of the fact. Only, they will often look for a cognate in the other's thesaurus for a word or an artifact drawn from their own.

To someone even casually surveying the literary landscape of medieval Bengal it will appear that the poets who revered the Prophet were often anxious to escape the time and place that they issued from. The result was several of their tales being located in Arabia and Persia rather than the native soil. It is almost as if they had self consciously attained a state of emotional secession from it. The seemingly prosaic act of expressing oneself in the language of the land could be a source of trepidation too. Thus, there is the fifteenth century poet Shah Mohammad Saghir trying to dispel this dread among his co-religionists. He assures his audience that the truth of the word does not depend on the language it is expressed in. Apparently, this dread existed for a long time without dissipating. Several poets like Mojammil Haq in the fifteenth, and Syed Sultan and Sheikh Mutalib in the sixteenth and seventeenth centuries AD, hint at opinion that disapproved of writing in Bengali. However, as our poets displayed defiance and composed verses in the tongue of the land, they also strove towards the "purity" of faith. Apparently, they viewed a sort of contradiction between the nature of their faith and the existing language with its given signifiers. As a result, acquiring a new faith also necessitated the construction of a new idiom with its own signifiers. This meant that our poets often took to creating fantasy worlds in which *Hinduāni* will be dissolved and which will furnish a new language adequate to convey the new belief system. We encounter this being attempted in several texts over the centuries. In the fifteenth century *Rasul Bijay* (রসুল বিজয়), for example, the poet Zainuddin had a fictional king of Iraq beaten by the Prophet. Interestingly, this king, though ruling a land far from Zainuddin's, followed the Vedas. In the next century, Syed Sultan began creation with the Indic deities in his *Nabibangśa* (নবিবংশ), a genealogy of the prophets. He also had the Vedas revealed to them by *Allāh.* But this creation had to be dissolved and another begun because of moral depravity. The Deity now had the Vedas cast in the ocean and sent down the *Qur'ān.* Interestingly, Syed Sultan displayed the Prophet fighting *Hinduāni* in his own family before he could establish Islam. The local reality was transferred to Arabia and defeated.

A tension thus came to permeate the articulations of the inhabitants of two distinct cultural complexes. There was, as it appears, also an attempt to speak across the chasm which was being opened up. We have already noted the instance of Daulat Qazi addressing *Allāh* as *niranjan.* We also see a Muslim character exclaim to a *qāzī* who is about to wreck the altar of goddess Manasa in the *Bāis Kabīr Manasā-Mangal bā Bāisā* (বাইশ কবির মনসা-মঙ্গল বা বাইসা) that both the Hindu and the Muslim are watched over by the same God. On occasions like these our poets seem to be consciously contrapuntal with their voices sounding like two entwined and distinct melodies played upon the same musical time. But unlike as in music, it does not appear that harmony was what they intended at. In their case one theme will always be louder and more distinct and will either muffle or subsume the other. The bigoted *qāzī* of *Manasā-Mangal* of course does not heed the well meaning Muslim. Insouciant, he goes on to desecrate the altar of Manasā. In the end, he is punished by the goddess in the most gruesome fashion and has to submit to her. In fact, the narrative of conquest or conflict appears in the works of non-Muslim poets more frequently than in their "Muslim" compatriots. We will come across several such instances, in the *Śrī Chaitanya Bhāgbat, Śrī Chaitanya Charitāmrita* (শ্রী চৈতন্য চরিতামৃত), *Śītalāmangal* (শিতলামঙ্গল) and *Annadāmangal* (অন্নদামঙ্গল). Each of these texts tells the story of the conquest and conversion of a Muslim. In the

Annadāmangal the Mughal Emperor Jahangir himself has to submit to the goddess Annapurna to save his capital from starvation and an army of ghouls.

With our path charted by the *kāvyas,* we shall move on to study the developments of the second half of the eighteenth century and the first half of the nineteenth. The *kāvyas,* it ought to be obvious by now, formed a monumental emotional inheritance as far as the mutual perceptions of individuals and groups striving to be "Hindu" and "Muslim" are concerned. The tradition lingered on till the early decades of the nineteenth century. The *kāvyas,* apparently, still displayed the tensions and anxieties of the earlier centuries. In Vishnu Pala's *Manasā Mangal* (বিষ্ণু পালের মনসামঙ্গল), dating to the cusp of the eighteenth and nineteenth centuries, we see the brothers Hasan and Husain emerging from the crescent upon lord Śiva's head. However, their divine origins notwithstanding, the goddess Manasā chastens the brothers pitilessly when they invite her wrath and spares them only upon earning their submission. There is also evidence that the *kāvya* tradition had begun to employ a hero-villain duality to narrate its stories. Despite all the conflict that they depict, we suggest, the medieval *kāvyas* had not employed this trope. The characters conflicting in them seem only to aid the conversation of two sacral universes. It is suggested that the cow killing villain of the *kāvya Gaurī-Mangal* (গৌরি মঙ্গল) is actually an allegorical representation of the British. The text dates to 1806 and was composed by one Raja Prithwichandra of the state of Pankur. This transformation and restructuring of the mode of tale telling, thus, couched the potential of investing a narrative with a political and ideological charge. Nevertheless, *kāvyas* produced by non-Muslim hands were now rare, but the "Muslim" versifiers were still as prolific as in the olden days. They, as the Satyapir and Manikpir *pānchālis* produced in the last decades of the eighteenth and the early years of the nineteenth century reveal, now produced conquest mythologies. These miracle working *pīrs* were excellent at forcing homage out of the unbeliever.

The language that the Muslims were writing had changed too. Seventeenth century onwards there had been a wont on the part of the Muslim authors to infuse words of Arabic and Persian extraction into Bengali. Now the trend came to a head as they created almost a distinct language later identified as *Musalmānī Bānglā.* By the early nineteenth century they seem to have commanded a rather obvious audience among a certain section of the Muslims. According to Sukumar Sen, it was the "illiterate people"[15] of Calcutta who read their works drawn from the Hindi, Urdu, and Persian popular romances. Rousing our curiosity further, he points out that this new "Muslim Bengali" was the work of the West Bengal Muslim authors. This intercrossed language found favour with their East Bengal co-religionists not before the end of the nineteenth century. Was the West Bengal Muslim reacting to a cultural anxiety brought forth by the extinction of the Nawabi state? Whatever the reason, there was a perceptible discomfiture with Sanskritised Bengali, as evidenced by authors like Mālé Mohammad and Mohammad Danesh. The discomfiture could only have been exacerbated as the Bengali language was more and more made to correspond to Sanskrit in the early decades of the nineteenth century.

Meanwhile, from the first half of the eighteenth century itself, the European intercessions were introducing the Bengali language to a set of seminal changes. Probably the first printed text in Bengali, *Crepar Xaxtrer Orth, bhed,* was produced by the Portuguese church at Dhaka.[16] In the absence of a Bengali type the Portuguese had to print the text in the Roman type. Later, in 1778, Charles Wilkins devised a Bengali type for the publication of Nathaniel Brassey Halhed's *Grammar of the Bengali Language.* Bengali, thus, moved into the age of print.

Bengali moved into the age of prose with the founding

of the Fort William College in 1800. The college entrusted the *munshis* and *pundits* in its employ with the task of producing literary and scientific works and translations in the Bengali language. As a part of this endeavour, *Rājā Pratāpāditya Charitra* (রাজা প্রতাপাদিত্য চরিত্র), discussed in the third chapter, was written by *pundit* Ram Ram Basu in 1801. The *Charitra* is the hagiography of a potentate who ruled the Jessore region in the early years of the seventeenth century and briefly resisted the Mughal advance. Though a nondescript effort in stuttering prose, it is significant for one reason. Basu's work seems to be an inheritor to the emotional world of the *kāvyas.* The *Charitra* purports to be history, but presents a fantastical landscape full of enchantment and eloquent with omens. It is worth noting that Basu heavily drew upon Bharatchandra's *Annadāmangal kāvya* dating to 1752 for putting together his tale. However, besides a numinous construction of the world, very likely inherited from the *kāvyas,* the *Chritra* displays something strikingly new. The narrative of the *Charitra* is seemingly privy to an ideological and political charge. The words put by Basu in the mouth of a character called Daud when he is plotting rebellion against the Emperor in Delhi reveal to us how the faultline[17] rested in our author's consciousness. Basu makes the character confess that India does indeed more genuinely belong to the Hindus. "This country belongs to the Hindus," Says Daud, "and the Muslims won it by the force of arms. The emperor at Delhi is a Muslim and so am I. Then on what grounds does he expect tribute from me and why at all should I pay him any":

> এ হেঁদুর দেশ তাহারদের অধিকার। মোছলমানেরা আপন পরাক্রমে এ রাজ্য করতলে করিয়াছেন। দিল্লিপতী মোছলমান আমিও সেই জাতি। তবে তিনিই বা কিমার্থে আমার কাছে কর লএন এবং আমিবা কেন তাঁহাকে কর দেই।[18]

The first native explorations of the craft of writing

"scientific" history in Bengali were also made in the first half of the nineteenth century. The groundbreaker in the area was Rajendralal Mitra, the librarian of the Asiatic Society from 1846 to 1856, started the journal *Bibidhārtha-Saṅgraha* (বিবিধার্থ সঙ্গ্রহ) in 1851. The *Bibidhārtha* tried to cast light on the various periods of Indian history, from the most ancient to the more recent Mughal past. Rajendralal, however, seems to have had a special fondness for the history of the Rājputs and the Marathas. Their history was indeed worth a special mention, the journal wrote in 1857. It was due to the reason that, unlike the rest of the country, despite lying under the dominance of the Yavans, they had not desisted from broadcasting the glories of the nobility and valour of their respective national greats:

> . . . মহারাষ্ট্র ও রাজপুত জাতীয়েরা যবনাধীন হইয়াও স্ব স্ব জাতীয় মহদ্যুক্তিদিগের মহত্ব ও বলবীর্যের গরিমা প্রকাশ করনে বিরত হয়েন নাই।[19]

From the very beginning *Bibidhārtha* saw itself as correcting the historical amnesia of the Indians. The very first issue of *Bibidhārtha* carried an instalment of the history of Sikhs, *Sikh Itihās* (শিখ ইতিহাস), meant to be continued in the subsequent numbers. It was introduced with the following words:

> The people of this country have an apathy for history. This is on account of the ancient texts current as history in our country being so full of supernatural actions. Valmiki's *Rāmāyana* and Vyasa's *Mahābhārata* have been anointed as histories and accepted and adored in the land by all. However, divine characters being so abundant in them, their fantastical descriptions can barely ever be imagined as the aspects of humans.
>
> পুরাবৃত বিষয়ে এতস্কেশিয় মনুষ্যেরা এক প্রকার বিতরাগই আছে। ইহার মুখ্য কারন এই যে পূর্ব্বপর যে সকল প্রাচিন গ্রন্থ অস্মদেশে প্রচলিত তন্মধ্যস্থ পুরাবৃত সকল আলৌকিক ক্রিয়াতে পরিপূর্ন। ভগবান বাল্মীকি ও বেদব্যাস কৃত রামায়ত ও মহাভারতাদি গ্রন্থ-সকল ইতিহাসস্থানে অভিষিক্ত হইয়া দেশমান্য ও সর্ব্বগ্রগন্যরূপে গনিত হইয়াছে বটে, কিন্তু তত্তদগ্রন্থে দৈব-চরিত্রের বাহুল্য-হেতুক তৎ সমস্ত উৎকট-বর্ননা মনুষ্য-

চরিত্রমধ্যে গ্রাহ্য করা দুরহ।[20]

The writer assumed that the readers will be eager to learn about the Sikhs, for even the proud Europeans accepted them as prodigiously and gloriously brave:

শিখদিগের উপাখ্যান-শ্রবনে কে না উৎসুক হইবেন ? . . . যাহাদিগের বিপুল সাহসের গৌরব স্বগৌরবে গর্ব্বিত ইউরোপিয়েরাও স্বিকার করেন। . . .[21]

The next issue introduced the Bengalis to the glories of the Rājputs in an article entitled "Rājputra-Itihās" (রাজপুত্র-ইতিহাস). It was thought important that the Bengali reader becomes aware of their achievements:

The Puranas and histories have been ever engaged in amply singing the glories of kings of the Lunar and Solar lineages. However, their achievements and relations with the present day population are yet to be popularised in the Bengali language. চন্দ্র ও সুর্য্য বংশিয় রাজাদিগের বিপুল মহিম-বর্ননে ও যশঃকীর্ত্তনে ইতিহাস ও পুরান-সকল নিয়ত নিযুক্ত আছে; কিন্তু তাহাদের এক্ষনকার জনগনের সহিত সম্বন্ধ-ধারা ও মহিমা বঙ্গভাসায় অদ্যাপি প্রচলিত হয় নাই।[22]

The article reminded the readers that,

The countries of Kabul, Kandahar, Bamiyan, and Balkh wherefrom Muslims deluged India and put out Hindu liberty were once under the sceptre of rulers of the Solar line. There was a time when the people of these lands spent their days obeying the Hindu. কাবুল, কান্ধাহার, বামিয়ন, বল্খ ইত্যাদি দেশ-সকল, যত্রত্য মোসলমানেরা ভারতবর্ষকে প্লাবিত করিয়াছে, ও হিন্দুস্বাধিনতা উৎসন্ন করিয়াছে, সেই সকল দেশ কোন কালে সৌর-রাজাদিগের দণ্ডাদধিন হইয়াছিল; কোন সময় তথাকার লোকেরা হিন্দু-আজ্ঞাবহ হইয়া কালযাপন করিত।[23]

Now the Bengali readers were told why it is so essential to know about the Rajputs:

> Most of the Solar lineages extant today dwell in the country of Rajwara. . . . The descendants of these lines possess great heroism and are the best among Hindus. As they bear the name "Rajputra" many take them to be born of miscegenation, but this is a delusion. The *kulāchāryas* (preceptors) of these lines possess genealogies with details of their descent and ancestry and there is no evidence to nurture the belief that all of them are untrue.
>
> যে সকল সৌর শাখা এ পর্য্যন্ত বর্ত্তমান আছে, তাহাদিগের অধিকাংশের আধুনিক বাসস্থান রাজবারা দেশ। . . . এদদ্বংশজাত ব্যক্তি বৃহেরা মহাতেজস্বি ও হিন্দুজাতি-শ্রেষ্ঠ। রাজপুত্র নাম হওয়াতে কেহ ২ ইহাদ্গিকে বর্নশঙ্কর জ্ঞান করে; কিন্তু সে ভ্রম মাত্র। রাজপুত কুলাচার্য্যদিগের গ্রন্থে ইহাদের বংশাবলির সমূহ বিবরন বিস্তার আছে; এবং ঐ কুলজি সমস্তই যে মিথ্যা এ কথার পোষক কোন প্রমান নাই।[24]

The journal seems to be encamped upon the bridgehead which was later occupied by historical fiction in the second half of the nineteenth century. What we notice unfolding here is probably the replacement of what was till now mere tradition or remembrance by ostensible empirical, positivist history. What was perhaps begun by Ram Ram Basu had now taken a more cogent shape. The past was now very explicitly a political and ideological formulation replete with the kind of hero-villain duality we see in the *Gaurī-Mangal kāvya.* The heroes were the brave Sikhs and Rajputs who had defended the land and fought the invader. The villains were the warlike Muslims who had deluged India and put out her freedom.

Thus, we seem to have the stage readied for the developments of the post 1857 decades. A framework of remembrance and a construal of the "other" had been handed down by the *kāvyas.* This inheritance was not just passively extant was but was still actively shaping and forming the new beliefs and subjectivities. This formation allied itself with the new positivist curiosity about India's past which phrased it as an ideological formulation. This formulation visualized the past centuries as a battleground upon which heroes and villains stood armed and arrayed. Thus was begotten, as it appears, the prolific genre of historical fiction of the later years. The Bankims, the Tagores, and their Muslim counterparts, the Kaikobads, are perhaps best locatable and made sense of in this context.

What strikes us about the literature of Hindu authorship in the post-1857 years is the diverse ways in which it alludes to the Muslims. Like the *kāvyas*, on occasions the Hindu authors are scathingly condemnatory and on others they are ambivalent. As those who authored the *kāvyas*, they too at times seem to be trying to subsume the other while suggesting some sort of subordinating gesture. On occasions like these, just like the poets of the yore, our authors seem to be following a strategy of speaking with two voices at the same time. Of course, in their case too one voice will inevitably make a serious attempt to overlap and silence the other.

A few examples should suffice to underline the above suggestions. Just as medieval Bengal had the *kāvyas*, the second half of the nineteenth century saw many long narrative poems being composed by several authors. In their breadth and scope they almost appear to be novels in verse. Perhaps, one of the first of these was *Padminī Upākhyān* (পদ্মিনী উপাখ্যান), composed by Rangalal Banerjee and published in 1858. Rangalal set his tale in a pristine Chittor undefiled by Yavan hands. The "hated" Muslim of his description had not yet got to this island of Hindu sovereignty. However, despite his very obvious antipathy for the *mlechchha* Muslim, Rangalal ascribed a very curious achievement to a character called Bapparao. He conquered the lands of the *mlechchhas*, such as Iran, Turan, and Kabul. He wedded the princesses of these lands and the alliances produced Pathans of the solar lineage:

জন্মিল অসংখ্য বংশ হিন্দু মুসলমান।
হিন্দু সূর্য্যবংশী খ্যাত যবন পাঠান॥[25]

Interestingly, a few years ago the *Bibidhārtha* too had ascribed this feat to Bapparao when describing his life and career in the article on the Rajputs.

Rangalal incorporates the other into his imagining, but only after subordinating him absolutely. It is worth noting that in a later panegyric devoted to Rana Pratap, *Śūrasundarī* (শূরসুন্দরী, 1868), he proclaimed the Hindus and Muslims to be like oil and water, predestined never to mix

তৈল যথা তোষ সহ সংমিলিত নহে।
. . . হিন্দু মুসলমানে হেন ভাব প্রতিকূল॥[26]

The writings of Nabinchandra Sen furnish a similar example of such a mode of accommodation of the "other." Nabinchandra published the long verse narrative of *Palāśīr Juddha* (পলাশীর যুদ্ধ) in 1875. He made the character of Sirajud-daula a libertine given to excessively indulging his senses. Such is his predatory nature that at one point Nabinchandra has Jagat Seth exclaiming that soon no chaste women may be left in the land of Bengal:

. . . এই দুর্নিবার নদী, কে বলিতে পারে,
কোথা হবে পরিনত ? কিছুদিন আর,
সতীত্ব-রতন এই বঙ্গের ভাণ্ডারে
থাকিবে না। . . .[27]

Unbridled licentiousness was attributed as the most pronounced aspect of the Muslim by Nabinchandra.

However, even this Nabinchandra thought it fit to weave into the narrative of *Palāśīr Juddha* a strong counter voice. When Jagat Seth and his accomplice Raja Krishnachandra Rai are plotting to depose the Nawab, the Raja asks his wife if what he is doing is right. Curiously, his wife decries him. The Yavan and the English both are of foreign, she says. Yet the former are different, for they have dwelt in this country for five hundred years. The Yavans and the descendants of the Aryans are now tied in a bond of affection. Now the Yavans are like the shrubs that grow at the foot of the great banyan and appear to be a part of its body:

> যবন ভারতবর্ষে আছে অবিরত
> সার্দ্ধপঞ্চশত বর্ষ।...
> হইয়াছে পরিনয় প্রণয় স্থাপিত;
> নাহি বৃথা দ্বন্দ্ব জাতি-ধর্ম্মের কারনে।
> অশত্থ-পাদপ-জাত উপবৃক্ষ মত,
> হইয়াছে যবনেরা প্রায় পরিণত।[28]

Yes, the Muslim could find inclusion in the vaguely imagined, incipient nation of Nabinchandra, but only as the foliage at its foot.

It is against the backdrop of this inherited literary culture that a Bankimchandra embarked upon his creative career. Hence, his depictions of the Muslim are best understood when seen as yet another set of responses that a literary and intellectual trend allied to an emotional inheritance elicited. Bankim was responding to his age in a very specific manner as many of us do. He was neither misshapen nor free-standing. Bankim's was only another voice in an intellectual polyphony.

Tagore's was a voice which added to or echoed various strains of the polyphony of the age. He began like any other, penning verses reminiscing Hindu valour and dedicating poems to the Sikh Gurus. However, we observe him growing to painting the Muslim with a finer brush. One calls to the mind the nobility he bestowed on the character of Aurangzeb in the poem *Mānī* (মানী). The Aurangzeb he drew appears free of all sentiments of vengeance. His armies are pursuing Yashwant, the fugitive king of Achalgarh. But upon his capture the Emperor is strangely free of ire. He is so impressed with Yashwant's bravery that he restores him to the throne without a moment's hesitation. Then, we have the story *Durāśā* (দুরাশা) in which Tagore's voice is obviously complicit with his protagonist, a Muslim woman who had been in love with a Brahman sepoy but was spurned by him. The Muslim of Tagore's making is a character and no caricature. This is especially important when one observes that he did come to realise that serious differences suffuse the relations of Hindus and Muslims in the country. Looking back on the anti-partition agitation of 1905, he wrote that it was no surprise that the Muslim's response to it had been lukewarm. It was because a primal sin haunts the dealings of the two communities. The two had shared the same earth for centuries and yet had failed to grow normal neighbourly ties demanded by religion and humanism:

> হিন্দু-মুসলমানের সম্বন্ধ লইয়া আমাদের দেশের একটা পাপ আছে . . . প্রতিবেশীর সঙ্গে প্রতিবেশীর যে সম্বন্ধ মনুস্যোচিত, ধর্মবিহিত, তাহা আমাদের মধ্যে হয় নাই।[29]

In the nineteenth century the Bengali-Muslim finally got rid of his ambivalence towards the Bengali language which he displayed so very often in the earlier ages. Interestingly, this happened as proselytising movements such as "Tarīqa-i-Mohammadiyā" and "Farāizi" brought him closer to the Islam and of the Book, the Holy *Qur'ān.* As the contemporary journals stressed, learning Bengali was now a practical necessity for the Bengali-Muslim. He had no alternative as he wrote and read no Arabic or Persian. Besides, the inclination for Bengali became more firm and pronounced with the emergence of a prosperous Bengali-Muslim peasantry. The resu'. was a proliferation of the *ashraf* in the countryside as most of them claimed a superior social status. But unlike the traditional *ashraf,* they were unread in Arabic and Persian. They also needed Bengali to compete with the Bengali-Hindu. From the middle of the nineteenth century, the Bengali-Muslim novelist, essayist or poet was a commonplace. This was remarkable when one observes that in the first-half of the century individuals from the community made absolutely no contribution to modern prose or verse. We shall study some of these contributions in the fifth chapter. When we are done, we hope, the "default position in narratives of Bengali modernity will not sound exclusively or primarily Hindu."[30]

Beginning with Mir Mosarraf Hosain in 1861, the Bengali-Muslim litterateurs avidly contributed their voices to the controversies of the times. Hosain attempted to dissuade his community from consuming cow flesh, while a contemporary, Usufji, meditated on the politics of the time and declared the intentions of Hindus untrustworthy. What is most striking is that these authors wrote a language as Sanskritised as their Hindu peers but used it to carve a distinctive Bengali identity qualified by Islam.

As it is with the Hindus, the literature of Bengali-Muslim authorship is a landscape with a prodigal diversity of features. The same fissures and crevices run across it. As with their Hindu counterparts, our Muslim authors respond variously to their existence. Some walk alongside them strongly affirming them, while some try to straddle them, trying to be two voices simultaneously, as we saw with some Hindu authors. The first among the Bengali-Muslim novelists was Mir Mosarraf Hosain. He published the fantasy tale *Ratnabati* (রত্নবতি) in 1861. All the characters of *Ratnabati* are Hindu and one almost feels that Hosain was trying to impersonate a Hindu author. In fact, when he published the verse work *Gorāi Brij Athabā Gauri Setu* (গোরাই ব্রিজ অথবা গৌরি সেতু) in 1873, so impressed was the journal *Bangadarśan* with his Sanskritised language that it declared that Bengali like his is beyond many Hindu authors. Of course, the journal revealed the assumption in the process that it is the Hindu who is the natural guardian of the Bengali language. Later, in an essay entitled *Go-Jiban* (গো-জিবন,1888), Hosain was to suggest that for the sake of concord with the Hindus-

Muslims ought to give up eating beef. He had his very Muslimness questioned for being a little too well meaning. Undaunted, Mosarraf published the essay *Sat-Prasanga* (সৎ-প্রসঙ্গ) in 1898 contesting the notion that there are any cogent causes behind Hindu-Muslim conflicts.

Hosain, thus, attempted to speak across the chasm. But, at the same time, one also observes him trying to be a truer Muslim telling the epic tale of the martyrdom of Ali in the three volume work *Biṣād-Sindhu* (বিষাদ সিন্ধু).[31] Besides, like his Hindu peers he too could inhabit and express seemingly contradictory emotional states. In the poem *Bartamān Musalmān Samājer Ekkhāni Chitra* (বর্তমান মুসলমান সমাজের একখানি চিত্র) published in 1897, he scathingly censured his co-religionists for being repeatedly duped by the Hindus:

চিরকাল হিন্দুগন
করিতেছে নির্যাতন
তবু জ্ঞান হল নারে হায়।
নিতেছে সকল টেনে,
চক্ষে ধাঁধা এমনি লাগায়॥[32]

In the novel *Gāzī Miār Bastāni* (গাজী মিএার বস্তানি) too the Hindu continued to be a knave. Hosain published this work in1898, the same year as *Sat-Prasanga.* Did the founding of the Indian National Congress and the beginnings of political agitation lie behind these sentiments? As we will go on to see, Usufji made almost a similar assessment of Hindus in the political context. Though important, this is a question beyond the purview of this book.

The contemporary politics might have been a reason why Hosain began to contemplate retreating to his side of the chasm and remaining there. There were, however, writers such as Sheikh Usman Ali who advised concord in the political sphere. He believed that it was sheer sloth because of which Muslims are not joining the Congress. He advised his co-religionists to stir themselves into activity and join the organisation.

Though seeking the location to be a political truce maker, Ali did not try to circumvent the social and cultural reality. He published *Debalā* (দেবলা), a long narrative poem of eight cantos, in 1901. Debalā's subject was the romance of prince Khizr, son of Allauddin Khilji, and the princess of Gujarat, Debala Rani. When Khizr despairs, the noble Debala consoles him saying that certain social conventions cannot be escaped. Trying to do so can only bring ignominy:

> . . . কেন বৃথা কর রোষ সমাজের প্রতি।
> সংঘিলে সমাজ বিধি হয় অধোগতি॥[33]

The emotional complexities of the age are underlined further by Mohammad-Kazem-al-Qureishi, better known as Kaikobad. He published his grand epic poem *Mahaśmaśān* in 1904. This grand, in excess of a thousand pages, effort by the poet was a paean to the crushing defeat inflicted by the Afghan arms upon the Marathas in 1761. However, as though to remind us of the kind of ambiguities that we are dealing with, Kaikobad refused to depict the Hindus as cowardly. In the introduction to the first edition of *Mahaśmaśān* he wrote:

> What do the Muslims gain if the Hindus are shown as unmanly, drenched in the colours of cowardice? Does Muslim gallantry lie in slaying cowards? A fox can be killed by even women, but it takes brave men to hunt lions. That is why I have not observed parsimony in depicting the bravery of the Hindus. I have only enhanced the bravery of the victorious Muslims by truthfully rendering the terrifying gallantry of the Hindus. The Muslim is a brave man, so is the Hindu, the warm blood of the two brave races has committed their glory and bravery to the eternal annals of history. The tales of their gallant deeds will testify to their courage as long the earth endures and history lasts. This redounds to the glory of both the races. But Hindus are the conquered and vanquished while the

Muslims are the victors and anointed with the glory of victory.
বিশেষতঃ হিন্দুদিগকে কাপুরুষ সাজাইয়া, ভিরুতার বর্নে রঞ্জিত করিয়া মুসলমানদিগের কি লাভ ? কাপুরুষ বধে মুসলমানদিগের কি বিরত্ব ? শৃগাল বধকরিতে রমনীরাও পারে, সিংহ বধ করিতে বিরেরই দরকার; তাই হিন্দুদিগের বিরত্ব প্রদর্শন করিতে আমি কৃপণতা করি নাই। আমি তাহাদিগের সেই ভিষন বিরত্ব যথাযথ ভাবে চিত্রিত করিয়া বিজয়ী মুসলমান বীর পুরুষদিগের বিরত্ব প্রদর্শন করিতে আমি কৃপণতা করি নাই। আমি তাহাদিগের সেই ভিষন বিরত্ব যথাযথ ভাবে চিত্রিত করিয়া বিজয়ী মুসলমান বীর পুরুষদিগের বীরত্বের মাত্রা আরও অধিক বৃদ্ধি করিয়াছি। মুসলমানগন বীর পুরুষ, হিন্দুগনও বীর পুরুষ, এই দুই বীর জাতি হৃদয়ের উষ্ণ শোনিতে আপনাদিগের জাতিয় গৌরব ও ভীষন বীরত্ব কালের অক্ষয় পটে লিখিয়া গিয়াছেন; যতদিন পৃথিবী থাকিবে, ইতিহাস থাকিবে, ইহাদিগের বিরত্ব ও জাতীয় গৌরবের কথা ততদিন, তাহার সাক্ষ্য প্রদান করিবে। ইহা উভয় জাতির পক্ষে গৌরবের কথা, তবে হিন্দুগন বিজিত ও বিধ্বস্ত, মুসলমানগন জয়দৃপ্ত ও বিজয় গৌরবে সম্মানিত।[34]

Proclaiming the glories of Islam he indeed was, but Kaikobad had apparently imbibed so much of the Sanskritic imagery that we also see him imagining Islam as a mother goddess. His Islam is evoked as a demon slaying Hindu goddess holding the *Qur'ān* in one hand and dispatching *kāfirs* with another:

পাপ তাপ হারিনী কাফের মর্দিনী
শত্রু সংহারিনী
ভীমা!
কোরান ধারিনী অধর্ম নাশিনী
অতুল গৌরবময়ী
বামা![35]

Members of the Bengali-Muslim intelligentsia were also expending a lot of thought on reviving the worldly fortunes of their community. In the pages of the journal *Islām Prachārak* (ইসলাম প্রচারক), for example, we see these ruminations being often set in words. In the Chaitra-Baishakh issue of *Islām Prachārak,* 1902–3, one Sheikh Fazlul-Karim suggested that Bengali-Muslims' lot will improve if only this drastic measure is taken:

> The warm blood of religion must be run through our society, a part of our lives must be expended for the world (*duniā*). . . . Today there is no one to administer medicine to our disease-weakened society, the servants of our society are not getting medication these days.
>
> . . . আমাদের সমাজের শরীরে ধর্ম্মের উষ্ণ রক্ত স্রোত বহাইতে হইবে; "দুনিয়ার" জন্যও আমাদের জিবনের এক অংশ ক্ষয় করিতে হইবে। . . . আজ আমাদের রোগ-ক্লিষ্ট সমাজের ঔষধ খাওয়াইবার কেহই নাই; আজ আমাদের সমাজ সেবকগন পথ্য পাইতেছেন না।[36]

The journal tried to reach out to the Hindus too. In its Magh (January–February), 1905 issue *Islām Prachārak* tried to dispel the Hindu loathing for Muslims. In an article entitled *Sottoi ki Musalmān Ghrinār Pātra?* (সত্যই কি মুসলমান ঘৃণার পাত্র ?) one Usman Ali argued that it is the Muslims who more resemble the Vedic Aryans, because they observe no caste, bury their dead and eat meat. Referring to some recent research which identified these as the features of Vedic society he averred,

> . . . If the aforementioned practices existed only in the Vedic age, and since we act in accordance with them, you concede that we are like those of the Vedic age.
>
> . . . উল্লিখিত বিষয়গুলি যদি কেবল বৈদিক যুগেই আচরিত হইত, তবে আমরা তৎসমুদয় আচরন করি বলিয়া আমরা নিতান্তই বৈদিক যুগের লোক স্বীকারই করিতেছ।[37]

However, as the anti-partition agitation began and picked pace, the journal abandoned these efforts at amity. Now we find the *Islām Prachārak* unequivocally choosing a distinct political destiny for the Bengali-Muslims. The Paush issue of the journal carried the article *Banga-Bibhāg O Swadeśi Āndolan* (বঙ্গ-বিভাগ ও স্বদেশি আন্দোলন), authored by someone who called himself Ebne Mauza:

> The cunning of the Hindus has hassled us on many occasions and deprived us of our wealth and lives. When the terrible conflagration of the sepoy mutiny engulfed all India in 1857, behind it all too were the clever Hindus. . . . In the end, the Muslims' fate was undone, the glory of the Mughals was extinguished forever.
> হিন্দুগনের চতুরতায় আমরা অনেক সময়েই বিড়ম্বিত হইয়াছি ও ধনে প্রানে মারা পড়িয়াছি। এই যে ১৮৫৭ খৃঃ অব্দে সিপাহি বিদ্রোহের ভিষন অগ্নি সমগ্র ভারত সত্ব প্রজ্জস্বলিত হইয়া উঠিয়াছিল, উহার মুলেও ছিলেন সুচতুর হিন্দুগন।...কিন্তু কার্য্যকালে মুসলমানেরই কপাল পুড়িল - মোগলের-গৌরব চিরদিনের জন্য অস্তমিত হইল।[38]

Mauza further added,

> We will no more be swindled by them (Hindus) and invite trouble for ourselves. We will do nothing unpleasant to the government. Our devotion towards the British government is unshakable. Though the foreign policy of the English is somewhat against our national interests, their India policy is wholly in our favour—this we must acknowledge in an uninhibited tone.
> আমরা আর তাহাদের ধোকায় পড়িয়া আপনাদের বিপদ ডাকিয়া আনিব না। আমরা গবর্নমেন্টের অপ্রীতিকর কোনও কার্য্যই করিব না। ব্রিটিশ গবর্নমেন্টের প্রতি আমাদের ভক্তি অচলা। যদিও ইংরেজের পররাষ্ট্র-নীতি কতকটা আমাদের জাতিয় স্বার্থের প্রতিকুল, কিন্তু ভারতের স্বরাষ্ট্র-নীতি আমাদের সম্পুর্ন অনুকুল—একথা আমরা মুক্তকন্ঠে বলিতে বাধ্য।[39]

Thus, as Bengal was cleaved, the majority of Bengalis, by now assuredly Muslim, aspired to a distinct political future. They had become Muslims, socially and politically, just as their compatriots, whose overtures they decided to ignore, had become Hindus.

References

1. New York: Vintage, 1966, p. 9. [Italics in original.]
2. New York: Harper Perennial Modern Thought, 2008, p. 430.
3. See Cynthia Talbot, "Inscribing the Other, Inscribing the Self: Hindu-Muslim Identities in Pre-Colonial India," in Richard M. Eaton, ed., *India's Islamic Traditions, 711-1750.* New Delhi: OUP, 2003, p. 84.
4. "Sacred Symbols as Mobilising Ideology: The North Indian Search for a 'Hindu' Community," in *Comparative Studies in Society and History* 22(4), pp. 597–625.
5. The founder of the Ilyas Shahi line was Shams al-Din Ilyas Shah (r. 1342–57).
6. The Husain Shahi dynasty was founded by Sultan 'Ala al-Din Husain Shah (r. 1493–1519) in 1493.
7. The armies of Akbar ventured into Bengal for the first time in 1574.
8. *The Rise of Islam and the Bengal Frontier, 1204–1760,* University of California Press, 1993.
9. Ibid., p. 270.
10. "First of all I bow down to the Supreme Deity [Prabhu], and secondly to (the same Omnipotent Being conceived as) the Creator [Srijan]; and thirdly to the benign Incarnation of Light. The Koran and the other scriptural texts I regard as revelation—the sacred utterance of the Lord [Prabhu] himself . . .," ibid., p. 271.
11. Ibid., pp. 234–36.
12. Joseph T. Connel, "The Word 'Hindu' in Gaudiya Vaishnava Texts," in *Journal of the American Oriental Society,* vol. 93, no. 3 (Jul–Sep 1973), pp. 340–44.
13. In the *Padmābati* (পদ্মাবতি).
14. In the prologue to *Lor Chandrāni O Sati Mainā* (লোর চন্দ্রানি ও সতি মইনা).
15. *History of Bengali Literature.* New Delhi: Sahitya Akademi, 1960, p. 157.
16. Likely to date to 1743. See Sushil Kumar De, *Bengali Literature in the Nineteenth Century (1757–1857).* Calcutta: Firma K.L. Mukhopadhyay, 1962, p. 61.
17. For a better elaboration of the idea of the cultural faultline see Shashi Joshi and Bhagwan Josh, "The Cultural Faultline and its Mirrors" (chap. 5), in *Struggle for Hegemony in India, 1920–47, Culture, Community and Power,* vol. III, 1941–47. New Delhi: Sage Publications, 1994, pp. 115–45.
18. *Rājā Pratāpāditya Charitra* (রাজা প্রতাপাদিত্য চরিত্র). Calcutta: Ranjan Publishing House, 1942, p. 5.
19. See Dilwar Husain, *Bānglā Upanyāse Mughal Itihāser Byabahār, 1857–1916* (বাংলা উপন্যাসে মুঘল ইতিহাসের ব্যেবহার, ১৮৫৭-১৯১৬). Dhaka: Bangla Academy, 1984, p. 40.

20. Published by the Baptist Mission Press of Calcutta, Kārtik (October–November), Śakābda 1773 (1851), vol. 1, issue I, p. 10. Calcutta: Asiatic Society Library.
21. Ibid., p. 11.
22. Ibid., vol. I, issue II, p. 17.
23. Ibid., pp.17–18.
24. Ibid.
25. Shantikumar Dasgupta and Haribandhu Mukhti, eds., *Rangalāl Rachanābalī* (রঙ্গলাল রচনাবলী). Calcutta: Duttachaudhari and Sons, 1974, p. 143.
26. Ibid., p. 216.
27. *Nabīnchandrer Granthābalī* (নবীনচন্দ্রের গ্রন্থাবলী), Calcutta, 1904, p. 424.
28. Ibid., p. 436.
29. *Byādhi O Pratikāra* (ব্যাধি ও প্রতিকার), 1907; *Rabindra Rachanābalī* (রবিন্দ্র রচনাবলী), vol. VII. Calcutta: Vishvabharati, 1975, p. 628.
30. We hope that our effort addresses this very genuine concern expressed by Dipesh Chakrabarty:

    [The] forgetting of the Muslim was deeply embedded in the education and upbringing I received in independent India. Indian-Bengali anti-colonial nationalism implicitly normalized the "Hindu." Like many others in my situation, I look forward to the day when the default position in narratives of Bengali modernity will not sound exclusively or primarily Hindu.

    See *Provincializing Europe, Postcolonial Thought and Historical Difference.* Princeton University Press, 2000, p. 21.
31. Published over seven years. The first volume *Mohurram* (মহরম) was published in 1885, the second *Uddhāra* (উদ্ধার) in 1887 and the third *Ezid Badh* (এজিদ-বধ) in 1891.
32. Dr Qazi Abdul-Mannan, ed., *Mośārraf Rachanā-Sambhāra* (মশাররফ রচনা-সম্ভার). Dhaka: Bangla Academy, 1984, vol. 3, p. 383.
33. Ibid., p. 308.
34. Kaikobad, *Mahāśmaśān Kābya Arthāt Pānipater Tritīya Juddha O Mahārāṣṭrīyadiger Patan* (মহাশ্মশান কাব্য অর্থাত পানিপতের তৃতীয় যুদ্ধ ও মহারাষ্ট্রীয়দিগের পতন), sec. edn. Dhaka: Published by Abdul-Khayer Saifuddin Ahmed, 1917, Introduction, pp.viii–ix.
35. See Manirujjaman Mohammad, *Ādhunik Bānglā Kābye Hindu-Musalimān Samparka, 1857–1920* (আধুনিক বাংলা কাব্যে হিন্দু-মুসলমান সম্পর্ক. ১৮৫৭-১৯২০). Dhaka: Bangla Academy, 1970, p. 340.
36. *Islām Prachārak,* Chaitra-Baishakh, 1309–10 (Bengali year) (ইসলাম প্রচারক

চৈত্র, বৈশাখ, ১৩০৯-১০), Dhaka University Library, p. 146.

Chaitra is the last month on the Bengali calendar. It corresponds to the period from mid-March to mid-April. Baishakh is the first month of the year and extends from mid-April to mid-May. The Bengali years 1309 and 1310 will be the Gregorian years 1902–3 and 1903–4.

37. *Islām Prachārak,* Magh, 1311 (Bengali) (ইসলাম প্রচারক, মাঘ, ১৩১১), p. 400. The Bengali year 1311 will be the Gregorian years 1904–5. The month of Magh extends from mid-January to mid-February.
38. *Islām Prachārak,* Paush, 1312 (Bengali) (ইসলাম প্রচারক, পৌষ, ১৩১২), pp. 361–62. The month of Paush extends from mid-December to mid-January. The Bengali year 1312 will correspond to the Gregorian years 1905–6.
39. Ibid., p. 368.

1

The Discourses Emerge 1342–1757

IN THE YEAR 1204, the capital of the Sena rulers of Bengal, Nabadwip, fell, allegedly to a band of mere eighteen Turkish horsemen. Lakhnauti, another major city of the Sena domains, fell soon after to the Turkish horse. These developments turned Bengal into a province of the Delhi Sultanate. Bengal was fated to remain so for the next almost century and a half. The year 1342 marked another watershed with the secession of Bengal from the parent empire and the accession of the Ilyas Shahis. There are many works of political history which narrate this course of events and the history that followed.[1] But they rarely, if ever, try to explore how Islam as a belief and a social and cultural system came to be disseminated in the region. None attempt to understand how the dissemination of this belief system which also subsumed within it a discourse of state power might have been perceived by those who did not belong to it. It has been said, after all, that for the new rulers there was no question of "seeking legitimacy within the framework of Bengali Hindu culture or of establishing any kind of continuity with the defeated Sena kingdom."[2] Lying on the other side of the political and cultural rupture, how did the conquered represent the adherents of Islam? And how, in turn, the protagonists of Islam perceived and represented those who did not belong to its cultural and political internality?

A noteworthy exception is the effort by Richard M. Eaton. He tries to explore the first of the above issues raised by us. According to Eaton, as stated above already, the earliest Muslim rulers sought no reason to "assert legitimate authority"[3] over the land they had subjugated and restricted themselves to a show of "coercive power."[4] Over the thirteenth century, as the rulers of the province engaged in rivalry with the sovereigns in Delhi, "they adopted a posture of strenuous religious orthodoxy"[5] and associated themselves with the office of the Caliph in Baghdad. To add to this, after gaining independence from Delhi, the rulers of Bengal adopted a "projection of Persian imperial ideology."[6] As it appears to us, for quite a while the framework of legitimacy remained one of hard power and the reference points for the same all exogenous. By the early fifteenth century, however, the edges of this state softened and it "evolved a secular modus vivendi with Bengali society and culture."[7] Our attention is drawn towards discrete emergences such as the royal mosques adopting "purely indigenous motifs and structural traits"[8] and the late fifteenth century poet Bijay Gupta paying a rhapsodic tribute to an Ilyas Shahi king.[9]

The expansion of Islam in Bengali society, a much more difficult project than constructing mosques with indigenous motifs, is placed in the period following Mughal annexation. This occurred despite the Mughal refusal to "promote the conversion of Bengalis to Islam."[10] Instead, Islamisation in Bengal "was but one aspect of a general set of transformations associated with an expanding economic frontier, which took place most dramatically in the Mughal period."[11] The spread of Islam was coincident with the expansion of the agrarian economy. The Mughal state, according to Eaton, "oversaw the establishment of both Hindu and Muslim institutions as new lands were opened up for cultivation."[12] But Islam had the edge because "the Muslim institutions proved by far the more numerous and influential."[13] Once established in an area they tended to integrate the local communities "into an Islamic ordered cultural universe."[14]

Strangely though, Eaton avoids telling us as to why the Islamic institutions were more numerous and influential. Did the state create a cultural climate which helped the flourishing of a certain faith? As about the question of integration, it could happen because these communities had not yet been incorporated into a Hindu social order. Eaton furnishes the example of Chittagong where allegedly this was the case.[15] Thus, according to Eaton, what happened in the end was a three tier process of inclusion, identification and displacement. In the first instance "Islamic superhuman agencies became accepted in local Bengali cosmologies alongside local divinities already embedded therein." In the second the two merged and finally the Islamic agencies replaced the older divinities.[16]

However, Eaton's schema is impaired by sweeping formulations which miss the internal dynamics of individuals and groups caught up in the process of becoming Muslims. His generalisations are too broadbrushed and, as we will see, cannot withstand the complexity of the available evidence suggestive of cultural contest and confrontation through which a section of the Bengali society came to embrace a certain kind of Islam. He, for example, argues that "in the corpus of pre-modern Bengali literature celebrating indigenous deities such as Manasa, Chandi, Satya Pir, Dharma, or Dakshin Ray, one readily sees local cosmologies expanding in order to accommodate new superhuman beings introduced by foreign Muslims."[17] We will study precisely this corpus in this chapter. As we will go on to see, the indigenous deities were rather less than alacrous to "accommodate new superhuman beings introduced by foreign Muslims." Besides, all Eaton cites in support of his claim is a scrap from an East Bengal ballad with which he tries to illustrate how the Islamic deity was being identified with the local deities.[18] Eaton also never quite tells us in concrete terms what the religious beliefs of those denizens of Eastern Bengal not yet integrated in the Hindu social order might have been like. No words are expended in outlining their nature to us. Hence, the beliefs of eastern Bengal remain but an assumption if not an assertion. Furthermore, the book itself is replete with tell-tale signs suggesting that the religious beliefs and practices of the region might have been anything but what Eaton terms them. Eaton refers to rebel potentates in the Chittagong, Sonargaon and Chota Pandua regions who issued coins with the legend "Sri Candi Carana Parayana" (devoted to the feet of Goddess Chandi) in the second decade of the fifteenth century.[19] We also have the example of the tiny kingdom of Tripura on the easternmost extremity of Bengal where Sanskritisation, apparently, had made more than sufficient progress. We have, for example, the lion motif appearing on the coins issued by the state. Eaton himself mentions the fact and acknowledges the motif to be a "generalized symbol of political authority in eastern Bengal."[20] The royal chronicle of Tripura, the *Śrī Rājmālā* (শ্রী রাজমালা), composed from the fifteenth till the eighteenth centuries, speaks of patronage and munificence being bestowed upon Brahmans by the court. The chronicle itself is the work of many Brahman authors.

Eaton, as we saw above, furnishes the example of Chittagong as being an area whose inhabitants were not yet incorporated in the Hindu social order. However, the kingdom of Tripura lay right across Chittagong's borders and seemingly upheld a very different order. The *Rājmālā* contradicts Eaton's assertions when giving an account of the generosity of Kalyan Manikya. We find that the rulers of Tripura could be as lavish when entertaining the Brahman as those in any other part of India. At the turn of the third decade of the seventeenth century the Mughal state briefly expanded into Tripura. After suffering an initial defeat, the Mughal occupation of the kingdom was soon brought to an end by the then ruler Kalyan Manikya. The king decided to celebrate his victory by declaring his son Govinda Narayan the heir apparent. On this occasion Kalyan Manikya mounted the weighing scale and had himself weighed in gold, jewels and clothes. All of these were gifted to the twice born. No less than fifteen thousand of them turned up to receive the gifts:

জাজ্ঞ হোম করিলেক ব্রাহ্মণের গনে।
তুলাতে বসিল রাজা ধর্ম্মের আসনে॥
অলঙ্কার বস্ত্র সমে তুলাতে বসিল।
আর আগে ধন রত্ন পরিমিত দিল॥
...তুলাপুরুষ কির্ত্তী হইল বিস্তর।
সেই কির্ত্তি গেল রাজার দেশদেশান্তরে॥
নৃপতি করয়ে দান উদয়পুরেতে॥
পঞ্চদশ সহস্র আসিছে দ্বিজগণ।
যাচক কাঙ্গালী যত না ছিল গণন॥[21]

More importantly for us, irrespective of whether actually fifteen thousand Brahmans were privy to the king's largesse, we witness that the ideal of patronising the Brahman existed for Tripura kingship as it did for Hindu kingship anywhere else in India. Govinda Narayan, assuming the throne as Govinda Manikya, kept up the practice in the wake of his father. Govinda lushly rewarded the Brahmans when performing the *śrāddha* ceremony upon Kalyan Manikya's death. The holy ones were sent away with cows that had calved:

বিধিমতে করে শ্রাদ্ধ গোবিন্দ নৃপতি।
নানা রাজ্য হইতে দ্বিজ আসিলেক অতি॥
বেশ্টিত হইয়া বসে দ্বিজগণ॥
...তার পরে মহাদান ছিল আরস্কন॥
সবৎসা কপিলা আদি গো দান করেন॥[22]

This is definitely not the picture of a diffuse, indeterminate religious universe as Eaton will have us believe. Not even in the farthest extremity of Bengal which culturally

Tripura was and still is.

Like the *Rājmālā,* we find several other contemporaneous texts produced in eastern Bengal almost burble evidence demonstrating that the religious universe of the region was not as diffuse as claimed by Eaton. Though often leavened by ambiguities, religious identities were definitely forming. To cite an example, all the Hindu deities extant today commanded worship then as well. Inevitably, we find the ballads composed by the poets of the region beginning with an invocation of the deities. The poets of *Līlā Kanyā-Kabi Kanka Pālā* (লীলা কন্যা-কবি কঙ্ক পালা), Nayanchand Ghosh, Raghusut, Srinath Bania and Damodar Das, pay homage to Narayan, Brahma, Śiva, Durga, Kartik, Ganapati, Lakshmi and Saraswati as they begin their yarn:

গোলক বৈকুণ্ঠপুরি পরথমে বন্দনা করি
তার মধ্যে বন্দি নারায়নে।
পদ্মযোনি বইন্দা গাই যাহা হইতে জনম পাই
যেহি দেব স্রজন কারনে॥
আরে কইলাশ পর্বত যথা শিব দুর্গা বন্দি তথা
তার সঙ্গে কার্তিক গনপতি।
সব দেব দেবি সার তাহার সঙ্গেতে আর
যোগমায়া লক্ষ্মী সরস্বতী॥[23]

Chandrabati Devi, a poetess who lived in the same century as Damodar, also begins her *Sundarī Maluā Pālā* (সুন্দরী মলুয়া পালা) with a lengthy salutation to the gods. Besides the Deity who is without a beginning (*anādi*), she invokes Śiva, Durga, Lakshmi, and Saraswati:

আদিতে বন্দিয়া গাই অনাদি ঈশ্বর।
দেবের মধ্যে বন্দিয়া গাই ভোলা মহেশ্বর॥
দেবির মধ্যে বন্দিয়া গাই শ্রিদুর্গা ভবানি।
লক্ষ্মী সরস্বতী বন্দুম যুগল নন্দিনী॥
ধন সম্পদ মিলে ভাই লক্ষ্মীরে পুজিলে।
সরস্বতী বন্দিয়া গাই বিদ্যা যাতে মিলে॥[24]

The same text yields evidence of the celebration of Durga Puja. Apparently, the Hindu festivals too had already taken the form in which we witness them today. Chandrabati tells us how when the country celebrated the Puja a peasant mortgaged his son to buy food:

> দেশে আইল দুর্গা পূজা
> দেবী জগত জননী।
> কুলের ছেইলা বান্ধা দিয়া
> কিরষান খায় ভাতপানি॥[25]

The seventeenth century *Deyānā Madina bā Ālāl Dulāler Pālā* (দেয়ানা মদিনা বা আলাল দুলালের পালা) by one Mansur too contains a description of the gaiety of the Puja. At a juncture in the tale, the step mother of the boys Alal and Dulal conspires to have them drowned and persuades them to take a boat ride. She entices them with a description of the sights of the festival of Durga Puja they will see on the way. "You will see Durga, the deity of the Hindus," she tells them, "who has an elephant headed son. She rides the tiger and slays a man. Beside her stands a damsel waving a lotus. She has another daughter who wields the lute (*dotārā*) and who has a brother standing upon a peacock":

> হিদুএ ঠাকুর দুগগা আইব তার ছাওয়ালের মাথা হাতি।
> রাইতের বেলা রোশনাই হইব জস্কইলল্যা ঝার বাতি॥
> সিঙ্গীর পিঠে দুগগা মাইয়া মরদ ধইর্যা মারে।
> তার কাছে আর এক মাইয়া পদ্ম ফুল লাড়ে॥
> আর এক মাইয়া আছে তার হস্তেতে দোতারা।
> তার আছে ভাই ময়রের পিঠে খাড়া।.[26]

That the cow was sacred as well, we gather from the *Līlā Kanyā-Kabi Kanka Pālā*. Garga, a character in the tale, unwittingly commits the sin of killing a cow. To expiate he had to make some severe penance, only then do the gods forgive him:

গো হত্যা জনিত পাপ কেমনে হইবে মাফ
সেই পাপে মুক্তির কামনা॥
অবশেষে অতি রুষ্ট দেবতা হইল তুষ্ট
তার অতি কঠোর সাধনে।[27]

Thus, the identities had had their beginnings. However, we also observe attempts of melding or juxtaposing the Islamic deity with the non-Islamic deities and artefatcs. Nevertheless, the effort generates its own tensions limiting its success. We note this in case of the anonymous *Pīr-Bātāsī Kanyār Pālā* (পীর-বাতাসী কন্যার পালা). In the first canto of this ballad the poet rhymes a salutation to the "Hindu" and the "Muslim":

সভাজনে বন্দুম রে ভাই হিন্দু মোছলমান।[28]

Having greeted his audience, he juxtaposes the holy places of the "Hindu" and the "Muslim"—Mecca, Medina, Kashi, and Gaya—and salutes them:

মক্কা মদিনা বন্দুলাম মুঁই কাশি গয়া থান।[29]

The eclectic piety notwithstanding, he displays a sure awareness of which pilgrimage belongs to whom. This poet too is conjectured to be of the sixteenth century. The non-Muslims forming a self-professed group in his eyes acquires more significance when we note that he is likely to have been a Muslim. He embarks on his versification seeking *Allāh*'s grace:

পরথমে বন্দনা করি গো আল্লা নিরঞ্জন।[30]

Works by non-Muslim poets too furnish similar juxtaposition of artefacts. The invocations at the beginning of Dwija Kanai's *Bāidyā Kanyā Mahuā* (বাইদ্যা কন্যা মহুয়া) consummately flit between the sacred universes of Muslims and non-Muslims. "In the east I salute the Sun," says the first invocation, "which lights up the quarters. I salute the ocean of milk in the south (*khīrnadī*) where Chandsadagar used to venture on business. I salute Mount Kailash which lies to the north and where dwell Śiva and Parvati. In the west I salute Kashi and Vrindavan, the abodes of Śiva and Krishna. I salute the four quarters of the earth, the gods of Hindus and *pīrs* of Muslims. I pay my respect at the feet of the Hindus and Muslims assembled. Finally, make obeisance at the feet of my guru":

পূবেতে বন্দনা করি পূবের ভানুশ্বর।
একদিকে উদয় রে ভানু চৌদিকে পশর॥
দক্ষিণে বন্দনা গো করি ক্ষীরনদী সাগর।
যেইখানে বানিজ্যে যাইতেন চান্দসদাগর॥
উত্তরে বন্দনা করি গো কৈলাশ পরবত।
যেইখানে বসতি করেন গৌরি মহেশ্বর॥
পশ্চিমে বন্দা গো করি কাশি বিন্দাবন।
যেইখানে আছেন শিব কৃষ্ণ প্রানধন॥
চাইরকুনা পিরথিমি বইন্দা মন করলাম থির।
হিন্দুর দেবতা বন্দি মুসলমানের পীর॥
সভা কইর্যা বইছ ভাই সব হিন্দু মুসলমান।
সবার চরনে আমি জানাই পরনাম॥
কিবা গান গাইবাম আমি বন্দনা করলাম ইতি।
উস্তাদের চরন বন্দি করিয়া মিন্নতি॥[31]

The second invocation contains exactly the same words as the first till salutations are made to Mount Kailash. The poet makes an interesting addition to Kailash's topography. He identifies it as the place where lies the boulder which Ali used to exercise with (*mālāmer pāthar*). He first salutes this rock and then Mecca before offering respect at the feet of the "Hindus" and "Muslims" making the audience. Then the poet salutes the four quarters of the earth, the warrior *pīr* Ghazi Zindapir who dwels in Sundarban, the Sun and the Moon and *al-Kitāb,* the Book of *Qur'ān*. Like the first, this invocation too ends with obeisances offered to the guru:

পূবেতে বন্দনা করলাম পূবের ভানুশ্বর।
একদিকে উদয় রে ভানু চৌউদিকে পশর॥
দক্ষিণে বন্দনা গো করলাম ক্ষীরনদী সাগর।
যেখানে বানিজ্য করে চান্দ সদাগর॥
উত্তরে বন্দনা গো করলাম কৈলাশ পরবত।
যেখানে পড়িয়া গো আছে আলির মালামের পাথর॥
পশ্চিমে বন্দনা গো করলাম মক্কা হেন স্থান।
উরদিশে বাড়ায় সেলাম মোমিন মুসলমান॥
সভা কইরা বইছ ভাইরে হিন্দু মুসলমান।
সভার চরনে আমি জানাইলাম সেলাম॥
চাইকুনা পিরথিমি বইন্দ্যা মন করলাম থির।
সুন্দরবন মুকামে বন্দলাম গাজী জিন্দাপীর॥
আশমানে জমিনে বন্দলাম সূরুজ আর চান।
আলাম কালাম বন্দুম কিতাব আর কুরান॥
কিবা গান গাইবাম আমি বন্দনা করলাম ইতি।
উস্তাদের চরন বন্দলাম করিয়া মিন্নতী॥

It does seem to us that, for the non-Muslim poets to pay respect to these sacred motifs, they must have appeared sufficiently well outlined to them and indicative of a distinct faith of human beings. The evidence yielded by our texts also clearly suggests that the non-Muslims of the age and the region themselves were well aware of the fact. They had begun recognising what makes for a difference of faith and clung to the symbols of their own belief and society to ensure that they are not violated. In the following pages we shall record a number of stories which will underline the process of the formation of a distinct universe of faith identified as 'Hindu.'

The *Līlā Kanyā-Kabi Kanka Pālā* tells the tale of the love of Lila and Kanka. At a point in the story, the hero Kanka accepts a *pīr* as his preceptor and invites censure. Kanka ate *prasād* at the *pīr*'s and learnt *kalāms* from him. The act is regarded tantamount to a loss of caste and *dharma* and he earns obloquy:

নিজের সে জাতি ধর্ম সকলি ভুলিয়া।
পীরের প্রসাদ খায় অমৃত বলিয়া॥...
পীরের নিকটে কঙ্ক শিখয়ে কালাম।
জাতি ধর্ম নাশ হইল রটিল বদনাম॥[32]

Kanka's master, the *pīr*, responds to the situation by suggesting that he compose an ode, a *pānchāli*, to the deity Satyapir. Kanka heeds his master and composes the ode. Since Satyapir commanded worship among both "Hindus" and "Muslims," the *pānchāli* earned Kanka fame and approval in his own and far off lands. All in the country sang his praise, now he was no more called a mere cowherd but was known as Kanka the poet. Garga, Kanka's foster father, was very pleased. Whoever, in whichever country, worshipped Satyapir read Kanka's *pānchāli* and praised him:

দেখিয়া শুনিয়া পির কঙ্করে করিলা থির
উপজুক্ত ভক্ত এই জন।
সত্যপীরের পাঁচালী কঙ্করে লিখিতে বলি
একদিন হইলা অদর্শন॥
গুরুর আদেশ মানি লিখিয়া পাঁচালীখানি
পাঠাইলা দেশ আর বিদেশে।
কঙ্কের লিখন কথা ব্যক্ত হইল জথা তথা
দেশ পুর্ন হইল তার যশে॥
কঙ্ক আর রাখাল নয় কবি কঙ্ক লোকে কয়
শুইন্যা গর্গ ভাবে চমৎকার।
হিন্দু আর মুসলমানে সত্যপীর সবে মানে
পাঁচালীর হইল সমাদর॥
জেই পুজে সত্যপীরে কঙ্কের পাঁচালী পড়ে
দেশে দেশে কঙ্কের গুন গায়॥[33]

But there was more trouble yet for Kanka. Kanka's opponents sought to harry him by upraising his past. He was born to a Brahman couple but his parents had died when he was still an infant. A *chāndāla* and his wife took him in and raised him till he was five. But they died too and Kanka was left an orphan once more. Providence, however, was again kind to him. The Brahman Garga noticed comely little Kanka when passing by the cremation ground on which he lived. The childless Garga took him home and raised him as his own son. Kanka's adversaries now bandied the fact that he was begotten by *chāndālas*. Garga found himself being impeached before an assembly of the learned for nurturing the sire of untouchables. Some of the *pundits* said that what Garga has done is nothing wrong. After all, Kanka ate the food of *chāndālas* when he was barely conscious. But the more zealous "Hindus" were not convinced, they shook their heads and disagreed. "One who takes in someone who has eaten the food of *chāndālas* after birth is not a Brahman. Faulty ways (*anāchār*) destroy *jāti* and *kula*, one does not pick up a flower that has been cast away on the earth," the detractors said:

পণ্ডিত সমাজিগনে একত্র করিয়া ভনে
"এই কঙ্ক ব্রাহ্মন তনয়।
জ্ঞানমানে নাই সে রয় চণ্ডালের অন্ন খায়
ঘরে নিতে নাইত সংসয়॥
এতেক শুনিয়া নন্দু আর জত গোঁড়া হিন্দু
কয় সবে মাথা নাড়াইয়া।
আমরা সম্মত নই আর শুন সবে কই
লও কঙ্কে মোদের ছাড়িয়া॥
জন্মিয়া চণ্ডালের অন্ন যেই জন খায়।
যে তারে সমাজে তুলে সেই ত ব্রাহ্মন নয়।
অনাচারে জাতি নষ্ট নষ্ট হয় কুল।
মাটিতে পড়িলে কেউ নাই সে তুলে ফুল॥"[34]

The traducers now let all know that not only is Kanka's master a "Muslim" but he is also born of untouchables:

রটাইলা কঙ্ক নয় শুধু চণ্ডালের পুত।
মুসলমান পীরের কাছে হয়্যাছে দীক্ষিত॥[35]

Maddened by hurt and grief, Garga decides to kill Kanka and then immolate himself to atone for the sin he has committed:

> শহস্তে করিবাম আমি কঙ্কেরে বিনাশ॥
> . . .
> তারপর প্রবেশিয়া জলন্ত আগুনে।
> পরাচিত্ত করবাম নিজ শরীর দাহনে॥[36]

Lila, Garga's daughter and Kanka's love, discovers her father's plan and she goes and asks Kanka to beware. The wounded Kanka decides to go and visit the pilgrimages. "Take good care of my father while I am away, only when he is cured of his delusions will I return home," he says to Lila. Besides, he tells Lila, "At the *pīr*'s I have learnt the oneness of *Allāh* and Ishvar. The diference of expression *(bhāṣā)* does not make God different. The good (*sādhu*) are the same in all faiths, they live and act the same way. All I know is that all beliefs are one. This is what I learnt from my father too, what I know is that all religions are one":

> শুন দেবি লিলাবতি আমার বচন।
> কিছুদিন করবাম আমি তীর্থ ভ্রমন॥
> রাখিবা পিতারে মোর অতি যত্ন কইরে।
> ভ্রম দূর হইলে পিতার আইব আমি ঘরে॥
> . . .
> পীরের কাছেতে আমি শিখ্যাছি যেইনা কথা।
> মোদের শাস্তরে আছে সেইসব বারতা॥
> যেই আল্লা সেই ঈশ্বর এক কইর্যা জানি।
> ভাষা ভেদে ঈশ্বর ভেদ নাই আমি সে আমি মানি॥
> সকল ধর্মেতে দেখ সাধু যেই জন।
> এক মতে থাকে তারা এক আচরন॥
> এইসব তত্বকথা পিতার মুখে শুনি।
> সব ধর্ম এক হয় এই তত্ব জানি॥[37]

One must not assume the censure faced by Kanka to be something exceptional. We observe several other instances of characters suffering similarly when they commit acts of transgression, however inadvertently. Chandrabati Devi's heroine Malua in the *Sundarī Maluā Pālā* suffers a fate similar to Sita's after she is abducted by the *qāzī* of the village. This *qāzī* was an unusually wicked man whose licentiousness knew no bounds. He had several wives and keeps, but never ceased ravishing women of other households:

পরে তো হইল কিবা শুন দিয়া মন।
লুচ্চা দুশমন কাজী কৈল বিড়ম্বন॥
ঘরে আছে বিবি-বান্দী গণ্ডা পাচ শাত।
তবুও দুশমনি তার নাই সে পড়ে বাদ॥
বড়ই দুরন্ত কাজী ক্ষেমতা অপার।
কুলের বধু বাইর করে অতি দুরাচার॥[38]

When he cast eyes on Malua, he carried her away and proposed marriage to her. The virtuous Malua managed to fend off his advances for three months. Finally, when she returns to her household all regard her defiled for having lived in a Yavan's house. "If we take her in, we loose caste," her husband's maternal uncle (*māmā*) says. "She has spent three months in a Muslim's house who is such a thug that he makes a tiger quail. There is no way now, she has been deprived of her *jāti* and *dharma.* The jaws of a tiger never spare a doe. Not even expiation can restore the *jāti* and *dharma* of a woman who has returned from the mansion (of the *qāzi*)," he laments:

বিনোদের মামা বলে হালুয়ার সঙ্কর।
"ঘরে যেই তুইল্যা লইব জাতি যাইব তার॥
তিন মাস আছিল বউ মোছলমানের ঘরে।
দারুন সে লুচ্চা দেওয়ান বাব কাপে ডরে॥
বাঘের মুখে পইড়্যা হরিনা নিস্তার না পায়।
জাতি ধর্ম সব গেছে না আছে উপায়॥
এই মত কত নারী হাউলী থাইক্যা ফির্যা।
জাতি ধর্ম নাই সে পায় পরাচিত্তি কইর্যা॥[39]

A fate like Malua's could befall men too. Jayananda, a character in Nayanchand's *Chandrābatī* (চন্দ্রাবতী), suffers a similar banishment from society because of his association with a Muslim woman. The principle of mutual exclusion once again points to the fact of the formation of two separate societies based on two different universes of faith.

Like the stories above, *Chandrābatī* is a tragedy. Sorrow visits the beauteous heroine, Chandrabati, when her betrothed, Jayananda, falls in love with Asmani, the village *qāzī*'s daughter. Asmani too reciprocates his affections. When the wedding day of Jayananda and Chandrabati arrives, seeking to claim her lover for herself, she complains to her father that Jayananda has cheated on and abandoned her. The wrathful *qāzī* has Jayananda bound and brought to him. He makes him recite the *kalimah* and weds his daughter. Thus Jayananda, the poem says, becomes Jayananda *Miyār*:

বিচার করিয়া কাজী কালেমা পড়াইল।
আশমানির সঙ্গে জয়ার সাদী দিয়া দিল॥
জয়ানন্দের সঙ্গে হইল আশমানির বিয়া।
জয়ানন্দ হইয়া গেল জয়ানন্দ মিয়া॥[40]

Following the incident, the neighbours berate Jayananda viciously for marrying a "Yavani" and losing his caste. "What indeed has fate made him do, this dandy (*nāgar*) has sunk in sin his fourteen forebears' names. By wedding a Yavani he has destroyed his caste," they say:

হেন কালে দৈবেতে করিল কোন কাম।
পাপেতে ডুবাইল নাগর চৈস্ক পুরুষের নাম॥
. . .
যবনী করিয়া বিয়া জাতি কৈল মার॥'[41]

We, thus, come across a local population increasingly becoming part of a universe based on a different belief system, much unlike what Eaton would have us believe. The texts we studied above provide no signs of a people not yet integrated in a distinct social order. Eaton, thus, only makes a set of assertions, he does not quite explain by which process Islam expanded its frontiers in Bengal. But this notwithstanding, we do gather that the spread of Islam in Bengal was protracted. Despite him arguing in the contrary, we have observed that there was a cogent vocabulary of belief in eastern Bengal. We can, thus, assume that the thesaurus of belief and culture that Islam represented had a counterpart to engage with when introduced in Bengal. The 'spread' of Islam for us shall mean only the introduction of this vocabulary and the breaches caused by it in the existing universe of belief because of its interaction with it through a contestatory process. We shall, as a result, begin by trying to follow the engagement and mutual perceptions of peoples speaking with the aid of two distinct thesauri. Perhaps it will be revealed to us how, in the process, the articulators shaped and chiselled their own and the 'other's' selves in sharper relief.

It has been argued that the "notion of a uniform, religious community readily identified as Hindu"[42] was absent in precolonial India. However, as we have seen, already by the fifteenth and sixteenth centuries, the dwellers of Bengal identified themselves as 'Hindus' in a denominational and societal sense. As the *kāvya* tradition that flourished in Bengal from the fourteenth to the eighteenth centuries reveals, its authors, both non-Muslims and Muslims, had an acute awareness of belonging to two distinct cultural complexes. This tradition, represented by *mangal kāvyas* and *vijay kāvyas*, will command our attention in this chapter.

"Around the ninth and tenth centuries," we learn from Niharranjan Ray, "two dialects as well as Sanskrit were spoken in Bengal."[43] Of the two dialects, Śauraseni Apabhraṁśa and Māgadhi Apabhraṁśa, the latter was "the oldest form of Bengali."[44] Ray's claim is attested by Suniti Kumar Chatterjee's study of the history of the Bengali language. "The earliest extant specimens of Bengali"[45] date to the middle of the tenth century, writes Chatterji in *The Origin and Development of the Bengali Language.* By this time, Chatterji tells us, Bengali had become distinctive as the "expression of the life and religious aspirations of the people of Bengal, with the nucleus of a literature uniting the various dialectal areas."[46] However, not much of this nucleus has survived into our times. The earliest surviving literature in the Bengali language are the *charyās.* This corpus, an anthology of fifty songs of eight to fourteen lines each, was discovered by Haraprasad Shastri[47] (1853–1931) in the durbar library of Nepal in 1907. He edited and published the collection in 1916. The earliest and the latest dates assigned to the *charyās* differ rather widely, from the eighth to the twelfth centuries. Most, however, seem to have accepted the tenth or the eleventh century as the probable age of composition[48] of these "highly mystic"[49] poems encoding esoteric Yogic and Sahajiya concepts. After the *charyās* we have a long quietude. "There is no definite evidence of any literature for four hundred years"[50] making it difficult for us to assume a long term historical perspective.

The stillness was broken only after the Ilyas Shahis assumed power in 1342. A fair portion of the new revived literature in Bengali composed of translations of the epics and Vaishnava literature.[51] But the most to be produced were the long narrative poems—the *mangal kāvyas* and *vijay kāvyas.* This literature "had a strong religious, even a sectarian character, and was obviously designed to spread the doctrines of the particular sects."[52] Thus, goddesses such Manasa and Chandi and later Chaitanya Mahaprabhu (1486–1534) had many such poems devoted to them. In fact, there is, in this oeuvre, an "almost complete lack of any secular writing"[53] before the eighteenth century. The stray exceptions are a few romances by Muslim poets. What makes this trove especially valuable as a source to study the religious attitudes or prejudices of the age is what has been called its "non-official"[54] character. In Bengali we do not have much of what might be termed "court poetry." Thus, the poets "either consciously or instinctively, addressed their writings to the broad strata of readers."[55] The *kāvyas* were thus 'popular' and also gave expression to a 'popular religion.' It also appears that they are the articulations of a liminal religious universe which was still in the process of incorporating and synthesizing new elements. T.W. Clark discerns in the *kāvyas* "pre-Brahmanic" and "pre-Aryan" elements. These, we gather, owed their presence in the religious universe to the preceding centuries when Brahmanism was reestablished under the Sena kings. "It is probable," writes Clark, "that their [Senas] inclination tended not towards the suppression of indigenous cults and their mythology, but towards the incorporation of them within a framework of Sanskritic myths, thereby in effect Hinduizing them."[56] It is interesting to observe that the non-Muslim authors of the *kāvyas* are frequently Brahmans, their caste being deducible from the *dwija* (twice-born) prefixed to their names. The Brahman scholar, according to Clark, was the "literary producer of a synthesis."[57] J.C. Ghosh too observes a "self assertion" of *laukik* (worldly) cults in the fifteenth century to which he credits the "resurgence" of Hinduism.[58] Representative of the "non-Brahmanic and non-Aryan masses and their culture" these cults were emerging to the surface "after centuries of submerged existence."[59] Dr Ashutosh Bhattacharya equates the *kāvyas* to the Puranic literature in Sanskrit. According to him, they represent a transition in religious expression similar to the one evinced by the Puranas. The Puranas, Bhattacharya argues, issued from Hinduism's effort to reclaim ground lost to Buddhism. They replaced the abstract Vedic deities by more immediate, graspable divinities. Bhattacharya will have us infer that a similar effort was needed in Bengal for the region was dominated by Buddhism till the eleventh century AD. Hence the *kāvyas* and their 'worldly' deities. Bhattacharya also suspects that the Mahayana Buddhism prevalent in Bengal might have interacted with certain local cults to produce the beliefs which find expression in the *kāvyas.*[60] Thus, the *kāvyas* of non-Muslim authorship lead us into a religious universe consciously forming and claiming room for itself. To borrow from Kunal Chakravarti's description of the role played by the Bengal Puranas, the Bengali *kāvyas* are replete with "linguistic codes" constituting "social and discursive formations."[61] Hence, when they take note of the Muslims we too must pay heed.

The non-Muslim *kāvya* authors will occasionally depict the Muslims in a value neutral tone. Sometimes a note of ambivalence will creep into their voices. The transition from a value neutral to an ambivalent tone could happen in the same verse or in the very next one. We, for example, can cite the part from Kavikankan Mukunda's *Chandimangal* (চণ্ডিমঙ্গল) wherein he alludes to the coming of "Muslims" to a new settlement and the treatment they received.[62] Mukunda's hero Kalketu founds the city of Gujarat at the behest of goddess Chandi. Mukunda describes how people left a city by the name of Kalinga for the city founded by Kalketu. Kalketu settled various peoples there. Among them were the "Muslims" who received the betel (*pān*) from Kalketu and were granted the western quarters. The *saiyads, maulānās,* and the *qāzīs* rode into the city of Kalketu and he generously allotted them dwelling places:

> কলিঙ্গনগর ছাড়ি প্রজা লয় ঘর-বাড়ি
> নানা জাতি বিরের নগরে
> বিরের পাইয়া পান বৈসে যত মুসলমান
> পশ্চিম দিগা বির দিলো তারে।
> আইসে চড়িয়া তাজি সৈয়দ মোলানা কাজি
> খইরত দেয় বির বাড়ি।[63]

The author is also clearly aware that they adhere to a different belief and have different cultural practices. Mukunda's verse tells us of the "Muslim" wont of rising at the hour of *fajr* and offering five prayers spreading red mats on earth. Further, we learn that they told beads reciting the names of the prophets and saints. They also lit lamps upon the graves of the saints:

ফজর সময়ে উঠি বিছাই লোহিত পাটী
পাঁচ বেরি করয়ে নমাজ
সোলেমানি মালা ধরে জপে পির পয়গম্বরে
পিরের মোকামে দেই সাঁজ।[64]

Our poet discovers many things admirable with the strangers. The "Muslims" decided disputes in groups of ten or twenty, they constantly read the *Qur'ān*. Mukunda calls the "Muslims" generous and not given to quarrelling. He adds that they do not give up on the *ramzān* fast even if they were to die. Describing the appearance of the "Muslims" Mukunda writes that they tonsure their heads and their beards cover their chests. The poet adds that they never keep their heads uncovered and wear trousers which are tied up with draw strings. Mukunda relates these features of their appearance almost with a measure of admiration:

দশ বিশ বিরাদরে বসিয়া বিচার করে
অনুক্ষন পডয়ে কোরান

. . .

বড়ই দানিসবন্দ কেহনা করয়ে দ্বন্দ্ব
প্রান গেলে রোজা নাহী ছাড়ি
ধরেয কম্বুজ-বেশ শিরে নাহি রাখে কেশ
বুক আচ্ছাদিয়া রাখে দাড়ি।
না ছারে আপন পথে সদাই টুপি দেই মাথে
ইজার পড়য়ে দড় নাড়ি[65]

However, his voice sounds faintly ambivalent when he tells us of a quirk of his subjects. He writes that they do not talk to those whose heads are uncovered, instead they cudgel them on the head:

জার দেখে খালি মাথা তার সনে না কহে কথা
সড়িয়া দণ্ডের মারে বাড়ি।[66]

The people he describes must have struck him as having a rather exacting standard of decorum.

Mukunda now moves on to other features. He dwells on the ways of the "Muslims" in some detail. It might have appeared strange to him that after dining they wipe their hands on a piece of cloth, the reason why he mentions the fact. Mukunda makes an account of "Muslims" of varied provenances, Surani, Lohani, Spani (Ispahani?), Kitapi, Bittani, Huni, and Pathan. He also describes the roles played by the *maulavīs*, that they read the *nikāh*, sacrifice chicken and goats, teach children in the *muqaddam* and are paid for in cowry shells for their services:

আটনা বাটনা নিঞা বসিল সকল মিঞা
ভুন্জিআ কাপড়ে মুছে হাথ
সুরানি লোহানি স্পানি কিতাপি বিট্টানি হুনি
পাঠান বসিল নানা জাত।
বসিল অনেক মিঞা আপন টবর নিঞা
কেহো নিকা কেহো করে বিহা
মোললা পড়াইয়া নিকা দান পায় সিকা সিকা
দোয়া করে কলমা পড়িয়া।
করে ধরি করা ছুরি মুরগি জবাই করি
দশ গণ্ডা দরে পায় কড়ি
বকরি জবাই জাথা মোললাকে দেই মাথা
দড়ে পায়ে কড়ি ছয় বুড়ী।
জত শিশু মুসলমান কড়িআ দলিজখান
মখস্কম পড়ায়ে পড়ানা[67]

After describing their social practices, Mukunda goes on to enumerate the professions followed by the "Muslims." He mentions many, the *julāhā*, the seller of paddy, the maker of sweet meats (*pithā*), the mason, the *tānti* who works the loom, the vender of icons, the healer, the paper maker and the *qalandar* who wanders day and night:

রোজা নামাজ না জানিঞা বোলাইল গোলা
তাসন করিয়া কেহ নাম ধরে জোলা।
বলদে বহিয়া ধান বলাইল মুগরি
পিঠা বেচিয়া নাম বলাইল পিঠাহারি।
...সানা বান্ধিয়া নাম ধরে সানাকর
জিবন উপায় তার পায়্যা তাঁতিঘর।
পট লৈয়া ফিরে কেহো নগরে নগরে
তিরকর হইয়া কেহো নিরাময় শরে।
কাগজ কুটিয়া নাম বলায় কাগতি
কলন্দর হইয়া কেহো ফিরে দিবারাতি।[68]

This verse ends interestingly with the author expressing a mild discomfiture with their presence. He addresses his audience as "Hindus," apparently implying a denominational category, and asks them to beware of these people:

নানাবৃত্তি করিআ বসিল মুসলমান
সাবধান হইয়া শুন হিন্দুর উঠান।[69]

Apparently, even when the new-comers were to be welcomed, it was important to be careful and circumspect about them as they were a people with different cultural practices.

Dwija Hariram writing in the same age as Mukunda begins with a similar value neutral depiction when alluding to the Muslims. Describing their advent into a town called Hasanhati, he writes that the Mughals and Pathans were welcomed as heroes and were granted the western quarters of the town. The Sheikhs and the Saiyads dwelt in the centre of Hasanhati:

বীরের সম্মান পায়্যা পশ্চিম দিগেতে গিয়া
বস্যে যত মোগল-পাঠান
হাসনহাটীর মাঝে সৈদ সকল বাজে
সেকজাদা বৈসে প্যায়া গান॥[70]

However, he goes on to call the Muslims people of wicked

and unkind speech, prone to passions and quarrelsome,[71] despite the fact that they were received respectfully and honourably. It is also interesting to note that both Mukunda and Hariram locate the Muslims in the western quarters of the cities they describe. Perhaps, it seemed natural to them in view of the fact that the Muslims genuflected facing west when offering prayers. The authors of the *kāvyas* also display a strong awareness of what they perceive to be the 'Hindu' way of life and can recognize its violations. This is manifest when one character in Mukunda's *Chandimangal* admonishes a woman for consuming non-vegetarian food though her husband is believed to be dead. She is accused of letting down her 'Hindu' birth with her actions:

> দনাঞি পণ্ডিত মোরে কহিল নিষ্ঠুর স্বরে
> কোনকালে মৈল ধনপতি
> মায়ের আইত হাতে ভোজন আমিস্য ভাতে
> মিছা হিন্দুকুলে উতপতি।[72]

One must remember in this context that an upper caste Bengali Hindu widow was expected to entirely abstain from non-vegetarian food.

The *kāvya* poets of medieval Bengal who strove to be 'Muslim' too display a very percipient knowledge of a cultural complex which is distinct and lies juxtaposed to their own. Their corpus is as large and diverse as that of their non-Muslim counterparts, if not more. Asim Roy contends that an "Islamic syncretistic tradition"[73] emanates from this literature. This tradition, he suggests, was constructed "rather consciously"[74] by Muslim "cultural mediators" "urged by a deep sense of obligation towards the masses of the believers, with their specific needs and demands in the social and cultural milieu of Bengal."[75] Why did they need to make this effort? This was because, Roy writes, "indigenous and low class origin"[76] of the Muslims of Bengal significantly informed the process of Islamisation in the region. Hence, the literature produced by the "mediators" is marked by an "anxiety to illumine the masses of Bengali Muslims"[77] who were ignorant of Arabic and Persian and still bore in their minds the detritus of their Hindu and Buddhist past. Besides the indigenous converts, there were the immigrant Muslims in Bengal, making up the other half of the community. There existed, we learn from Roy, a "total absence of cultural contact and communication"[78] between the two groups. This, in turn, indicated the possibility of the relapse of the indigenous "isolated majority into the amorphous sponge-like body of Hinduism."[79]

As their non-Muslim coevals, the "Muslim" poets, Roy's 'mediators,' too appear to trace their roots to the more privileged social groups. Of course, this is to be expected in the authors of a literary tradition in the pre-modern period. They "comprised both the descendents of immigrant families and those of indigenous converts."[80] "There were quite a few *saiyids* among these writers" and "there were a very large number of them bearing the doubtful title of *sheikh*."[81] Whatever their origins, indigenous or foreign, we are told that they tried to "make their religious traditions available to the Muslims in terms familiar and intelligible to them."[82] This meant that they reduced the "Islamic struggle against infidelity in general to that against Hinduism."[83] The Muslim versifiers did not shrink from bringing "the prophet himself in line with the comparable symbols of Hindu traditions."[84] Thus, the Islamic concepts of *nabī* and *rasūl* were collapsed with the Hindu idea of the *avatār*. As illustrated by Roy, the Muslim poets do appear to have interacted with the parallel sacral universe and even borrowed artifacts from it, ironically, to sharpen their own sense of singularity and apartness, to 'become' more of Muslims. To us it does not appear like 'syncretism' was what they were intending at, consciously or otherwise.

The 'Muslim poets' interaction with the parallel universe is displayed often and variously, like in the tribute paid by the seventeenth century Arakanese poet Alaol to his guru Magan Thakur. Describing the virtues of his master he writes that there lived in the country a great soul, a truthful Muslim of Siddiqui birth. Alaol praises the infinite creative ways of the creator who has placed amid his creation such learned ones. His guru knew Arabic, Persian, Magha, and *Hinduāni.* He was skilled in many ways and was an interpreter of signs:

. . . এক মহাপরূস আছিল সেই দেসে।
মোহাসত্য মছলমান ছিদ্দিকের বংসে॥[85]
...কতার শ্রীজন রূপ কহিতে অনন্ত।
তাহাতে করিল বিধি নানা গুনমত্ত॥
আরবি ফারসি আর মঘা হিন্দু আনি।
নানা গূনে পারগ সঙ্কেত জ্ঞাতা গুলি॥[86]

So, Alaol's guru knew Arabic, Persian, Magha (the Arakan language) and *Hinduāni.* The last mentioned could be the Awadhi language that had found its way into the Arakan court.[87] Or could it be Bengali, the language in which Alaol was writing? Irrespective of the identity of this language, it seems as though Alaol recognizes it as an artifact that does not belong to his cultural universe. It is likely, because we find that when the non-Muslim *kāvya* poets of the same age are putting the term in the mouth of a Muslim character it implies 'the way of the Hindus.' Generally, the Muslim character in question will employ the nomenclature in a condemnatory or pejorative tone. We come across *qāzīs* who do this in certain of the *kāvyas.* The pontiffs, however, will not stop at expressing reprobation, they will also vow to put down *Hinduāni.* One such example is furnished by a rough contemporary of Alaol in the *Bāiś Kabir Manasā-Mangal bā Bāiśā* (বাইশ করিব মনসা-মঙ্গল বা বাইশা) wherein we have a *qāzī* who went about forbidding *Hinduāni*:

আপনিই কাজি সেই গোষ্ঠী তার জোলা।
কিতাব কোরান পড়ি করে কাজিয়ালা॥

নগরে ফিরে হিন্দুর পুজা করি মানা।
'ভুত পুজা' বলি তারে করে বিডম্বনা॥
তার যত গোষ্ঠী জোলা কলিমা জানিয়া।
কাজির ভাই কাজির শালা সব হইল মিঞা।[88]

As the verse above puts it, this *qāzī* was a *julāhā* who read the *Qur'ān* to discharge his office. Our *qāzī* censured the rites of "Hindus" as the "worship of ghosts" and wandered the town proscribing *Hinduāni*. The poet seems to hint that he was a neo-convert. He writes that the *qāzī*'s kin *became* "Muslim" by learning the *kalimah*. It seems that sometimes it was the neo-converts to what was considered an Islamic way of life who were the most zealous in spreading their newly acquired faith.

We come across zealot *qāzīs* in other places too. In the *Śrī Chaitanya Bhāgbat* (শ্রীচৈতন্যভাগবত) by Sri Brindabandas Thakur, for example. In this text a *qāzī* is chafed at the sight of a congregational prayer, a *kīrtan*, organised by Chaitanya in the town of Nadia. The *qāzī* swears that if he has his way he will punish this display of *Hinduāni*:

কাজি বোলে "হিন্দুয়ানি হইল নদীয়া।
করিমু ইয়ার শাস্তি নাগালি পাইয়া॥[89]

They appeared in the earlier centuries too. There is a like *qāzī* in the late fifteenth century *Padmāpurān* (পদ্মাপুরান) by Bijay Gupta, another poem dedicated to goddess Manasa. His two sons, Hasan and Husain, took great delight in putting down all display of *Hinduāni*. These rather boistrous youths will speak ill of the Vedas whenever they could:

হাসন হুসন দুই কাজির নন্দন॥
মহা দুরন্ত তারা কোন ভয় নাই।
ধর্ম্ম কর্ম্ম বেদ নিন্দা করে ঠাই ঠাই॥[90]

If they came across someone with his forehead anointed

with *tulsi* (basil) leaves they beat him dragging him by the hair. They took particular pleasure in insulting a Brahman:

> তুলসীর পত্র পায়ে জাহার মাথাতে।
> চুলে ধরি আনে তারে আপনা সাক্ষাতে॥
> সোগার তলে মাথা থুইয়া মারে উভাকিল।
> . . . ব্রাহ্মনে অপমান করে পৈতা পাইয়া কান্ধে।[91]

One must recall that this same Bijay Gupta had extolled an Ilyas Shahi king providing Eaton an example of the evolution of an ostensible modus vivendi that the dynasty had come to share with Bengali culture. What we propose is that the acceptance of Islam as the state need not necessarily mean an acceptance of its cultural manifestations and representatives at the local level. *Qāzīs*, writes Eaton, were "the most visible representatives of royal authority vis-à-vis non-Muslims, since they were charged with maintaining public order generally."[92] However, what this contact with the 'other' meant in terms of cultural encounter, Eaton does not ask. As the above verses above illustrate, the *qāzī* definitely vexed.

Thus, *Hinduāni* was a parallel universe lying on the other side of a cultural and emotional breach. Occasionally, the two universes came into contact with implications for our narrative. What is most significant for us is that someone like Alaol could espy this universe even while being in the court of Arakan which lay across the frontiers of Chittagong. This is an area which, according to Eaton, was yet to be integrated into the Hindu social order. One must also remember that he was writing in the middle of the seventeenth century, a time not very long after the Mughal expansion in the region. In the contiguous kingdom of Tripura we have the author of the *Rājmālā* bitterly complaining of the Mughals forbidding the observance of *dharma* and the worship of goddess Kalika and the *chaturdaśdebatā,* the fourteen guardian deities of Tripura, during their brief occupation of the state. This was before the invaders had been repelled by Kalyan Manikya:

পাপিষ্ঠ মগল জাতি দুষ্ট দুরাচার।
ধর্ম্ম কর্ম্ম নিষেধিল নগরে রাজার॥
চতুর্দ্দশ দেবপূজা নিষেধে যবন।
কালিকা দেবীর পূজা করিল বারণ॥[93]

From the very early days, any flirtation with this parallel universe could give a 'Muslim' poet reason for anxiety. We have Shah Mohammad Saghir, the very first of the lot to write in Bengali in the closing years of fourteenth or in the beginning of the fifteenth century, assuring his audience that the sacred word could indeed be translated in the native language. Saghir wrote that people, he obviously meant his co-religionists, are wary of composing in it because they fear condemnation. But he had come to realise that such fears are unfounded for it is not the language that makes the 'word' true:

নানা কাব্য-কথা-রসে মজে নরগন।
যার যেই শ্রধীএ সন্তোষ করে মন॥
না লেখে কিতাব কথা মনে ভয় পায়।
দুষিব সকল তাকে ইহা না জুয়ায়॥
গুনিয়া দেখিলুঁ আক্ষি ইহ ভয় মিছা।
না হয় ভাষায় হয় কথা সাচা॥[94]

The mid-fifteenth century poet Mujammil too expressed similar sentiments. In a tone bearing a tinct of defiance he wrote the following in his *Nītiśastra Bārtā* (নিতিশাস্ত্র-বার্তা):

People do not understand Arabic. So that all may comprehend, I will compose these verses. Let people say what they will, I have written what I wanted to . . . Mojammil has composed a sweet cadent *pānchāli* in the tongue of the country (*deśi bhāṣe*).

আরবি ভাষায় লোকেঁ না বুঝে কারন।
সভারে বুঝিতে কৈলুঁ পয়ার রচন॥
যে বলে বলৌক লোকেঁ করিলুঁ লিখন।

ভাকে ভাল মন্দে মন্দ না যাএ খণ্ডন ॥
রচিলেক মোজাম্মিল পঞ্চালি সুছন্দ।
দেশি ভাষে রচিলুং মাঝে মৃদু মন্দ ॥
নীতিশাস্ত্র-বার্তা যে জন পড়এ শুনএ।
আপ্তযশ বাঢ়ে জান দারিদ্র্য খণ্ডএ ॥[95]

This anxiety must have been common, as we will see 'Muslim' poets of the later centuries too expressing it often. Many who followed Saghir consciously sought to come to terms with it. Apparently, a means they adopted to dispel their guilt was to direct their verses against local paganism. In their tales, the artifacts of local paganism were frequently transported back to Arabia of the Prophet's days and destroyed at his hands. One such instance is provided by the poem *Rasūl Bijay* (রসুল বিজয়) by Zainuddin. *Rasūl Bijay* narrates the tale of the conquest of Iraq by the Prophet. In the poem, the country is ruled by a fictional king called Zaikum. At one point in the story the warrior Zonabil, a devout follower of the Prophet, delivers an oration on the battlefield. Incidentally, we gather from it that the Vedas are sacred books in the kingdom of Zaikum too:

> The brave one let out a leonine roar on the battlefield and spoke aloud. Come and adore the feet of the Prophet and retain your life, he said. The Prophet is an ocean of compassion, hasten to seek his audience. Whoever recites his *kalimah* rids himself of the sins of ten million births. Know that his *kalimah* contains the Vedas too. . . . And if you refuse to trust my word look in the Vedas yourself. They indeed contain peans to the *kalimah*.

রনস্থলে গিয়া বীর সিংহনাদ ছাড়ি।
কহিতে লাগিলা বীচ উচ্চ স্বর করি ॥
শুন, করতার তুহ্মি বোল গিয়া ধাই।
নৃপতির সৈন্য লৈয়া আইস ঝাটাই ॥
আসিয়া নবির পদ প্রনামিয়া।
নিজ প্রান রাখউক ইমান আনিয়া ॥
কৃপার সাগর নবী আসিছে নিকট।
ঝাটে করি ভেট আসি তাহার নিকট ॥

তাহান কলিমা কহএ মন্ত্র জপএ।
কোটিক জন্ম পাপ সেইখানে ক্ষএ॥
আপন জন তান কলিমা বাখান।
শীঘ্র চল বেদ আছে বিদ্যমান॥[96]...
প্রত্যয় না হয় যদি আহ্মার বচন।
সে বেদ বিচারি তবে চাহত আপন॥
কিবা চারি বেদ মধ্যে শাস্ত্র সব জান।
কলিমা বাখান জান আছে তান স্থান॥[97]

It is interesting to observe that earlier in the narrative the same Zainuddin had employed a very Indic imagery to praise the valour of Ali:

Valiant as Brahma and leonine, he bore a mace of a thousand *mun.*
The sight of him stunned even the Lord of Death (Yama).

ব্রহ্মসম তেজবন্ত মৃগেন্দ্র সমান॥
সহস্র মনের গদা ধরি বীর দাপ।
যমরাজা দেখি তস্ক হৈল মনস্তাপ॥[98]

There were others like Saiyad Sultan who tried to bring the Prophet in line with the local cosmogony but definitely not with the intention of validating it. He started composing *Nabibangśa* (নবিবংশ), a genealogy of the prophets, at some point between 1584 and 1586.[99] Sultan begins the work with an invocation of the God who is without a beginning and end and has created the fourteen worlds:

প্রথমে প্রনামি প্রভু অনাদি নিধান
নিমিষে সৃজিছে যেই এ চৌস্ক ভুবন
আদি অন্ত নাহি তার নাহি স্থান স্থিতে[100]

Sultan's conception of the divine is quite on the Indic lines. Suggesting that he might have been familiar with the Sāṁkhya system of philosophy, Sultan ascribes to the deity three dominant humours—*rajas, sattva,* and *tamas.* With the first he created, *sattva* helped him nurture his creation while *tamas* urged him to destroy:

রজঃ গুন ধরি প্রভু সংসার সৃজএ
সত্বগুন ধরি প্রভু সংসার পালএ।
তমগুন ধরি প্রভু করে সংহার॥[101]

Sultan presents a cosmogony that incorporates Indic elements. But in his work it evolves in a way so as to render inevitable the Islamic revelation. The world, in Sultan's view began like this:

> After having placed the earth, the Formless One thought of laying a creation upon her. Hence, he made a great fire from which to draw his creation. He stirred the fire to bring forth a man. The Creator called him Marich. Marich recited the name of the Lord in an unwavering tone. Pleased with his devotion, the Creator ordered a woman into existence from left of Marich's body. She was beauteous and the Lord called her Marijat.

প্রথিবি স্থাপন যদি কৈলা নৈরাকার
ইচ্ছা হৈল তাহাতে যে সৃষ্টি করিবরে।
তবে এক আনল সৃজিলা করতারে
যে আনল হোন্তে প্রভু সৃষ্টি করিবার।
বিনি ধুমে আতস সৃজিল নিরঞ্জন
তা হোন্তে করিলা এক পুরুষ প্রধান।
আনল মথিয়া যদি পুরুষ সৃজিলা
তার নাম করতারে মারিচ রাখিলা।
চিরকাল মারিচ রহিয়া একসর
প্রভু নাম জপিতে লাগিলা নিরন্তর।
তার ভক্তিভাব দেখি প্রভু নিরঞ্জন
আজ্ঞা কৈলা নারি এক হৈতে সৃজন।
মরিচের বাম অঙ্গ হোন্তে এক নারী
জন্মিয়া নিকলে নারি পরম সুন্দরী
'মারিজাত' নাম প্রভু থুইল সে নারীর[102]

The 'Hindus,' says Sultan, know this pair as Ishvar and Parvati. They had two sons—Brahma and Vishnu:

এহি নারি-পুরুষক যত হিন্দুগনে
ঈশ্বর-পারতী বুলি কহে সবজনে।
ঈশ্বর-পারতী হোন্তে হৈল দুই সুত
একে ব্রহ্মা আরে বিষ্ণু রুপে অদ্ভুত।[103]

A busy course of events is now set into motion. Parvati gave birth to a son called Jan. After Jan, Marich and Parvati begot a daughter. When the two grew up Marich married his daughter to his son. First the *asura* Janbil was born of this union and then a daughter. As his father, Janbil made his son wed his sister when they grew to be youths. As their parents and grandparents, Janbil and his spouse begot a son and a daughter. Loyal to precedents, the son, the *asura* Ajajil, took his sister as wife upon attaining maturity. Their fecund union produced many offspring, an equal number of *asuras* and *suras*. Initially both dwelt in the sky. Later Niranjan put the *asuras* upon earth. The *asuras* did his will and served him with devotion. However, as the old among them died, the *asuras'* piety eroded and they yielded to sin. When Niranjan saw what they have come to, he chose an *asura* named Am to be the sovereign of earth. Niranjan dispatched his angels to Am who taught him the *śāstras* and tutored him in ethics. Am was instructed to hand down to the *asuras* what he has learnt and directed them not to do sin again. But when Am tried to do as bidden his charges slew him. Soon after, the *suras* defeated the *asuras* aided by the angels and won the sovereignty of the earth:

সুরগনে সমে রহি ফিরিস্তা সকল
অসুরক মারিলা করিয়া রসাতল।[104]

Thus, the *suras* dwelt upon earth. The demons lost on account of their sins. The *suras* served the lord punctiliously and never committed evil:

রহিলেন্ত সুর সব পৃথিবী উপর
সবে নিরঞ্জন এবা করে অনিবার।

হারিলেক দৈত্য সব পাপের কারন
দৈত্য সকলেরে প্রভু করিলা নিধন।
যত্ন করি প্রভু সেবা করে প্রতিনিত
পাপ কর্ম সে সবে না করে কদাচিত।[105]

However, Niranjan was to be disappointed again as even the *suras* gradually gave in to sin. The earth then made a plaint to him not being able to bear the weight of ill deeds. Heeding her laments, the wrathful Niranjan burnt the *suras* to death sparing only a few who had not sinned much. Their descendants, the *naras* (humans), again peopled the earth. When the *naras* too began to lapse from their early piety, Niranjan sent down the four Vedas to help them tell good from bad:

ঐহি যে আলোপ হই আছে সুরগন
তার বংশে পুনি ক্ষিতি হইল ভরন।
সে সবের নর নাম হৈল প্রথিবীত
দান ধর্ম সৎকর্ম করিলেন্ত নিত।
চিরদিন হৈল যদি গঞিল বিশেষ
একে একে করিলেন্ত পাপেত প্রবেশ।
নর সবে পাইবারে পাপ পুন্য ভেদ
চারি মহাজনে পাঠাইলা চারি বেদ।
চারি বেদ পাঠাইয়া দিলা নিরঞ্জন
নীতি শাস্ত্র সামবেদ নামিল তখন।[106]

He handed the *Sāmaveda* to Brahma so that the humans might draw knowledge. *Yajurveda* was sent with Vishnu. Then the Lord created Śiva and charged him with the *Ṛgveda*. The fourth to be created was Hari and he was entrusted with the *Atharvaveda*. In all the four books the Creator testified to the inevitability of the manifestation of Mohammad. However, the people were unable to read these texts, as they were unlettered. Then an angel from the heavens taught a few to read. The descendants of those who learnt to read came to be known as the *dwija* (twice born):

সাম বেদ ব্রহ্মাত পাঠাইল নৈরাকার
নর সব সেকালেত জ্ঞান পাইবার।
তবে বিষ্ণুর হইল উতপন
যজেবেদ তাহানে পাঠাইলা নিরঞ্জন।
তৃতীয় মহেশ যদি সৃজন হইলা
ঋকবেদ তার স্থানে পাঠাইয়া দিলা।
চতুর্থে যদি সে হরি হইলা সৃজন
অথর্ববেদ তাহানে পাঠাইলা নিরঞ্জন।
এ চারি বেদেতে সাক্ষি দিছে করতার
অবশ্য অবশ্য মুহম্মদ ব্যক্ত হইবার।
মুর্খ সব আছিল না জানে পড়িবার
পড়িতে না পারি সবে হৈল ধন্ধকার।
তবে অন্তরীক্ষে থাকি এক ফিরিস্তাএ
সেই পত্র পড়িবারে সবারে সিখাএ
যে-সকলে সে পত্র লাগিল শিখিবার
পৃথিবীতে দ্বিজবর নাম হৈল তার[107]

Thus some time passed. The age of Rama dawned upon Earth. After Sita disappeared in her depths, the Earth again pleaded before the Creator that she is no more being able to suffer the weight of the sin that is committed upon her. Hearing her lament, the Creator decided to create Adam and entrust Earth to him. In all of creation, the Creator decided, there will be nothing equalling him:

সতী নারি সীতা দেবি অনাল হইয়া
মোহোর উদরে ছিল বহু দুঃখ পাইয়া।
এ দেখিয়া মো হইল ফাফর
নিবেদন কৈলঁ প্রভু তোমার গোচর।
এ পাপের ভর আমি না পারি সহিতে
পাতালে মজ্জিব আমি রহিব নিচিন্তে।
কথেক সহিব আমি এ পাপের ভার
সহজে ললাটে হেন লিখন আমার।
ক্ষিতির কাকুতি শুনি প্রভু নিরঞ্জন
ক্ষিতি-রক্ষা ফিরিস্তারে বুলিলা বচন।
নিশ্চয় জানহ মুত্রি আদম সৃজিমু
সে আদম হোতে ক্ষিতি নিশ্চয় পালিমু।

ক্ষিতি হোতে মাটি আনি সৃজিমু আদম
সৃষ্টি মধ্যে কেহ যেন নহে তার সম[108]

Niranjan destroyed all evils that preceded Adam one by one. He summoned an angel and said that it has been futile creating the Vedas as no one abides by them. He directed him to cast the Vedas in the ocean:

আদমের আগে যথ ছিল দুরাচার
একে একে নিরঞ্জনে করিলা সংহার।
ফিরিস্তারে আজ্ঞা দিলা প্রভু নিরঞ্জন
না ধরিল পাপি সব বেদের বচন।
বেদ শাস্ত্র সৃজিয়া না কৈলা কোন কাজ
রাখ নিয়া চারি বেদ সমুদ্রের মাজ।[109]

The books had failed and so had, as we understand, their recipients. Of all the demigods to whom the Creator had handed down books, Hari had been the most ignominious failure. Sultan also informs the "Hindus" as to why Hari was unsuccessful in discharging the responsibility the Deity had entrusted him with. "Your Hari was created," Sultan writes, "so that you might know scripture. But Hari was trailed by *iblīs* (Satan) in the guise of sage Narada. He taught Hari tasks good and bad. Thus, the doer of foul deeds lived with Hari":

তোহ্মার হরির এবে হইল সৃজন
তোহ্মা সবে তত্ব জ্ঞান পাইবারে কারণ।
সে হরির সনে রহি ইব্লিস দুবার
ধরিয়া আছিল পাপী মুনির আকার।
ইব্লিস নারদ পাপী হরির সহিত
ভাল মন্দ কার্য যে শিখাএ প্রতিনিত।
হরি সনে যেই রূপে আছিল দুরাচার
কহি শুন হএ নহে করিতে বিচার।[110]

Besides condemning the deities of non-Muslims, Saiyad Sultan also describes how the categories of believers and unbelievers had their beginning. This was when the Creator summoned all to make obeisance to the refulgence (*nūr*) of Mohammad. Those who saluted this light were born as believers (*momin*) in the world. There were the ones who performed salutations thrice, they were born as the good. But there were those who made no supplication, they were born as the unbelievers (*kāfir*). Some saluted later, they were born among "Hindus" but later became "Muslims." And there were some who saluted first but not later. Though they were born among "Muslims" they lived as *kāfirs*:

যে সবে সে নূর দেখি কৈলা পরনাম
জগতে জন্মিল সেই মুমীন উপাম।
প্রনমিলা নূরেরে যে সবে তিনবার
জগতে জন্মিল সেই ভাল ব্যবহার।
যে সবে নূরেরে দেখি প্রনাম না কৈলা
কাফির হৈয়া সেই জগতে জন্মিলা।
আগে না প্রনমিয়া যে পশ্চাতে প্রনমিলা
হিন্দুকুলে জন্মি পুনি মুসলমান হৈলা।
যে আগে প্রনাম করি পাছে না করিল
মুসলমানকুলে জন্মি কাফির হইল।[111]

The most curious discovery for us is that Mohammad too was born a "Hindu" and *Hinduāni* is what Arabia observed. The local paganism which must have displeased Sultan so is transposed upon Arabia and the Prophet himself is made to speak against it. When Mohammad is still a boy he earns the ire of his uncle Abu Jehel for doing so. Abu said to him, "You are my brother's son still you preach foul thoughts. Though born of Hindus, you speak ill of *Hinduāni*. You seek to preach the *Musalmāni* ways. First I will make a Hindu out of you, only then merit will be bestowed on you in the moments of death. If you follow the beliefs of your clan you will be saved in afterlife. I will tattoo an image (*murati*) on your forehead, then I will sling the sacred thread upon your shoulder. After that I will teach you all our ways (*āchār*). I will make you perform the ablutions and *tarpan.* In the end, I will make you burn in fire. If you want to meet a good end in afterlife, cast *Musalmāni* out of your heart":

শিশুকে বুলিলা আবু জেহেল দুর্মতি
তুহ্মি মোর ভ্রাতৃসুত প্রচার কুমতি।
হিন্দুর তনয় হই নিন্দ হিন্দুয়ানি
প্রচারিতে চাহসি আচার মুসলমানি।
প্রথমে তোহোরে হিন্দু করিবাম আহ্মি
মৃত্যু কালে তবে পুন্য পাইবেক তুহ্মি
আপনা বংশের যদি করিলা আচার
পরকালে ভাল গতি হইব তোহ্মার।
প্রথমে ললাটে তোর মৃরতি লেখিমু
দ্বতীএ তোহ্মার কান্ধে পৈতা চড়াইমু।
তৃতীয়ে যথেক আছে আচার আপনার
একে একে জানাইমু সে সব প্রকার।
চতুর্থে করাইমু তোরে স্নান তর্পণ
পঞ্চমে করাইমু তোরে আনলে দাহন।
পরলোকে তবে সে তোহোর ভাল গতি
মন হোন্তে মুসলমানি তেজ সম্প্রতি।[112]

All conflict, universally, is about difference, whether of race religion or nationality. Sultan universalises the conflict between 'Hindus' and 'Muslims' to the point that the differences causing it find their echos in the imaginary, supernatural world too. We observe "Hindus" among the fairies too. One such mischief making "Hindu" fairy lurked in an idol in Abu Jehel's house:

পরীর মেলেতে বহু হিন্দু পরি আছে
এক হিন্দু পরী গিয়া মূর্তিতে রহিছে।
আবু জেহেলের ঘরে মূর্তির ভিতর
রহিয়াছে হিন্দু পরী অধিক দুষ্কর।[113]

We also observe beings out of Indic mythology being converted by the Prophet. Hearing of Mohammad's glories, once the king of the *gandharvas* comes to see him. He takes the Prophet to where he lived. Then all *gandharvas* embrace *īmān*. All the fairies too turn up to offer the *namāz*. Mohammad acts as the *imām* as they perform the *namāz*. The king of *gandharvas* dispatches scouts and musters all of his kind. Then they all recite the *kalimah* and become "Muslims":

নবির মহিমা শুনি গন্ধর্ব নৃপতি
রসুলের সাক্ষাতে আইলা শিঘ্রগতি।
রসুলক লই গেলা আপনার স্থান
গন্ধর্ব সকলে মিলি আনিল ইমান।
নামাজ পড়িতে যতে পরীগন আইলা
রসুল ইমাম হই নামাজ পড়িলা।
গন্ধর্ব নৃপতি যথ সব চর পাঠাইয়া
আনাইলা গন্ধর্ব সকল ডাকাইয়া।
সকল গন্ধর্ব মিলি হইল মুসলমান
নবীর কলেমা পড়ি আনাইল ইমান।[114]

However, despite relating his monumental tale in Bengali, Sultan too displays the same trepidation about writing in the language as did Saghir two centuries ago. He pauses the narration and expends a few verses to tell us how he did not have a choice in the matter. "Ill-fate has bred Bengalis in Bengal," writes Sultan, "they do not understand the Arabic word. Not comprehending a word of their faith, they remain as animals. My heart pains seeing them read the tales of Rama and Krishna always. They have all not understood a word of their faith. Having no knowledge of this world and the other, they are all immersed in sin":

কর্মদোষে বঙ্গেতে বঙ্গালী উতপন
না বুঝে বঙ্গালী সব আরবী বচন।
আপনা দীনের বোল এক না বুঝিল
পশুর চরিত্র হই সে সব রহিল।
সদাএ পঠএ রাম-কৃষ্ণের যে কথা
শুনিয়া মোহের মনে লাগে অতি ব্যথা।

এ সবে দিনের বোল এক না বুঝিল
পরাপন জ্ঞান না ছিল পাপেতে মজিল।[115]

It is very clear from the above verse that even when groups and individuals had formally accepted the new faith they were still lapsing into the cultural mould indicated by the master signifiers of Rama and Krishna. Obviously, it was found a painful experience by those local cultural leaders who were engaged in the process of helping them to cross over to a new universe of faith.

Hence, we find Sultan's quandary genuine enough. He indeed had no other means of taking the sacred word to his co-religionists who were ignorant of the tongue in which it was originally revealed. But, apparently, there were people in his times who were unsympathetic to his efforts. In the lines which follow the above ones, Sultan very obviously refers to his detractors. "They say that I have violated the Book," Sultan offers his defence, "but in the country of Bengal I can make no one understand the Arabic word":

কিতাব ভাঙ্গিল করি দূষ এ আহ্মারে।
. . .
বঙ্গদেশি সকলরে কিরূপে বুঝাইব
বাখানি আরবি ভাষে বুঝাইতে নারিব।[116]

In another of his works, *Śab-i-Mirāj* (শব-ই-মিরাজ), Sultan again hints at pesky detractors:

> Those who cannot read their own language blame me for composing this *pānchāli.* As I have made the language of this book *Hinduāni* they call me a phony Muslim (*monāfiq*).
> যে সবে আপনা বোল না পারে বুঝিতে।
> পঞ্চালি রচিলুং করি আছএ দোষিতে॥
> মোনাফেক বলে মোরে কিতাবেত পড়ি।
> কিতাবের কথা দিলুম হিন্দুয়ানী করি॥[117]

Sultan's references and laments point to an intense debate on the irreplacibility or otherwise of the sacred language. The question at the heart of the disputation seems to be, can the Prophet's 'sacred word' be conveyed in a language other than Arabic? Such debates must have continued for a long time before it was settled that Bengali could indeed be the vehicle for conveying the Prophet's teachings and various aspects of the Islamic ritual universe.

The 'Muslim' poet's fear of opprobrium for writing in Bengali existed consistently without dissipating. Sheikh Mutalib in the seventeenth century sounds almost as apologetic as Saghir did in the fourteenth. In his *Kifāetul Musallīn* (কিফাইতুল মুসল্লীন) he writes:

> Not everyone understands good and bad in Arabic. That is why I compose this text in Bengali.
>
> আরবীতে সকলে না বুঝে ভাল মন্দ।
> তে কারনে দেশী ভাষে রচিলু প্রবন্ধ॥[118]

But he too must offer a timid defence like Saghir and Sultan. Unlike them he even accepts that he has done something deserving of censure. "I know that I have incurred many sins," Mutalib owns and hopes, "for I have rendered into Bengali the *Musalmāni śāstra.* But in my heart there is the assurance that the believers (*momin*) will understand and pray for me. The blessings of the believers will earn me merit. Definitely, *Allāh* too will forgive my sin":

> মুসলমানী শাস্ত্র কথা বাঙ্গালা করিলু।
> বহু পাপ হয় মোর নিশ্চয় জানিলু॥
> কিন্তু মাত্র ভরসা আছয়ে মনান্তরে।
> বুঝিয়া মুমীন দোয়া করিব আমারে॥
> মুমীনের আশীর্বাদে পুন্য হইবেক।
> আবশ্য গফুর আল্লা পাপ খেমিবেক॥
> এ সব জানিয়া জদি করয়ে রক্ষন।
> তবে সে মোহোর পাপ হইবে মোচন॥[119]

Mohammad Khan who wrote the *Maktūl Husain* (মকতুল হুসেন) around 1645, a retelling of the life of Husain, writes the following explaining as to why he chose to undertake the task:

> The folks in Hindustan do not understand the Book. Ignorant, they daily commit great sins. That is why I have composed this *pānchāli* in brief without caring for good or bad, sin or merit. Upon reading this *pānchāli* fear will strike the people's hearts and they will go and listen to (readings of?) the Book. They will know *Allāh*'s commands from the Book and will be munificent and commit meritorious deeds. Hence, all have blessed me. The blessings of the good folk will counter error. As I cannot violate the command of my *pīr*, I have composed the *pānchāli* for his sake:
>
> হিন্দুস্থানে লোক সবে না বুঝে কিতাপ।
> না বুঝি না শুনি নিত্যি করে মহাপাপ॥
> তেকাজে সংক্ষেপে করি পঞ্চালী রচিলুং।
> ভাল মন্দ পাপ পুন্য কিছু না জানিলুং॥
> পঞ্চালী পড়িতে সব মনে ভয় পাই।
> অবশ্য কিতাব কথা শুনিবেক যাই॥
> কিভাবে আল্লার আজ্ঞা শুনিবেন্ত যবে।
> দান বর্ন পুন্য কর্ম করিবেন্ত তবে॥
> অবশ্য মোহোরে সবে দিলে আশীর্বাদ।
> মহাজন আশীর্বাদ খণ্ডিবে প্রমাদ॥
> বিশেষ পীরের আজ্ঞা না যায় লংঘন।
> রচিলুং পঞ্চালিকা তাহার কারন॥[120]

Another seventeenth century poet, Abdul-Hakim, challenges opinion biased against writing in Bengali in his *Nūr Nāmā* (নূর নামা):

> Those not used to reading the Book expressed their desire to me (to read the Book?). I dedicated myself to the task of rendering it in the Bengali word. Thus I labour to please all. I bear no anger for Arabic and Persian . . . our *prabhu niranjan* understands the language spoken in a country without effort. He understands Arabic and *Hinduani*, the language of Bengal or any other tongue. . . . Those who have not learnt *mārfat* are jealous of the letters of the

"Hindus." Dwelling in Bengal those who resent the Bengali tongue, I do not know of whom they are born. The ones whose hearts are not pleased by the language and the knowledge of the country, why do not they leave the land and go some place else? My mother and grand-parents have been of Bengal, it is preachings in the local speech which please me the most:

কিতাব পড়িতে যার নাহিক অভ্যাস।
সে সবে কহিল মোতে মনে হাবিলাষ॥
তে কাজে নিবেদি বাংলা করিয়া বচন।
নিজ পরিশ্রম তোষি আমি সর্বজন॥
আরবি ফারছি শাস্ত্রে নাই কোন রাগ।...
যেই দেশে যেই বাক্যে কহে নরগন।
সেই বাক্য বুঝে প্রভু আপে নিরঞ্জন॥
আরবাক্য বুঝে প্রভু কিবা হিন্দুয়ানী।
বঙ্গদেশী বাক্য কিবা যত ইতি বানি॥
মারফত ভেদে যার নাহিক গমন।
হিন্দুর অক্ষর হিংসে সে সবের গন॥
যে সবে বঙ্গেতে জন্মি হিংসে বঙ্গবাণী।
সে সব কাহার জন্ম নির্ণয় না জানি॥
দেশি ভাষা বিদ্যা যার মনে না জুয়ায়।
দেশী ভাষা ত্যাগী কেন বিদেশে না যায়॥
মাতা পিতামহ ক্রমে বঙ্গেতে বসতি।
দেশী ভাষা উপদেশ মনে হিত অতি॥[121]

In another of his efforts, *Śihābuddin Nāmā* (শিয়াহাবুনি নামা), Hakim concedes that Arabic is indeed the best knowledge, but if ignorant of it there are other options, of which the last is the local language:

Learning Arabic you understand the glories of the *śāstras.* Of all knowledge Arabic is supreme. If you cannot read Arabic then read Persian. And if you cannot read Persian either, then study the *śāstras* in the language of the country:

আরবি পড়িয়া বুঝ শাস্ত্রের বাখান।
যথেক এলেম মধ্যে আরবি প্রধান॥
আরবী পড়িতে যদি না পার কদাচিত।
ফাড়ছি পড়িয়া বুঝ পরিনাম হিত॥

ফারছি পড়িতে যদি না পার কিঞ্চিত।
নিজ দেশী ভাষে শাস্ত্র পড়িতে উচিত॥[122]

Thus, it is authors like Sultan, Sheikh Mutalib, Mohammad Khan and Abdul Hakim who seem to have tilted the 'language debate' in favour of Bengali.

However, while some were conveying the Prophet's teachings in Bengali, others were celebrating in eloquent verse the heroism and martial spirit inspired by the new faith. Amhed Sharif quotes the following eulogy dedicated to his *pīr* by Mohammad Khan in the *Maktūl Hosain.* We gather from this panegyric that Khan's *pīr* was a sword wielding holy man who won Chattagram (Chittagong) for Islam polishing off some simian like infidels:

> Salute with an unwavering mind Kadal Khan Ghazi Pir, the essence of three worlds. He felled in battles infinite hosts of foes; some sank to the bottom of the sea of his fear. The unchallenged ruler (of the land?) was left without life. Conquering the foes he put Chattagram beneath his thrall. The *kāfirs* lived on the tree branches, the trees were felled and the infidels slain. The book will grow longer so I do not name them, but his eleven companions won Chattagram and made it "Muslim":
>
> একমনে প্রনাম করম বারেবার।
> কদল খান গাজি পীর ত্রিভুবন সার॥
> যার রনে পড়িল অক্ষয় রিপুদল।
> ভএ কেহ মজ্জি গেল সমুদ্রের তল॥
> একেশ্বর মহিম হইল প্রানহীন।
> রিপু জিনি চাটিগ্রাম কৈলা নিজাধীন॥
> বৃক্ষডালে বসিছিলা কাফিরেরগন।
> সেই বৃক্ষ ছেদি সবে করিলা নিধন॥
> তান একাদশ মিত্র করম প্রনাম।
> পুস্তক বাড়এ হেতু না লেখিলুঁ নাম॥
> তান একাদশ মিত্র জিনিয়া চাটিগ্রাম।
> মুসলমান কৈলা চাটিগ্রাম অনুপাম॥[123]

Apart from the above two categories of poets, there was

another. They seem to have been of the opinion that best means of broadcasting the Prophet's teachings was to illustrate the new faith through catechisms. With the clamant object of making good believers, the catechism literature emerged in the eighteenth century. An example from the genre is *Gadā-Mālikā Sambād* (গদা-মালিকা সম্বাদ) by Sheikh Sa'di. Sa'di was a native of Tripura and Ahmed Sharif, the editor of the text, dates it to 1712. *Gadā-Mālikā Sambād* is a dialogue between the princess Malika and the youth Gada who will win her hand if he answers the questions posed by her. One of the questions is:

> "How did *Hinduāni* come to be?" The *faqīr* (Gada is disguised as a *faqīr*) thought and replied, "Quran and Puran two *śāstras* were created, Hindus and Muslims were marked. Purans were pure in the beginning but were later fouled by Satan (*iblīs*). The Hindus hold on to the hand of Satan."
>
> হিন্দুয়ানী কিরূপে হৈল শুনি
> ফকিরে কহিলা তবে নিজ মনে গুনি।
> পুরান-কোরান দুই শাস্ত্র যে সৃজিল
> হিন্দু মুসলমান দুই পরিচিহ্ন কৈল।
> পূবে পুরান শাস্ত্র আছিলেক শুদ্ধ
> অখনে ইব্লিসে পাইয়া করিছে অশুদ্ধ।
> ইব্লিসের হস্ত ধরি হিন্দু সব চলএ[124]

Gada's answers seem to collapse Judaic and Indic cosmogonies. He says, for example, that Hinduism was brought forth by an Adam like first man created by the Deity:

> A man called Anadi was created. *Hinduān* emerged of him.
>
> অনাদি নামেতে এক পুরুষ সৃজন।
> অনাদির হতে হইছে কথা হিন্দুয়ান
> তাহার কথন কহি শুন দিয়া মন।[125]

Brahma emerged of Anadi in a manner which is again faintly redolent of Indic theogony. This Anadi, the limitless one, resembles Vishnu of whose navel Brahma had come out:

> A luminous man called Brahma issued from the mouth of Anadi.
>
> অনাদির মুখ হতে পুরুষ প্রধান
> নিঃসরিল ব্রহ্মা নামে অতি তেজবান।[126]

Sa'di was probably familiar with the Puruṣa Sūkta hymn of the *Ṛgveda.* The manner in which he has Gada describe the beginning of castes suggests so:

> The Brahmans were born of Brahma. Of his (Brahma's) arms Kshatriyas emerged. The Vaiśyas were born of the heart and Śudras of the feet. Thus these four brothers came to be known in the world.
>
> তবে যদি ব্রহ্মা হতে জন্মিল ব্রহ্মান
> বাহু হতে যথ ক্ষেত্রি হইল উৎপন।
> হৃদ হতে বৈশ্য হৈল শূদ্র চরণেত
> হেনমতে চারি ভাই ভুবন বিদিত।[127]

However, the coalescing of Judaic and Indic world views notwithstanding, Sa'di does not let his character suffer any doubts about which is the more correct of the two. Gada ends his answer thus, pleasing the bonny princess immensely:

> "Hindus" are descended of the son of Adam—Kabil. The Book says that they are *kāfirs.* No more than four castes of "Hindus" are born, they all have been deluded by Satan. They follow his scriptures, they will lighten their sins in hell.
>
> আদমের তনয় কাবিল বংশ হতে
> কাফির হইল হিন্দু কহে কিতাবেতে।
> চারি জাতির বেশী তবে হিন্দু না জন্মিছে
> আর যথ ভোলাইয়া ইব্লিসে করিছে।
> সেই শাস্ত্র ধরিয়া চলএ হিন্দু সব
> নরকে পড়িয়া পাপী পাইব লাঘব।[128]

Nasrullah Khondkar wrote a similar work seeking to make observant Muslims in 1749. Entitled *Sharī'atnāmā* (শরীয়তনামা),

among its many instructions was that Muslims must not plaster the floors of their houses with cow dung. The act displeases *Allāh* and pleases Satan. In fact, a house with its floor plastered with dung becomes Satan's mosque:

> গোবরে লেপিলে ঘর শাস্ত্রে বহু দোষ।
> অষন্তোষ রসুল ইবলিস পরিতোষ॥
> ইবলিসের মসজিদ জান সেই ঘর।[129]

Ideas of the 'self' and the 'other' had apparently solidified by the eighteenth century and the rupture had been opened wide. But even in this century we catch sight of an occasional poet who presented a cosmogony constructed entirely of Indic elements. Ali Raza had the world originating thus in *Sṛṣṭitattva* (সৃষ্টিতত্ব):

> The Formless One lost himself in the Humour of Love. He beheld the light (*nūr*) of Mohammad in the state. As they beheld each other with love, they sweated in the heat of this humour. Then, the Creator (*karatār*) who is without a beginning (*anādi*) and attributeless (*nigun*) formed the world with that sweat. He brought forth the three worlds from it and all that is hidden and manifest. The *mahāmantra*, the knowledge of *brahmā*, the four Vedas and the fourteen *śāstras* were all made of that sweat. Without an aim, the Creator built twenty-seven universes with this sweat. He created the twin lights (*jyoti*) of the souls of the creatures (*jīvātmā*) and the Supreme Spirit (*paramātmā*). The angels and the Throne of the Lord too were formed of this sweat.

> নৈরাকার মগ্ন হইল প্রেমরস ভাবে।
> নুর মোহাম্মদ পর দর্শিলা গৌরবে॥
> অন্যে অন্যে প্রেমরসে দর্শন করিল।
> প্রেম রস তেজ হইতে দোহান ঘর্মিল॥
> তবে অনাদি নিগুন প্রভু করতার।
> সেই ঘর্মে নীর হইতে সৃজিল সংসার॥
> সেই ঘর্ম হইতে কৈল এ তিন ভুবন।
> গুপ্ত ব্যক্ত যতদূর প্রভুর সৃজন॥
> সেই ঘর্মে মহামন্ত্র যত ব্রহ্ম জ্ঞান।
> চারি বেদ চৌদ্দশাস্ত্র হইল নির্মান॥

সাতাইশ ব্রহ্মাণ্ড প্রভু সে ঘর্মে নির্মিল।
বিনি লক্ষ্যে কবতারে এ সব করিল॥
জীব আতমা পরাতমা এ দোহান জ্যোতিঃ।
অনুলক্ষে সৃজন করিল জগপতি॥
সেই ঘর্মে হইল ফেরেশ্তা যতজন।
আর্শ কুর্সি হইল প্রভুর সিঙ্ঘাসন॥[130]

The *kāvyas* penned by poets aspiring at 'Muslimness' are an enthralling continent, a land which never ceases to fascinate and surprise. They reveal the complexity of the manifold processes through which passed the "becoming" of the Muslim. They reveal to us individuals inhabiting multiple subjectivities and occasionally being torn between them. These poets obviously are people who are recipients of a new world view and are in the process of struggling to create a coherent universe with it. The confusion and the frequent ambiguities that mottle their works are but a proof of this and of the demands of the effort. Sometimes, the contrasting worlds were blended without any apparent tension or contradictions. We see this in case of the transposition upon Arabia of the local religious beliefs or the fusing of the Judaic and the Indic cosmogonies. Of course, in both cases the local is subsumed and the new ideas are demonstrated to be dominant. But there are also times when our poets turn into what might be termed 'divided selves' or are haunted by the apparition of what R.D. Laing has termed a 'false self.' Their repeated apologetic justification of the decision of writing in Bengali, accompanied by laments that their audience is ignorant of Arabic, might be cited as an example. This is the expression of a part of their self which "is occupied in maintaining [its] identity and freedom by being transcendent, unembodied."[131] It aspires to attain a "Muslimness" free of the time and place its bearers inhabited. This goal being unattainable, and our poets being condemned to write and speak Bengali, many a times they regarded their "objective existence as the expression of a false self."[132] However, let it be emphasised that in our study we also infuse this concept of a 'false self' with a different meaning in order to underline the split nature of the subjective world of those who come to absorb elements of a new vision, that is, a certain kind of Islam, and begin to follow them in every day practice. For us both the selves, the one before the absorption of a new vision and the one developed organically afterwards, are equally real selves. Of course, each is now located in a culturally dynamic process of struggling to integrate with its other half and seeking new coherence in search of an emotionally stable mental equilibrium. An individual caught up in the process of emotional and intellectual transformation, a world of changing convictions, sometimes labelled as religious 'conversion,' will certainly have its own share of anxieties hopes, and sometimes, may be, uncertainties. The attempt to bridge the chasm between the old and new vocabularies would certainly generate an unstable dynamic struggling between the two selves, one old and the other new, to attain a sense of stable equilibrium. In terms of historical time this process continued for long. It apparently continues in Bengal even today as the course run by Bangladesh, oscillating between its Bengali and Muslim identities, in the four decades of its existence suggests.

Seeking cultural coherence and mental equilibrium, our poets attempted the absorption and rearticulation of new vocabularies and changing the cultural complexion of the Bengali language. This resulted in the creation of new selves. This seems to be the case with many of the poets whose works we studied above. Our poets were surely responding to expectations from certain quarters which could not reconcile to the expression of the sacred word in the tongue of the heathens. Hence, they denounced *Hinduāni* all the more vehemently in the language they were expressing themselves in to justify its use. In the end, our poets come across as individuals in which three types of 'Muslimnesses' twined. They struggled to create a coherent whole with new ideas, they differentiated themselves from other sections of the population whom they recognised as non-Muslims, and they struggled to reconcile the 'Muslim' and Bengali writing halves of their selves. It is this complex process that resulted in a new hybrid indetity which we would label as 'Bengali-Muslim.' Their struggle also becomes "a persivient cycle of loss and recovery, damage and repair" and the expression of an "increasing anxiety"[133] over the credibility of their existence. Observing them being outwardly engaged in this effort it might well seem as though they are living 'syncretic' lives when they were actually fashioning a vocabulary to demarcate their apartness and forge a new identity. Thus, Asim Roy errs in the other extreme as Eaton in suggesting a wilful obliteration of boundaries, a consciously created 'syncretism,' while Eaton posited a complete absence of any boundaries.

If Islam, as Eaton says, was merely fusing into an indeterminate and uncontesting or unresisting religio-cultural complex why is it that our poets express a ceaseless anxiety lest the local beliefs and language contaminate their faith? Besides, despite Eaton's claim that the Ilyas Shahis evolved a secular modus vivendi with Bengali society and culture and despite their mosques employing purely indigenous motifs and structural traits, it does not seem like the ideal of hard power was entirely given up. We come across an inscription upon a sixteenth century mosque built at Pabna by the Ilyas Shahi king Nasir al-din Nusrat Shah (r. AD 1519–32) which evokes the almighty to give the king opportunity to "uproot the enemies of Allah from among the unbelievers and polytheists."[134] We do not propose that the king actually proceeded to do this. But the vanquishing of polytheists definitely still existed as a desirable ideal and cultural agenda before the Ilyas Shahi kingship which it would evoke to legitimise itself among the believers. This nature of the state, whenever manifest, could only have served to widen the cultural and emotional difference slowly leading to the opening of more tensions.

As we saw above, 'Muslim' poets do indeed borrow Indic motifs and vocabulary to shape their religious ideas and universe. Their intention, however, is to devise a more effective mode of contestation to vanquish their opponents. As a result, the emotional tensions and ambiguities are laid bare very perceptibly. For example, we saw Saiyad Sultan repeatedly refer to the Creator as Niranjan. However, Sultan invalidated the entire Sanskritic pantheon and world view. Another example is Daulat Qazi who bestows the same epithet upon *Allāh* in the prologue to his poem *Sati Mainā O Lor Chandrāni* (সতি ময়না ও লোর চন্দ্রানি):

বিসমিল্লাহ প্রধান এক নাম নিরন্জন॥[135]

But Qazī also firmly states that the *sharī'ah* is the only way to the Almighty:

সরিয়ত নৌকা কর ইমান প্রদিব ধর
বসুল সোহাএ হইবা পার॥[136]

Thus, it appears plausible that these are not examples of "religious capitulation" but are attempts to locate "commensurate analogues."[137] These examples are also an indication that a representation of the 'other' or an incorporation from the 'other's' universe could occasionally take a contrapuntal[138] form. Just as in this musical troupe two distinct motifs or themes attain simultaneity upon the same musical time, the authors of the *kāvyas* too will sometimes juxtapose opposing artifacts or voices. Dwija Bangshidas in *Bāis Kabīr Manasā-Mangal* does so when he has a Muslim trying to stop the zealot *qāzī* who forbids *Hinduāni* from wrecking the altar of the goddess Manasa. Bangshidas has him say that *Hinduāni* must not be put down because the same God watches over both the "Hindu" and the "Muslim." The ways of all peoples are created by God, he says to the *qāzī*, it is no good being rude in these matters:

তার মাঝে একজন জাতি মুসলমান।
সে বলে, "উচিত নহে রাখ হিন্দুয়ান॥
একই ঈশ্বর দেখ হিন্দু-মুসলমানে।
যার তার কর্ম, সেই করে ধর্মজ্ঞানে॥
সকলের কুলাচার স্রজিলা গোঁসাই॥
পাষণ্ড হইয়া তাতে কোন কার্য নাই॥[139]

The intolerant *qāzī* of course does not heed the well-meaning Muslim and tries desecrating the altar of the goddess. But her devotees, a group of shepherds, keep him and his followers from doing their will. The shepherds give them chase and the zealots run for their lives. This *qāzī* goes to another *qāzī* named Hasan and reports the audacity of the devotees:

"ধর ধর, মার মার" বলে গোপগনে।
মিঞা সব পলাইল ভয় পায়্যা মনে॥
. . .
মিনা কাজি পলাইল গণিয়া প্রমাদ।
হাসনের কাছে গিয়া করিল ফৈরাদ॥[140]

Hasan *qāzī* goes with his cortege and chastens the shepherds. Manasa then dispatches her snakes to his house ending his and his sons' lives. His wife wails and wishes he had not forbidden *Hinduāni* or he would still be alive. She accepts Manasa as the mother of "Hindu" and "Yavan" both:

"কলিযুগে, মাও তুমি সাক্ষাৎ দেবতা।
হিন্দু কি যবন তুমি সকলের মাতা॥"[141]

In fact, quite a few of the *Mangal Kāvyas* and *Vijay Kāvyas* authored by the non-Muslim poets display a similar belligerence in depicting the 'other' who is cowed and converted. Their works illustrate violent cultural conflicts but also many attempts to contain them. The non-Muslim poets often have their characters try their best to curb the violent eruptions, some of them even try to drive home the wisdom that both sides are children of the same supreme being. But, we see the intolerant *qāzīs* appearing in these texts meeting a dreadful fate in all instances, be it the *Chaitanya Bhāgbat, Padmapurān* or the *Manasā-Mangal.* After threatening to score out *Hinduāni,* the *qāzī* in *Chaitanya Bhāgbat* began policing the town in the company of louts looking for people performing the *kīrtan.* Disquieted by the scrutiny, the terrified town dwellers will hide from him. More so since this *qāzī* beat "Hindus" whenever he could:

এইমত প্রতিদিন দুষ্টগন লৈয়া।
নগর ভ্রময়ে কাজি কীর্ত্তন চাহিয়া॥
দুঃখে সব নগরিয়া থাকে লুকাইয়া।
হিন্দুকে কাজি সব মারে কদর্থিয়া॥[142]

The disciples of Chaitanya go to him and tell him of the *qāzī*'s terror. The saint is roused into a paroxysm of anger. He decides to march all of Nabadwip singing the *kīrtan* in the company of his followers. Besides, Chaitanya declares that he is going to burn down the *qāzī*'s house:

সর্ব্ব-নবদ্বীপে আজি করিমু কির্ত্তন।
দেখোঁ মোরে কোন কর্ম্ম করে কোন জন॥
দেখ আজি কাজির পোড়াঙ ঘরদ্বার।
কোন কর্ম্ম করে দেখ রাজার বা তাহার॥[143]

The *kīrtan* led by Chaitanya turns out to be a passionate affair. Singing and dancing, he and his followers experience an eloquent ambit of emotions. One moment they will laugh and another they will cry. Thus promenading the town they arrive at the *qāzī*'s house. The livid Chaitanya raged and thundered at the *qāzī*'s threshold. He ordered his disciples to tear down the *qāzī*'s house. Mesmerised by Chaitanya, many disciples scampered up the house to do as bidden, some broke the doors while some kicked about and yelled. They also utterly destroyed the orchards which surrounded the house. The branches of the mango trees were snapped, the plantain grove too was destroyed with shouts of "Hari." Finally, Chaitanya commanded that the house be set afire too as he wished to bring *pralaya* to all "Yavans." He is, however, dissuaded by certain of his close companions. "You have insulted him enough for now," they say, "more errors from him and you take his life":

আসিয়া কাজির দ্বারে প্রভু বিশ্বম্ভর।
ক্রোধাবশে হুঙ্কার করয়ে বহুতর॥...
মহামত সর্ব্বলোক চৈতন্য আবেশে।
ঘরে উঠিলেন সভে প্রভুর আদেশে॥
কেহো ঘর ভাঙ্গে কেহো ভাঙ্গয়ে দুয়ার।
কেহো লাথি মারে কেহো করয়ে হুঙ্কার॥
আম্র-পনসের ডাল কেহো ভাঙ্গি ফেলে।
কদলেক-বন ভাঙ্গি কেহো 'হরি' বলে॥...
অগ্নি দেহ' ঘরে তোশরা না করিহ ভয়।
আজি সব যবনের করিমু প্রলয়॥"...
করিলা ত কাজির অনেক অপমান।
আর যদি ঘটে তবে সংহারিহ প্রান॥"[144]

Thus, having destroyed the *qāzī*'s abodes, this army of the devout went away dancing in great joy chanting the name Hari:

কাজির ভাঙ্গিয়া ঘর সর্ব্ব-নগরিয়া।
মহানন্দে 'হরি' বলি যায়েন নাচিয়া॥[145]

A similar face-off is described in *Chaitanya Charitāmṛta* (চৈতন্য চরিতামৃত) too. It occurs when, ordered by the master, all households in the town of Nabadwip began to perform the *kīrtan*:

নগরিয়া লোকে প্রভু যবে আজ্ঞা দিল।
ঘরে ঘরে সংকীর্তন করিতে লাগিল॥[146]

When the Yavans heard of this they were angered, they came and complained to the *qāzī* of the town. Blinded by rage, the *qāzī* stormed into a house one evening where the *kīrtan* was being sung. Obviously, the *kīrtan* had emerged as a site of cultural contestation, peaceful or otherwise. The *qāzī* broke the *mṛdanga* and asked the gathering, "Till now you did not display *Hinduāni*, what strength makes you do this so brazenly now? May no one sing the *kīrtan* in the town. I forgive you today, but if I discover you again engaged in *kīrtan*, I will punish you and destroy your caste." The town dwellers sorrowed greatly and came and made their plaint before the master. Chaitanya said, "Go and perform the *kīrtan*, today I will destroy all Yavans." But he knew that people fear the *qāzī* and are not at ease with hearts filled with dread. He called them and said, "I will sing the *kīrtan* in the town, let all decorate their houses in the evening and light lamps. I will see which *qāzī* can forbid me":

শুনি যে ক্রুদ্ধ হৈল সকল যবন।
কাজী পাশে আসি সব কৈল নিবেদন।
ক্রোধে সন্ধ্যাকালে কাজী একঘরে এল।
মৃদঙ্গ ভাঙ্গিয়া লোকে কহিতে লাগিল॥
এতকাল কেহ নাহি কৈল হিন্দুয়ানি।
এবে যে উদ্যম চালাও কার বল জানি॥
কেন কীর্ত্তন না করিহ সকল নগরে।
আজি আমি ক্ষমা করি যাইতেছি ঘরে॥
আর যদি কীর্ত্তন করিতে লাগ পাইনু।
সর্ব্বস্ব দণ্ডিয়া তার জাতি যে লইনু॥
এত বলি কাজী গেল নগরিয়া লোক।
প্রভু স্থানে নিবেদিল পাইয়া বড় শোক॥

প্রভু আজ্ঞা দিল যাহ করহ কীর্ত্তন।
মুঞি সংহারিমু আজি সকল যবন॥
ঘরে গিয়া সব লোক করয়ে কীর্ত্তন।
কাজী ভয়ে স্বচ্ছন্দ নহে চমকিত মন॥
ত সবার অন্তরে ভয় প্রভু মনে জানি।
কহিতে লাগিলা লোকে শিঘ্র ডাকি আনি॥
নগরে নগরে আমি করিমু কির্ত্তন।
সন্ধ্যাকালে কর সবে নগর মণ্ডন (ঘ)॥
দেখি কোন কাজী আসি মোরে মানা করে।
এত কহি সন্ধ্যাকালে চলে গৌররায়॥[147]

True to his word, Chaitanya wandered the town singing the *kīrtan* with his companions. Wandering, he arrived at the *qāzī*'s door and raged and raised a din. But the *qāzī* had hid himself hearing the strains of singing, he did not venture out. Encouraged by Chaitanya, his followers were as if mad. They took to destroying the *qāzī*'s garden insolently. Then the master sat down at the *qāzī*'s door and had him brought over by some decent folk (*bhabyalok*). The *qāzī* came with his head lowered, the master seated him with all respect. The master said, "I am your guest and seeing me you hide. What strange ways are these." The *qāzī* replied, "You come in anger, to calm you I hid myself. Now that you are soothed, I come and meet you. I am lucky to have a guest like you. Nilambar Chakravarti of your village happens to be my uncle (*chāchā*), and since he is your grandfather you are my nephew. Ties of the village are truer than the ties of the flesh. An uncle must bear with a nephew's anger. A nephew, on his part, must ignore an uncle's mistake." Does the poet suggest here that the *qāzī* is a neo-convert, bringing up as he is kinship bonds with Hindus? If this is what we are meant to infer, then we observe that by evoking the warm and affectionate discourse of Hindu kinship relations both the parties are able to relate to each other more sensibly without anger.

Thus, Chaitanya and the *qāzī* talked without anyone understanding what is being implied. Then Chaitanya said, "I have come to your place to ask questions." The *qāzī* replied, "Ask whatever you have in your mind." The master queried, "You consume milk hence the cow is your mother. The bull helps you to grow crops and is your father. What *dharma* makes you slaughter and eat your mother and father. With what certitude do you perform such an ill-deed?" It is clear from Chaitanya's question that by the time he became a significant voice in Bengali society beef eating had become a fairly widespread cultural practice. His question also points to the fact that a large section of Bengali society had also acquired the cultural sensibilities and sensitivity of the new faith they had adopted.

The *qāzī* answered, "The way you have your Veda and Puran, I have the Qur'ān as my *śāstra*. This *śāstra* tells me what is to be consumed and what is to be abstained from. There is no fear of sin when you kill what the *śāstra* allows you to. Even your Vedas talk of the killing of kine. The great sages of the olden days slaughtered them." The master said, "The Vedas forbid cow-killing. That is why no Hindu kills a cow. The Vedas and the Puranas say that you may kill only what you can restore to life. So the sages killed old cattle and then resurrected them. Thus, old kine were young again. This only did them good. But in the age of *kali* the Brahmans do not have this power, so they no more kill cows":

এমত কির্তন করি নগরে ভ্রমিলা।
ভ্রমিতে ভ্রমিতে প্রভু কাজিদ্বারে গেলা॥
তর্জ্জন গর্জ্জন করি করে কোলাহল।
গৌরচন্দ্র বলে লোক প্রশ্রয় পাগল॥
কীর্তন ধ্বনিতে কাজী লুকাইল ঘরে।
তর্জ্জন গর্জ্জন শুনি না হয় বাহিরে॥
উদ্ধত লোকে ভাঙ্গে কাজীর পুষ্পবন॥

বিস্তারি বর্ণিলা ইহা দাস বৃন্দাবন।
তবে মহাপ্রভু তার দ্বারেতে বসিল।
ভব্যলোক পাঠাইয়া কাজী বোলাইল॥
দূরে হৈতে এলা কাজী মাথা নোঙাইয়া।
কাজীরে বসাইল প্রভু সম্মান করিয়া॥
প্রভু বলে আমি তব হই অভ্যাগত।
আমা দেখি লুকাইলা এ ধর্ম্ম কেমত॥
কাজী কহে তুমি আইস ক্রুদ্ধ হইয়া।
তোমা শান্ত করাইতে রৈনু লুকাইয়া॥
ইবে তুমি শান্ত হৈলে আসি মিলিলাম।
ভাগ্য মোর তোমা হেন অতিথি পাইলাম॥
গ্রাম সম্বন্ধে চক্রবর্ত্তী হয় মোর চাচা।
দেহ সম্বন্ধ হৈতে গ্রামসম্বন্ধ সাঁচা॥
নীলাম্বর চক্রবর্ত্তী হয় তোমার নানা।
সে সম্বন্ধে হও তুমি আমার ভাগিনা॥
ভাগিনার ক্রোধ মামা অবশ্য সহয়।
মাতুলের অপরাধ ভাগিনা না লয়।
এই মতে দোহার কথা হয় ঠারে ঠারে।
ভিতরের অর্থ কেহ বুঝিতে না পারে॥
প্রভু কহে প্রশ্ন লাগি এনু তব স্থানে।
কাজী কহে আজ্ঞা কর যে তোমার মনে॥
প্রভু কহে দুগ্ধ খাও গাভি তোমার মাতা।
বৃষ অন্ন উপাজেয় তাতে তেহোঁ পিতা॥
পিতা মাতা মারি খাও এবা কেন ধর্ম্ম।
কোন বলে কর তুমি এমত বিকর্ম্ম॥
কাজী কহে তোমার যৈছে বেদ পুরান।
তৈছে আমার শাস্ত্র কেতাব কোরান॥
সেই শাস্ত্রে কহে প্রবৃত্তি নিবৃত্তি মার্গ ভেদ।
নিবৃত্তি মার্গে জীব মাত্র বধের নিষেধ॥
প্রবৃত্তি মার্গে গোবধ করিতে বিধি হয়।

শাস্ত্রাজ্ঞায় বধ কৈলে নাহি পাপ ভয়॥
তোমার বেদেতে আছে গোবধের বানী।
অতএব গোবধ করে বড় বড় মুনি॥
প্রভু কহে বেদে কহে গোবধ নিষেধ।
অতএব হিন্দু মাত্রে না করে গোবধ॥
জীয়াইতে পারে যদি তবে মারে প্রানী।
বেদ পুরানে আছে হেন আজ্ঞা বাণী॥
অতএব জরদ্গব মারে মুনিগন।
বেদমন্ত্রে সিদ্ধ করে তাহার জীবন॥
জরদ্গব হই হএা যুবা হয় আরবার।
তাতে তার বধ নহে হয় উপকার॥
কলিকালে তৈছে শক্তি নাহিক ব্রাহ্মণে।
অতএব গোবধ না করে এইক্ষণে॥[148]

"You can only kill but not restore life," Chaitanya continued, "nothing can save you from hell. A cow killer suffers hell for as many years as there are hair on a cow's body. The creators of your *śāstras* were deluded to order what they did." The *qāzī* was stunned and could not talk. The *qāzī* pondered and said, "I accept defeat. What you say is indeed true. My *śāstras* are all fantasy but still I abide by them to oblige my people." Now the *qāzī* confided a nightmare in Chaitanya. "The day I went to a Hindu household and forbid the *kirtan* breaking the *mṛdanga*, when sleeping in the night a terrifying lion pounced upon my breast and gnashed its teeth and laughed." "I will rip open your chest for splitting the *mṛdanga*, I will destroy you for forbidding the *kīrtan*," the beast said:

তোমরা জীয়াতে নার বধ মাত্র সার।
নরক হইতে তোমার নাহিক নিস্তার॥...
শুনি স্তব্ধ হৈল কাজী নাহি স্ফুরে বাণী।
বিচারিয়া কহে কাজী পরাবভ মানি।

তুমি যে কহিলে পণ্ডিত সেই সত্য হয়।
অধুনা মোর শাস্ত্র বিচারসহ নয়।
কল্পিত আমার শাস্ত্র আমি সব জানি।
জাতি অনুরোধে তবু সেই শাস্ত্র মানি।...
কাজী কহে যবে আমি হিন্দু ঘর গিয়া।
কীর্ত্তন করিলুঁ মানা মৃদঙ্গ ভাঙ্গিয়া॥
সেই রাত্রে এক সিংহ মহা ভয়ঙ্কর।
নরদেহ সিংমুখ গর্জ্জয়ে বিস্তর॥
শয়নে আমার উপর লাফ দিয়া চড়ি।
অট্ট অট্ট হাসে করে দন্ত কড়মড়ি॥
ফাড়িমু তোমার বুক মৃদঙ্গ বদলে॥
কির্ত্তন মানা করিস করিমু তোরে ক্ষয়।[149]

The same day another portent indicted the *qāzī.* "On that day a retainer of mine came and said that when he went to break up a *kīrtan* a meteor struck him on the face. His beard was burnt and eruptions appeared on his face. Since then I live in great fear," the *qāzī* confessed:

সেদিন আমার এক পেয়াদা আইল॥
আসি কহে গেলু মুত্রি কির্ত্তন নিষেধিতে।
অগ্নি উল্কা মোর মুখে লাগে আচম্বিতে॥
পুড়িল সকল দাড়ি মুখে হৈল ব্রণ।
যেই পেয়াদা যায় তার এই বিবরন॥
তাহা দেখি রহিনু মুত্রি মহাভয় পাএা।[150]

Muslims visited the *qāzī* and reported strange happenings. One said, "Since the day I ridiculed Hindus, my tongue does not cease uttering the name 'Krishna.' I do not know what charms are known to the Hindus." Then the *qāzī* said to Chaitanya, "Narayan, the god of the Hindus is indeed greater, may be you are him after all, my heart says":

আর ম্লেচ্ছ কহে শুন আমি ত এমতে।
হিন্দুকে পরহাস কৈল সে দিন হইতে॥
জিহ্বা কৃষ্ণনাম করে না মানে বর্জ্জন।
না জানি কি মহৌষধি জানে হিন্দুগণ॥...
হিন্দুর ঈশ্বর বড় যেই নারায়ণ।
সেই তুমি হও হেন লয় মোর মন॥[151]

The master heard the *qāzī* and smiled. Chaitanya touched the *qāzī* and said, "How strange it is that your tongue speaks the name 'Krishna,' you have been ridden of sin and rendered pure. You have taken the three names, 'Hari,' 'Krishna,' and 'Narayan.' You are lucky and bearer of great merit." Hearing this, the *qāzī*'s eyes streamed tears. He held the feet of the master and spoke, "Your grace has removed evil from my mind, let me always have this same faith in you." The master replied, "I seek a charity from you, let the *kīrtan* never be forbidden in Nadia." "I will swear all who will take birth in my line to never proscribe the *kīrtan*," the *qāzī* assured Chaitanya:

এত শুনি মহাপ্রভু হাসিয়া হাসিয়া।
কহিতে লাগিলা প্রভু কাজিরে ছুঁইয়া॥
তব মুখে কৃষ্ণ নাম এ বড় বিচিত্র॥
পাপক্ষয় গেল হৈলা পরম পবিত্র॥
হরি কৃষ্ণ নারায়ন লৈলে তিন নাম।
বড় ভাগ্যবান তুমি বড় পুন্যবান॥
এত শুনি কাজির দু'চক্ষে পড়ে পানি।
প্রভুর চরণ ধরি বলে প্রিয় বানি॥
তোমার প্রসাদে মোর ঘুচিল কুমতি।
এই কৃপা কর যে তোমাতে বহু ভক্তি॥
প্রভু কহে এক দান মাগিয়ে তোমায়।
সঙ্কীর্তন বাদ যৈছে নহে নদীয়ায়॥

কাজি কহে মোর বংশে যত উপজীবে।
তাহাকে তালাক দিব কির্ত্তন না বাধিবে॥[152]

The *qāzī* is not the only opponent from another creed whom Kaviraj's Chaitanya converts to his own. There is an episode in the *Charitāmrita* wherein Chaitanya has a lengthy altercation with a band of Pathan troopers. He shows the most pious among them the error of his ways and converts them all in the process. This happens when the companions of Chaitanya, the Rajput Krishnadas, Balbhadra Bhattacharya and two other Brahmans, suggest that they visit the Mahavan surrounding Vrindavan. The master and his disciples board a boat and journey to their destination sailing down the Ganga. They stop on the way to rest beneath a tree when, of a sudden, a cowherd grazing his cows in the vicinity plays on his flute. Hearing the strains, Chaitanya is overcome by passion and falls down in a swoon foaming at the mouth. A band of ten Pathan troopers who were passing by witness the scene and halt. The Pathans deduce that Chaitanya has been drugged by his companions whom they take for robbers. They bind them all as well as the cowherd and decide to execute them. Chaitanya comes to when Krishnadas is parleying with his captors. Chaitanya awakes with a roar chanting Hari. The *mlechchhas* are terrified at the sight of him dancing with his arms raised, uttering loud cries in a state of trance. Cowed, they release the five they had arrested:

হেনকালে মহাপ্রভু চেতন পাইল॥
হুঙ্কার করিয়া উঠে বলে হরি হরি।
প্রেমাবেশে নৃত্য করে উর্দ্ধবাহু করি॥
প্রেমাবেশে প্রভু যবে করেন চিৎকার।
ম্লেচ্ছের হৃদয়ে যেন লাগে শেলধার॥
ভয় পাইয়া ম্লেচ্ছ ছাড়ি দিল পঞ্চজন।[153]

The *mlechchhas* bowed at the feet of the master. They said to him, "These five are robbers. They drugged you to have you go insane and took your money." The master replied, "These are not robbers but my companions. I am a renunciate beggar and have no wealth. I only had a fit and was unconscious. In compassion they were tending to me." Among the *mlechchhas* there was a very grave one. He was dressed in black and was known as a *pīr.* His heart melted at the sight of the master. The *mlechchha* engaged in a discourse with him on non-duality (*advaya*) and *brahma.* But the master refuted all that his scriptures said. In the end, he was stunned and without answers. Chaitanya said to him, "In the end, your scriptures too speak of the same God. He is dark hued and bearer of all glories, He is all joy and absolute *brahma,* all spirits, all knowing and all forms. Creation (*sṛṣṭi*), the continuation of creation (*sthiti*) and its dissolution (*pralaya*) all issue from Him. He is the refuge of the manifest and unmanifest worlds, the cause of all causes, devotion to Him and serving Him alone redeems all lives from the world."

The *mlechchha* said, "All you say is indeed true. What is written in my scriptures, no one has imbibed. But you explained all with ease. You verily are God manifest. Be kind to this worthless one. I have seen enough of the *mlechchha* scriptures. They do not explain cause, effort and matter. Seeing you my tongue utters the name 'Krishna.' The pride I had in being learned is gone." Having said this he fell at the feet of the master. The master said, "You have taken Krishna's name. You have cleansed yourself of the sins of ten million births." The master named him Ramdas. There was another Pathan in the group who was a prince. His name was Bijuli Khan. Ramdas and the rest were his servants. He too placed his head upon the feet of the master. He bestowed his grace upon them all. They all turned renunciate Vaishnavs and sang the glories of the master everywhere:

ম্লেচ্ছগন আসি প্রভুর বন্দিল চরন।
প্রভু আগে কহে এই ঠক পাঁচ জন॥

এই পঞ্চ মিলি তোমা ধুতুরা খাওয়াইয়া।
তোমা ধন লইল তোমা পাগল করিয়া॥
প্রভু কহে ঠক নহে মোর সঙ্গী জন।
ভিক্ষুক সন্ন্যাসি মোর নাহি কিছু ধন॥
মৃগি ব্যাধিতে আমি হই অচেতন।
এই পাঁচ দয়া করি করেন পালন।
সেই ম্লেচ্ছ মধ্যে এক পরম গম্ভীর।
কাল বস্ত্র পরে তাকে লোকে কহে পীর॥
চিত্ত আর্দ্র হইল তার প্রভুকে দেখিয়া।
নির্ব্বিশেষে ব্রহ্ম স্থাপে স্বশাস্ত্র উঠাইয়া॥
অদ্বয় ব্রহ্মবাদ সেই করিল স্থাপন।
তার শাস্ত্র যুক্তে প্রভু করিল খণ্ডন॥
যেই যেই কহিল প্রভু সকলি খণ্ডিল।
উতর না আসে মুখে মহা স্তব্ধ হৈল॥
প্রভু কহে তোমা শাস্ত্র কহে নির্ব্বিশেষে।
তাহা খণ্ড সবিশেষ স্থাপিয়েছে শেষ॥
তব শাস্ত্র কহে শেষে একই ঈশ্বর।
সর্ব্বৈশ্বর্যপুর্ন তিঁহ শ্যাম কলেবর॥
সচ্চিদানন্দ দেহ পুর্ন-ব্রহ্মস্বরূপ।
সর্ব্বাত্মা সর্ব্বজ্ঞ নিত্য সর্ব্বাদিস্বরুপ॥
সৃষ্টি স্থিতি প্রলয় তাঁহা হইতে হয়।
স্থুল সূক্ষ্ম জগতের তিঁহো সমাশ্রয়॥
সর্ব্বশ্রেষ্ঠ সর্ব্বারাধ্য কারনের কারন।
তাঁর ভক্ত্যে হয় জিবের সংসারতারন॥
তাঁর সেবা বিনা জিবে না যায় সংসার। . . .
ম্লেচ্ছ কহে যেই কহ সেই সত্য হয়।
শাস্ত্রে লিখিয়াছে কেহ লইতে না পারয়॥
নির্ব্বিশেষ গোঁসাঞি লঞা করেন ব্যাখ্যান।
সাকার গোসাঞি সেব্য কার নাহি জ্ঞান॥
সেইতে গোসাঁঞি তুমি সাক্ষাৎ ঈশ্বর।

মোরে কৃপা কর মুঞি অযোগ্য পামর॥
অনেক দেখিনু মুঞি ম্লেচ্ছ শাস্ত্র হৈতে।
সাধ্য সাধন বস্তু নারি নির্দ্ধারিতে॥
তোমা দেখি জিহ্বা মোর বলে কৃষ্ণনাম।
আমি বড় জ্ঞানি এই গেল অভিমান॥
কৃপা করি বল মোরে সাধ্য সাধনে।
এত বলি পড়ে মহাপ্রভুর চরনে॥
প্রভু কহে উঠ কৃষ্ণনাম তুমি লৈলে।
কোটি জন্ম পাপ গেল পবিত্র হইলে॥
কৃষ্ণ কহ কৃষ্ণ কহ কৈল উপদেশ।
সবে কৃষ্ণ সবা হৈল প্রেমাবেশ॥
রামদাস বলি প্রভু তার কৈলা নাম।
আর এক পাঠান তার নাম বিজুলি খান॥
অল্প বয়স তার রাজার কুমার।
রামদাস আদি পাঠান চাকর তাহার॥
কৃষ্ণ বলি পড়ে সেই মহাপ্রভু পায়।
প্রভু শ্রিচরন দিল তাহার মাথায়॥
তা সবারে কৃপা করি প্রভুত চলিলা।
সেইত পাঠান সব বৈরাগি হৈলা॥
পাঠান বৈষ্ণব বিল হৈল তার খ্যাতি।
সর্ব্বত্র গাইয়ে বুলে মহাপ্রভু খ্যাতি।[154]

Chaitanya succours the humiliated and banished Shubuddhi Rai in the same text. When Shubuddhi Rai ruled Gauda, Syed Husain Khan was in his employ. He ordered Husain Khan to excavate a tank. But, when Shubuddhi discovered a breach in the tank dug by Husain, he had him whipped. Later, when Husain became the king of Gauda he bestowd a very high position upon Shubuddhi Rai. One day, his wife saw the whip cuts on his back and asked him to punish Shubuddhi. Husain replied, "This cannot be. He fed me and was a father to me. I cannot strike him." Then his wife said, "If you cannot take his life, destroy his caste." "He will not live if I destroy his caste," Husain protested. But when his wife threatened to die he was left with no choice and did what she had demanded. Shubuddhi left all worldly affairs and went to Benares. He asked the *pundits* there how should he expiate. Some asked him to drink boiling butter and die. When the master came to Benares, Shubuddhi narrated all to him. Chaitanya said to him, "All you need to do for deliverance is chant Krishna's name":

পুর্ব্বে যবে সুবুদ্ধি রায় ছিলা গৌড় আধিকারী।
সৈয়দ হুঁসেন খাঁ করে তাহার চাকরি॥
দীঘি খোদাইতে তারে মনসীব কৈল।
ছিদ্র পাঞা রায় তারে চাবুক মারিল॥
পাছে যবে হুসেন খাঁ গৌড়ে রাজা হৈল।
সুবুদ্ধি রায়রে তিহঁ বহু বাড়াইল॥
তাঁর স্ত্রী তাঁর অঙ্গে দেখে মারনের চিহ্নে।
সুবুদ্ধি রায়কে মারিতে কহে রাজা স্থানে॥
রাজা কহে আমার পোষ্টা রায় হয় আমার পিতা।
তাহারে মারিব আমি ভাল নহে কথা॥
স্ত্রী কহে জাতি লহ যদি প্রানে না মারিবে।
রাজা কহে জাতি নিলে ইহা নাহি জীবে॥
স্ত্রী মরিতে চাহে রাজা সঙ্কটে পড়িলা।
কারোয়ার পানি তার মুখে দেয়াইলা॥
তবে সুবুদ্ধি রায় সেই ছদ্ম বাঞা।
বারানসী আইলা সব বিষয় ছাড়িয়া॥
প্রায়শ্চিত পুছিল তিঁহ পণ্ডিতের গনে।
তাহা কহে তৃপ্ত ঘৃত খাঞা ছাড় প্রান॥
কেহ কহে এত নহে অল্প দোষ হয়।
শুনিয়া রহিল রায় করিয়া সংশয়॥
তবে যদি মহাপ্রভু বারানসী এলা।

তারে মিলি রায় আপন বৃতান্ত কহিলা॥
প্রভু কহে ইয়া হৈতে যাহ বৃন্দাবন।
নিরন্তর কর কৃষ্ণনাম সঙ্কীর্তন॥[155]

Not just Chaitanya himself, but his disciples too are ascribed feats of conquest and conversion. Srila Brindabandas renders one such account in the *Chaitanya Bhāgbat*. The hero of this tale is Haridas. Haridas was born a Muslim but had accepted Chaitanya as his preceptor and lived the life of a Vaishnav. A *qāzī* called on the sovereign of the land and reported the matter to him. "There is a *yavan* practicing Hindu manners, you must summon and try him," he said:

কাজি গিয়া মুলুকের অধিপতি-স্থানে।
তহিলেন তাহান সকল বিবরনে॥
"যবন হইয়া করে হিন্দুর আচার।
ভাল-মতে তারে আনি করহ বিচার॥"[156]

Haridas was produced before the Sultan who asked him, "Why are your ways so strange? When it is such great fortune to be a *yavan*, why do you immerse your mind in Hindu manners? We give up a meal if we are to even look at a Hindu [when eating]. Being so well born, why do you transgress your *jāti* and *dharma*? You will not be spared in after life for the errors you have committed in ignorance. Recite the *kalimah* and rid yourself of sin." When Haridas heard the words of the "deluded one," writes Brindabandas, he laughed aloud and said, "What *māyā* of Vishnu." Then sweetly he answered, "Listen! God is one for all. Hindu and *yavan* are but distinctions of name. The *paramārtha* is the same in both Qur'ān and Puranas. There is one Pure, Eternal and Indivisible who sits in and fills the hearts of all. This Lord stirs our hearts as he pleases and we perform our *karma* accordingly. It is this Lord whose glories all sing according to their scriptures. This God takes charge of us all. Committing violence means doing violence to him. Such is indeed my God who has taken my heart, I do what he directs my heart to. Among Hindus there are Brahmans who become Yavan of their own accord. The Hindus leave them to their *karma*, it is pointless to kill someone already dead. Now, if you regard me guilty, please try me O noble one." The Yavans were all convinced of the truth of Haridas's words. But the "wicked *qāzī*" said to the Sultan, "You must punish his evil, for he will turn others to evil. He will bring ignominy to Yavans. Hence, chasten him severely, or else, make him recite his own *śāstra*. Hearing this the lord of the land said, "O brother, if you recite your own *śāstra* you have nothing to fear. If you don't, all the *qāzīs* will punish you." Haridas replied, "One can only do what God makes him. You all must know that God has a comeuppance for unfair demands. Even if my body is hacked into small bits, I won't leave the name of Hari." Hearing Haridas, the lord of the land asked [the *qāzī*], "what do we do unto him?" The *qāzī* said, "Have him beaten in twenty-two market places (*bāzārs*), I have no other justice for him":

আপনে জিজ্ঞাসে তানে মুলুকের পতি।
"কেনে ভাই! কিরূপ তোমার দেখি মতি॥
কত ভাগ্য দেখ তুমি হৈয়াছ যবন।
তবে কেনে হিন্দুর আচারে দেহ মন॥
আমরা হিন্দুরে দেখি নাহি খাই ভাত।
তাহা তুমি ছাড় হই মহাবংশজাত॥
জাতি ধর্ম্ম লঙ্ঘি কর অন্য-ব্যবহার।
পর লোকে কেমতে বা পাইবা নিস্তার॥
না জানিঞা যে তুমি করিলা অনাচার।
সে পাপ ঘুচাহ তুমি কমিলা-উচ্চার॥"
শুনি মায়ামোহিতের বাক্য হরিদাস।
"অহো বিষ্ণু-মায়া!" বলি হৈল মহা-হাস॥

বলিতে লাগিল তারে মধুর উতর।
"শুন বাপ! সভারই একই ঈশ্বর॥
নাম মাত্র ভেদ করে হিন্দুয়ে যবনে।
পরমার্থ এক কহে কোরানে পুরানে॥
এক শুদ্ধ নিত্য বস্তু অখণ্ড অব্যয়।
পরিপূর্ণ হই বসে সভার হৃদয়॥
সেই প্রভু যারে যেন লওয়ায়েন মন।
সেই মত কর্ম্ম করে সকল-ভুবন॥
সে প্রভুর নাম গুন সকল জগতে।
বোলেন সকল মিত্র নিজ-শাস্ত্র-মতে॥
যে ঈশ্বর সে পুনি সভার ভার লয়।
হিংসা করিলেও সে তাহান হিংসা হয়॥
এতেকে যে আমারে সে ঈশ্বর যেহেন।
লওয়াইয়াছেন চিতে, করি আমি তেন॥
হিন্দুকুলে কেহো যেন হইয়া ব্রাহ্মান।
আপনেই গিয়া হয় ইচ্ছায় যবন॥
হিন্দুরা কি করে তারে, যার যেই কর্ম্ম।
আপনে যে মৈল তাঁরে মারিয়া কি ধর্ম্ম॥
মহাশয় তুমি এবে করহ বিচার।
যদি দোষ থাকে, শাস্তি করহ আমার॥"
হরিদাস ঠাকুরের সুসত্য-বচন।
শুনিঞা সন্তোষ হল সকল যবন॥
সবে এক পাপি কাজি মুলুকগতিরে।
বলিতে লাগিলা "শাস্তি করহ ইহারে॥
এই দুষ্ট, আরো দুষ্ট করিবে অনেকে।
যবনকুলের অমহিমা আনিবেক॥
এতেকে উহার শাস্তি কর ভাল মতে।
নহে বা আপন শাস্ত্র বলুক মুখেতে॥"
পুন বোলে মুলুকের পতি "আরে ভাই!
আপনার শাস্ত্র বোল, তবে চিন্তা নাই॥

অন্যথা করিব শাস্তি সব-কাজিগনে।
বলিবাও পাছে, আর লঘু ইবা কেনে॥”
হরিদাস বোলেন “যে করান ঈশ্বরে।
তাহা বই আর কেহো করিতে না পারে॥
অপরাধ-অনুরোধ যার যেন ফল।
ঈশ্বরে যে করে, ইহা জানিহ সকল॥
খন্ড খন্ড হই দেহে যদি যায় প্রান।
তভো আমি বদনে না ছাড়ি হরিনাম॥”
শুনিঞা তাহান বাক্য মুলুকের পতি।
জিজ্ঞাসিল “এবে কি করিবা ইহার প্রতি ?”
কাজি বলে বাইশ-বাজারে নিঞা মারি।
প্রান লহ, আর কিছু বিচার না করি॥[157]

The Sultan decreed that Haridas be whipped in twenty-two *bāzārs*. If he still lived his words will be accepted as true. The Sultan directed his soldiers to whip Haridas so that life leaves him. Only death will redeem him of the sin of practicing *Hinduāni* while being a Yavan, the Sultan exclaimed:

বাইস-বাজারে মারিলেহ যদি জীয়ে।
তবে সব জানি, জ্ঞানি সাঁচা কথা কহে॥”
পাইক-সকলে ডাকি তর্জ্জ করি কহে।
“এমত মারিবি, যেন প্রান নাহি রহে॥
যবন হইয়া যেন হিন্দুয়ানি করে॥
প্রানান্ত হইলে শেষে এ পাপেতে তরে’॥[158]

But even after being whipped in twenty-two market places Haridas still lived. Seeing the disappointment of his tormentors he said, "If my life injures you so, look, here I die." Saying this, Haridas immersed himself in meditation. The same instant his body stilled and ceased to breathe.

The Yavans were struck by wonder and they bore the apparently lifeless form before the Sultan. The Sultan ordered them to bury Haridas. But the *qāzī* forbid them. If Haridas receives a burial, the pontiff said, he stands a chance of redemption in the next world. But Haridas was unworthy of it as he had performed base deeds. Instead, the *qāzī* asked them to cast Haridas's body in the Ganga:

"আমি জিলে তোমাসভাকার মন্দ হয়॥
তবে আমি মরি এই দেখ বিদ্যমান।"
এত বলি আবিষ্ট হইলা করি ধ্যান॥
সর্ব্ব-শক্তি-সমন্বিত প্রভু হরিদাস।
হইলেন অচেষ্ট, কোথাও নাহি শ্বাস॥
দেখিয়া যবনগন বিস্মিত হইল।
মুলুকপাতির দ্বারে নিয়া ফেলাইল॥
"মাটি দেহ নিঞা" বলে মুলুকের পতি।
কাজি কহে "তবে ত পাইব ভাল গতি॥
বড় হই করিলেক নিচ-কর্ম্ম।
এতএব ইহারে জুয়ায় এই ধর্ম্ম॥
মাটি দিলে পরলোকে হইবেক ভাল।
গাঙেগ ফেল, যেন দুঃখ পায় চিরকাল॥[159]

However, even after being cast in the river Haridas's body remained afloat. In the moments that followed he regained consciousness and climbed ashore full of joy. With a joyous appearance Haridas walked into the city chanting 'Krishna.' Witnessing Haridas's powers the Yavans' ill will was dispelled. They all, including the Sultan, accepted him as a *pīr* and made obeisance to him. The Sultan sought Haridas's forgiveness saying that verily there is no one in the three worlds capable of comprehending him. He permitted Haridas to live in a cave by the Ganga and granted him the liberty to do what he pleased:

হেনমতে হরিদাস ভাসেন গঙগায়।
ক্ষনেকে হইল বাহ্য ঈশ্বর-ইচ্ছায়॥
চৈতন্য পাইয়া হরিদাস মহাশয়।
তীরে আসি উঠিলেন পরানন্দময়॥
সেইমতে আসিলেন ফুলিয়া নগরে।
কৃষ্ণনাম বলিতে বলিতে উচ্চশ্বরে॥
দেখিয়া অদ্ভুত শক্তি সকল যবন।
সভার খণ্ডিল হিংসা ভাল হইল মন॥
পীর-জ্ঞান করি সভে কৈল নমস্কার।
সকল যবনগন পাইল নিস্তার॥...
সসম্ভ্রমে মুলুকপতি জুড়ি দুই কর।
বলিতে লাগিলা কিছু বিনয়-উতর॥
"সত্য সত্য জানিলাঙ তুমি মহা-পীর।
এক জ্ঞান তোমারে সে হইয়াছে স্থির॥...
তোমা চিনে হেনজন ত্রিভুবনে নাঞি॥
চল তুমি, শুভ কর আপন ইচ্ছায়।
গঙগা তিরে থাক গিয়া নির্জ্জন-গোফায়॥[160]

Thus, as the *Chaitanya Charitāmṛta* and *Chaitanya Bhāgbat* display, a combination of persuasion and superior piety, besides coercion and chastisement, are resorted to in the *kāvyas* of non-Muslim authorship for converting the 'other.' This pattern begins to emerge when we take into account similar episodes found in the Manasa literature.We came across one such instance in the *Bāis Kabīr Manasā-Mangal,* the *Padmapurān* furnishes us another. The mischief making brothers Hasan and Husain in the *Padmapurān* try destroying an urn which is the emblem of goddess Manasa. The two charge at the urn chanting *Allāh* but receive a very sound beating from a group of shepherds who were making worship to it. The shepherds let them go only when they are contrite and offer a thousand salutations to each of them:

আল্লা আল্লা বলিয়া যায় ঘট ভাঙ্গিবার।
হাতে ধরি রাখাল সবে লাগে মারিবার॥[161]
মুছাপের দোহাই দেয় সাতবার।
জনে জনেরে প্রনাম করে হাজারে হাজার॥
এতেক শুনিয়া রাখাল সবে সদয় হইল।
দিব্য করিয়া তবে মোল্লা ছাড়ি দিল॥[162]

Hasan and Husain go and report the matter to the *qāzī*, also called Hasan. "Where will you now go as the land is taking to *Hinduāni?*" they ask of him. The *qāzī* is bestirred and collects a large posse for punishing the shepherds. As the bearded *mullahs* set off for where the shepherds were they say, "Today we will make all Hindus we find eat beef and detroy their caste":

হেন কালে মোল্লা আসি কহিল কাজির ঠাই।
হিন্দুআন হইয়া গেল যাইবা কোন ঠাই॥[163]
মোল্লা সব চলে মুখে বড় বড় গোপ।
ইষকারি কুতা চলে দিতে চাহে ছোপ॥
যদি গিয়া পাম যতেক হিন্দুয়া।
জাতি নাশ করিব আজি গোস্ত খিলাইয়া॥[164]

The *qāzī*'s retinue beats the shepherds and burns down their houses. They then tie them up with the intent of feeding them beef and destroying their caste:

চোপড় চোপড় মারে যত পেয়াদাগনে॥
ঘর ভাঙ্গে তারা করে ছারখার।
পুরিয়া ফেলায়ে সব করে মার মার॥[165]

. . .

রাখোলালগনেরে রাখিল বান্ধিয়া।
জাতি নাশ করো সবের গোস্ত খিলাইয়া॥[166]

The goddess Manasa now calls forth her snakes to aid her devotees. The snakes go to the *qāzī*'s house and deal the fatal sting to his three wives. The *qāzī* tries charms and the verses of the *Qur'ān* to rid them of the venom but nothing avails. However, the goddess is moved to pity by the laments of the *qāzī*'s mother. She grants her a vision and says that what has befallen them is because Hasan and Husain caused her great pain. However, she says, she can still spare them all. Manasa demands that the *qāzī* must provide the shepherds with all they need for her worship (*pūjā*). The *qāzī* is both amazed and troubled. He, however, supplies the shepherds' *pūjā* daily and lives happily ever after:

কাজির ঘরে ভাঙ্গা ঝাপ তাহা দিয়া সামাইল সাপ
বিবরে খাইল বিষম ঠাই।
ছোট বিবি লর পারে মাঝিয়া বিবি গরি পারে
বড় বিবিকে খাইল বিষম ঠাই।
কিতাব কোরান এর আপোনে ফু দিয়া ঝাড়
প্রান যায় দেখিবারে নাই।
মশারি টানাইয়ারে ফুক দিয়া বিশ ঝাড়ে
কাজির বিবি জিবার [আশা] নাই॥[167]

. . .

মোরে বড় দুঃখ দিয়াছে হাসান হোসেন॥
সেই কোপে তাহারা আমি করিল সংহার।
আখন আমি সভারে করিব নিস্তার॥
আমার পুজার সজ্জা দেও রাখাল নগর।
তবে রক্ষা পাইবে তোমার সকল নগর॥[168]...
বিস্মিত হাসন কাজি চিন্তিত হইয়া মতি॥
নিত্য নিত্য পুজার সজ্জা দেয় পাঠাইয়া।
হরষিত হইয়া কাজি রহিলা বষিয়া॥[169]

Sometimes, in the world of a *mangal kāvya*, we see a Muslim holy man battling a semi-divine Hindu sovereign. We witness this in the *Rāimangal* (রায়মঙ্গল) composed by

Krishnaram Das. The text dates to 1686 and narrates how the holy warrior Bodo Khan Ghazi came to fight Dakhin Rai, the lord of a region called Atharobhati in the Sundarbans. The two begin as friends but quarrel later. It requires God himself to descend upon earth to restore amity between them:

শুন্যছ বড়খাঁ গাজি পরতেক পীর।
ঠাকুর দক্ষিণরায় আঠারোভাঁটীর॥
দুইজনে দোস্তানি হইয়াছিল আগে।
তারপর হুড়াহুড়ি মহাযুদ্ধ লাগে॥...
বিরোধ ভাঙ্গিয়া দিল আসিয়া ঈশ্বর।
তারপর দোস্তানি পাইল দোহকার॥[170]

The dispute between the two great heroes is sparked by an act of indiscretion committed by the merchant Dhanpati. When setting off for a land called Patan on a trading expedition, he offers worship to Dakhin Rai but not to the Ghazi. Not even when followers of Bodo Khan, some *faqīrs*, ask him to make the necessary obeisance does he do that. The *faqīrs* go and report the matter to the Ghazi. An enraged Bodo Khan orders them to break idols. Besides doing that, the rather overzealous *faqīrs* also end up ripping sacred threads of the shoulders of Brahmans:

ধনপতি সদাগর যাইতে পাটনে।
একঘাটে চাপাইল বিধির বিধানে॥
দক্ষিনরায়ের যারা দেখলেক কূলে।
হরবরপুত্র জানি পুজে গন্ধ ফুলে॥
নানা রত্নভুষণ তেমনি দিবা কেবা।
বিদায় মাগিল শেষে জোড়হাথে সেবা॥
বড়খাঁ গাজির পুজা না করিয়া যায়।
অনেক ফকির গিয়া ঘিরিলেক তায়॥[171].
উনকি মূরতি তোম সব ইতি বেরি তোর॥

একেতে ফকির রুঢ়া আরে এই বোল।
দড়বড় আসিয়া ভেজায় গন্ডগোল॥
বামুনেরে ধরিয়া জনুর নিল কেড়্যা।[172]

The savage quarrel which thus begins between Dakhin Rai and the Ghazi is settled only when the Deity descends from the heavens. Interestingly, we observe that the poet has created a strange, composite figure to restore friendly relations between the two. This Deity has half his head tonsured and a queue dangles from the other half, like Lord Krishna he holds the glittery *banmālā* in his hand. As about the body, it is half white and half blue. One hand of him bears the *Qur'ān* and the other carries the Puranas. Dakhin Rai and the Ghazi prostrate at his feet and the Lord of the Universe persuades them to be friends again:

অর্দ্ধেক মাথায় কালা একভাগে চূড়া টানা
বনমালা ছিলিমিলি হাথে।
ধবল অদ্ধেক কায় অর্দ্ধনীল মেঘ প্রায়
কোরান পুরান দুই হাথে॥
এইরূপ দরশন পাইয়াছে দুইজন
ধরিযা পড়িল দুই পায়।
তুলিয়া অখিলনাথে বুঝাইয়া হাথে হাথে
দুইজন দোস্তানি পাতায়॥[173]

Another of Krishnaram Das's works is *Śītalāmangal* (শীতলামঙ্গল). The poem is dedicated to Sitala, the goddess of smallpox. This story too assumes a course similar to the previous one. Early in the *Śītalāmangal* the sage Narada calls on the goddess when she is reposing in her golden throne fanned by the nymphs. The sage tells her something which the goddess apparently did not know till then. Narada tells her that she does not command worship among all on earth. There are some people who do not revere her and one among them is a *qāzī* named Akbar who esteems no one but his *pīr.* Narada suggests that the goddess teach him a lesson so that he knows better:

সবেমাত্র পৃথিবীতে আছে জন কত।
না করে তোমার পূজা অন্যদের মত॥
মুনি বলে নাম একবর কাজি।
পির বিনে নাহি ভাবে পরম দাগাবাজি।
শেখাও তাহারে জেন ভালমত জানে॥[174]

The goddess's vanity is pricked and her ire is roused. At her behest numerous maladies afflict the *qāzī*, his *pīr* and those who followed the two. In the end, the *qāzī* has to acknowledge the greatness of Sitala, he also agrees to offer worship at her feet. The *qāzī* concedes that Sitala is the essence of everything and the mistress of all maladies. He realises that those who speak ill of her receive sorrow. He also admits to have contemplated and discovered the indistinguishability of the *Qur'ān* from the Puranas. It is only a few customs, the *qāzī* says, which tell the "Hindu" from the "Muslim." Thus, as the goddess's anger is assuaged and the Muslims are cured, they joyously found a temple in her honour:

এখন বুঝিলাম ভাবি শিতলা পরম দেবি
পুজিব তাহার পদযুগ।
তিনি সকলের সার যতো ব্যাধি আদি তার
নিন্দি অধম পায় দুখ॥
বিচার করিএ দেখি কোরান পুরান একি
সারদা বসতি সবঘটে।
হিঁদুকি মোচোলমানে পয়দা একই স্থানে
আচারেতে জুদাজুদা বটে॥[175]

. . .

ব্যাধি হইল হত (তবে) মোচোলমান।

পূজিতে শীতলাদেবি হরষিত মন॥
গ্রামের ভিতর দিল উতম মন্দির।[176]

A more striking instance of the engagement of the two contending universes is to be found in the *Śūnyapurān* (শূন্যপুরান). This text contains a canto called *Śrī Niranjaner Rūśmā* (শ্রীনিরঞ্জনের রূষ্মা) in which we see the Hindu deities descending upon earth in the guise of Muslims to rid a town called Jajpur of the tyranny of some grasping Brahmans. There were sixteen hundred households of *vedis* in the town of Jajpur, the poet tells us. All of the *vedis* were wicked. They went about demanding *dakṣiṇā* and whoever refused them they cursed. They did this to all, making no distinction between their kin and strangers. The priests were powerful and ten or twenty of them together did not mind destroying a coreligionist. The Brahmans chanted the Vedas and cast offerings in the fire. All trembled at their sight. Their hearts wounded, the people prayed to Dharma pleading to be saved from the twice-born who were laying the entire creation waste. Dharma heeds the prayers and comes down on earth. The god assumes the form of a Yavan, a black cap covering his head and a gun gracing his hand. The rest of the gods too gladly put on the *izār* (a kind of pajamas worn by Muslims). Brahma becomes Mohammad and Vishnu the *paighambar* (the poet does not seem to have known that the two are one). Lord Śiva appears as Adam, while Ganesh chooses the role of a *ghāzī*. Kartik takes the appearance of a *qāzī*. The *munis* all become *faqīrs*. Narada changes garb to become a *sheikh* and Indra, the chief of gods, a *maulānā*. Lesser gods such as Chandra and Surya become foot soldiers to the major deities, together they play (martial?) music. Goddess Chandika becomes Eve and Padmabati (?) Bibi Nur. Thus, all gods enter Jajpur together and smash temples:

শ্রীনিরঞ্জনের রুষ্মা

জাজপুর পুররাদি সোল সঅ ঘর বেদি
বেদি লয় কেবোল দুর্জ্জন।
দাখিন্যা মাগিতে জায় জার ঘরে নাহি পাঅ
সাঁপ দিয়া পড়াএ ভুবন॥
মালদহ লাগে কর না চিনে আপন পর
জালের নত্রিক দিস পাস।
বলিষ্ট হইল বড় দস বিস হয়্যা জড়
সদ্ধর্ম্মিরে করএ বিনাস॥
বেদ করে উচ্চারন বের্যাঅ অগ্নি ঘনে ঘন
দেখিয়া সভাই কম্পমান।
মনেতে পাইয়া মর্ম্ম সভে বোলে রাখ ধর্ম্ম
তোমা বিনা কে করে পরিতান॥
এইরূপ দ্বিজগন করে সৃষ্টি সংহারন
ই বড় হোইল অবিচার।
বৈকুন্ঠে ডাকিয়া ধর্ম্ম মনেতে পাইয়া মর্ম্ম
মায়াতে হোইল অন্ধকার॥
ধর্ম্ম হৈল্যা যবনরূপি মাথাএত কাল টুপি
হাতে সোভে ত্রকচ কামান।
চাপিআ উতম হয় ত্রিভুবনে লাগে ভয়
খোদায় বলিয়া এক নাম॥
নিরঞ্জন নিরাকার হৈলা ভেস্ত অবতার
মুখেতে বলেত দম্বদার।
জতেক দেবতাগন সভে হইয়া একমন
আনন্দেতে পরিল ইজার॥
ব্রহ্মা হৈল মহাঁমদ বিষ্ণু হৈলা পেকাম্বর
আদম্ফ হৈল সুলপানি।
গনেশ হইয়া গাজি কাতিক হৈল কাজি
ফকির হৈল্যা জত মুনি॥
তেজিয়া আপন ভেক মারদ হইলা সেক
পরন্দর হইল মলানা।
চন্দ্র সুর্য্য আদি দেবে পদাতিক হইয়া সেবে

সভে মিলি বাজায় বাজনা॥
আপুনি চণ্ডিকা দেবি তিহুঁ হৈল্যা হায়া বিবি
পদ্মাবতি হল্য বিবি নুর।
জতেক দেবতাগন হয়্যা সভে একমন
প্রবেশ করিল জাজপুর॥
দেউল দেহারা ভাঙ্গে কাড়্যা ফিড়্যা খায় রঙ্গে
পাখড় পাখড় বোলে বোল।[177]

The *Annadāmangal* (অন্নদামঙ্গল) composed in 1752 by the poet Bharatchandra makes the Emperor Jahangir submit to goddess Annapurna when she sends an army of ghosts and goblins to the city of Delhi. The irate goddess's *casus belli* is an insult meted to her devotee, Bhabananda, by the Emperor. Bhabananda was a Brahman employee of Pratapaditya, a chieftain in the Jessore region of Bengal, to whom the third canto of *Annadāmangal* is devoted. Pratapaditya is defeated by an expeditionary force dispatched by Jahangir. Mansingh, the general of the force, decides to make a ghoulish gift to the Emperor. He fries the body of his beaten and slain enemy in butter and caries it back to Delhi. He takes along Bhabananda too. As Mansingh's army marches back to Delhi, it is caught in a great thunderstorm for seven days. Many of the troopers die in the deluge. Those who survive are left without supplies and starve. When all appears hopeless, Bhabananda redeems the imperial army from despair. He prays to goddess Annapurna and works a miracle. The clouds part and food appears for the army. Upon his return, Mansingh narrates the incident to the Emperor praising the Brahman Bhabananda:

গিয়াছিনু বাংগালায় ঠেকেছিনু বড় দায়
সাত রোজ দারুন বাদলে।
বিস্তর লস্কর মৈল অবশেষে জাহা রৈল
উপবাসী সহ দলবলে॥
ভবানন্দ মজুন্দার নাম খুব হস্তশিয়ার

বাংগালি বামন এই জন।
সপ্তাহ খোরাক দিল সকলেরে বাঁচাইল
ফতে হৈল ইহারি কারন॥
অন্নপুর্ণা নামে দেবী তাঁহার চরন সেবি
কেরামত কামাল ইহার।
সে দেবির পুজা দিয়া ঝর বৃষ্টি মিটাইয়া
যোগাইল সকলে আহার॥[178]

The Emperor, however, is not convinced. Instead, he begins to utter copious invectives against everything "Hindu." The Brahman worshipping Annapurna and conjuring food, he rails, was a trick by Satan. It was but the worship of a ghost. What he knows of the religion of "Hindus," Jahangir warns, will embarrass Mansingh. He accuses the "Hindus" of having surrendered to the Satan and reading the Puranas in vain as the *Qur'ān* was not revealed to them:

বামন খোরাক দিল অন্নদা পুজিয়া॥
সয়তান দিল দাগা ভূতের পূজায়।
আল চাউল বেঁড়ে কলার ভুলাইয়া খায়॥
আমারে মালুম খুব হিন্দুর ধরম।
কহি জদি হিন্দুপতি পাইবে সরম॥
সয়তানে বাজী দিল না পেয়ে কোরাণ।
ঝুট মূট পড়ি মরে আগম পুরান॥[179]

Moreover, this was only one of their flaws. Jahangir reprobates almost the entire compass of "Hindu" existence. A great range of things about the "Hindus" offended him, even something as innocuous as the shaving of facial hair. After all, it was God who, when creating man, had caressed his face had endowed him with the beard and the moustache. Jahangir found it very disagreeable that the Brahman shaved away this dispensation of divine grace:

গোঁসাই মৰ্দ্ধর মুখে হাত বুলাইয়া।
আপনার নুর দিলা দাড়ি গোঁফ দিয়া॥
হেন দাড়ি বামন মুডায় কি বিচারে।
কি বুঝিয়া দাড়ি গোঁফ সাঁই দিল তারে॥[180]

Jahangir finds fault with the "Hindu" method of slaughtering cattle, for they do not resort to *zabīhah*. All ways of the "Hindus" are reckoned to be profane by him. The Emperor cites varied reasons for his scorn. They do not accept the *qāzīs* as the Prophet's deputy, upon the death of the husband they do not remarry a widow:

আর দেখ পাঁঠা পাঁঠী না করি জবাই।
উভ চোটে কেটে বলে খাইল গোসাঁই॥
যত কাম করে হিন্দু সকলি নাপাক॥
ভাতের কি কব পান পানীর আয়েব।
কাজি নাহি মানে পেগম্বরের নায়েব॥
আর দেখ নারির খসম মরি যায়।
নিকা নাহি দিয়া রাঁড় করি রাখে তায়॥[181]

The Hindus make images of wood, earth and stone. They imagine to be with life what only man has made. Thus, they worship their many goblins. The Merciful One (*Karīm*) gave humans the head out of benevolence, but, mired by error, the "Hindus" do not realise this. They are not discriminating with their religious homage, they bow their heads at all places:

. . .

মাটি কাঠ পাথরের বনাইয়া মুরুত।
জীউ দান দিয়া পুজে নানামত ভুত॥
আদমীতে বনাইয়া জীউ দেয় যারে।

. . .

করিম দিয়াছে মাথা করম করিয়া॥
মিছা ফান্দে পড়ি হিন্দু তাহা না বুঝিয়া।
যারে তারে সেবা দেই ভুমে মাথা দিয়া॥[182]

Finally, he gets rather radical and expresses the wish of converting every "Hindu" that he sees by forcing him to undergo circumcision and recite the *kalimah. Hinduāni*, he says, is nothing but deceit and the very sight of a Brahman ignites his wrath. "This Annapurna is nothing but a spook that the Brahman swindled you by conjuring," Jahangir says to Mansingh. But he is not the kind to be taken in by such tricks, he has seen enough of the hobgoblins of "Hindus". The Emperor ends the rather too grouchy address by promising Mansingh a little more reward if the Brahman can summon the same spectre for him to see:

আমার বাসনা হয় যত হিন্দু পাই।
সুন্নত দেওয়াই আর কলমা পড়াই॥
. . .
মিছা লয়ে ফির বেইমানি হিন্দুয়ানি॥
দেহ জব্বলি যায় মোর বামন দেখিয়া।
. . .
ভুলাইল বামন তোমারে বাজী দিয়া॥
এমন হিন্দুর ভুত দেখেছি বহুত।
মোরে কি ভুলাবে হিন্দু দেখাইয়া ভুত॥
আর কিছু ইনাম মাগিয়া লহ রায়।
বামনেরে বল ভুত দেখাক আমায়॥[183]

Bhabananda steps forward to answer the Emperor. He seeks to diffuse the petulant intolerance of Jahangir with a strain of thought by now familiar to us. Bhabananda tries to persuade Jahangir to see that both "Hindus" and "Muslims" worship the same Deity. "It is strange that you speak ill of

Narayan who is formless and yet with form and whose manifestation are the three worlds," he says. There is but one god for the "Hindu," the "Muslim" and all sentient beings, nor is there anything in the *Qur'ān* which is not in the Puranas, Bhabananda argues. Bhabananda asks the Emperor to realise this before he thinks of the "Hindus" and "Muslims" as being apart:

এ কথা কব কেমনে। নর নিন্দে নারায়নে॥
যেই নিরাকার সেই সে সাকার
তাঁরি রুপ ত্রিভুবনে।

. . .

মজুন্দার কহে জাহাঁপনা সেলামত।
দেবতার নিন্দা কেন কর হজরত॥
হিন্দু মুসলমান আদি জীব জন্তু যত।
ঈশ্বর সবার এক নহে দুই মত॥
পুরানের মত ছাড়া কোরানে কি আছে।
ভাবি দেখ আগে হিন্দু মুসলমান পাছে॥[184]

Having said this Bhabananda attempts to defend the "Hindu" way with a little more verve. If there is anything sacred about facial hair, and the shaving of one's chin is so bad, why does the Emperor dislike "Hindus" wearing a queue? What good will it do if the "Hindus" cropped the queue and shaved their heads? If the piercing of ears is bad how much more loathsome is circumcision?:

ঈশ্বরের নুর বলি দাড়ির যতন।
টিকি কাটি নেড়া মাথা এ যুক্তি কেমন॥
কর্নবেধে যদি হয় হিন্দু গুনাগার।
সুন্নতের গুনা তবে কতে গুন তার॥[185]

Bhabananda's voice now begins to ring with a mite of

aggression. The Puranas and *Qur'ān* both, he says, trace God in everything, be it earth, wood or stone. Those who make images of earth, wood and stone discover the form of the Formless Supreme. And those who deprive the Supreme of form and think of him as the formless alone are only scooping up manure leaving aside gold:

মাটি কাঠ পাথর প্রভৃতি চরাচর।
পুরানে কোরানে দেখ সকলি ঈশ্বর॥
তাঁহার মূরতি গড়ি় পুজা করে যেই।
নিরাকার ঈশ্বর সাকার দেখে সেই॥
সাকার না ভাবিয়া যে ভাবে নিরাকার।
সোনা ফেলি আঁচলে গিরা সার।[186]

Gradually, Bhabananda raises the register of his defence and lets go of restraint altogether. He equates the remarrying of widows to a cow being serviced by several bulls. Moreover, he argues, if the word of God evinced by the Vedas and Puranas is Satanic then, undoubtedly, the divine word of the *Qur'ān* is equally Satanic:

খশম ছাড়িয়া যেবা নিকা করে রাঁড়।
একে ছাড়ি় গাই যেন ধরে আর ষাঁড়॥
ঈশ্বরের বাক্য বেদ আগম পুরান।
সয়তান বাজী সেই এ যদি প্রমান॥
সেই ঈশ্বরের বাক্য কোরান যে কয়।
সেহ সয়তান বাজী কহিতে কি ভয়॥[187]

Now Bhabananda fends for the catholic, indiscriminating piety of the "Hindu." "The lord has given us the head for it to be bowed," argues he. "In all the world there is nothing but His image, the Hindu regards all His forms inseparable, that is why he bows his head before all and everything,"

Bhabananda clarifies:

প্রনাম করিতে মাথা দিল যে গোসাঁই।
সংসারে যে কিছু মূর্তি তাহা ছাড়া নাই॥
ভেদজ্ঞানি নহে হিন্দু অভেদ ভাবিয়া।
যারে তারে সেবা দেয় ভুমে মাথা দিয়া॥[188]

Having put up his defence, Bhabananda assumes a tone similar to Jahangir's and launches an assault on the ways of the "Muslims." The sun rises as the light of the Deity in the east, the "Hindu" faces east when offering worship and realises Knowledge. The "Muslim's" way is senseless for he genuflects facing west where the sun sets. The "Muslims" observe no taboos of food, they say the beads with the impure left hand. Nor do they follow any rules of purity and pollution, they think it is enough just to acknowledge the existence of God:

সুর্য্যরুপে ঈশ্বরের পূর্ব্বেতে উদয়।
পূর্ব্বমুখে পুযে হিন্দু জ্ঞানোদয় হয়॥
পশ্চিমে সুর্য্যের অস্ত সে মুখে নামাজ।
যত করে মুসলমান সকলি অকাজ॥

. . .

না মানে না করে খানাপিনার আয়েব॥
বাম হস্ত নাপাক তসবি জপে তায়।
হিন্দুরে নাপাক বলে এ ত বড় দায়॥

. . .

শৌচ আচমন নাহি যাহা পায় খায়।
কেবল ঈশ্বর আছে বলে এই দায়॥[189]

A piqued Jahangir has Bhabananda imprisoned. The prison-guards threaten to destroy his caste by making him recite the *kalimah* and drink their spittle:

না হোয় সুন্নত দেকে কলমা পড়াঁও লোকে
জাতি লেঁউ খেলায়কে থুক॥[190]

Bhabananda sits down to invoke Annapurna seeking deliverance from the rather difficult situation. The goddess heeds her devotee's postulation and numerous ghosts, goblins and ogres descend upon the city of Delhi. Many are possessed by them and they stubbornly refuse to be exorcised. Worse, food disappears of the city and the people are left with nothing to eat. In the end, the proud Jahangir admits defeat after he has a terrifying vision of the goddess. He summons Bhabananda and concedes that his goddess is true indeed. He orders that Annapurna be worshipped in every household of Delhi:

পাতশা কহেন শুন বামন ঠাকুর।
দেবি পুজা করি মোর পাপ কর দূর॥
সে পদ পুজিলে পাব সেই পদে ঠাঁই।
হায় রে পুজিব কিসে কোন চিজ নাই॥

. . .

জাহাঁগির কহেন ঠাকুর মোরে বাঁচা।
ভালমতে বুঝিনু তমার দেবি সাঁচা॥
জাহাঁগির ঢেড়ি দিল সকল শহরে।
অন্নপুর্ণাপুজা সবে কর ঘরে ঘরে॥[191]

The poet, thus, has the supernatural come out victorious over the resisting regime of reality. May be, here the poet is accomplishing something in the world of imagination which he desired for real.

As the middle of the eighteenth century dawned the conversation of the two sacral universes progressed apace like the shifting sands in a desert. But, soon, unvarying hills were to replace the permuting dunes.

References

1. Take, for instance, Sir Jadunath Sarkar, ed., *The History of Bengal. Muslim Period, 1200–1757*, repr. Delhi: B.R. Publishing Corporation, 2003.

   The story of eighteen horsemen capturing the Sena capital was lent credence to by Minhaj-i-Siraj's *Tabaqāt-i-Nāsirī*, composed in the second half of the thirteenth century. Sarkar provides the following translation of Minhaj's account of the facile triumph:

   . . . Muhammad Bakhtyār got his troops ready, started from Bihar and suddenly entered the city of Nadia, so fast that no more than 18 troopers could keep up with him, while the rest of his army were coming up behind him. When he reached the gate of the city he did not molest any one, but (proceeded) silently and modestly, so that none could imagine that it was Muhammad Bakhtyār, but most probably the people thought that the (new-comers) were traders who had brought high-priced horses for sale. When he reached the gate of the residence of Rāi Lakhmaniya, he drew his sword and began to slaughter the infidels. At that time the Rāi . . . was seated at his meal . . . when cries rose up from the gate of his palace and the middle of the city. By the time that he learnt what the circumstances were, Muhammad Bakhtyār had run into his palace and *harem* and cut down a number of people; (so) the Rāi fled away by the back door with bare feet. . . . (pp. 6–7)
2. Richard M. Eaton, *The Rise of Islam and the Bengal Frontier, 1204–1760*, University of California Press, 1993, p. 34.
3. Ibid., p. 69.
4. Ibid.
5. Ibid.
6. Ibid.
7. Ibid.
8. Ibid., pp. 60–61.
9. Ibid., p. 68.

   The encomium goes like this:

   সুলতা [ন] হুসেন রাজা পৃথিবীপালক ॥
   সমরে দূর্জয় রাজ্য বিপক্ষের যম।
   দানে কল্পতরু রাজা রূপে কামসম॥
   সমরে দূর্জয় রাজ্য বিপক্ষের যম।
   দানে কল্পতরু রাজা রূপে কামসম॥
   যাহার পালনে প্রজা সুখে ভুঞ্জে [অ]ধিক

   [Sultan Husain is the nurturer of the world. Invincible in battle, he is Death (*yama*) to his foes. He is giving as the *kalpataru* (a mythical tree that produces what one wishes for) and in appearance beautiful as the God of Desire (*kāma*). Ruled by him the subjects are happy and eat more.]

See Jayanta Kumar Dasgupta, ed., *Kabi Bijaygupter Padmapurān* (কবি বিজয় গুপ্তের পদ্মপুরান), Calcutta University, 1962, p. 9.

10. Ibid., p. 178.
11. Ibid., p. 234.
12. Ibid., p. 231.
13. Ibid.
14. Ibid., p. 264.
15. Ibid., pp.234–36.
16. Ibid., p. 269.
17. Ibid., p. 270.
18. "First of all I bow down to the Supreme Deity [Prabhu], and secondly to (the same Omnipotent Being conceived as) the Creator [Srijan]; and thirdly to the benign Incarnation of Light. The Koran and the other scriptural texts I regard as revelation—the sacred utterance of the Lord [Prabhu] himself . . .," ibid., p. 271.
19. Ibid., pp. 54–55.
20. Ibid., p. 59.
21. Kaliprasanna Sen, ed., *Śrī Rājmālā, Tripur-Rajanyabarger. Itibritta, Tritīa Lahar, Pandit Prabar Swargia Gangādhar Siddhāntabāgīś Birachita* (শ্রীরাজমালা, ত্রিপুর-রাজন্যবর্গের ইতিবৃত্ত, তৃতীয় লহর, পণ্ডিত প্রবর স্বর্গিয় গঙ্গাধর সিদ্ধান্তবাগীশ বিরচিত)), Agartala State Press, 1931 (ত্রপুরাব্দ), pp. 74–75. Sen opines that the *Tritīa Lahar* was composed in the seventeenth century (Introduction, p. i). According to Sen, Mughals occupied Tripura from 1623 to 1625 (p. 237).
22. Ibid., p. 77.
23. Kshitishchandra Maulik, ed., *Prāchīn Purbabanga Gītikā* (প্রাচীন পুর্ববঙ্গ গীতীকা). Calcutta: Firma K.L. Mukhopadhyay, 1971, vol. 3, p. 10. This text is dated to the sixteenth century (pp. 3–4).
24. *Prāchīn Purbabanga Gītikā,* vol.1, p. 99.
25. Ibid., p. 102.
26. *Prāchīn Purbabanga Gītikā,* vol. 2, p. 276. The age of the text is determined by the editor (p. 252).
27. *Prāchīn Purbabanga Gītikā,* vol. 3, p. 61.
28. Ibid., vol. 2, p. 169.

    Whenever I put "Hindu," "Muslim," *yavan* and *mlechchha* within double inverted commas, I imply the use of these terms by the author of the text.
29. Ibid.
30. Ibid.
31. *Prāchīn Purbabanga Gītikā,* vol.1, p. 6. According to the editor, the work depicts the circumstances of the first half of the fifteenth century

(p.4). These invocations, the editor opines, might be the work of poets other than Kanai (p. 5), but that in no way weakens our argument

32. *Prāchīn Purbabanga Gītīkā*, vol. 3, p. 36.
33. Ibid., p. 37.
34. Ibid., p. 38.
35. Ibid., p. 39.
36. Ibid., p. 40.
37. Ibid., p. 47.
38. Ibid., vol.1, p. 143.
39. Ibid., p. 191. The text is dated to the end of the sixteenth century by the editor (p. 94).
40. Ibid., p. 229. As determined by the editor, *Chandrābati* was composed in the sixteenth century (p. 205).
41. Ibid.
42. Romila Thapar, "Imagined Religious Communities? Ancient History and the Modern Search for a Hindu Identity," in *Cultural Pasts: Essays in Early Indian History*. New Delhi: OUP, 2000, p. 978.
43. See *History of the Bengali People from the Earliest Times to the Fall of the Sena Dynasty*, trans. John W. Hood. New Delhi: Orient Blackswan, 2013, p. 499.
44. Ibid.
45. *The Origin and Development of the Bengali Language*, third edn. New Delhi: Rupa & Co., 2002, p. 82.
46. Ibid.
47. Noted Sanskrit scholar and historian of Bengali literature, Shastri was appointed Head of the Sanskrit Department at Presidency College in 1895. From 1900 to 1908 he acted as the Principal of the Sanskrit College. Shastri quit the post to join the government's Bureau of Information. Also, from 1921–24, he was Professor and Head of the Department of Bengali and Sanskrit Faculties at the Dhaka University.
48. See Dusan Zbavitel, *Bengali Literature*. Otto Harrassowitz, 1976, p. 124.
49. See *The Origin and Development of the Bengali Language*, p. 112.
50. See J.C. Ghosh, *Bengali Literature*. London: OUP, 1948, p. 31.
51. Ibid.: Drawing a connection between the revival of Bengali and the accession of Muslim rule in Bengal, Dineshchandra Sen ascribed the development to the interest the new rulers took in listening to translations of the "Hindu" scriptures in their courts. As a result, he says, even the "Hindu" potentates and *zamindārs* could not ignore the language that the rulers of Bengal now encouraged. The rulers' example came to followed by all:

. . . মুসলমান সম্রাটগন পাত্রমিত্র পরিবেষ্ঠিত হইয়া হিন্দুশাস্ত্রের বঙ্গানুবাদ শূনিতে আগ্রহ প্রকাশ করিতেন...গৌড়েশ্বর যে ভাষাকে উৎসাহ প্রদান করিলেন, হিন্দুরাজগন তাহাকে অগ্রাহ্য করিতে পারিলেন না। সম্রাটগনের দৃষ্টান্ত পল্লির জমিদারগন পর্য্যন্ত অনুসরন করিতে লাগিলেন...

See *Bangabhāṣā O Sāhitya. Ingrāj Prabhāber Pūrba Parjanta* (বঙ্গভাষা ও সাহিত্য, ইংরাজ প্রভাবের পূর্ব্ব পর্যন্ত্য), eighth edn. Calcutta: Dasgupta and Company Ltd., 1949, pp. 74–75.

52. See J.C. Ghosh, *Bengali Literature,* p. 31.
53. See Zbavitel, *Bengali Literature,* p. 122.
54. Ibid., p. 121.
55. Ibid.
56. "Evolution of Hinduism in Medieval Bengali Literature: Śiva, Caṇḍi, Manasā," in *Bulletin of the School of Oriental and African Studies, University of London,* vol. 17, no. 3 (1955), pp. 503–18.
57. Ibid., p. 515.
58. See J.C. Ghosh, *Bengali Literature,* p. 18.
59. Ibid.
60. *Bānglā Mangalkābyer Itihās* (বাংলা মঙ্গলকাব্যের ইতিহাস), fourth edn. Calcutta: A Mukherjee & Co. Pvt. Ltd., 1964, Introduction, pp.1–2.
61. See *Religious Processes: The Purānas and the Making of a Regional Tradition.* New Delhi: OUP, 2001, Introduction, p. 20. Bhattacharya's ideas appear plausible in the light of what Kunal Chakravarti has to say about the Bengal Puranas' attitude towards Buddhism. They, he writes, "projected Buddhism as brahmanism's external and deviant 'other,' and urged kings and householders to make gifts and pay honorarium to *brāhmanas* for conducting sacrifices and other rituals on their behalf." (Introduction, p. 33.)
62. See Dr Sukumar Sen, ed., *Chandimangal* (চণ্ডিমঙ্গল), Sahitya Akademi. New Delhi, 1986, Introduction, p. 45. [The completion of the work is dated to CE 1555 or 1556 by Dr Sukumar Sen.]
63. Ibid., p. 78.
64. Ibid.
65. Ibid.
66. Ibid.
67. Ibid.
68. Ibid., p. 79.
69. Ibid.
70. Quoted by Dilwar Husain in *Bāngla Upanyāse Mughal Itihāser Byabahār, 1857–1916* (বাংলা উপন্যাসে মুঘল ইতিহাসের ব্যেবহার, ১৮৫৭–১৯১৬). Dhaka: Bangla Academy, 1984, p. 4.
71. Anisujjaman, *Swaruper Sandhāne* (স্বরুপের সন্ধানে). Dhaka: Jatiya Sahitya Prakashani, 1976, p. 41.

72. *Chandimangal*, p. 227.
73. *The Islamic Syncretistic Tradition in Bengal*, Princeton University Press, 1983, Preface, p. xii.
74. Ibid.
75. Ibid.
76. Ibid., p. 58.
77. Ibid.
78. Ibid., p. 60.
79. Ibid., p. 70.
80. Ibid., p. 72.
81. Ibid.
82. Ibid., p. 82.
83. Ibid., p. 90.
84. Ibid., p. 95.
85. Debnath Bandyopadhyay, ed., *Padmābati, Jāisī O Alāol* (পদ্মাবতি, জায়সী ও আলাওল). Calcutta: West Bengal State Book Board, 1985, p. 15. According to the editor the composition of the text was finished at some point between 1645 and 1652.
86. Ibid., p. 17.
87. Debnath Bandyopadhyay's opinion in ibid.
88. Dr Ashutosh Bhattacharya, ed., *Bāis Kabīr Manasā Mangal bā Bāisā* (বাইশ কবির মনসা-মঙ্গল বা বাইসা). Calcutta University, 1962, p. 69. The *Bāisā* is an anthology of poetry dedicated to Manasa by poets of various ages. The quoted verses are by Dwija Bangshidas who is surmised to have been born in the mid-seventeenth century by the editor (Introduction, p. xlv).
89. Satyendranath Bose, ed., *Śrīla Brindābandās Thākur Birachita Śri Chaitanya Bhāgbat* (শ্রীল বৃন্দাবনদাসঠাকুর বিরচিত শ্রীচৈতন্যভাগবত). Calcutta: Deb Sahitya Kutir, 2001, p. 264. According to Bose, Brindabandas was born in the year 1518 or 1519 (p. viii).
90. *Kabi Bijaygupter Padmapurān*, p. 123.
91. Ibid., p. 124.
92. *The Rise of Islam and the Bengal Frontier*, p. 101.
93. *Śri Rājmālā, Tritīa Lahar*, pp. 63–64.
94. Dr Mohammad Enamul Haq, ed., *Shāh Mohammad Saghir Birachita Usuf-Jolekhā* (শাহ মুহম্মদ সগীর বিরচিত ইউসুফ -জোলেখা), sec. edn. Dhaka: Moula Brothers, 1998, p. 115. In his work *Muslim Banglā Sāhitya [Bānglā Sāhitye Muslim Abadāner Saṁkṣipta Itihās]*, (মুসলিম বাংলা-সাহিত্য [বাংলা সাহিত্যে মুসলিম অবদানের সংক্ষিপ্ত ইউসুফ), Haq claims that Saghir was an employee of Sultan Ghiasuddin Azam Shah (r. 1389–1410), this places Saghir in the cusp of the fourteenth and fifteenth centuries. See Mansur Musa, ed., *Mohammad Enāmul Haq Rachanābali* (মুহম্মদ

এনামুল হক রচনাবলী). Dhaka: Bangla Academy, 1991, vol. I, p. 232.

95. See "Muslim Banglā Sāhitya," in *Mohammad Enāmul Haq Rachanabali*, p. 244.
96. Ahmed Sharif, ed., *Rasul Bijay* (রসুল বিজয়), published by the University of Dhaka, 1964, p. 45. Sharif dates the text to 1474 (Introduction, p. 11).
97. Ibid., p. 46.
98. Ibid., p. 25.
99. Ahmed Sharif, ed., *Saiyad Sultān Birachita Nabibangśa*, Pratham Khanda (সৈয়দ সুলতান বিরচিত নবিবংশ [প্রথম খণ্ড]). Dhaka: Bangla Academy, 1978. (For the editor's dating of the text see Introduction, p. ix.)
100. Ibid., p. 1.
101. Ibid., p. 2. Kshiti Mohan Sen describes *Sāṁkhya* thus:

    [An] important *Sāṃkhya* contribution to Hindu thought is the doctrine of *triguṇa*, the three qualities of nature. The three qualities are *sattva* (light, purity, harmonious existence), *rajas* (energy, passion), and *tamas* (inertia, darkness). These three conflicting aspects of *prakṛti* play different parts in its evolution. *Sattva* is primarily responsible for the manifestation of *prakṛti* and the maintenance of its evolution. *Rajas* causes all activity and *tamas* is responsible for inertia and restraint. *Hinduism*, Penguin Books, 2005, p. 68.

    In the light of Sen's description, Sultan's interpretation of these ideas does appear somewhat unorthodox. Nevertheless, from our point of view, it is his familiarity with them which is important.
102. Ibid., p. 7.
103. Ibid., p. 8.
104. Ibid., p. 23.
105. Ibid.
106. Ibid., p. 24.
107. Ibid., p. 25.
108. Ibid., p. 38.
109. Ibid., p. 65.
110. Ibid., p. 469.
111. Ahmed Sharif, ed., *Saiyad Sultān Birachita Nabibangśa, Dwitīa Khanda* (সৈয়দ সুলতান বিরচিত নবিবংশ [দ্বিতীয় খণ্ড]). Dhaka: Bangla Academy, 1978, pp.7–8.
112. Ibid., pp. 42–43.
113. Ibid., p. 159.
114. Ibid., p. 193.
115. Ibid., p. 479.
116. Ibid., p. 480.
117. See "Muslim Banglā Sāhitya," in *Mohammad Enāmul Haq Rachanabali*, p. 308.

118. Ahmed Sharif, ed., *Madhyajuger Kābya-Saṅgraha* (মধ্যযুগের কাব্য-সংগ্রহ). Dhaka: Bangla Academy, 1962, p. 131.
119. Ibid., p. 132.
120. See "Muslim Banglā Sāhitya," in *Mohammad Enāmul Haq Rachanabali*, p. 328.
121. Ibid., pp. 338–39.
122. Ibid., p. 341.
123. Ahmad Sharif, ed., *Muhammad Khān Birachita Satya-Kali-Bibād-Sambād bā Jug-Sambād* (মুহম্মদ খান বিরচিত সত্য-কলি-বিবাদ-সংবাদ বা যুগ-সংবাদ). Department of Bengali, University of Dhaka, 1959, p. 99.
124. Ahmed Sharif, ed., *Soāl Sāhitya* (সওয়াল সাহিত্য). Dhaka: Bangla Academy, 1976, p. 62.
125. Ibid., p. 63.
126. Ibid.
127. Ibid., p. 64.
128. Idid., p. 65.
129. Ahmed Sharif, *Madhyajuger Sāhitye Samāj O Sanskritir Rūp* (মধ্যযুগের সাহিত্যে সমাজ ও সংস্কৃতির রূপ). Dhaka: Muktadhara, 1977, p. 155.
130. *Madhyajuger Kābya Saṅgraha*, p. 207.
131. See R.D. Laing, *The Divided Self*. Penguin Modern Classics, 2010, pp. 94–95.
132. Ibid., p. 95.
133. See Charles Morgan and James R. Averill, "True Feelings, the Self, and Authenticity," in Monica Greco and Paul Steiner, eds., *Emotions: A Social Science Reader*. New York: Routledge, 2008, p. 161.
134. Abdul Karim, *Corpus of the Arabic and Persian Inscriptions of Bengal*, Asiatic Society of Bangladesh, 1992, p. 128.
135. Debnath Bandyopadhyay, ed., *Lor Chandrāni O Sati Moina* (লোর চন্দ্রানি ও সতি মইনা), fourth edn., Calcutta: Sahitya Sansad, 2006, p. 1. (According to the editor, the poem was very likely composed over the third and fourth decades of the sixteenth century.)
136. Ibid., p. 3.
137. Tony K. Stewart, "In Search of Equivalence: Conceiving the Hindu-Muslim Encounter through Translation Theory," in Richard M. Eaton, ed., *India's Islamic Traditions, 711–1750*. New Delhi: OUP, 2003, p. 387.
138. *The International Library of Music for Home and Studio*, vol. II (New York: The University Society, Inc., Educational Publishers, 1961) defines contrapuntal thus:
    [from Latin *contra-punctus*, against the point]. Notes were originally called points, hence when another set of points were added above or below the points of the theme, they were called counterpoints. In

modern use counterpoint may be defined as the art of making two or more parts move together with such freedom that they seem to be independent, each with a design of its own (p.743).

139. *Bāis Kabīr Manasā-Mangal bā Bāisā*, p. 69.
140. Ibid, p. 70.
141. Ibid., p. 74.
142. *Śrī Chaitanya Bhāgbat* (শ্রীচৈতন্যভাগবত), p. 264.
143. Ibid., p. 265.
144. Ibid., pp. 275–76.
145. Ibid., p. 276.
146. Dilip Muhopadhyay, ed., *Śrī Śrī Chaitanya Charitāmrita, Śrīla Kṛṣṇadās Kabīrāj Goswāmī Birachita* (শ্রী শ্রী চৈতন্য চরিতামৃত, শ্রীল কৃষ্ণদাস কবিরাজ গোস্বামী বিরচিত). Calcutta: Benimadhab Seal's Library, 2006, p. 134. The work is "the most authoritative biography of Chaitanya in Bengali" and was "written within a hundred years of Chaitanya's death," says J.C. Ghosh in *Bengali Literature* (p. 51). Since Chaitanya died in 1534, we can assume that the *Charitāmrita* dates either to the last decades of the sixteenth century or the early ones of the seventeenth.
147. Ibid., p. 135.
148. Ibid., p. 136.
149. Ibid., p. 137.
150. Ibid.
151. Ibid., p. 138.
152. Ibid.
153. Ibid., p. 355.
154. Ibid., pp. 355–56.
155. Ibid, p. 484.
156. *Śrīla Brindābandas Thākūr Birachita Śri Chaitanya Bhāgbat*, p. 91.
157. Ibid.
158. Ibid., p. 93.
159. Ibid.
160. Ibid., p. 94.
161. *Kabi Bijaygupter Padmapurān*, p. 123.
162. Ibid., p. 125.
163. Ibid., p. 126.
164. Ibid., p. 127.
165. Ibid., p. 130.
166. Ibid., p. 133.
167. Ibid., p. 141.
168. Ibid., p. 143.
169. Ibid., p. 145.
170. Satyanarayan Bhattcharya, ed., *Kabi Kṛṣṇarām Dāser Granthābalī* (কবি

কৃষ্ণরাম দাসের গ্রন্থাবলী), University of Calcutta, 1958, p. 180.

171. Ibid., p. 181.
172. Ibid., pp.182–83.
173. Ibid., p. 201.
174. Ibid., p. 258.
175. Ibid., p. 263.
176. Ibid., p. 264.
177. Bhaktimadhab Chattopadhyay, ed., *Rāmāi Panditer Śūnya Pūrān* (রামাই পণ্ডিতের শূন্য পূরান). Calcutta: Farma KLM Limited, 1977, pp.159–60. The editor opines that the original poem can be dated to the thirteenth or fourteenth century, but the extant structure of the poem is not older than the sixteenth century.
178. Brajendranath Bandyopadhyay and Sajanikanta Das, eds., *Bhāratchandra-Granthābalī* (ভারতচন্দ্র-গ্রন্থাবলী), third edn. Calcutta: Bangiya Sahitya Parishad, 1962, p. 304.
179. Ibid., p. 305.
180. Ibid.
181. Ibid.
182. Ibid., p. 306.
183. Ibid.
184. Ibid., pp. 306–7.
185. Ibid., p. 307.
186. Ibid.
187. Ibid.
188. Ibid., p. 308.
189. Ibid.
190. Ibid., p. 310.
191. Ibid., p. 320.

2

The Inheritance and Auguries 1757–1857

THE ENGLISH VICTORY IN 1757, followed by the one in 1764, brought about the extinction of the seat of the Nawab. Bengal now lay under a new state. Despite the seismal nature of the transition, and its obvious impact on Bengali society, the old literary culture endured a while. The *kāvya* tradition, now flourishing for more than four hundred years, held out for a few decades more. However, before being interred into the crypt of the bygone, its final spasms etched marks on the emotional landscape which mingled with the footprints of what followed.

We encounter what are perhaps the last of the *kāvyas* in the second half of the eighteenth and the first three decades of the nineteenth centuries. Though seemingly moribund, the tradition was still very much a carrier of the anxieties we described earlier. The manner in which they were sought to be negotiated also appears to be the same. Partly, it was one of incorporation while being aware that what is being incorporated into one's cosmos comes from outside its pales. And part it was one of absolute subordination while incorporating, following which the artifact in question will be cast to the fringes of one's world.

The above is what we observe in Vishnu Pala's *Manasā Mangal* (বিষ্ণু পালের মনসামঙ্গল). The redaction in which it has come down to us is derived from a manuscript dating to "sometime between 1775 and 1825." The text might have enjoyed a floating, oral existence in the interiors of eastern

Bengal sung by itinerant bards. It "gives us the version (or versions) that were used by the singers who came from the common people."[1] At one point in this curious poem, the brothers Hasan and Husain emerge out of the crescent upon lord Shiva's head. This happens when it falls off his matted locks upon earth and breaks into two:

> আধখানা চন্দ্র প্রভুর ভুমিতে পড়িল।
> হাসেন হোসেন দুই ভাই তাহাতে জন্মিল॥[2]

The divine parentage, however, does not help when running an errand for their father and master they offend the goddess to whom the text is dedicated. She inflicts the most gruesome punishment on the two, sending after them snakes by the thousands. They submit to her and promise to win her the earth if she spares their lives:

> এই ভুম তোমার শাসন করিয়া দিব
> দুটি ভাএর রাখহ পরান।[3]

There were similar pugnacious rejoinders from the other side. We encounter several such in the *pānchālis* dedicated to Satyapir and Manikpir written in the closing years of the eighteenth century. There was an apparent spurt around the time in their following as also in the literature dedicated to their cults. Though the corpus of Satyapir's literature had been forming since the sixteenth century, it really swelled now, as pointed out by Tony K. Stewart, "in the period of easy excess to inexpensive printing and the concomitant creation of great entrepreneurial fortunes."[4] Satyapir is often presented as the Islamic transliteration of the Hindu deity Satyanarayan and the outcome of a process termed "syncretism." Stewart, for example, proffers the idea that "the common concerns framing the invocation of Satya-pīr were not those defined by membership in a religious group."[5] According to him, the Satyapir texts instead reveal "structures of authority" "considerably more complex and subtly nuanced than the basic categories of Hindu and Muslim could ever recognise, and they often imbricate what are traditionally thought of as either exclusively Hindu or Muslim attitudes and acts."[6] However, as we will observe in the texts below, irrespective of an "imbrication," both Satyapir and Manikpir very doubtlessly further the triumph of Islam over the unbeliever. Both borrow motifs from the unbeliever's universe, even become his deities, but their final intent of conquest and conversion remains unaltered. Both are supremely confident of the superiority of Islam and their capacity to demonstrably establish this superiority with their spiritual and worldly accomplishments. The contests they engage in with this object form a thread binding their diverse tales together into one coherent whole.

The *pānchāli Ājodyār Kechchā* (আজদ্যার কেচ্ছা)[7] was composed by one Gharib Taiyab and it does not seem like 'syncretism' was what he had in mind when he made Satyapir battle and defeat Hanuman in his poem. "There are many Muslims in the world," writes Gharib setting the tone for his tale, "who are familiar with the prodigies (*karāmāt*) of Satyapir. But since the Hindus are not, they do not worship him":

দুনিঞাতে জত লোক আছে মোছলমানে। সত্তপিরের কারামত তারা সবাই জানে।
হিন্দু লোকে নাহি জানে দেত্তান সত্তপিরে। তেকারনে হিন্দুলোকে পুজা নাহি করে।[8]

What follows in the wake of the assertion is a by now familiar story of conquest of the sacred universe of the "other." The story begins with Satyapir deciding to visit Ayodhya. Being quite engrossing we reproduce all of it here.

"Girdle up," one day Satyapir said to his disciple Siddiqui, "we will go to Ayodhya." When Siddiqui heard this, he lowered his head and mulled. He said to Satyapir, "Going to Ayodhya is verily death. There the ruler is Daśaratha, the crown of the solar lineage. Even gods and *gandharvas* worship him":

দেত্তান বলেন বাত ছিদ্দিকা নফরে। বান্ধহ কোমর জাব আজস্কা নগরে॥
নফর ষুনিল জদি দেত্তানের কথা। ভাবিতে লাগিল তবে হেষ্ঙ কর্যা মাথা॥
ছিদ্দিক বলেন দেত্তান ষুনহে বচন। অজধ্যা নগরে যাবে মরিবার কারন॥
ষুর্জ্জুবংসে চুড়ামনি দসরত রাজা। দেবগন্ধর্ব্বলোকে জারে করে পূজা॥[9]

Siddiqui also warned his master of Daśaratha's sons. "The four brothers are the masters of war," Siddiqui continued, "their arrows make the three worlds quake. You wanting to appear in Ayodhya is like an ant growing wings at the approach of death." When Satyapir heard this he laughed heartily and said, "They might be masters of war and brave but I am a mere poor *faqīr* who begs his food. I know nothing of quarrel or war. They might be armed with the bow, but my only weapon is the *Qur'ān.* I will strike them with the verses (*āyats*) of the Book":

চারি ভাই জুদ্ধ্যাপতি ঐচ্ছে বলমান। জার বানে ত্রিভুবন হয় কম্পবান॥
জাহির হইতে চাহ অজর্দ্ধা নগরে। পিপিড়াকে পাখ উঠে মরিবার তরে॥
এতেক বচন জখন দেত্তান জিউ ষুনি। খল খল হাঁসেক জগত্তের মুনি॥
বাছা তারা যুর্দ্ধ্যাপতি বিরে মহাবির। আমি কেবল বাছা কাঙ্গাল ফকির ॥
কাঙ্গাল ফকির আমি ভিক্ষা মাগি খাই। না জানি ঝগড়া বাছা না জানি লড়াই॥
তারা বটে যুর্দ্ধ্যাপতি হাতে গণ্ডিবান। আমার হাতিআর কেবল আএত কোরান॥
কোরানের আএত জদি ফিকিঞা মারিব। হুকুম আল্লার তথে গাওবত কর্যা দিব॥[10]

Apparently, Satyapir is supremely confident of his capacity of attesting the superiority of the spirituality articulated in the *Qur'ān.*

As Satyapir resolves to visit Daśaratha's capital, Gharib takes us to the hovel of a poor Brahman in Ayodhya. He was without a child. The unhappy Brahman propitiated Lord Śiva for twelve years and the god blessed him with two sons:

এক কাঙ্গাল ব্রহ্মণ আছে অজর্দ্ধানগরে। পুর্ব্ব হইতে কথা কহি সভাকারে॥
ভিক্ষ্যা মাগ্যা খাএ দিজ দুখ বাড়া। পুত্র নাহিক তার জনম আঁঠকুড়া॥
বড়ই দুক্ষিত ব্রহ্মন ভাবেন অন্তরে। বার বর্শ্ছর একভাবে শিবপুজা করে॥
বার বর্শ্ছর পুজা করে সেই যে ব্রহ্মন। তুষ্ট হইয়া পুত্রবর দিল যে ত্রিলোচন॥[11]

Once there was no food in the Brahman's house for three days. For three days and nights he was without a meal. Finally, he went to the town to beg:

বিভার ফের হৈল ষুন তাহার বাত । তিন রোজ ব্রহ্মনের ঘর্রে নাহি ভাত।
তিন দিন তিন রাত্রি রঞা অনাহারে । সহরে চলিয়া যায় ভিক্ষ্যার খাতিরে ॥ [12]

After the Brahman left, his wife prepared the day's meal and went to a lake to bathe. She left her sons on the bed. Satyapir had by now appeared in Ayodhya. Wishing to weave some *māyā*, he decided to steal the Brahman's children. He tucked the two infants in his armpits and entered the netherworld (*pātāl*):

ব্রহ্মন ঠাকুর গেছে ভিক্ষার লাগিঞা । সকল রন্ধন করি ছিন্নান করিঙ্গা ॥
দুটি বালক দুটি পালঙ্গ ওপরে । সিন্নান করিতে নারি জায় সরবরে ॥
আছমানে হইছে দেখ দেড় পহর বেলা । সত্তপির নানামতে পাতে মাএআ খেলা ॥
ছাহেব অনাথের নাথ ভাবে মাএআ করি । ব্রহ্মনের দুটি বালক আমি করি চুরি ॥

. . .

দুই বালক দুই বগলে দাবি লঞা । পা[তা]লের পুরে গেল ষলঙ্গ বাহিঞা ॥ [13]

Finding their sons missing the couple were inconsolable. The Brahman told his sorrowing wife what Śiva had warned him of. "My blessings will bring you two sons," the god had said, "but you must know that if the parents sin then the sons will die. And if the king sins then too they will die." The Brahman thought hard but could trace no sin in him:

আমার বরে হবে তোমার কোলে নোন্দন । মাতা পিতার পাপ হৈল পুত্রের মরন ॥
মা বাপের পাপ জদি না থাকে সংসারে । রার্জ্জিধর হয়[না] জদি পাপকর্ম্ম করে ॥
রাজার পাপ থেকে জদি ষুন হে ব্রার্হ্মন । বরে পাইলে দুই পত্র অবস্য মরন ॥
খেতিতলে পড়া ব্রার্হ্মন এই মনে করে । কোন পাপফলে আমার দুটি পুত্র মরে ॥
মনে মনে ব্রার্হ্মন যুক্তি বিচারিল । আপনার পাপের লেষ দেখিতে না পেল্য ॥ [14]

Then the Brahman went to the court and said to Lakshman, "Your sins have killed my sons. Ravana abducted

Sita and kept her in the Ashokavan. The *māyā* of a demon is beyond fathoming, he must have sported with Sita for long. Many sins were thus committed in that Ashokavan. You rescued that woman and brought her back to the house. You have immersed the three worlds in sin. That is why my sons have died":

ষুনহ লক্ষন ঠাকুর বলি জে তোমারে । তোমাদের পাপে আমার দুটি পুর্ত্র মরে॥
সিতাকে করিল চুরি লঙ্কার রাবনে । চুরি কর্যা রাখে সিতা অসকের বনে॥
রাক্ষসের মাএআ কেবা বুঝিবেক পারে । সিতা লইয়া রাবন রাজা কত কৃড়া করে॥
কত পাপ কইল সেই অসোক ভিতরে । তাকেহ উর্দ্ধারিএগ পুনু রাখে জে ঘরে॥
পাপে মজিল রাজ্য ই তিন ভুবন । তে কারনে মৈল মর পুর্ত্র দুই জন॥[15]

Lakshman vowed to immolate himself if he fails to rescue the sons of the Brahman:

বাচাইতে নারি জদি তোমার নোন্দন । অগ্নিকুণ্ড কর্যা তবে তেজিব জিবন॥[16]

On the other hand, after some time, the Brahman's wife bore a son again:

বিধাতার মাএআ কিছু বুঝা নাঞি গেল । পুনুরুপি ব্রাহ্মনি গর্ব্ববতি হইল॥[17]
. . .
চন্দ্রবদনি নারি য়বনি লোটায় । ছাত্তাল মানিক এক প্রসবিল তায়॥[18]

The Brahman feared remembering the past and came to Lakshman again and said to him, "Listen O Lakshman, a son has been born to me fair as sunshine. I have come to give you the news so that you may protect him." Anxious, Lakshman took Hanuman along and came to keep watch outside his house:

পুর্ব্বকথা ব্রহ্মনের পড়্যা গেল মোনে । এক কথা কহিএগছিল ঠাকুর লক্ষ্যনে ॥
সেই কথা ব্রার্হ্মনের পড়্যা মোনে গেল । পুনুরুপি লক্ষনের কাছেতে আইল॥
কহিতে লাগিল কথা ষুন হে লক্ষ্যন । হএগছে বালক মোর ষুর্জ্জের কিরন॥

আপুনি কহিঞাছিলে বাচাবার তরে । সোমাচার দিতে আইলাম তোমারে॥
চঞালিতা হৈল তবে ঠাকুর লক্ষ্যন । হনুমানকে সঙ্গে করি করিল গোমন॥[19]

One morning, as the Brahman was away begging and Lakshman was keeping watch, Satyapir came up a tunnel and emerged in the Brahman's house. The Brahman's wife was sleeping with the infant in her lap. Satyapir snatched the child and entered the seventh layer of the netherworld:

ষুলঙ্গ বাহিঞা আইলেন সর্ত্তপির । ব্রাহ্মনের ঘরে হইলেন জে হাজির॥
জননি জাইছে নির্দ্রা পুর্ত্র কোলে নিঞা । কোলে হইতে সর্ত্তপির নিল ছনাইঞা॥
. . .
জতন করিঞা নিল আপনার কোলে । প্রবেস করিল এস্যা সপ্তম পাতালে॥[20]

When Lakshman learnt what has happened he said to Hanuman that now he must enter the fire:

ষুন বাছা পবননন্দন । বাচাইতে নারিলাম মুনির নন্দন॥
সত্যাবন্দি আছি মোঁ ইহার বালকের তরে । নির্শ্ছয় মরিব আমি অগ্নির ভিতরে॥[21]

Hanuman implored Lakshman to wait for three days within which he promised to look for and rescue the lost sons:

সমাচার দ্দিগা গোসাঙ্কি রঘুনাথ গোচরে । তিন দিন পরে মর প্রভু বলিএ তোমারে॥
তিন দিন কাবার করি দোহাই দিঞা । তিন দিনের মধ্যে বালক দিব জে আনিঞা॥[22]

After taking leave of Lakshman, Hanuman searched in every direction, he traversed the earth four times but did not the find the Brahman's sons. Angry, he went to the Hall of Death:

বিদায় হইঞা হনু করিল্যা গোমন । পুর্ব্ব পশ্ছিম উত্তর দক্ষিন করিল ভ্রমন॥
চারিকুন প্রিথিমি সকল ভ্রমিল । খোজ্রিজা মুনির পুত্র কথুই নাই পাইল॥
[৩৬ ছাত্তাল না পাইঞা চঞ্চলিত মন । কোর্দ্ধগত হঞা গেল জোমের ভুবন॥[23]

Death asked Chitragupta to look through his records. Ordered by Yama, Chitragupta searched sixteen thousand bales of paper but found no mention of the children of the Brahman. He reported his failure to Yama:

চিত্তগোপ্তকে ডেক্যা বলে মনে দিখ্য বাড়া। একে তর্ল্লাস কর জত কাগজের গোড়া॥
জোমের আজ্ঞ্যা পাএ্যা কাগজ ঢণ্ডিতে লাগিল । সোল হাজার কাগজের গোড়া তর্ল্লাষ করিল॥
না পাইল ঢণ্ডিএ্যা কথু মুনির ছাত্তাল । জোমরাজার কাছে কহিল ততকাল॥[24]

Hanuman wept in despair and went to Vibhishan. But Vibhishan refused help, he asked Hanuman to do the searching on his own. Weeping, Hanuman came to his mother:

কান্দিতে কান্দিতে হনু করিলা গোমন । বিবিস্বনের কাছে জাএ্যা দিল দরসন॥
. . .
ষুন বাপু হনুমান এই সকল কথা । আপনে তর্ল্লাস কর ঢোড় জোথাতোথা॥
চলিলেন হনুমান কান্দিতে কান্দিতে । অবিলম্বে গেলা হনু মাএর সাক্ষ্যাতে॥[25]

"Nowhere do I find the offspring of the sage, hence, I come to you," he said to his mother, Anjana. When Hanuman spoke thus, Anjana meditated. Meditation had bestowed on her the powers of realising the goings on of the four worlds. She discovered that the children have been carried away by Satyapir and said as much to her son. "To perform a prodigy he has stolen the children and hidden them in the seventh layer of the netherworld," she informed her son:

কোথাও না পাইলাম মুনির নন্দন । তে কারনে আইলাম তোমার সদন॥
[৪১ এমনি বচন জখন হনুমান কহিল । ষুনিএ্যা অঞ্জনা ধিয়ানে বসিল॥
ধিআনে ভকতা মাতা ধিআনে সকতা । ধিয়ানে জানে চারি জুগের বারতা॥
ব্রর্ম্মনে বালেকে পির হর্যা নিএ্যা ছিল । সেই কথা অঞ্জনা ধিআনে জানিল॥
অঞ্জনা বলে বাছা হনুমান বির । মুনির পুত্র হর্যাছেন দেত্তান সর্তপির॥
জাহিরের লগ্যা হর্যাছে মুনির ছাত্তালে । লুকাএ্যা রেখ্যেছেন সপ্তম পাতালে॥[26]

Joyous and remembering Rama, Hanuman travelled beneath the earth. He wondered, "How will my mind cope (with the task), where do I go to find the children." Meanwhile, the Ocean of Compassion (Satyapir) camped beneath the earth where there was a lake. He asked the children to fetch him water:

তিনটি বালক সহ আনন্দিত মন । পাতালপুরি গেল হনু কর্যা রাম সোঙরন॥
হনুমান বলে আমি বুর্দ্ধি কি করিব । কোনখানে কোথা গেলে সিষুরে পাইব॥
জেখানে আসেন আছে দয়ার সাগর । তাহার নিকটে আছে একটা সরবর॥

. . .

সেই সময় সর্ত্তাপির হইয়া মেহেরবানি । সিষুরে বলেন আনি দেহ অক্ষরপানি॥[27]

As providence will have it, the children meet Hanuman when they set off to bring Satyapir water. When Hanuman urged the children to leave with him they replied, "O sire of the wind god, you are putting a noose around your neck. Satyapir is the saviour of all, your ignorance makes you speak what you do. If you indeed want to take us along, go and plead with Satyapir, if he lets us go you may take us":

ছাত্তাল বলেন ষুন তুমি পবননোন্দন । মরিবার অউষদ কর গলাতে বন্ধন॥
সর্ত্তিনারায়ন নাম ভুবন প্রচার । জার নামে ভবসিন্ধু হঞা জাব পার॥
হেন সর্ত্তপির ঠাকুর সংসারে তারন । না বুঝিঞা হেন বাক্য বল অকারন॥
জদি তোমা মনে থাকে আমাদিগে নিতে । মিনতি করগা আগে পিরের সাক্ষ্যাতে॥
তেনি জদি ছেড়্যা দেন কৃপাযুক্ত হইঞা। তবে নিঞা জেত্যা পাব সোন মন দিঞা॥[28]

Hearing the children say that he is putting a noose around his neck, Hanuman burnt in anger and cried, "Listen, children of the sage, do not think that I am a mere wild beast. You do not know what strength I bear. If I wish I may carry you away with all of the netherworld. You ask me to plead with Satyapir, but I, a devotee of Rama, I fear no one":

নহে তুমি হেন বাক্য বল অকারন । মরিবার অউখদ কর গলায় বন্ধন॥
[৫০ এতেক বচন জদি বলিল ছাত্তালে । ষুনিঞাত হনুমান কোর্দ্ধে বড় জলে॥

ষুন অরে মুনির পুর্ত্র বলি উর্চ্চস্বরে । বনের পষু বল্যা পারা জান্যেছ মোরে ॥
বাহুবল মধ্যে মুঞি হেন সক্তি ধরোঙ । পাতাল সমেত উপুড়্যা নিঞা জেত্যা পারোঙ ॥
মিনুতি করিতে বল ফকিরের পাত্র । রামের কৃপাতে আমি কাথে পায় ভয় ॥[29]

Having spoken, Hanuman lifted the children upon his shoulder. Satyapir, on the other hand, wondered what is keeping the children as the hour of the *namāz* was drifting by. He meditated and the doings of Hanuman were revealed to him. The clairvoyant Satyapir knew that Hanuman intends to run with the children:

হনুমান নাঞি ষুনে ছাত্তালের বচনে ॥ কন্ধের ওপরে সিষু নিল তিনজোনে ॥
পআন করিল হনু কর্যা অহঙ্কার । অন্তরে জানিল তাহা পির অবতার ॥
সর্ত্তপির দেত্তান ভাবেন মোনে মোনে । দিরকু হইল সিষু নাঞি এল্য কেনে ॥
পানি আনিবারে তিন সিষু গেল । নামাজের বেলা জায় কেনে নাই আইল ॥
বেআনে বৈসেন মঞা দেত্তান সর্ত্তপির । হনুমানের সব কথা হইল জাহির ॥
অন্তরজামিনি ছাহেব অন্তরে জানিঞা । আমার ছাত্তাল হনু মিঞা জায় পালাইঞা ॥[30]

Satyapir went and sat by the road Hanuman had taken. When he went by, he saw the three children with him:

জেই পথে হনুমান জেছ্যে পালাইঞা । তার আগুপথে পির রঞাছে বসিঞা ॥
হেন বেলায় হনুমান সেই পথে জায় । তিন সিষু দেত্তানে দেখিবারে পায় ॥[31]

When Hanuman came by Satyapir confronted him. Hanuman, on his part, reproved Satyapir. "Your ways are not of a *faqīr*, you go about claiming others' children as your own. You run before I insult you more," said Hanuman censuring Satyapir. "Why do you speak unkind words O son of Pavan?" asked Satyapir of Hanuman. "I have seen no children of a sage, they are mine, you may ask around and find out. Do not carry away the children of a *faqīr,* I have raised them since they were little":

ফকির হইয়া তোমার এই সব রিত । পরের পুর্ত্র আপন বল ই কোন চরিত ॥
যে হবার তাই হৈল ফকির জাও পলাইঞা । নহে অপমান পারি কহি দড়াইঞা ॥

দেত্তান বলেন সুন পবননোন্দন । কঠুর বচন তুমি কহ কি কারন॥
কোথা মুনির পুর্ত্র দেখিনি নজরে । আমার ছত্তাল বটে ষুদাও ঘরে ঘরে॥
[৫৮ ছোট হৈতে তিন সিষু করিলাম পালন। ফকিরের ছাত্তাল নিঞা জায় কি কারন॥[32]

Hanuman refused to yield to the *faqīr*'s persuasion. Instead, he angered and attempted to uproot a tree to strike the *faqīr* with:

ষুনিঞা ত হনুর কোর্দ্ধ বড় হইল । ফকিরে মারিতে হাত গাছে বাড়াইল॥[33]

But no matter how hard he tried, the tree won't be ripped of the earth. Crushed, Hanuman collapsed upon earth and wept. Nevertheless, the next instant he rose to his feet and charged at Satyapir. That is when Satyapir uttered *āyats* of the *Qur'ān* depriving Hanuman of strength and wits. The weak and witless Hanuman looked around bewildered, then he collapsed and rolled in the earth. But he drew on his store of courage and once again rushed upon Satyapir intent on striking him:

কোরানের আএত মিঞার মুখে বারাইল । হনুমানের বল বুদ্ধি সব হরা নিল॥
বল বুর্দ্ধি নাহি হনু চারি পানে চায় । ভুমিতে পড়িঞা হনু গড়াগড়ি জায়।
তমুত সাহস করে মারিবার তরে । কোথা পালাইঞা জ[া]বে ষুন রে ফকিরে॥[34]

Satyapir was immensely saddened by the sight and spoke a malediction. The curse blinded Hanuman:

তখন দেত্তানে চিত্তে দুক্ষ্য বড় হৈল । মুখে হইতে বদ দোয়া বাহির হঞা গেল॥
সেইত অক্ষ্যর ভাই বড়ই বিবন্ধ। গজবে পড়িঞা হনু হঞা গেল অন্ধ॥[35]

The beaten Hanuman decided to hang himself:

অসার সংসার ইহাতে না রহিব আর মরিব গলাতে দিয়া দড়ি॥[36]

Seeing Hanuman's death certain the children of the Brahman addressed him. "We see only one way," they tried to reason with him, "the fire that can burn us to death can warm us too. Only Satyapir, the very incarnation of Truth (*satya*) can save you. Dwell on his name with an unwavering mind and you will be redeemed." Hanuman obeyed the children and took Satyapir's name seven times. Then he asked them to take him into the presence of the *pīr*:

মরন নির্শ্চয় কথা ষুনিঞা নিদানে । কহিতে লাগিল কথা মুনির নন্দনে॥
ইহার উপায় হনু আর নাহি দেখি । জে আগুনে পুড়ে মরি সে আগুনে সেকি॥
সেই সর্ত্তপির ছাহেব সর্ত্তি অবতার । দেনি বা তরাইতে পারেন হইঞা কাণ্ডার॥
একচির্ত্তে সর্ত্তাপির কর সোঙরোন । উর্দ্ধার করিয়া নিবেন পতিতপাবন॥
[৬৭ ছাত্তালের বচন সুনি পবনকুমার । সর্ত্তপির সর্ত্তপির বলে সাতবার॥
পুনরুপি হনুমান লাগিল কহিতে । নিঞা জাইতে পার একবার পিরের সাক্ষাতে॥[37]

Thus, after putting up a tough resistance, Hanuman was compelled to recognize the spiritual power of the *pīr*.

When the children led him to where Satyapir was Hanuman held his feet and cried. He begged forgiveness for raising a hand to strike the *pīr*. "Forgive me and show me compassion as a disciple. Not knowing better, I parleyed with you. You have given me what I deserved," Hanuman said weeping at the *pīr*'s feet. Pity welled in the The Lord of Compassion (Satyapir). With his unfathomable *māyā* Satyapir took the form of Raghunath (Vishnu):

তোমাকে মারিতে ছাহেব হাত বাড়াইলুঁ । ছাহেবের চরনে বড় অফরাদি হইলুঁ॥
অফরাদ কর ক্ষেমা ঘুচাইঞা মাএআ । নফর বলিয়া গোসাঞি পুনু কর দএআ॥
না জানিঞা তোমা সনে বাদ কৈলাঙ আমি । তেমতি উচিত ফল দিখাইলা তুমি॥
চরনে পড়িয়া হনু কান্দিতে লাগিল । দএআর ঠাকুর সর্ত্তপিরের দওআ উপজিল॥
বিসম পিরের মাএআ বুঝা নাই গেল । রঘুনাথের মুর্ত্তি ছাহেব ততক্ষ্যনে হৈল॥
দুর্ব্বাদলস্বাম গোসাঞি অমৃত রসাল । দির্ঘ নাসিকা চারি চৌরস কপাল॥[38]

But the blinded Hanuman could not behold this form. "Return me my vision," he begged writhing and holding the *pīr*'s feet, "all the secrets of the three worlds have been uncovered to me. I will take your name for eons now, for as long as I live in this world":

অন্ধক আছিল হনু দেখিতে না পায় । লোটাঞা লোটাঞা ধরে সর্ত্তপিরের পায়॥
[৬৯ কৃপা করি আখি দান দেহ সর্ত্তপির। ই তিন ভুবনে কথা হইল জাহির॥
যুগে যুগে তোমার নাম অভিরত নিব । সয়াল ভুবনে আমি জতকাল জিব॥[39]

Rama's mighty devotee was now completely broken. The surrender of Hanuman was complete and he accepted defeat with utter humility.

The generous *pīr* returned and increased Hanuman's vision, strength and wits four folds:

অনাথের নাথ পির হইয়া মেহেরবান । অন্ধ আছিল হনু আঁখি পাইল দান॥
বল বুর্দ্ধি জত কিছু হরা নিঞাছিল । পিরের দোয়াতে হনু চতুর্গু[ন] পাইল॥[40]

When Hanuman opened his eyes and saw the form of Raghunath he was confounded. He asked the *pīr*, "Why are you in *pātāl* leaving Ayodhya. You had asked me to fetch the children O Narayan, but you have beaten me to the task":

নআন মেলিঞা জদি দেখিতে লাগিল । রঘুনাথের মুর্ত্তি দেখ্যা মনে ধন্দ হৈল॥
কহিতে লাগিল তবে পিরের সন্নিধানে । অজদ্যা ছাড়িয়া তুমি পাতালপুরে কেনে॥
আপনে করিলে আজ্ঞ্যা সিষুর কারন । আমাকে ভাণ্ডাঞা আগু এস্যছ নারায়ন॥[41]

"I understand Hari," he went on, "it is you who have handed me sorrow. You yourself stole the children of the Brahman. I know not what *māyā* you have wrought." Then Satyapir said, "I am not Raghunath but Satyapir." "If it is so," Hanuman demanded, "let me see you in a *faqīr*'s appearance":

বুঝিলাঙ আপনে দুখ দিঞাছ শ্রীহরি । আপনে ব্রার্ক্ষনের পুর্ত্র করা এন্যছ চুরি॥
এমন বিসম মাএআ কে বুঝিতে পারে । এতখানি কর তুমি নফরের তরে॥
দেত্তান বলেন হনু তেরা হযুর কই । রঘুনাথ নই আমি সর্ত্তাপির হই॥
হনুমান বলে যদি সর্ত্তপির দেত্তানে । ফকিরের মুর্ত্তি একবার দেখাও নআনে॥[42]

Satyapir consented to grant Hanuman a vision of his as a *faqīr*. He asked Hanuman to turn his back to him and turn around at his command. Upon assuming the visage of a *faqīr*, Satyapir directed Hanuman to turn around and look at him. However, a terrible fear seized Hanuman when he viewed Satyapir in his original form and he dropped down senseless. Satyapir asked Hanuman to rise and open his eyes. Upon regaining consciousness, Hanuman said to the *pīr* that he verily is Narayan, the one who has been incarnate in the four *yugas*:

ষুনিঞা দেত্তানের কথা ফিরিয়া চাহিল । ছাহেবের রুপ দেখ্যা মুর্শ্ছাগত হইল ॥
মুর্শ্ছাগত হইঞা পড়িল খেতিতলে । নিজহস্তে সর্ত্তপির হনুমানে তোলে ॥
উঠ উঠ অরে বাছা চক্ষু মেল্যা চাও।৭১] [৭২ আমি ত ফকির মুঝে কথা কের্নে কয় ॥
হনুমান বলে গোসাঞি কথা কব কি । তোমার বরনে মুর্শ্ছাগত হইঞাছি ॥
নির্শ্ছয় জানিলাঙ তুমি সর্ত্তিনারায়ন। নআনে দেখিঞা গোসাঞী জানিল এখন ॥[43]

. . .

হনুমান বলে গোসাঞি কি বলিব আর । চারি যুগ ধর তুমি চারি অবতার ॥[44]

"When your name (*harinām*) quenches the world, why do you still need to take the name Satyapir," Hanuman asked. "Sin has filled the earth," the *pīr* replied, "hence I have become Satyapir to redeem the world with my hands which bear the lotus." "Pay heed Hanuman, I am Satyapir to Muslims and Narayan to Hindus. The Muslims call a Mullah and offer me *shīrīnī*, the Hindus call a Brahman to offer me worship (*pūjā*)":

হরিনামে তরা গেল জগতসংসারে । আবার সর্ত্তপির নাম ধর কিসের খাতিরে ॥
দেত্তান বলেন বাছা মন করহ স্থির । এ কারনে নাম আমি ধরি সর্ত্তিপির ॥
মন দিয়া ষুন তুমি সেই সোমাচার । যে কারনে হইল আমার পুজার প্রচার ॥
পাপে হইল পুন্য দেখ মর্তভুবন । রসাতল জায় পুরি পাপের কারন ॥
তেকারনের অরে বাছা সর্ত্তরুপ হঞা । সংসার তারন কৈলুঁ পদ্মহস্ত দিঞা ॥
[৭৪ সোন সোন অরে বাছা ব্বির হনুমান ঃ আমি মোছলমানের সর্ত্তপির হিন্দুর নারায়ণ ॥
মোছলমান সির্ন্নি দেয় মোল্লাকে ডাকিঞা । হিন্দু সব পূজা করে ব্রার্ক্ষন আনিঞা ॥[45]

Finally, Satyapir sent away Hanuman with a message, "I forgive you Hanuman for you are my servant. You take the children of the Brahman with you and propagate my worship in Ayodhya. You go and tell this all to Raghunath. Ask him to offer me *shīrīnī* in person":

সোন বাছা হনুমান সোন মন দিঞা । অফরাদ কৈলুঁ ক্ষমা সেবক বলিঞা ॥
[৭৫ সঙ্গে করা লঞা জায় ব্রার্হ্মনের নন্দন । অজদ্যাতে কর জাঞা পুজার প্রতন ॥
রঘুনাথে সব কথা বল তুমি জাঞা । জেন সর্ত্তপিরের সর্ন্নি করে আপুনি আসিঞা ॥[46]

Not content with vanquishing Hanuman, Satyapir also seeks the surrender of Rama through him.

Satyapir exacts worship in a similarly coercive fashion in *Postak Kechchā Mānik Saudāgar* (পোস্তক কেচ্ছা মানিক ছওদাগর).[47] Only in this case the victims are not Hindu deities but ordinary human beings. Unlike Gharib, however, Balk Mian, the author of this text, begins with an apparently "syncretic" invocation. "Satyapir is the incarnation of the age of *kali*," he writes, "to sing his glory is beyond everyone's talents. He has revealed himself to Hindus and Muslims both. Satyapir is the way to Truth (*satya*). He taught the Muslims as a Yavan and Hindus as Satyanarayan. The Muslims call a Mullah and offer him *shīrīnī*, the Hindus invite a Brahman and offer him *pūjā*:"

সর্ত্তযুগে সর্ত্তপির কলিতে অবতার । মহিমা করিতে পারে কুদরত কাহার ॥
কিব্যা হিন্দু মোছলমান সকলেই জাহির । কলিযুগে অবতার নাম সর্ত্তপির ॥
ভেদাভেদ নাহি জ্ঞান অভেদ সরির । সর্ত্তের সাধন বটেন নাম সর্ত্তপির ॥
মোছলমানে সোমঝাইলা হইঞা জবন । হিন্দুলোকে বুঝাইলা সর্ত্তনারায়ন ॥
মোছলমান করিবে সির্ন্নি মোল্লা ডাকিঞা । হিন্দুলোক করিবেক পুজা ব্রার্হ্মন ডাকিঞা ॥[48]

This tale too begins with the *pīr* deciding to go somewhere and reveal his glories. One day, Satyapir said to Siddiqui, "Sash your waist, we will go to Manik's house. He lives in the Gujarat town, we will appear in his house." When Siddiqui heard Satyapir, he got thinking. "If you appear in his house," he warned, "it will be like tying a pestle to one's neck for dying (drowning?). If you go to his house you will indeed lose your life. He is a vile *kāfir* who cannot stand the sight of a Yavan *faqīr*."

দেত্তান বলেন বাছা ছির্দ্দিকা নফর । কোমর বান্ধ জাব তবে মানিকসাধুর ঘর ॥
[৬ মানিকসাধুর ঘর আছে গুজরাটসহরে । জাহির হইব বাছা জাইব তাহার ঘরে ॥
সির্দ্দিক ষুনিল যদি সর্ত্তপিরের কথা । ভাবিতে লাগিল তখন হেষ্ট করা মাথা ॥
জাহির হৈতে জাহ তুমি মানিকসাধুর ঘরে । গলাতে আউখদ বান্ধিলে মারিবার তরে ॥
মানিকসাধুর ঘর জদি জাইবে দেত্তান । জানিল কারন তবে হারাইবে পরান ॥
বড়ই নামাকুল কাফির দুনিআর ভিতরে । জবন ফকির কভু না দেখে নজরে ॥[49]

It is interesting to observe that though the poet tried his best to establish Satyapir as a "syncretic" figure in the previous verses, he is now simultaneously revealing his subject for what he actually is—a Muslim *faqīr* accompanied by a Muslim follower, Siddiqui.

The intrepid Satyapir ignored his disciple's warnings. The *pīr* went to Manik's house and called out standing at his threshold. Inside, Manik quaked in anger. He picked up a staff to beat the *pīr*.

দুআরে দেত্তান ফকির জিকির করতে লাগিল । ঘরে থাকি মানিকসাধু গোর্শ্বাএ জলিল ॥
আপনার গোর্শ্বাএ বেটা কাঁপে থরহরে । হাথে লাঠি নিল বেটা মারিবার তরে ॥[50]

The *faqīr*'s incomprehensible *māyā* made Manik's junior daughter-in-law emerge from the house before he could. When she saw a *faqīr* she offered *salām*. Satyapir recited a *kalām* and blessed her. Her name was Kamlabati, she was virtuous and fair as the full moon. She joined her palms and said to the *pīr*, "Why have you come to such a sinful one. If he catches sight of you, you will lose your life:"

বিসম ফকিরের মাএআ বুঝা নাই গেল । মানিক সাধুর ছোট বহু নিকলিঞা আইল ॥
ফকিরে দেখিয়া কন্যা করিল ছার্ল্লাম । দোত্তা করিলেন দেত্তান পড়িঞা কাল্লাম ॥
কোমলাবতী নাম পরম সুন্দরি । রুপে গুনে পুর্ন্নসসি জেন মঞ্জদরি ॥

করপুট হঞা কন্যা করে নিবেদন । পাপিষ্টির এখানে কেন হারাবে জিবন॥
এখনি তোমাকে জদি দেখিবেক নআনে । জিবন হারাবে গোসাঞি মরিবে পরানে॥[51]

Satyapir said, "Listen, child, give me something to eat so that I live." Kamlabati replied, "Heed what I say, holy one. I do not know from where to get *bhāt* (boiled rice) for you. I am an enemy to all here, I rarely get to enter the kitchen. You ask some other householder for food:"

দেত্তান বলেন বাছা ষুন গ বচন । থোড়া অন্য দিঞা আগু রাখ জিবন॥
কোমলাবতি বলে গোসাঞি ষুন মন দিঞা । কোথা পাব ভাত আমি তোমারে লাগিঞা॥
১০]
[১১ সভারি দোসামন আমি হাড়ি নঞী হাতে । কদাচিত নাঞী পাই হেঁসেলঘর জেতে॥
ষুন গ দেত্তানজি ষুন মেরা বাত । আর এক গ্রহস্তের মাগ্যা খাও গা ভাত॥[52]

But the *pīr* was adamant. "Mother," he protested, "if you bring me no food, I will die at your door." Then Kamlabati said, "I can get you some *bhāt* if I get to cook." The *pīr* said, "By my blessings you will." The very moment, Manik loudly called out to Kamlabati. She hastened to her father-in-law and showed herself. Manik said, "Daughter, listen to what I say, today you will cook for all:"

মা গো জদি অর্ন্ন এন্যা না দিবি এখন । তোমার দুআরে আমি তেজিব জিবন॥
কমলাবতি বলে গোসাঞী ষুন গ বচন । তবে ভাত দিএ জদি করিতে পাই রন্ধন॥
[১২ দেত্তান বলেন মা গো ষুন গো বচন । আমার দোত্তাতে আজি করিবে রন্ধন॥

. . .

ছোট বৌ বল্যা মানিক সাধু ডাকে উর্চ্চস্বরে । ঘরে বস্যা ছিল কন্যা পাইল ষুনিবারে॥
আস্তবেস্ত হঞা রামা করিলা গোমন । সষুরের নিকটে জেঞা দিল দরসন॥
মানিক সাধু বলে কন্যা বলে মা গো সোন মন দিঞা । সিতাবি করিঞা অর্ন্ন দেহো) পাকাইঞা॥[53]

Having prepared the afternoon meal, Kamlabati put some *bhāt* on a plate of gold and carried it to the *pīr*. She offered *salām* to Satyapir and asked him to go elsewhere and eat. But Kamlabati was noticed talking to the *pīr* by the senior daughter-in-law of Manik. She hurried to Manik and said,

"Your junior daughter-in-law has trimmed your beard:"

আগহাড়িতে ভাত কন্যা ষুবর্ন্নের থালে লঞ । ফকিরের কাছে কন্যা ছার্ল্লাম কৈল জেঞা ॥
অর্ন্নগুলি নামাইঞা কহিছে বচন । অন্যর্ত্তরে জেঞা ছাহেব কর গো ভক্ষ্যন।

. . .

ফকিরের সাথে কথা কমলাবতি কয় । মানিক সাধুর বড় বহু দেখিবারে পায় ॥
ফকিরে দেখিয়া হৈল কলপতি মোন । সষুরের কাছে জেঞা কহিছে তখন ॥
ষুন ষুন অগো সষুর দেখইসে তড়াবড়ি । ছোট বহু হঞা তোমার হেষ্ণ করিল দাড়ি ॥[54]

Manik picked a cane and rushed out to beat the *faqīr* with fury in his heart. But the prescient *faqīr* knew what Manik intended. He said to Kamlabati, "Your father-in-law comes to beat me. He is an ingrate and will not get to see me. I take leave of you and go home. Remember that I am Satyapir, call me when in peril:"

খুব এক সোটা তখন হাতে করা লঞা । ফকিরে মারিতে জয় গোছাদিল হইঞা ॥
[১৫ ফকিরে মারিতে মানিকসাধু চলিল । অন্তজামিনি পির অন্তর জানিল ॥
দেত্তান বলেন তখন কন্যার হুযুরে । তোমার সষুর আসিছে মারিবার তরে ॥
বেইমান দেখা নাই দিব গ অতপর । বিদায় হঞা মা জাই আপন ঘর ॥
সর্ত্তপির নাম মর ষুন গ বচন । বিপদ পড়ীলে মোরে কর সোঙরন ॥[55]

Manik came out the same instant, not seeing the *faqīr* he was angry and grabbed Kamlabati by the hair. "A Yavan has agitated your heart, or else why should you bring him *bhāt*," he arraigned Kamlabati:

কোন ছাহেব এস্যাছিলেন ছলিবার তরে । হেনকালে মানিকসাধু আইল বাহিরে ॥
ফকিরে মারিতে না পেঞা গোছা হইল দিলে । লাফ দিঞা ধরিলেক কমলাবতির চুলে ॥
[১৬ জবন দেখিঞা তোমার কলপিত মোন । আঘাডিতে ভাত তুঞি দিলি কি কারন ॥[56]

Manik called out for his younger son. He came and stood before his father. Manik said to him, "What do I tell you of the virtues of your wife, she brought a Yavan food on a plate of gold and made many a talk with him. I went out and saw this myself. Know that your wife has strayed. Exile her to the forest, I will have you married a second time." When he heard Manik speak, the son felt the sky collapse upon him. "Feeding a *faqīr* is no loss of *jāti*," he protested, "it only adds to the prestige of the *kula*." "Forgive her this once," he pleaded, "if she repeats the act you drive her away." But Manik's anger flared even more, like a fire fed by butter. He told off the younger son and called for the elder one. Manik said to him, "The junior daughter-in-law has destroyed our *jāti*, take her to the forest and exile her." "As you command," the elder son said and bowed his head:

ছোটবেটা বল্যা তখন ডাকিতে লাগিল । বাপের হুযুরে জেঞা তখন খাড়া হৈল ॥
মানিক সাধু বলে বাছা ষুন সমাচার । ছোট বহুর গুনের কথা কি কহিব আর ॥
ষুবর্ন্নের থালে অন্য দিঞাছিল জবনে । নানামত কথ কহিল ফকিরের সনে ॥
বাহির হঞা আমি দেখিলাম আপনি । তোমার স্ত্রি বাছা হইল দোচারিনি ॥

. . .

ইহাকে বনবাস দেহ ষুন মন দিঞা । অন্যতরে দিব বিভা উর্ত্তম দেখিঞা ॥
[১৭ বাপের মুখে ষুনিল জবে ই সব খবর । আকাস ভাঙ্গিঞা পরে মাথার ওপর ॥
ফকিরে দিলে ব ভাত নাঞি জায় জাতি । আপনা আপনি কর কুলের খিআতি ॥

. . .

এইবারকার দোস বাপ কিছু না লইয় । আর জদি এমন করে তবে দূর করা দিয়।
ষুনিয়া মানিক সাধু গোর্শ্ছায় জলিল । জলন্ত অনলে জেন ঘৃত ঢেল্যা দিল ॥
দূর দূর বলিঞা তারে দিল খেদাড়িঞা । আপনার বড়বেটাকে আনিল ডাকিঞা ॥
বড়বেটা গেল তবে বাপের কাছে । কহিছে মনের কথা জত কিছু আছে ॥
ছোটবহু আমাদের জাতি করিল নাস । এ বহুকে লঞা বাছা দেহ বনবাস ॥
বড়বেটা ষুনিঞা তবে বাপের কথা । যে আজ্ঞা বলিয়া তখন নোঙাইল মাথা! ॥[57]

The elder son was crazed by worry but walked a long way. When he reached the forest he addressed Kamlabati and said, "Kamlabati, this is what was fated for you. Do not fear the days and nights here for both now are same to you. Your father-in-law has banished you not knowing the truth. But you must be here while I go home:"

চিন্তায় আকুল হঞা গেল অনেক দূর । জঙ্গলে জাইঞা বলে কন্যার ভাষুর ॥
ষুন মা কোমলাবতি আমার বচন । তোমার কপালে এই আছিল লিখন ॥

[২৪ রাত্রিদিন বনমর্দ্ধে না করিয় মনে ডর । দিবস রজনি তোমার এক বরাবর॥
না বুঝিয়া বনবাস দিল তোমার সষুরে । তুমি বনে থাক মা গ আমি জাই ঘরে॥[58]

As willed by fate, the girl remained in the forest. The elder son returned home as dusk was falling. He went to Manik and informed him that he has done as bidden. "I am glad now," said Manik, "we have got some waste out of the house:"

কপালের লিখনে কন্যা রহিল বনে । ২৪] [২৫ ভাষুর আইল ঘর বেলা অবসানে॥
মানিকের বড় বেটা প্রবেসিল ঘরে । সমাচার দিল গিয়া বাপের হুযুরে॥
মানিকসাধুর বেটা বলে যুন সমাচার । বহুকে রাখিঞা এলাম অরন্যামাঝার।
মানিকসাধু বলে আমি হইলাম খোসাল । ভাল হইল বেরাইল ঘরের জঞ্জাল॥[59]

In the forest Kamlabati wailed aloud calling Satyapir. "Beyond you I know nothing, neither good nor bad, ferry me across, I put my trust at your feet," she cried. When Satyapir felt that she has remembered him, he hastened to her:

কান্দে কন্যা উর্চ্চস্বরে মনে করি সর্ত্তপিরে তোমাঁ বিনা কিছু নাহি জানি।
ভালমন্দ নাই জানি পার কর গুনমনি ভরসা চরন দুইখানি।
ইআদ করিল বনে ছাহেবের হৈল মনে আস্তবেস্ত করিল গমন।[60]

Satyapir appeared before Kamlabati. "You let me no peace my child. Though misfortune has befallen you, *Allāh* willing, I will see you through," he comforted her. "You are my helmsman, ferry me across this misfortune," Kamlabati held his feet and said. "Do not wallow in the dust of the forest and cry," Satyapir replied, "wait, I will make you a temple of gold:"

কাঙ্গাল ফকির হঞা পির করিলা গমন । কমলাবতির কাছে পির দিলেন দরসন॥
আহা মরি মরি বাছা সোন গো বচন । স্থির হঞা রহিতে নারি তোমারি কারন॥
পড়িল বিপদ আজি তোমারি ওপরে । পার করিঞা নিব আজি আল্লা জদি করে॥
ছাহেব তোমার চরন আমি করিলুঁ সার । সঙ্কটে তরাইঞা লেহো হইঞা কাণ্ডার॥

পির বলে ধুলায় পড়্যা কান্দিছ এখন বনের ভিতর । তোমাকে বনাঞা দিব সোনার মন্দিরঘর ॥[61]

Then, Satyapir called Hakim Lukman. Lukman came and stood before Satyapir with joined palms. He asked, "For what have you called me?" Satyapir asked Lukman to construct a house. "As you order," Lukman said and lowered his head. He began constructing the house in the forest:

তখন যে পির দেখ কি কাম করিল । লোকমান হাকিমে বোলাইঞা নিল ॥
দেত্তানের হুজুরে লোকমান জোড়করে । আমাকে বোলাইয়া কিসের খাতিরে ॥
দেওত্তান বলেন তবে সোন মন দিঞা । সিগ্র করি হেমগ্রহো দেহো বনাইঞা ॥
যে আজ্ঞা করা তখন ছির নোঙাইল । বনের ভিতর ঘর বনাইতে লাগিল ॥[62]

After settling Kamlabati in comfort in the forest, Satyapir decided to humble Manik's pride. The poet makes Manik a very wealthy and powerful man of the locality. Apparently, his defeat and surrender was meant to have a great impact on lesser folk. Manik had a herd of sixteen hundred cows which his twelve cowherds grazed in the woods. Satyapir went where the cowherds were and enquired whose cattle they were grazing. "We graze Manik's cows and prepare for hell," the lads replied:

সোল স পাল আছে মানিকসাধুর ঘরে । দোয়াদস বাগালে রাখে বনের ভিতরে ॥
এইরুপ আইলা সর্ত্তপির নারায়ন । ধেনুর বাথানে পির দিলা দরসন ॥
ধেনু নিঞা আছে তারা দোয়াদেষ বাগালে । সেইখানে দেত্তান গেলেন কুতুহালে ॥
দেত্তান বলেন বাছা সব বলিএ তোমারে । কার গরু চরাও তোমারা জঙ্গল ভিতরে ॥
ষুনিঞা রাখালগন দেত্তান হযুরে । মানিকসাধুর গরু চরাই দোজখ খাতিরে ॥[63]

"Go and have your meal while I graze the cows," Satyapir said to the cowherds. "When you return fetch me a little *bhāt*," the *pīr* demanded of the boys:

তোমরা চল্যা জাহ বাছা ভাত খাবা তরে । গরুগুলি চরাই আমি বনের ভিতরে ॥
এখন বস্যা থাকিয় ঘরে ষুন মেরা বাত । সভে মেল্যা মোর তরে আনিয় থোড়া ভাত ॥[64]

When the cowherds left for their repast, the *pīr* put all the sixteen hundred cows in his bag. Then he leaned against a rock and rested. Meanwhile, the boys ate and returned to Satyapir for the cows. Standing in the middle of the meadow, they looked around for the animals. Upon not finding them, they were as though their lives had flown their forms:

সোল সত পাল পির থুলির ভিতর খুঞা। বসিঞা রহিলেন তবে ঢিলে ঠেষ দিঞা॥
এখানে রাখাল সব ঘরে অন্য খাঞা । ফকিরের কাছে জায় ধেনুর লাগিঞা॥
মাঝমাঠে জেঞা তারা চারিপানে চায় । গরু না দেখিলে তাদের প্রান উড়ে যায়॥[65]

When they enquired about the cows, Satyapir said, "I have not seen the cows. I do not know whither they went, I had had *bhāṅg* and *dhatūrā* and snoozed:"

ছাহেব বলেন বাছা যুন আমা ঠাঞী । কাঙ্গাল ফকির আমি গরু দেখি নাঞী॥
ভাঙ্গ ধতুরা খাইঞা আমার গিআন নাঞী । কোন্দেগ্যে গেল ধেনু আমি দেখি নাঞী॥

The cowherds saw no way they could return home, they knew not what explanation to offer. They rolled in the dust and wept:

কি বলিঞা ঘর জাব নাহিখ উপায় । ধুলায় লোটাঞা কান্দে বল্যা হায় হায়॥[66]

Then the *pīr* said, "Come with me down the path in the forest, I will show you all the cows:"

পির বলেন বাছা সব আইস মোর সাতে । দেখাব সকল গাবি চলহ বনপথে॥[67]

Satyapir took the cowherds inside the forest and kept them all with the cows where Kamlabati was:

[৩৮ আজিম কুদ্দরত ছাহেবের কে কহিতে পারে।রাখালসমেত গাবি নিল বনের ভিতরে॥
কমলাবতির ঘর বাড়ি যেখানে আছিল । রাখালসমমেত সব ধেনু সেখানে থৈল॥[68]

Manik thus lost all his cattle. He also had a lot of wealth in his house, but since the *pīr* was displeased with him all of it too was taken by the thieves. His prestige was now in ashes:

আছিল অনেক ধন মানিকসাধুর ঘরে । পির বৈমুখ হৈল সকলি নিল চোরে ॥
মালমার্ত্তা ধন ধান সব হইল হত। খাক হইঞা গেল মান আছিল হে জত ॥[69]

Now Manik's family husked rice for a living. The whole family shed tears and occasionally sold utensils of the house to buy food:

নিদানে বেরুন করা ধান্য কুটে খায় । পরিবার সম তারা কান্দিঞা বেড়ায় ॥
[৪২ থালা কাঁসা ঘটি গাড়ু সব দেচ্যা খায় । বিদাহে হাতের খাড়ু রক্ষ্যা নাহি পায় ॥[70]

Thus, the confrontation with the *pīr* brought disaster and calamity upon the entire household.

Manik wept and conferred with his seven sons. He asked them to go to the house of Kinu Banik and seek work as *munshīs*:

বড়ই কসনা পাঞা সাধু কান্দিতে লাগিল । সাত বেটা লঞা যুক্তি করিতে লাগিল ॥
. . .
যুন যুন অরে বাছা বলিএ উস্কিস্ব । কিনু বন্নিকের ঘরে জাহ খাটিতে মুনিস ॥[71]

Kinu was a virtuous man who used to be an employee of Manik. He had grown rich by the grace of Satyapir. One day, the *pīr* went to the poor man's house and called out for alms. His wife emerged and saluted him reverentially. She joined her palms and asked, "For what have you come?" The *pīr* replied, "What do I tell you child, if I get a fistful to eat I will bless you." Joyously, Kinu's wife served the *pīr* a plateful of edibles:

. . .
ঘরে হৈতে বিবি তবে আইল নিকলিঞা। ফকিরের হযুরে খাড়ি ছাল্লাম করিয়া ॥
ছাহেবের আগে মাই হইলেন খাড়া । কহিতে লাগিল বিবি দস্ত করিঞা জোড়া ॥
[৪৬ কি কারনে এস্যছ পির ছাহেব দেত্তান । দেত্তান বলেন বাছা যুন ফরমান ॥

ছাহেব বলেন বাছা তোমারে সোমজাই । একমুঠি খানা পাইলে দোত্তা করা জাই॥
ষনিঞা বিবি বড় খোসালিত হইঞা । একবাসন খানা মাই দিলেন আনিঞা॥[72]

The *pīr* went on eating and demanding helpings, he ate all the food the pious woman had prepared. Kinu's family had to fast that day.

সব খানা খাইল ফকির ষুন দিঞা মন । উপবাস রহিল দেখ তাহার চারি জন॥[73]

The next day, Satyapir visited Kinu's house again when the family was about to sit down at the meal and asked for food. Once again, he ate all the food prepared. Kinu and his wife bore with the hunger but their child could not and dropped unconscious. Kinu's wife wailed cradling him in her arms:

একে একে চারি বাসন সকলি খাইল । সেহদিন তাহার উপবাসি রহিল॥
তাহার দুইজনা দেখ অমনি রহিল । অবোধ বালক দেখ ভোকছানি লাগিল॥
গরলিঞা পড়িল বাছা হইল অচেতন । বাছারে করিঞা কোলে জননির রোদন॥[74]

Satyapir asked them to bring the child to him. Kinu's wife happily put him in his lap:

ছাহেব বলেন বাছা ষুন সোমাচার । কি আজব হঞাছে বাছায় আন একবার॥
এতেক ষুনিঞা বিবি আনন্দিত হঞা। ফকিরের কোলে বাছায় দিলেন তূলিঞা॥[75]

The *pīr* caressed the child with his left hand and it revived. The boy opened his eyes as though awaking from sleep:

[৫১ বাম হাত জিন্দা বুলাইলেন গায় । নিদাইঞা চিল জেন আঁখ মেল্যা চায়॥[76]

Pleased with Kinu's devotion, the *pīr* said, "I will give you seven pot loads of wealth." He took him to a site and asked him to dig. Kinu dug a neck deep pit and struck seven pots of wealth:

অরে অরে কিনু বাছা ষুন রে বচন । তোমাকে দিব আমি সাত ঘড়া ধন॥
আমার জম্বিনে থোড়া ভুজা নেহ ত এখন । পানি পিঞা তোমারা রাখ গা জিবন॥

. ..

পির বলে অরে বাছা ষুন রে বআন । এই জায়গাতে আছে সাত ঘড়া ধন॥ ৫১]
[৫২ খুদিতে লাগিল মাটি পিরের ফরমান । কাটিতে লাগিল চেপা পাহাড়ের ষুমান॥
গলাসমান করিঞা তবে গাড় জে খুদিল । পিরের হুকুমে সাত ঘড়া ধোন পাইল॥[77]

"I am beholden to you for you fed me," the *pīr* said to Kinu, "that is why I have given you seven pots of wealth. Remember, if you offer me *shīrīnī* with devotion, I will always be kind to you." "Let me tell you something more," the *pīr* added, "I will inflict great sorrow on Manik. I will bring his seven sons to your threshold. You must make them drudge":

খানা খিলাঞা বন্দি করিঞা ছ আমারে । সাত ঘড়া ধন বাছা দিলাম তোমারে॥
একচির্ত্ত হঞা করিহ পিরের সিরিনি । হামেসা তোমায় হবেন মেহেরবানি॥
আর এক কথা বাছা বলিএ তোমারে । বড় দুখ দিব আমি মানিকসাধুরে॥
সাত বেটা আছে মানিকসাধুর ঘরে । সাতজোনাকে আনিব তোমার দুআরে॥
সবাইকে খাটাবে বেটা ষুন রে বচন । আপনার দাদ বাবা বুঝ্যা নিবে এখন॥[78]

The poet obviously brings in the Kinu interlude to invest his story with dynamic tension between two alternative, contrasting attitudes vis-à-vis the *pīr*. Besides carrying the narrative forward, this tension also serves to illustrate which of the two attitudes is valid. The tale counterpoises opposition and hostility towards the *pīr* with piety and supplication. The character demonstrating the former, as we saw, is severely punished by the *pīr* with his spiritual powers. One the other hand, the characters who surrender to the *pīr* are bestowed with riches and prosperity.

One day, obeying their father, the seven sons of Manik came to Kinu seeking work. Kinu said to them, "I have bought some land but no plough or oxen, all you brothers must take their place":

কি কর কি কর ভাই কিনু আপনার ঘরে । আমরা সাত ভাই আইলাম বেরুন করিবারে ॥
এতেক সুনিঞা কিনু লাগিলা বলিতে । সাত ভাই তোমরা আমার খাটিতে ॥
কাদামাঠে লঞাছি জমি হালবলদ নাঞী। সেইখানে খাটিতে চল তোমরা সাত ভাই ॥[79]

Back at their home, Manik rolled in the earth in despair. He had not eaten for three days and could barely speak. His struck his head on the floor in frustration. Manik asked his seven daughters-in-law to borrow grain so that his sons may be relieved of their drudgery:

গর্জ্জব হইল পির কি কহিব তায় । মানিকসাধু ঘরে পড্যা গড়াগড়ি জায় ॥
তিনদিন উপবাস মুখে নাহি কথা । জমিনে পড়িঞা সাধু ঠুকিছেন মাথা ॥
. . .
সাত বেটা গেল আমার খাটিবার তরে । ধার সাধিঞা তোমরা লঞা আইস ঘরে ॥[80]

When Manik spoke thus, his seven daughters-in-law began to weep. The women went to a friend of Kinu's who gave them a *ser* and-a-half of paddy. But when they were returning home happy, they dropped all of it as Satyapir was displeased with them. Maddened by sorrow, they wallowed in the dust and wept. With his *māyā*, Satyapir appeared at the spot the very moment. "Whose daughters-in-law are you?" he asked them. "What do we tell you lord," they replied, "we unfortunate ones are the daughters-in-law of Manik." "Ask him to offer me *shīrīnī*," Satyapir said to them, "and he will get what he asks for":

সষুরের কথা ষুন্যা লাগিল কান্দিতে । সাত জায় তখন বেরুন সাধিতে ॥
. . .
আধন্য আধামাটি মিসাল করিঞা । ডের সের করা ধান্য দিলেন মাপিয়া ॥
হরসিত হঞা ধান্য লইঞা জায় পথে । সর্ত্তপির বিড়ম্বনে সব পড়িল পথে ॥
মাথা হইতে ধান্যগুলি জমিনে পড়িল । হা হা হুতাসন করি কান্দিতে লাগিল ॥
গড়াগড়ি সাত জন ধুলায় পড়ি কান্দে ॥ সেইখানে গেলা পির করা মায়াছান্দে ॥
[৫৯ পুছিতে লাগিলা পির আপনে মায়া করি । কাহার বহুআরি তোমরা কার ঝিআরি ॥
বহু সকল বলে ঠাকুর তোমাকে যে বলি । মানিকসাহার বহু মোরা জনমপুড়লি ॥
সর্ত্তপিরের সির্ন্নি দিতে বল গা সষুরে । জা মানিবে তাই পাবে পিরের বরে ॥[81]

The narrative now presents Manik with an opportunity to surrender to the superior powers of the *pīr* and regain his former prosperity and comfort.

The women reported to Manik what the *pīr* wished and had promised. But Manik was still adamant on not paying Satyapir homage. "If you saluted that *faqīr*, you have dishonoured my *kula,*" Manik admonished his daughters-in-law. "I had rather beg than serve a Yavan *faqīr,*" he added:

ফকিরে দেখিঞা যদি করাছ নমস্কার । তবে ত হইল আমার কুলের খাঁকার॥

. . .

সাধু বলে ভিক্ষা মাগিব তেপান্তরে । তথাপি না সেবিব জবন ফকিরে॥[82]

The poet introduces a measure of stubbornness in Manik before, as we can anticipate, he will make his surrender to the *pīr.* The idea behind this is to point out that greater the stubbornness and resistance offered to the *pīr,* the greater is the superior potential of his spiritual force. The tale seems to underline that, come what may, the *pīr*'s spiritual powers are irresistible. All foolish resistance will be ultimately and inevitably vanquished.

Manik, thus, was not persuaded. His daughters-in-law now went to husk the paddy. When they finished the task, Satyapir made all the grain disappear leaving behind only the husk. Manik said to the women, "Do not weep, serve us the husk so that we live." Meanwhile, Kinu released the seven brothers and they came home restless with hunger. They returned to find their wives rolling in the dust and weeping. The sons went to Manik and asked, "Why do they cry when there is paddy?" But when the paddy was brought to them they saw there was only husk and not a single grain:

ধান্যগুলি নিঞা মার্ত্র দিল ঢিকীর গড়ে । পার দিতে ঢিকিতে চারি জোনা চড়ে॥
[৬১ ধান্য কুট্যা চালু লঞা জান বাচাইব । তাহাতে ছাহেব দেওান বিবাদে লাগিব॥
এছাবি গজ্জব হইল দেখ সর্ত্তপির দেব । তুষগুলি রাখিঞা চাল করিলেন গা!এব॥

. . .

সাধু বলে মা না কর গো রোদন । তুষ কাট্যা দে গ বাছা বাচুক জিবন॥

. . .

এতক্ষনে কিনু সভে বিদায় করিল । কোদালি মাঠে থুঞা ভাত খাই আইল॥
খিদাতে আকুল হঞা চল্যা এল্য ঘরে । ছয় বহু পড়্যা কান্দিছে ধুলা ধোসরে॥
বাপের সাক্ষাতে জেঞা পুছে সাত ভাই । ধান্য সাধ্যা এন্যা কেনে কান্দিছে সবাই॥
ধান্যগুলি নিঞা আনিল মোর কাছে । একটি চালু নাহি তাহে সকল তুষ আছে॥[83]

The seven brothers again set out to look for work. They all wept together. Satyapir met them on the way robed as a Vaishnav. "Why do the seven sons of Manik weep," the *pīr* asked the lachrymose brothers. The disenchanted brothers saw and saluted the *pīr*. "Suddenly great sorrows have befallen us, O holy one," they replied. "Even the pious sometimes suffer with the impious if they live with them," Satyapir said to them:

দএআ করি সর্ত্তপির আসিছেন তাদের ঠাঞী । বেরুন করিতে তারা জেছেন সাত ভাই॥
দেত্তান সর্ত্তপির পুনু] হইলেন সখা । রাহের উপরে জেঞা তাদিগ্যে দিল দেখা॥
সাত তাই তারা কান্দিছে একসাত । বৈষ্ণমের বেশে পির ডেক্যা পুছে বাত॥
মানিকসাধুর বেটা তোমরা সাত জন । কোন আসস্কাবে তোমরা করহ ক্রন্দন॥
বৈরাগ্যবেস তারা নআনে দেখিল । করজোড় করিঞা তারা নমস্কার কৈল॥
মানিকসাধুর বেটা বলে গোসাঞী ষুন কথা । আচাম্বিতে মহাদুখ দিলেন বিধাতা ॥
[৬৪ ধার্ম্মিক লোকের কাছে জদি অধর্ম্মি থাকে । সেই দুখ পায় বাছা অফরাদি পাপে॥[84]

The *pīr* then went to Kamlabati and said, "I am bringing your folks here, prepare a meal. They are unfed for seven days. I will feed them *bhāt*." "Where do I find rice and water? I have no ingredients and do not know where to find any," Kamlabati complained. "Remember me and put the meal on fire, by my grace all will be done," Satyapir said:

দুইজনার মননিষ্টা জানিল বিনদিনি । তোমার গোষ্ঠি সকল বনে আনিব আমি॥
এখন রন্ধন কর মা গ ষুন মেরা বাত । ইহারা সাত দিন উপবাসি খিলাইব ভাত॥
কোথা চালু জল পাব করি নিবেদন । সরঞ্জাম কোথা পাব করিব রন্ধন॥

দেত্তান বলেন বাছা ষুন মোর বচন । সর্ত্তপিরে সোঙরিঞা চাহাপ রন্ধন॥
রন্ধন চাপাহ গিঞা আপনার ঘরে । সমপুর্ন্ন হইব সব সর্ত্তপিরের বরে॥[85]

The seven sons of Kinu were brought to the forest and fed by the *pīr*. After finishing the meal they washed and chewed on camphor and betel with contentment. "Who is this woman?," they asked Satyapir. "The girl you had banished to the forest," the *pīr* smiled and replied. "Bring the rest of your family to this forest and take my mother [Kamlabati] home," the *pīr* ordered the brothers. Heeding the *pīr*'s advice, the brothers came back home:

ভ্রজন করিঞা সভে করিল আচবোন । কর্প্পুর তামুল খায় মুখের সোধন॥
বৈরাগ্য কাছে গিঞা করিছেন বিনয় । কাহাদের রমনি এই কহ মহাসয়॥
হাসিঞা কহেন পির দআর সাগর । যে কন্যায় সাখিঞা গেলে বনের ভিতর॥
...
পরিবার সকলে বাছা আন এই বনে । মেরা মাকে লঞা জায় আপনা ভুবনে॥
উপদেষ পাঞা সভাই করিল গমন । আপনার বাড়িতে আসি দিল দরসন॥[86]

The seven brothers returned with their wives and took Kamlabati home. As she was leaving, Satyapir asked Kamlabati to offer him *shīrīnī* to relieve her father-in-law of sorrows. The next moment he vanished into the blades of grass. The temple of gold too disappeared:

ষুন ষুন আ গ মা গ সোন সমাচার । তোমার সষুরে এতদিন গেল দুখভার॥
আপনার ঘর জাহ ষুন বিনদিনি । ঘর জেঞা করিহ সর্ত্তপিরের সিরিনি॥
মিলাইঞা গেলেন পির দূর্ব্বাদলের বস । সোনার মন্দিঘর হঞা গেল ভস॥[87]

Such texts, underlining the superior spiritual power of *pīrs*, continued to be produced in the next century. We come across an adventure by Manikpir (also known as Badar) composed in the second decade of the nineteenth century in which he humbles and attains the devotion of the river goddess Ganga. *Mānikpīrer Jahurānāmā* (মানিকপীরের জহুরানামা)[88] by Zairaddi opens with *Allāh* sitting with twelve *āuls* (saints).

Addressing them the Almighty says, "Heed me, the one who visits earth and performs prodigies there will receive its charge from me." He also told the *āuls* that in the age of *kali* there will be an incarnation called Manik. The very moment Badar called on the Almighty and took it upon him to reveal *Allāh*'s glories:

একদিন আর্ল্লা সাহেব দরগায় বসিলা বার আউলে লইয়া কিছু কহিতে লাগিলা।
খোদায় বলেন কেবা মেরা বাত লবে দুনিঞায় গিয়া কেবা জহুরা করিবে।
সেইজনে দিব আমি দুনিয়ার ভার কলিকালে মানিক নামে হবে য়বতার।

. . .

হেনকালে হাজির বদর আল্লার হজুর দুয়া করতার করিব জাহির।[89]

Badar bowed in the court of *Allāh* and made his submission. "I will visit the earth as a *faqīr*," he said to *Allāh*:

আর্ল্লার দরবারে বদর নোঙাই[ল] মাথা খোদার হুজুর তবে কহিছে বারোতা।
বদর বলেন খোদা এক বাত কহিব ফকির [মু]রসিদ বেসে দুনিঞায় জাব।[90]

The saint wandered and arrived in Delhi from where he went to Lahore. Garbed as a *faqīr* he begged for alms in the city:

দিল্লির সহর জান জাহিরা করিতে উপনিত লাহুর সহর অচ্ছিম্বিতে।
ফকির বেসে লাহুর সহরে ভিখ্য মাগে দাম দাম মাদার বলি ফুকারে দূর ভাগে।[91]

Finally, he reached Triveni where he saw hundreds of *ṛṣis* and *munis* (ascetics) practicing penances. Many had reeds growing out of their bodies, so severe were their austerities:

ত্রিবিনির ঘাটে তবে আইলা তখন তপিস্ব্যা করয় তথা রিসি মুনিগন।
নলখাকড়া কারো য়ঙ্গেতে বেরোয় সত সত মুনিগন তপিস্বে করয়।[92]

The ascetics sought a vision of the river goddess Ganga. But as their eyes and hearts were restless Ganga did not appear before them. The *faqīr* (Badar) approached them and asked, "Why do you all sit here?" They stirred and a few replied, "Now listen to this shaven headed *faqīr*. We propitiate Ganga and it is none of your business":

চঞ্চল নআন কারো চঞ্চল আছে মন তেকারনে নাঞি পায় গঙ্গা দরসন।
হেনকালে ফকির সভায় কয় কথা কি লাগিয়া বসি আছ কহিবে বারতা।
কেহ বলে নেড়িয়া ফকির কয় কি গঙ্গারে তপস্যা করি তেরা বাপ কি।[93]

"What kind of a *faqīr* are you and where do you dwell? For twelve years we are performing austerities," they inveighed, "and reeds have emerged from our limbs. Yet, the mother of Brahma does not appear":

কাঁহাঁকা ফকির তুঞি কাঁহাঁ তেরা ডেরা দ্বায়াদস বৎসর বসে তপিস্য করি মোরা।
নলখাকড়া অঙ্গে ব্যারয় অমনি তবু নাঞি দিল দেখা ব্রহ্মার জননি।[94]

Flames of anger were kindled in Badar. He performed his ablutions and sat on a tiger skin to meditate. "Appear O Ganga," Badar prayed, "your elder brother calls you." When Badar remembered Ganga thus, she was pleased and revealed herself to sight. The moment they beheld her, the ascetics turned four armed (like Vishnu) and ascended to *brahmalok* (the abode of Brahma).

এতেক বলিয়া বদর হইল কোপানলে উজা করি তপিস্যায় বসিল বাগছালে।
করতার কর পার এইবার এইবার দেখা দেহ গঙ্গা ডাকে বড় ভাই তোমার।
এই বাক্ক বলে বদর গঙ্গা স্মঙরিয়া দেখা দিল গঙ্গাদেবি আনন্দিত হয়া।
জেইমাত্র গঙ্গাদেবি দেখিতে পাইল চতুর্ভুজ [illegible] মুনি ব্রহ্মালোকে গেল।[95]

"Ganga, Ganga!," Badar called. But the goddess refused him a vision for he was a "Yavan." "Let my eyes know your visage," Badar pleaded. Ganga said, "Only if you can survive seven of my waves." "By *Allāh*, I cannot endure seven waves," Badar implored. But Ganga proceeded to raise the waves. Seeing them Badar thought, "Now I have landed in trouble."

Badar remembered *Allāh.* Sitting in his *vimān, Allāh* knew that Badar has remembered him. *Allāh* summoned Pavan, the wind-god, and asked him to ensnare Ganga in a bag. Pavan took the form of a little white fly and went to Badar forthwith. He told Badar of *Allāh*'s design. Badar held his bag open as Ganga emerged as seven waves almost touching the sky. They made the earth tremor. Badar remembered *Allāh* and Ganga was caught in his bag:

> গঙ্গা গঙ্গা বলি বদর ডাকিতে লাগিল জবন বলি দেবি দেখা নাঞি দিল।
> বদর বলে তব যুরৎ দে[খি]ব নয়ানে গঙ্গা বলে সপ্ত ঢেউ সহ যদি প্রানে।
> ষুনিঞা দাত্তান মনে আনন্দিত হই না সহিব সপ্ত ঢেউ আল্লার দোহাই।
> মাই গঙ্গা হইল তবে সপ্ত ঢেউ তাল দেখিয়া ভাবেন বদর পড়িল জোঞ্জাল।
> মোনে মোনে ভাবে বদর সঙরী করতার এদ আল্লা এদ আল্লা বল এইবার এইবার।
> আল্লা বলে বদর স্বঙর করিল বিমানে বসিয়া [আল্লা] এ সব জানিল।
> পবন ডাকিয়া আল্লা বলেন তখন ঝোলা বন্ধিতে গঙ্গা বলিবে এখন।
> সেত মাছি রুপে রুপে পবন চলিল সর্তর বদর মুর্ষিদে আসি বলে তরাপর।
> ষুনিঞা বদর মুর্ষিদ ঝোলা জে পাতিল সপ্ত ঢেউ গঙ্গামাতা তথায় হইল।
> সপ্ত ঢেউ তাল মাথা হইল সর্ত্তর আসমানে উঠে ঢেউ জমিন থরথর।
> বদর পাতেন ঝুলি স্বঙরন করতার সস্কাইল গঙ্গাদেবি ঝোলার ভীতর।[96]

Thus, the very name of *Allāh* produced a miraculous result emphasising to us that in all the world there is no name greater.

Ganga pleaded, "Let go of me, you were indeed my elder brother in some previous life, I have realised." Badar said, "What you must do Ganga is repent, if you repent I will untie the mouth of my bag." Ganga repented and Badar released her. The seven waves were cast forth like fire:

> গঙ্গা বলে মর তরে ছাড়ে দেহ তুমি পুৰ্ব্বে বড় ভাই ছিলে বুঝিলাম আমি।
> বদর বলেন গঙ্গা এক বাত কব অবসাদ মানিলে ঝোলার মুখ ছাড়ে দিব।
> অবসাদ মানে গঙ্গা ঝোলার মুখ ছারে অগ্নি উথরল জেন সাত ঢেঔ পড়ে।[97]

"I let you go O Ganga," Badar said, "but you must keep a wish of mine. You must get me stones, I want to perform a prodigy in Triveni." Ganga did as Badar bade. She was now not just willing to surrender but also to discharge Badar's wishes. Ganga got Badar the stones of Rama's *setu* (bridge). Ganga's grace made the stones buoyant. They floated upon her and reached Badar. Seeing the stones he was pleased and summoned the god Vishwakarma, the artificer. Badar offered him *pān* (betel) and fruits and enjoined him to raise a mosque (with the stones) in seven days and nights. Vishwakarma agreed but said, "You must keep it dark for seven days and nights. If night segues into dawn I will remain no more. The edifice will be left half done." Badar exclaimed, "This is too simple. I will direct Night not to cease." Badar called Night and asked her not to cease. As Badar made Night do as he wished, Vishwakarma began his work. Thus, two days passed. Sitting in his *vimān, Allāh* lamented. *Allāh* sorrowed that now the glory of Mecca and Medina will be surpassed. He commanded Hazrat Ali to take the form of a white crow and go to the site (of construction). Upon arrival, the crow formed Ali sat on the branch of a *champā* (frangipani) tree and began to caw. As he did, the sun rose. Vishwakarma flung his axe and disappeared leaving the building half done:

ছাড়্যা দিলাম গঙ্গা বলেন বদর এক বাত গঙ্গাদেবি রাখিবেন জে মোর।
পাথর আনিঞা দিবে আমার হুজুর ত্রিবেনিতে আর এক করিব জহুর।
যুনিঞা দাত্তানের কথা এড়াইতে নারে সেতবন্ধ হইতে এক আনিল পাথরে।
দরিয়ায় ভাসিল পাথর দেবির ক্রপায় ভাসিতে ভাসিতে পাথর আইল তথায়।
খোসালিত হইল বদর পাথর দেখিয়া বিস্বকর্ম্মার তরে তবে আনিল ডাকিয়া।
পান ফল দিয়া বদর বলেন বচন সাত দিবা রাত্রে বাড়ি মসিদ গঠন।
বিসাই বলেন বদর আরতি কুলাবে সাত দিবা রাত্রি তুমি আন্ধার করিবে।
প্রভাত হইলে নিসি আমি নাঞি রব পড়িয়া রহিবে বাড়ি আমি চলে জাব।
বদর বলেন বিসাই এই কোন বাত নিশিকে ডাকিব আমি না পোহাবে রাত।
নিসিকে ডাকিয়া দাত্তান বচন বলিল বিস্বকর্ম্মা বাড়ি ঘর গড়িতে লাগিল।
ঐরূপে দুই দিন গুজরিয়া জায় বিমানে বসিয়া আল্লা করে হায় হায়।
বাড়ি ঘর বিসাই করিবে নির্ম্মান ভেস্তে মক্কা মদিনা যে পাড়ুয়া অপমান।
এতেক ভাবিয়া খোদায় হজ্জৎ আলি তরে সেঁট কাক হওয়া তুমি জায় তরাপরে।

ষুনি করতার কথা তখনি চলিল   চাঁপাডালে বসি আক ডাকিতে লাগিল।
উদয় দিল অস্ত্রগিরি আপনি করতার   কুড়ুল ফেলে পলাইল অর্দ্ধ বাড়িঘর।[98]

The rather disappointed Badar called out the name of Daraf Khan Ghazi. The Ghazi responded to the call and appeared before long. The two decided to go and see the Emperor in Delhi and then make an appearance in Chittagong. Having made up their minds, they set forth and appeared in the court of the Emperor:

বদর বলেন মমিন এক বাত কব   দিৰ্ল্লির ষুলতান বাদসার হুজুর জাব।
মমিন বলেন চল বাদষার হুজুর   পশ্চাতে চাটিগা সহর করিব জহুর।
এতেক ভাবিয়া দেত্তান করিল গমন   বাদসার দরবারে গিয়া দিল দরসন।[99]

When the two called on the Emperor he asked his *dewān*, "Why do they come to my court?" Before he could reply, Badar said, "O king promise me the alms I desire. Only when you do will I speak" Hearing the *faqīr*, the king flared (in anger). He yelled and hollered and said, "Wherefrom you come O *faqīr* and where do you dwell? How dare you speak so before me?" Badar said, "You have no reason to fear me O Emperor for I am as though your son-in-law has come to your court":

বাদষা জিজ্ঞাসা করে দেয়ানের তরে   কি লাগে আইলে কহ আমার দরবারে।
ফকির বলেন বাদস্বা রাখ মেরা বাত   এক ভিক্ষা মাগি সত্য কর মোর সাত।
আগে সত্য কর তবে কহিবে বচন   উজির ষুনিঞা বাত ভাবে মনেমান।
ফকিরের বাত ষুনি বাদস্বা যে জলিল   তৰ্জ্জন গৰ্জ্জন করে কহিতে লাগিল।
কাঁহাকা ফকির তেঞি কেঙ তেরা ডের[া] মেরা হুজুর বাত কহ এসা বুক তেরা।
বদর বলেন বাদস্বা তেরা ভয় নাঞি   দরবার ভিতর জেন বসি তোর জামাই।[100]

The Emperor insulted Badar and drove him off.

The same night, Badar had the princess, Dudbibi, abducted by a posse of tigers and brought to the garden of the Emperor's palace. "Who are you and why have you brought me here?" the princess asked. Badar said, "I was insulted in the court. That is why I sent the tigers and had you brought here. Now you marry me joyously." Dudbibi replied, "I am under a vow. In the *tretā* age I was Rama's devotee. Then I was a *gopī* in Gokul feeding butter to the son of Nanda (Krishna). Let me tell you, I will wed only the one who can assume a four-armed form." Badar said, "Dudbibi listen to me and close your eyes." Dudbibi happily shut her eyes. Now Badar took the form of Rama, he bore the bow in his left hand and the quiver in his right, Lakshman held the umbrella upon his head. Seeing him the Dudbibi was struck by wonder. Then, Badar assumed the form of Krishna, adorned with *śaṅkha, chakra, gadā,* and *padma,* playing the flute in the company of Balaram. Dusky hued, Badar stood beneath a *kaḍamba* tree. Dudbibi rejoiced and put the garland around Badar's neck:

বিবী বলে কহ দেখি তুমি কোন জোন   কাননের মধ্যে আন কিসের কারন।
দেওান বলে এসব তর্ত্তেতে দেহ মন   দরবার ভিতর বা[দ]স্বা কৈল অপমান।
তেকারনে আনিলাম বাগ ভেজাইয়া   করহ আমারে সাদি আনন্দিত হয়া।
দুদবিবী বলে আমার আছে এক পোন   ত্রেতা যুগে ভজি আমি রামনারায়ন।
তার পরে থাকি আমি গুকুলে গুপিনি   নন্দের নন্দনে সদা খায়াইতেম ননি।
চতুভুজ রুপ হয়া দেখাবে আমারে   তাহারে করিব সাদি বলিনু তোমারে।
বদর বলেন বিবী মেরা বাত রাখ   নয়ান মুদিত করি সেই রুপ দেখ।
মুদিত নয়ান বিবী আনন্দে হইল   ফকির বেস তেজি বদর রাম রুপ হল।
বাম হাথে ধনুক দিক্ষন্যা সরাসন   সিরেতে ধরিছে ছত্র ঠাকু[র] লর্ক্ষন।
দেখিয়া বা[দ]স্বার বেটি লাগে চমৎকার   পুনুরুপি হইল বদর কানাই অবতার।
দেখিয়া বাদস্বার বেটি লাগে চমৎকার   পুনুরুপি হইল বদর কানাই অবতার।
সঙ্খ চঞ্র গদা পদ্ম বনমালা ধরি   বলরাম সঙ্গে করি বাজায় মুরারি।
কদম্বতলাতে দাড়াইল হয়া কালা   হরসিত হয়া বিবী গলে দিল মালা।[101]

In the palace, the Emperor wailed and cried upon not finding his daughter. The queen, Dhanbibi, beat her forehead and rolled in the earth in sorrow. He called his minister and ordered him to send people to far and foreign lands. People rushed to the four quarters in search of the king's daughter but nowhere did they find her:

হায় হায় করে বাদস্বা কি হইল বেটি ধনবিবী সিরে ঘাত ভুমে জায় লুটি।
উজর ডাকিয়া বাদস্বা বলেন বচন দেস দেসান্তরে সভে কর অন্যসন।
হুকুম পাইয়া সভে চারিদিগে ধায় কোথায় বাদস্বার বেটি দেখা নাঞি পায়।

The minister, on the other hand, suggested that they search in the garden:

হেনকালে উজির বাদস্বার কয় কথা কাননের মর্দ্ধে চল খুজিব সর্ব্বতা।[102]

Hearing the footfalls, the fearful Dudbibi asked Badar, "My father comes with the minister, how do we deceive him?" "Listen Bibi," Badar said, "we will deceive them by becoming Rama and Sita." Thus, Badar transformed into Rama and on his left Dudbibi stood as Sita. They were as though two moons had risen in the woods. Seeing this, the Emperor wondered, "Why do I see Rama and Sita in the garden? Who has stolen Dudbibi?" He said to his minister, "I do not understand, where is Dudbibi, who has stolen her?" Then Badar asked the Emperor to shut his eyes. The Emperor obeyed and the true form of Badar and Dudbibi was revealed to him. The Emperor asked his daughter, "Why have you come to the woods from the palace?" Dudbibi replied, "Badar has been my husband through several lives. He came to your court wanting to marry me but you insulted him and tried to cast him in prison." The Emperor surrendered and gave his consent to the marriage:

আসিচে আমার বাপ উজির সংহতি কিরূপে ছলনা করি বল সির্গ্রগতি।
বদর বলেন বিবী ষুন [৮খ বচন রামসিত্য হয়া দ্বোহে করিব ছলন।
বামে হইল সিত্য বিবী বদর হইল রাম বনমর্দ্ধে দুই চন্দ্র উদয় অনুপাম।
এহাত দেখিয়া বাদস্বা ভাবে মনে মন বনমর্দ্ধে রাম সিতা দেখি কি কারন।
কহ কহ উজির বুঝিতে না পারি দুদবিবী কোথা গেল কেব কৈল চুরি।
হেনকালে বদর দেত্তান বলে[ন] বচন মুদিত করই নয়ন দেখিবে এখন।
এত ষুনি উজির বাদস্বা নয়ন মুদিত বদর দুদবিবী রুপ হইল অসচম্মিত।
বদস্বা বলেন বেটি এ আর কেমন মহ[ল হ]ইতে বনমর্দ্ধে আইল কি কারন।
দুদবিবী বলে বাপা না জান ভারতি জন্মে জন্মে বদর আমার হয় পতি।

সাদি করিবারে আইল তোমার দরবারে অপমান করিতে চাহ বন্দি কারাগারে।
বাদস্বা বলেন বেটি রাখ মেরা বাত আনন্দে করহ বিবাহ চল মেরা সাত।[103]

The *karāmāti pīr,* thus, proved his superiority over temporal authority. Faced by the *pīr*'s spiritual prowess, the Emperor could only struggle in vain and finally concede defeat.

As we saw in the last chapter, and again in this, *kāvyas* and *pānchālis* often told tales in which two spiritual worlds clashed—one Muslim and the other non-Muslim. However, we opine that the characters appearing in this tales are not cast in the mould of the archetypal heroes and villains. They are more like means for two sacral worlds to debate and are not ideologically motivated. But, by the turn of the nineteenth century, we have evidence that the *Mangal Kāvya* genre, in a transformed narrative structure, employed the duality of heroes and villains, casting the English in the latter role. As though boding what the next few decades were to bring, the duality also appears to bear the charge of political ideology. It is also worth noting that the genre had taken absolutely no note of the English for the century and a half they had been around. The author of a *kāvya* deigned to notice them only after they attained political power and the society to which he belonged experienced a fresh seism of violence, both physical and emotional. It is suggested that the villain in the *kāvya Gauri-Mangal* (গৌরি-মঙ্গল) is an allegorical depiction of the new hated *mlechchha,* the English.[104] "The most significant feature of the work is its veiled political import," writes Kalinikinkar Datta in the introduction to the Asiatic Society edition of the work. Talking of the villain of the story, Madrasena, Datta adds:

> The author does not state explicitly that Madrasena, who conquered Avanti from King Salavahana, represented the English invaders of India. But his description leaves little doubt on a discerning reader. Madrasena is described as coming from a northern region. He had no scruple in killing cows, polluting the

water of the sacred river Gomati with their blood and even in eating their meat.[105]

As we saw in the previous chapter, the poets striving to be "Muslim" were always in search of exotic landscapes where they had their characters confront new challenges and adversaries. Thus, many of their tales blossomed in the deserts of Arabia or Persia. But now they were no more content with having their yarns unfold in these far-away places. A trend afoot for almost three centuries was now coming to a head.[106] Due to some reason the Muslim poet was feeling an even greater discomfiture with the land of his birth. This is probably why we now observe him heavily clothing Bengali in words of Arabic and Persian derivation. It has been suggested that political developments far off aided the process. Anisujjaman, for example, holds the Shi'as who migrated to Bengal in the wake of the dissolution of the Safavid empire responsible for making the Persian influence widespread in the seventeenth century.[107] Interestingly, this trend appears to have been more pronounced in the western half of Bengal. By the early nineteenth century we have evidence of the existence of a class of Muslim writers who wrote for a sufficiently broad based Muslim audience. As Sukumar Sen puts it, they addressed "the illiterate people residing in Calcutta, and they drew largely from Persian, Hindi, and Urdu popular romances."[108] "Their language," Sen adds, "was so much saturated with Perso-Arabic and Hindi words that it was often unintelligible to persons not acquainted with those tongues."[109] This "Muslim Bengali," we are told, was the creation of the West Bengal Muslim writers and was not taken up by their East Bengal co-religionists till the end of the nineteenth century.[110] From our point of view, we feel curious as to whether the fact had anything to do with West Bengal being the seat of the Nawabdom. Further, it seems apposite to ask whether the trend could be seen as being reflective of a cultural anxiety.

Did the need to further indurate cultural exclusivity stem from the loss of the cultural overarch of the Nawabi state? Apparently, eastern Bengal was not left entirely untouched of the process. Sen refers to the Muslims of Sylhet who remained "more or less in cultural isolation" never having "lost contact with their west country co-religionists."[111] Strangely though, they bound themselves apart with artifacts which their west country co-religionists were to renounce as Hindu sometime later. This they did by cultivating Hindi poetry and keeping up the use of the Kayathi script.

While the above drifts were in progress, the European presence in Bengal was making interventions which were to fundamentally alter the nature of the Bengali language. The eighteenth century was when the first printed texts appeared in Bengali, the earliest of them brought out by the missionaries. Mention might be made in this context of the catechism *Crepar Xaxtrer Orth, bhed* printed by the Portuguese church at Dhaka.[112] In the absence of a Bengali type the text had to be printed in the Roman character. In 1778, Nathaniel Brassey Halhed, who was in the employ of the East India Company, published the *Grammar of the Bengali Language.* For the publication of this work Charles Wilkins devised a Bengali type and ushered the language into the age of print. Bengali took another sprightly and important stride as a print language with the publication of the Bengali Bible by William Carey's Srirampur Mission in 1801.

Earlier, on August 18, 1800, the College of Fort William had been established by a Minute in Council of the East India Company. The college undertook to produce literary and scientific works and translations in the Bengali language. *Munshis* and *pundits* were employed to accomplish the task. Working in these capacities, individuals such as Ram Ram Basu, Chandicharan Munshi, Mṛtyunjay Bidyalankar, Haraprasad Ray, and others produced the earliest prose works in the Bengali language. The earliest of them all was Ram Ram Basu's *Rājā Pratāpāditya Charitra* (রাজা প্রতাপাদিত্য চরিত্র)

published in 1801. The work is the hagiography of the same potentate who appeared in Bharatchandra's *Annadāmangal* in 1752. The prose of the *Charitra* has a staccato feel to it revealing the discomfiture of the language with the form. Bengali was making a difficult transition departing from cadent verse. However, despite the formal shift, the *Charitra* betrays faint indications of being privy to the emotional inheritance and the ruptures of the past centuries. The work also reminds one of the *kāvyas* at places with its fantastical landscape which foretells the doom of the hero with omens. The author though is hard pressed to present the fantastical as "history" in this case. We now seem to be at the juncture where a framework of remembrance replete with an emotional charge is fusing into what is at least ostensibly empirical history. In the second half of the nineteenth century the same heady mixture was to feed into the genre of historical fiction.

Pratapaditya's father was a vassal under the Afghan chief Daud who had to accept Mughal suzerainty towards the close of the sixteenth century. At the beginning of the *Charitra* we have Daud plotting to regain his independence. The words with which Basu has the character validating his action is an indication of how the faultline existed in his head. Besides, it appears that in his mind the past carried a faint political and ideological charge as he makes Daud admit that it is the Hindus who are the genuine owners of the country. "This country belongs to the Hindus," says Daud, "and the Muslims won it by the force of arms. The emperor in Delhi is a Muslim and so am I. Then on what grounds does he expect tribute from me and why at all should I pay him any":

> এ হেঁদুর দেশ তাহারদের অধিকার । মোছলমানেরা আপন পরাক্রমে এ রাজ্য
> করতলে করিয়াছেন । দিল্লিপতী মোছলমান আমিও সেই জাতি । তবে
> তিনিইবা কিমার্থে আমার কাছে কর লএন এবং আমিবা কেন তাঁহাকে কর দেই।[113]

Later, after Daud has been defeated and chastened, Mughal envoys Todarmal and Umrao Singh send for the father and uncle of Pratapaditya, Vikramaditya, and Vasantrai. The reason they cite for seeking truce is that they all are Hindus and there must not be any bitterness amid them:

> তাহারা হিন্দু লোক আমরাও সেই একি বর্ন।[114]

The next five decades saw the gradual coming of age of the fledgling Bengali prose as it attained a lithe expressiveness. A steady stream of literary works lent maturity to the language and the power to express sophisticated thought. Mṛtyunjay Bidyalankar, an assistant of William Carey at the Srirampur Mission, translated the *Batris-Sinhāsan* (বত্রিস সিংহাসন) and *Hitopdeś* (হিতোপদেশ) from Sanskrit. He also wrote two original works, *Rājābalī* (রাজাবলী, 1808) and *Prabodh-Chandrikā* (প্রবোধ-চন্দ্রিকা, 1813). The likes of Bhabanicharan Bandopadhyay and Akshay Kumar Dutta also contributed to the growing corpus of prose works. The former is famous for the *Nababābubilās* (নববাবুবিলাস, 1825) and *Nababibibilās* (নববিবিবিলাস, 1831). Akshay Kumar Dutta, who edited the *Tattwabodhinī Patrikā* (তত্ত্ববোধিনী পত্রিকা) for twelve years, produced *Chārupāṭh* (চারুপাঠ) and *Bhāratbarṣiya Upāsak Sampradāy* (ভারতবর্ষিয় উপাসক সম্প্রদায়).[115] He wrote on science too. Ishwarchandra Vidyasagar's quill yielded *Betāl Pancabiṃśatī* (বেতাল পঞ্চবিংশতী, 1847), *Sītār Banabās* (সীতার বনবাস, 1860), *Saṃskṛta Bhāṣā O Saṃskṛta Sāhitya Biṣayak Prabandha* (সংস্কৃত ভাষা ও সংস্কৃত সাহিত্য বিষয়ক প্রবন্ধ, 1853), a critical work on Sanskrit language and literature, and *Bhrāntibilās* (ভ্রান্তিবিলাস, 1869). Tarashankar Tarkaratna wrote *Kādambarī* (কাদম্বরী, 1854).

These years were apparently good for the newspaper trade too and several were launched. Srirampur Mission began publishing the *Samāchār Darpan* (সমাচার দর্পন) in1818, *Sambād Kaumudi* (সংবাদ কৌমুদি) was started in 1821 by Rammohan Roy, *Samāchār Chandrīkā* (সমাচার চন্দ্রীকা), edited by

Bhabanicharan Bandopadhyay, had its beginning in 1822. Nilratan Haldar and Ishwar Chandra Gupta founded the *Bangadūt* (বঙ্গদূত) and *Sambād Prabhākar* (সংবাদ প্রভাকর) in 1829 and 1831, respectively.

While Bengali prose matured it was progressively Sanskritised. As Sudipta Kaviraj has observed, Bengali was expected to perform two "mutually opposed functions" in the nineteenth century, it had to be a language of solemnity and ceremonial like Sanskrit and also of science and law. Hence Bengali "had to enter into a peculiar relation of transaction with both Sanskrit and English."[116] Bengali's "transaction" with Sanskrit had been on for some time. J.C. Ghosh has pointed out how "The Pundits of Fort William College, the British missionaries, and the other native and foreign writers before Vidyāsāgar, had overloaded their language with Sanskrit words and had added an unnaturalness and unintelligibility by blindly following the syntax either of Sanskrit or of English."[117] He regards Vidyasagar an exception because according to him he "borrowed no more than could be harmoniously blended with Bengali and was necessary to strengthen and clarify its native genius."[118] But was he an exception? Kaviraj writes about the language of *Sītār Banabās* that while the language is grammatically Bengali "the words are almost entirely Sanskrit."[119] According to Kaviraj, "He wished to create a Bangla that denied the language's somewhat mean and mixed ancestry by making Sanskrit more *internal* to the Bangla linguistic structure."[120] The development drew a response from elements in the Muslim community of Bengal. As we have already seen, writers from the community were introducing Arabic and Persian words into Bengali for some time. Apparently, the precipitous Sanskritisation of Bengali now spurred them further. According to T.W. Clark, "The removal by Sanskritists of words of Perso-Arabic origin in the Bengali vocabulary and their replacement by Sanskrit neologisms offended them and prompted them to increase the number of Perso-Arabic words in their own writings."[121] The new language thus birthed was named Musalmāni Bānglā in 1854 by Reverend James Long (1814–1887).[122] This was so much unlike the medieval times when, opines Clark, "a Muslim poet can in general be distinguished from a Hindu poet by the subject matter of his works; but he cannot be distinguished by the language he wrote in."[123] The contemporary literature too yields evidence of the rupture that now ran through the Bengali language riving it into two. Anisujjaman draws our attention to *Saifulmulūk Badiujjamāle* (ছয়ফলমুলুক বদিউজ্জামালে) composed in 1828 by one Mālè Mohammad. The text is based on an earlier work by Alaol on the same theme—the love story of Saifulmulūk and Badiujjamāl. In a verse introducing the work Mohammad writes that when this book was composed in the olden days it was in Sanskrit and *sādhu bhāṣā* (Sanskritised Bengali) and people found it tough reading, so he has written it in "popular Bengali" (*chalita Bāngālā*):

এই পুথি সায়েব ছিল আগু জমানার।
সংস্কৃত সাধু ভাষায় হৈল তৈয়ার॥
পড়িতে বুঝিতে লোকের বড়ই কসেল্লা।
এ কারনে অধীন রচে চলিত বাঙ্গালা॥[124]

Mohammad Danesh, a mid-nineteenth century poet, also owned to have been quickened by similar concerns in the introduction to his work *Chahār Darbeś* (চাহার দরবেশ). "I wrought this tale in *chalita Bāngālā*," he wrote, "so that all may comprehend. Not all know true Bengali, that is why, O brothers, I do not write in it":

চলিত বাঙ্গালায় কেচ্ছা করিনু তৈয়ার।
সকলে বুঝিবে ভাই কারনে ইহার॥
আসল বাঙ্গালা সবে বুঝিতে না পারে।
এ খাতেরে না লিখিলাম সোন বেরাদরে॥[125]

In both instances "popular Bengali" meant a language in the thrall of the Persian and Arabic lexicon.

The first half of the nineteenth century is also when we witness the first 'scientific' attempt of engaging with the craft of history writing in Bengali. A pioneer in the field was Rajendralal Mitra who was employed as the librarian in the Asiatic Society from 1846 to 1856. Mitra started a journal which he called the *Bibidhārtha-Sangraha* (বিবিধার্থ-সঙ্গ্রহ) in 1851. The *Bibidhārtha* made the most eclectic forays into India's past, from the most ancient to the more recent Mughal times which were still a part of the living memory. The journal seems to be bivouacked upon the bridgehead which was later occupied by historical fiction in the second half of the nineteenth century. What we notice unfolding here is probably the replacement of what was till now mere tradition or remembrance by ostensible empirical, positivist history. What was perhaps begun by Ram Ram Basu had now taken a more cogent shape. The past was now very explicitly a political and ideological formulation replete with the kind of hero-villain duality we saw the *Gauri-Mangal kāvya* employing. This is apparent in the reason that the journal cited justifying its special emphasis on the history of the Rajputs and the Marathas. There had been a dissipation of the historical consciousness in India following her conquest by the *mlechchhas*, the *Bibidhārtha* wrote in 1857. Enslaved, the denizens of the land had not been enthusiastic about preserving the accounts of their loss of freedom. The exceptions had been the Rajputs and the Marathas who, despite lying under the dominance of the Yavans, had not desisted from broadcasting the glories of the nobility and valour of their respective national greats:

> . . . মহারাষ্ট্র ও রাজপুত জাতীয়েরা যবনাধীন হইয়াও স্ব স্ব জাতীয় মহদ্যুক্তিদিগের মহত্ব ও বলবীর্যের গরিমা প্রকাশ করনে বিরত হয়েন নাই।[126]

Thus, the villain was the Yavan, and the heroes were those

who, despite being beaten by him, had not allowed their selves to be cowed.

From its very inception *Bibidhārtha* embarked upon its mission of reenergising pride in India's past with an expressive earnestness. The very first issue of *Bibidhārtha* carried an instalment of the history of Sikhs, *Sikh Itihās* (শিখ ইতিহাস), meant to be continued in the following numbers. The effort was justified with the following words:

> The people of this country have an apathy for history. This is on account of the ancient texts current as history in our country being so full of supernatural actions. Valmiki's Ramayana and Vyasa's Mahabharata have been anointed as histories and accepted and adored in the land by all. However, divine characters being so abundant in them, their fantastical descriptions can barely ever be imagined as the aspects of humans.
> পুরাবৃত বিষয়ে এতদ্দেশিয় মনুষ্যেরা এক প্রকার বিতরাগই আছে। ইহার মুখ্য কারন এই যে পূর্ব্বপার যে সকল প্রাচিন গ্রন্থ অস্মদেশে প্রচলিত তন্মধ্যস্থ পুরাবৃত সকল অলৌকিক ক্রিয়াতে পরিপূর্ণ । ভগবান বাল্মীকি ও বেদব্যাস কৃত রামায়ন ও মহাভারতাদি গ্রন্থ-সকল ইতিহাসস্থানে অভিষিক্ত হইয়া দেশমান্য ও সর্ব্বগ্রগন্যরূপে গনিত হইয়াছে বটে, কিন্তু তত্তদ্গ্রন্থে দৈব- চরিত্রের বাহুল্য-হেতুক তৎ সমস্ত উৎকট-বর্ননা মনুষ্য-চরিত্রমধ্যে গ্রাহ্য করা দুরহ।[127]

This is why some "real" history was needed and somehow it was thought best to begin with the history of the Sikhs:

> The majority of individuals are not guided by their own intellect in discharging worldly affairs, they wander about allowing the instances and examples of others defeat the radiance of their own knowledge. It has to be unanimously agreed that a study of history augments the awareness of such people and helps them tell good from bad. Today, the noble souls who dream of propagating the Bengali language ought to acquire the expertise of composing and translating histories and do what is needed to get the average folks interested in the discipline. This journal is dedicated to and will be ever engaged in the said task. Here we present the history of the Sikhs.

. . . জগতের অধিকাংশ লোক স্বিয় বুদ্ধি-বৃতিদ্বারা সাংসারিক ব্যাপার নির্ব্বাহ করে না, কিন্তু পরকিয় দৃষ্টান্তের আলোকদ্বারা স্বিয় জ্ঞানরূপ প্রভাকে পরাজিত করিয়া ইতস্তত ভ্রমন করে; পুরাবৃত-পাঠে যে ঐ সকল মনুষ্যের জ্ঞানবৃদ্ধি হয়, বহু দর্শন, ও সদ-সৎ বিবেচনার ক্ষমতা হয়, ইহা সর্ব্বতোভাবে স্বীকার করিতে হইবেক । এক্ষনে যে সকল মহাত্মারা বঙ্গভাষা প্রচলিতা করিবার কল্পনায় ব্রভি হইয়াছেন তাঁহাদিগের কর্ত্তব্য যে আদৌ ইতিহাসাদির রচনা ও অনুবাদ-করনে নিপুন হইয়া তব্দিষয়ে সাধারনের যাহাতে অভিরুচি জন্মে তাহাই করেন । এত পত্র উক্ত-ব্রতের ব্রতি, এবং তন্নিয়ম সাধনে সর্ব্বদা নিযুক্ত থাকিবেক । সম্প্রতি শিখদিগের ইতিহাস প্রস্তাব করা যাইতেছে।[128]

The writer assumed that the readers will be very keen on learning about the Sikhs, for even the proud Europeans have accepted them as prodigiously and gloriously brave:

শিখদিগের উপাখ্যান-শ্রবনে কে না উৎসুক হইবেন ? . . . যাহাদিগের বিপুল সাহসের গৌরব স্বগৌরবে গর্ব্বিত ইউরোপিয়েরাও স্বিকার করেন. . .[129]

After extolling Sikh bravery, the first instalment of *Sikh Itihās* provided an account of the life and activities of Guru Nanak. A significant step was thus taken, we argue, towards infusing the cultural differences with an ideological vision with which to guide one's gaze upon India's past. Mitra did this by presenting Sikh history as a sort of ideological template. This ideological template was further developed by assembling Rajput histories and underlining the idea of Hindu resistance to Muslim rulers.

The Agrahayan (March–April 1852) issue of the journal introduced its readers to the history of the Rajputs in an article entitled *Rājputra-Itihās* (রাজপুত্র-ইতিহাস). The historical amnesia of the Indians was loudly lamented while this was done:

The Puranas and histories have been ever engaged in amply singing the glories of kings of the Lunar and Solar lineages. However, their achievements and relations with the present day population are yet to be popularised in the Bengali language.

চন্দ্র ও সুর্য্য বংশিয় রাজাদিগের বিপুল মহিম-বর্ননে ও যশঃকীর্ত্তনে ইতিহাস ও পুরান-সকল নিয়ত নিযুক্ত আছে; কিন্তু তাহাদের এক্ষনকার জনগনের সহিত সম্বন্ধ-ধারা ও মহিমা বঙ্গভাসায় অদ্যাপি প্রচিল হয় নাই।[130]

The article reminded the readers that,

The countries of Kabul, Kandahar, Bamiyan, and Balkh wherefrom Muslims deluged India and put out Hindu liberty were once under the sceptre of rulers of the Solar line. There was a time when the people of these lands spent their days obeying the Hindu. কাবুল, কান্ধাহার, বামিয়ন, বল্খ ইত্যাদি দেশ-সকল, যত্রত্য মোসলমানেরা ভারতবর্ষকে প্লাবিত করিয়াছে, ও হিন্দুস্বাধিনতা উৎসন্না করিয়াছে, সেই সকল দেশ কোন কালে সৌর-রাজাদিগের দণ্ডাদধিন হইয়াছিল; কোন সময় তথাকার লোকেরা হিন্দু-আজ্ঞাবহ হইয়া কালযাপন করিত।[131]

The idea of 'Hindu liberty,' it strikes us, is now being used to collate local histories and to elevate them to the status of 'national history,' a standard history of all India. In *Bibidhārtha*'s telling, all of India suffered the loss of the liberty that the denizens of the north-west of the country had borne at the hands of the invaders.

Reciting the virtues of the Rajputs, *Bibidhārtha* also evoked colonial authority. The article quoted Colonel Todd as saying that had the history of the rulers of the Solar line been written by the likes of Herodotus and Xenophon their deeds would have been universally celebrated and extolled:

রাজপুত্র সম্বন্ধে ইতিহাসবেত্তা টড সাহেব জাহা লিখিয়াছেন তাহা সৌর ও চন্দ্র বংশীয় সমস্ত রাজাদিগের প্রতি উত্তমরূপে প্রয়োগ হয়। "হিরোডোটাস এবং জিনোফেন জদ্রূপ গ্রিক দেশের ইতিহাস লিখিয়া তদ্দেশীয় মহাত্মাদিগের কীর্ত্তি সকল বর্নন করত চিরস্মরনীয় রাখিয়াছেন, সূর্য্যবংশীয় রাজাদিগের ইতিহাস তদ্রূপ সুচারু লেখকদ্বারা সুরচিত হইলে তাঁহাদের কীর্ত্তি-সকল তুল্যরূপে মান্য ও পুজনিয় হইত"।[132]

Following this, it almost broke into a loud wail:

But, alas! The histories of India are extinct! Lord Rama's valour

> and glory made known to the world by the great poet Valmiki captured our minds, the echoes of the encomiums paid to the Lunar line by Vedavyas still resound in our hearts. But what became of these lineages later, how their branches spread across India, what noble deeds they performed and how they came to be extinct, despite there being several descriptions to the effect they have not been collated by the historians till date, nor have they collected their essence.
>
> কিন্তু, হায়। ভারতবর্ষের ইতিহাস সকল লোপ হইয়াছে। মহাকবি বাল্মীকিদ্বারা শ্রীরামচন্দ্রের পৌরুসপ্রতাপ জগদ্বিস্তৃত ও সকলের মনে বিকসিত হইয়াছে; এবং ভগবান ব্যাসদেব ইন্দুবংশের যে গুনগান করিয়াছেন তাহার প্রতিধ্বনিদ্বারা অদ্যাপি সকলের অন্তঃকরন ব্যাপিত আছে; কিন্তু ঐ বংসদ্বয়ের পর কি অবস্থা হয়, তাহাদের শাখা সকল ভারতবর্ষে কি প্রকার বিস্তৃতা হয়; কোন দেশে কোন শাখা স্থাপিতা হয়; তাহাদের দ্বারা কি ২ মহৎ কর্ম্ম নিষ্পাদিত হয়; এবং তাহাদের কি প্রকারেই বা লোপ হয়, তাহার নানা বিধ বিবরন সত্বে কোন ইতিহাসবেত্তা তাহার সার সমন্বয় ও সার-সঙ্গহ করেন নাই।[133]

The author is clearly pronouncing his intention of collating and valourising the new Indian history that he is engaged in writing. Also, implicit in this declaration of intent, is the author's view that there has been a rupture of memory in the Indian mind which he saw himself as healing.

Now the Bengali readers were told why it is so essential to know about the Rajputs:

> Most of the Solar lineages extant today dwell in the country of Rajwara. . . . The descendents of these lines possess great heroism and are the best among Hindus. As they bear the name 'Rajputra' many take them to be born of miscegenation, but this is a delusion. The *kūlāchāryas* (preceptors) of these lines possess genealogies with details of their descent and ancestry and there is no evidence to nurture the belief that all of them are untrue.
>
> যে সকল সৌর শাখা এ পর্য্যন্ত বর্ত্তমান আছে, তাহাদিগের অধিকাংশের আধুনিক বাসস্থান রাজবারা দেশ।...এতদ্বংশজাত ব্যক্তি বুহেরা মহাতেজস্বি ও হিন্দুজাতি-শ্রেষ্ঠ। রাজপুত্র নাম হওয়াতে কেহ ২ ইহাদ্গিকে বর্নশঙ্কর জ্ঞান করে; কিন্তু সে ভ্রম মাত্র। রাজপুত্র কুলাচার্য্যদিগের গ্রন্থে ইহাদের বংশাবলির সমূহ বিবরন বিস্তার আছে; এবং ঐ কুলজি সমস্তই যে মিথ্যা এ কথার পোষক কোন প্রমান নাই।[134]

But there was still but a thin partition between 'myth' and 'history.' This is revealed to us when the writer makes an account of the life of the Rajput hero Bapparao. He is given credit for siring a whole line of Pathans:

> Having ruled Mewar for many years Bapparao installed on the throne Aparajita, a son he had begotten from the princess of Saurashtra. Then he embarked on the conquest of the western regions. He conquered countries such as Kashmir, Kabul, Kandahar, Iran, Turan, Ispahan, and Kafristan and took their princesses as wives. A hundred and thirty sons were born of their wombs. Their descendents are today known as the 'Naushera Pathans.'
>
> তদনন্তর বহুকালাবধি মিবার রাজ্য ভোগ করত পূর্ব্বোক্ত মহিষী-জাত অপরাজিত-নামা পুত্রকে ঐ রাজ্য প্রদান করিয়া বাপ্পা পশ্চিম প্রদেশ জয় করনে যাত্রা করিলেন। পরে ক্রমশঃ কাশ্মির, কাবুল, কন্ধহার, ইরান, তুরান, ইস্পহান, এবং কাফ্রিস্থান দেশ সকল জয় করত তত্তদ্দেশের রাজকন্যা সকলকে বিবাহ করেন ঐ রাজকন্যা সকলের গর্ভে একশত ত্রিশ পুত্র জন্মে। ঐ সকল পুত্রদিগের বংশ "নৌশেরা পাঠান" নামে অদ্যাপি বিখ্যাত আছে।[135]

History dissolved into myth once again when the circumstances of his death were described:

> He (Bapparao) grew old and died. A riotous controversy emerged between his Hindu sons and those of the other race when his last rites were to be performed. The *kshatriyas* were impatient to cremate him, his sons of the other race sought to bury him. But when they raised the shroud covering the corpse they found only a few blooming lotuses.
>
> বয়ঃক্রম তাঁহার মৃত্যু হয়; এবং তৎ সময়ে তাঁহার হিন্দু ও অপ্র জাতিয় পুত্রদিগের মধ্যে তাঁহার অন্তিম-ক্রিয়োপলক্ষে এক তুমুল বিবাদ উপস্থিত হয়। পূর্ব্ব পক্ষীয়েরা হিন্দুরীত্যনুসারে বাপ্পার শবদাহন করাই কর্ত্তব্য জানিয়া তদ্বিষয়ে ব্যগ্র হইল; এবং তাহার বিজাতিয় পুত্রেরা তাঁহার সমাধি অর্থাৎ গোর দেয়নে উদ্যত হইল; কিন্তু ঐ শবোপরিস্থিত বস্ত্র উত্তোলন সকলে দেখিল যে শব নাই, এবং তৎস্থানে কতকগুলি প্রস্ফুটিত পদ্ম পুষ্প রহিযাছে।[136]

This account, interestingly, corresponds exactly to a

popular legend about Kabir. His corpse too is said to have metamorphosed into so many flowers, disappointing the Hindus and Muslims who were fighting over it. Apparently, Bengali prose now cast forth some very interesting tales. They aspired to be 'history' and were ready to herald Bengal into some very interesting times.

References

1. Dr Sukumar Sen, ed., *Vishnu Pāla's Manasā Mangal* (বিষ্ণু পালের মনসাঁমঙ্গল). Calcutta: Asiatic Society, 1968, Work no. 289, Issue no. 1587. (Sukumar Sen's views, Introduction, p. i.)
2. Ibid., p. 14.
3. Ibid., p. 41.
4. See "Alternate Structure of Authority. Satyapīr on the Frontiers of Bengal," in David Gilmartin and Bruce B. Lawrence, eds., *Beyond Turk and Hindu. Rethinking Religious Identities in Islamicate South Asia,* University Press of Florida, 2000, p. 25.
5. Ibid., p. 23.
6. Ibid., p. 27.
7. Panchanan Mandal, comp., *Punthi-Parichai* (পুঁথি-পরিচয়), Visvabharati, 1980, vol. IV. Mandal dates the manuscript of this text to *c.* 1794. Its provenance is the Birbhum district of West Bengal (p. 1).
8. Ibid., p. 1.
9. Ibid.
10. Ibid., p. 6.
11. Ibid., p. 4.
12. Ibid.
13. Ibid.
14. Ibid., p. 5.
15. Ibid., p. 6.
16. Ibid., p. 7.
17. Ibid.
18. Ibid.
19. Ibid.
20. Ibid., p. 8.
21. Ibid.
22. Ibid., p. 12.
23. Ibid.
24. Ibid., p. 13.

25. Ibid.
26. Ibid., p. 14.
27. Ibid., p. 15.
28. Ibid., p. 16.
29. Ibid., p. 17.
30. Ibid., p. 18.
31. Ibid.
32. Ibid., p. 19.
33. Ibid., p. 20.
34. Ibid.
35. Ibid.
36. Ibid., p. 22.
37. Ibid., p. 23.
38. Ibid.
39. Ibid.
40. Ibid., p. 24.
41. Ibid.
42. Ibid.
43. Ibid.
44. Ibid., p. 25.
45. Ibid.
46. Ibid.
47. Ibid. The manuscript of this text is too assigned the same date and provenance as the previous one by Mandal (p. 359).
48. Ibid., p. 359.
49. Ibid., p. 360.
50. Ibid.
51. Ibid., p. 362.
52. Ibid.
53. Ibid.
54. Ibid., p. 363.
55. Ibid.
56. Ibid.
57. Ibid., p. 364.
58. Ibid., p. 366.
59. Ibid., p. 367.
60. Ibid., p. 368.
61. Ibid.
62. Ibid., p. 369.
63. Ibid., p. 370.
64. Ibid.
65. Ibid.
66. Ibid. p. 371.

67. Ibid.
68. Ibid.
69. Ibid.
70. Ibid., p. 373.
71. Ibid.
72. Ibid., p. 374.
73. Ibid., p. 375.
74. Ibid.
75. Ibid.
76. Ibid., p. 376.
77. Ibid.
78. Ibid.
79. Ibid., p. 377.
80. Ibid.
81. Ibid., p. 378.
82. Ibid., p. 379.
83. Ibid.
84. Ibid., p. 380.
85. Ibid.
86. Ibid., p. 381.
87. Ibid., p. 382.
88. Panchanan Mandal, comp., *Punthi-Parichai* (পুঁথি-পরিচয়), vol. II, Visvabharati, 1958. The manuscript of this text is dated to 1817 by Mandal (p. 305). No provenance is cited.
89. Ibid., p. 305
90. Ibid., p. 306.
91. Ibid.
92. Ibid.
93. Ibid., p. 307.
94. Ibid.
95. Ibid.
96. Ibid.
97. Ibid., p. 308.
98. Ibid.
99. Ibid.
100. Ibid., p. 309.
101. Ibid., p. 311.
102. Ibid., p. 312.
103. Ibid.
104. *Gaurī-Mangal* (গৌরী-মঙ্গল) was composed by Raja Prithvichandra of Pankur in the year 1806.
105. Bimanbehari Majumdar, ed., *Gaurī-Mangal* (গৌরী-মঙ্গল), Asiatic Society, 1971, Introduction, p. vii.

106. Suniti Kumar Chatterji finds that "quite a number of Persian words" found their way into the Bengali language by the sixteenth century. By the seventeenth century, this trickle had turned into a "preponderant influence" of Persian upon Bengali. *The Origin and Development of the Bengali Language*, pp. 203–4.
107. See *Muslim-Mānas O Bāngla Sāhitya (1757-1918)* [মুসলিম-মানস ও বাংলা সাহিত্য], Calcutta, 1971, p. 111.
108. *History of Bengali Literature.* New Delhi: Sahitya Akademi, 1960, p. 157. The same trend was espied by S.K. Chatterji too. Looking back upon the nineteenth century, he ascribed the creation of "Musalmani Bangla" to Urdu knowing Maulvis. A "considerable literature" was produced in it, comprising of 'Jang-namahs' (narration of the tragedy of Karbala) and adaptations of the 'Sikandar-namah' and the 'Shah-namah', etc. *The Origin and Development of the Bengali Language*, p. 210.
109. Ibid., p. 158.
110. Ibid.
111. Ibid.
112. Likely to date to 1743. See Sushil Kumar De, *Bengali Literature in the Nineteenth Century (1757–1857)*. Calcutta: Firma K.L. Mukhopadhyay, 1962, p. 61.
113. *Rājā Pratāpāditya Charitra* (রাজা প্রতাপাদিত্য চরিত্রঃ). Calcutta: Ranjan Publishing House, 1942, p. 5.
114. Ibid., p. 13.
115. Published in two volumes, the first came out in 1871 and the second in 1883.
116. See "The Two Histories of Literary Cultures in Bengal" in Sheldon Pollock, ed., *Literary Cultures in History. Reconstructions from South Asia*, New Delhi: OUP, 2003, p. 542.
117. See *Bengali Literature*, p. 125.
118. Ibid.
119. See "The Two Histories of Literary Cultures in Bengal," in *Literary Cultures in History. Reconstructions from South Asia*, p. 543.
120. Ibid.
121. See "Encounter and Growth in Bengali Literature. A Survey of Modern Bengali Literature," in Edward C. Dimock, Jr., ed., *Bengali Literature and History*. Asian Studies Center, Michigan State University, 1967, p. 85.
122. A member of the Church Mission Society, he led the Mission in Thakurpukur, Calcutta. Long was associated with institutions like Calcutta School-Book Society, the Bethune Society, the Bengal Science Association and the Asiatic Society. He also published the English translation of the play *Nīl Darpan* (নীল দর্পন) by Dinbandhu

Mitra in 1861. He had to face libel charges for the act and was sent to jail for a short duration.

123. See "Encounter and Growth in Bengali Literature. A Survey of Medieval Bengali Literature," in *Bengali Literature and History*, p. 16.
124. See *Muslim-Mānas O Bāngla Sāhitya (1757–1918)*, p. 140.
125. Ibid., p. 136.
126. See Dilwar Husain, *Bānglā Upanyāse Mughal Itihāser Byabahār, 1857–1916*, pp. 84–85.
127. Published by the Baptist Mission Press of Calcutta, Kārtik (October-November), Śakābda 1773 (1851), vol. 1, issue I, p. 10.
128. Ibid. pp.10–11.
129. Ibid., p. 11.
130. Ibid. vol. I, issue II, p. 17.
131. Ibid., pp.17–18.
132. Ibid., p. 18.
133. Ibid.
134. Ibid.
135. Ibid., pp. 22–23.
136. Ibid., p. 23.

3

Becoming Hindus 1857–1905

DURING THE ANTI-PARTITION AGITATION IN 1905, one Girindramohini Dasi penned a song she called *Swadeśīnī* (স্বদেশীনী). The fourth stanza of the lyric, entitled *Rākhimantra* (রাখিমন্ত্র), piously hoped that the Hindu and the Muslim will now be united in a brotherly bond never to be severed. She wished that this sacred bond will lend their arms the strength of *vajra* in the world of action:

অচ্ছেদ্য বন্ধনে; হিন্দু মুসলমান ভুলি;
যে আশায়—দৃঢ়তম—অটুট রহুক
সেই ভ্রাত্রবন্ধন; এ প্রার্থনা চির,—
কর্মক্ষেত্রে যেন এই পবিত্র বন্ধন
দানে সদ বজ্র-শক্তি ও বাহুযুগলে।[1]

Kaliprasanna Kabyabisharad, another from the vast multitude of minstrels the movement had provided an occasion and a voice, attempted to write a song entirely in *Musalmāni Bānglā*. "Where is the Muslim faith now," Kaliprasanna asked his targeted audience, "all around are Christian (*nāchār*) glories. No one anymore puts his heart upon the path of *Khudā*. The dead Nawab was a debauch; the Khan Bahadurs are lions of their villages. Greedy for fame, they have forgotten their duties. Forgetting all concerns of the other world, they pull down their brothers in faith. Those who were Emperors without abilities, now they groan in servitude. In blind greed they drive knives into the throats of their brothers. The fate is now to be a *khānsāmā*, at most a Sub-registrar. Food, I hear, is always short, the *salāms* of servitude are wasted. How many in the country now get two fistfuls of rice twice daily? Do not think what you were two days ago. Whose forebears ever went without food in Bengal? To what pass those days have come, where are those crops now and where those crafts. Where is respect now and where affection. Now it is hard to gather food. Some have come from far away and looted and carried away things of our *bāzārs*. We have made our habit such that we cannot remove the poverty of our land. We carelessly gave away the jewels of the land and received nothing in return. The poet says awake, do not keep your eyes shut. The land in which you were born is the essence of the world":

গান
বাউলের সুর-মুসলমানি বাংলা
এখন মুসলমানের ইমান কোথা,
নাছারের বাহার।
দেখি খোদাতালার রাহার পরে
দেল রাখে না কেহ আর॥
ফোতো নবাব মস্ত ধিঙ্গি
খান বাহাদুর গাঁয়ের সিঙ্গী,
নামের লোভে কাম ছেড়ে সব -
দেনা করে দেয় বাহার॥
আখেরের সব ভাবনা ভুলে,
জাতি ভাইকে ফেলছে তলে,
যারা বাদসা ছিল এলম বিনে,
তারাই গোলাম আর গোঙায়।
কি লোভে সব ভায়ের গলায়
অন্ধ হয়ে ছুরি চালায়,
আখেরে খানসামাগিরি
(এখন) বড় জোর ছব্রেজিষ্টার॥
সদাই শুনি অন্নকষ্ট
গোলামগিরির সেলাম নষ্ট,

দু'বেলা দুই মুঠো ভাত (পেটভরে)
    জুটছে দেশে ক'জনার ?
দু'দিন আগে কি ছিলে ভাই,
দোলের আগে ভেব না তাই,
খানা বিনা কেটেছে দিন
    বাঙালায় কার বাপ-দাদার ?
সে দিনের কি এই আখিরি –
কোথায় সে চাষ কারিগিরি,
কোথায় কদর কোথায় আদর –
    এখন অন্ন জোটা ভার॥
কোথা থেকে কারা এসে
লুটে নে জায় নিজের দেশে
বাহিরের চটকে লালছ –
    আমাদের কই হাট বাজার ?
করেছি হায় এয়েছা স্বভাব
নিজের দেশে জায় না অভাব
অযত্নে বিলালাম রত্ন –
    বদলি মিললো ফক্কিকার॥
সায়ের বলে জেগে দেখো –
নয়ন কেন মুদে রাখ
যে মাটিতে পয়দা হলে
    সেই মাটি সার দুনিয়ার॥[2]

These attempts at addressing the Muslim were unique and unprecedented. They came at the head of an almost fifty year long literary tradition in which Muslims were always spoken of but never spoken to.

The Bengali-Hindu author was frequently and diversely prolix *on* the Muslim but uniformly silent *towards* him. We shall engage in a survey to fully comprehend the import and scope of this diversity, and the uniformity of the silence, in this chapter. Our starting point is the immediate aftermath of the fateful rebellion of 1857. The dust raised by the uprising of 1857 had barely settled on the plains of north India when one of the very first works of historical fiction appeared in Bengal. This was Rangalal Banerjee's

(1827–87) *Padminī Upākhyān* (পদ্মিনী উপাখ্যান), written in verse and published in 1858. This was only the beginning of what was to become very soon a minor deluge. Muslims figured consistently in these works. The consistency is enough for us to suspect that they formed the *raison d'être* for this genre. As we observed and discussed in the previous chapters, the encounter with the 'other' had commenced five centuries ago within the bounds of the literary effusions made by the Bengali language. This engagement now entered a new phase in an altogether unprecedented context, one in which a political nationhood for India was soon to be imagined and wrought.

The representation of the Muslim in the literature of Hindu authorship is an expansive terrain. It is also a terrain which displays remarkable heterogeneity of landscapes. They reveal quite many of the same emotional ruptures that we caught sight of in the very beginning, now broadenings into crevices. Equally often, the contrapuntal melodies that we discussed earlier come drifting to us upon these landscapes.

The history of Bengal was barren in one regard for the nineteenth century Bengali-Hindu writer. He could not see himself as being the inheritor to a martial history. The land of Bengal had witnessed sporadic warfare when Mughal sway was extended to the region. Almost two centuries later the hosts of the Nawab and the English clashed on this verdant land. But the forebears of the Bengali-Hindu had been mere bystanders to these wars. They did not wield arms themselves. Perhaps that is why we see many writers locating their tales in the north-west of the country, mostly in the Rajputana, and appropriating the past of the region for a Hindu nationalist history. That is where *Padmini Upākhyān* unfolds. Rangalal echoes the sentiments expressed in the *Bibidhārtha-Sangraha* when he tells us as to why he had to narrate this tale. It was because, following the extinction of India's freedom, it was in the Rajputana that the remnants of the heights of Indian genius and valour had been preserved:

> এই নির্দ্দিষ্ট কালমধ্যে এদেশের পূর্ব্বতন উচ্চতম প্রতিভা ও পরাক্রমের যে কিছু ভগ্নাবিশেষ, তাহা রাজপুতানা দেশেই ছিলো।[3]

Obviously, for Rangalal the extinction of Indian freedom had occurred with the conquest of the subcontinent by Muslim dynasties. The Muslims are now cast in a monolithic history which counterpoised the *other* history of Hindus' struggle for liberty against the medieval Muslim rulers.

The Chittor that Rangalal creates in his epic poem is a Hindu utopia undefiled by foreign touch. The fort bore no impression of the touch of Yavan hands:

> যবনের কার্য্য তাহে নহে দৃশ্যমান।[4]

Curiously though, despite the pristine nature of the setting, an achievement that he ascribes to one of his heroes is of producing Hindus and Muslims who are also a little of the other. This he does by re-telling the story of Bapparao. Bapparao, a forebear of the heroes of the tale, conquered the lands of the *mlechchhas.* He extended his fiat to Iran, Turan, Kabul, etc. He struck terror in the hearts of the dwellers of these lands and they scattered in his wake. Bapparao wedded many princesses of these countries. Thus were born many lineages of Hindus and Muslims, among them were Pathāns of the Solar lineage:

> জন্মিল অসংখ্য বংশ হিন্দু মুসলমান।
> হিন্দু সূর্য্যবংশী খ্যাত যবন পাঠান॥[5]

Is it possible that Rangalal had drawn inspiration from the account of Bapparao's life that had appeared in the *Bibidhārtha*?

The remainder of the tale follows the traditional rendering. The author, however, seems to have greatly added to the sexual rapacity of Allauddin. Rangalal reminds us of the tenor of the medieval Bengali *kāvyas* when Allauddin vows to destroy the *Hinduāni* that offends him so:

ছাড়াইব হিন্দুয়ানি ব্রত পুজা যাগ।[6]

In response we have Padmini's husband Bhimsingh retorting that this is probably not what the word of God revealed in the *Qur'ān* teaches:

এই কি কোরানে তোর লিখেছে ঈশ্বর ?[7]

The Muslim in *Padmini Upākhyān* consistently remains a hated ogre. However, as we notice above, the author does make an attempt, albeit faint, of incorporating him into his own world. But it could happen only after they had been reduced to political subordination and brought under Hindu cultural hegemony as is achieved by Bapparao. His nuptials producing Pathāns of the Solar lineage is faintly like Śiva being the father of Hasan and Husain. Rangalal's attempted incorporation obviously draws from a definite emotional history.

Rangalal published another long narrative poem entitled *Śūrasundarī* (শূরসুন্দরী) in 1868. The poem recounts Rana Pratap's defiance of the Mughal Empire ruled by Akbar. In its very first canto he affirms the differences of Hindus and Muslims to be irreconcilable. They were like the primordial elements of nature, predestined to be opponents. Like oil and water the Hindus and Muslims could never mix. The presence of one made the other burst forth in flames, just as butter did in the proximity of fire. One reacted to the other as the mongoose reacted to the serpent:

তৈল যথা তোয সহ সংমিলিত নহে।
হবি যথা অনল পরশ পেয়ে দহে॥
ভুজঙ্গের প্রতি যথা বিরাগী নকুল।
হিন্দু-মুসলমানে হেন ভাব প্রতিকূল॥[8]

Nevertheless, Rangalal remains an example of how complex the Hindu writer's sentiments towards Muslims often could be. He bestows upon Akbar the sobriquets "ocean of compassion" and "incarnation of dharma":

যে আক্‌বর করুণার সাগর অপার॥
যে আক্‌বর সুবিচারে ধর্ম্ম অবতার।[9]

It is Mansingh who incites him to destroy the Hindu faith after being insulted by Rana Pratap and he vows to do so:

সেই গুণসিন্ধু শাহ শ্যালকবচনে।
হিন্দুধর্ম্ম-সংহারে প্রতিজ্ঞা করে মনে॥[10]

The Muslim continued to be etched in the most lurid colors in the writings of Hemchandra Banerjee (1838–1903) and Nabinchandra Sen (1847–1909). For both, the Muslim could be nothing but a fiend hopelessly addicted to blood lust. The Muslim was also a sexual predator preying upon innocent Hindu women. In the medieval Bengali *kāvyas,* we saw, the Muslim is only occasionally prone to blood lust and gratuitous violence. We also observed that the *kāvyas* never display sexual anxiety, a rare exception being Chandrabati Devi's *Sundarī Maluā Pālā* discussed in the first chapter. But sexually anxiety pervaded the writings of Hemchandra and Nabinchandra. The emotional crevice was definitely widening in the literature of the times and the character of the Muslim was seemingly debasing beyond any hopes of redemption. In his *Bīrbāhu Kābya* (বীরবাহু কাব্য, 1864) Hemchandra had a fictional Muslim ruler ravishing Hindu women by the hundreds:

. . . একজন যবন ভূপতি।
শত হিন্দু নারি ধরে করয়ে দুর্গতি॥[11]

Nabinchandra too made the character of Sirajuddaula in his *Palaśīr Juddha* (পলাশীর যুদ্ধ, 1875) an unrestrained libertine.

His depravity is of a degree that Raja Rajballabh fears at one point in the narrative that soon no chaste women may be left in the land of Bengal:

. . . এই দুর্নিবার নদী, কে বলিতে পারে,
কোথা হবে পরিনত ? কিছুদিন আর,
সতীত্ব-রতন এই বঙ্গের ভাণ্ডারে
থাকিবে না. . .[12]

Nabinchandra presents Bengal as having been utterly blighted by the terror inflicted by the Yavans. The state of the land is such that even the stars in the sky choose to be concealed behind clouds. They dared not look at what lies beneath lest the sight stained their purity:

যবনের অত্যাচার করি দরশন,
বিমল হৃদয় পাছে হয় কলুষিত,
ভয়েতে নক্ষত্র-বালা লুকায়ে বদন।[13]

Nonetheless, despite the sidereal disapproval of the Nawab's regime, *Palaśīr Juddha* is not an unmitigated damnation of Sirajuddaula. Nabinchadra's blank verse speaks in many voices. We first note this when Sirajuddaula's minister makes his appearance in the narrative. This is a moment when the plotters against the Nawab, Raja Rajballabh, Jagat Seth and Raja Krishnachandra Rai, are trying to persuade him to be an accomplice to their scheme. The minister refuses to be a party to the plot. He cannot be an ingrate, he tells them, for it is a great sin. Nor is he so foolish as to hack the hand that has fed him, an ingrate's heart is hell indeed. Even if someone has done you the smallest good, to harm him means to tar one's soul with sin, he says:

"কৃতঘ্নতা মহাপাপ! বল না আমায়
যেই করে করে মুখে আহার প্রদান,
কোন মূর্খ সেই কর কাটিবারে চায় ?

কৃতঘ্নহৃদয় আহা! নরক সমান!
সামান্য যে উপকারি, তার অপকার
করিলে, পাপেতে আত্মা হয় কলুষিত।"[14]

But, besides the purely ethical, Sirajuddaula's minister cites some other reasons for choosing not to betray his master. Bengalis are easily enfeebled and have been ever suppressed. They have suffered the servitude of five hundred years. Apparently, the poet is referring to the five hundred years of Muslim rule in Bengal. Being so long fettered, Bengal has been rendered bereft of strength and valiance. Bengalis can no longer defend their country, they are too feeble. The minister advises the plotters to garb for war only if they are strong enough to rule the land and subdue the Nawab. And if not, it is sufficient to be subjects and thank providence for the little rewards of royal offices and ministerial positions that subjecthood brings:

"সহজে দুর্ব্বল মোরা চির-পরাধীন।
পঞ্চ শত বৎসরের দাসত্ব-জিবন
করিয়াছে বঙ্গদেশ শৌর্য্য-বীর্য্য-হীন,
রক্ষিতে আপন দেশ অশক্ত এখন।
শাসিতে বাঙ্গালা-রাজ্য আপনার বলে
পার যদি, নবাবেরে করিতে দমন,
সাজ তবে রনসাজে; . . .
নতুবা অধিন থাক এখন যেমন।
রাজপদে, মন্ত্রিপদে, আছি বিরাজিত,
অদৃষ্টকে ধন্যবাদ দাও সমুচিত।[15]

Sirajuddaula is indeed unbridled, cruel and wicked, the minister concedes. But do not humans use their wits to tame a lion or a venomous snake, he asks? Similarly, he argues, the Nawab's uncurbed nature will be tamed if his heart is introduced to righteousness, statecraft and a fear for sinfulness. Once this is done, the indomitable, wicked Nawab will be tender as a garland of flowers and a fragrant, heavenly peace will prevail in Bengal:

সিরাজ দুর্দ্দান্ত অতি, নিষ্ঠুর পামর,
মানি আমি। কিন্তু লোকে বনের শার্দ্দুল
পোষে না কি, পোষে না কি কালবিষধর,
বুদ্ধির কৌশলে ?—তবে কেন হেন ভুল?
ধর্ম্মনীতি, রাজনীতি, পুন্য-পাপ-ভয়
সবে মিলি কর যদি হৃদয়ে সঞ্চার,
এই যে দুর্দ্দমনীয় দুষ্প্রবৃত্তিচয়,
হইবে কোমল যেন কুসুমের হার।
শীতল সৌরভরপে শান্তির বিধান
হইবে সমস্ত বঙ্গে, স্বর্গের সমান।[16]

The minister's interlocutors are not convinced. Jagat Seth loudly laments the Bengali habit of never agreeing upon anything. This wont, he argues, is the reason why foreigners stomp upon the Bengalis, snatch possession of Bengal's throne and inflict hundreds of insults daily. Even if heaven and earth exchange places, says Jagat Seth, Bengalis will not be unanimous on anything:

"মন্ত্রিবর!
সাধে কি বাংগালি মোরা চির-পরাধীন ?
সাধে কি বিদেশী দলি পদভরে
কেড়ে লয় সিংহাসন? করে প্রতিদিন
অপমান শত শত চক্ষের উপরে?
স্বর্গ মর্ত্ত্য করে যদি স্থান-বিনিময়,
থাপি বাংগালি নাহি হবে এক-মত;[17]

Having censured the minister the Seth launches into a tirade which he ends avowing vengeance against the Nawab:

প্রতিহিংসা-প্রতিহিংসা-প্রতিহিংসা সার,
প্রতিহিংসা বিনা মম কিছু নাই আর!"[18]

Raja Rajballabh now joins in terming Nawab's wickedness

and tyranny as being beyond ordinary human nature:

> বোধ হয় পাপিষ্ঠের অত্যাচার যত;
> নর প্রকৃতিতে নাহি সম্ভব কথন।[19]

As we have already seen, the Raja points at the growing prurience of the Nawab and what it might augur for Bengal. He then shudders remembering the Black Hole Tragedy which occurred after the Nawab conquered Calcutta:

> কলিকাতা-জয়-কালে-কাঁপে কলেবর
> অন্ধকুপ-অত্যাচার করিলে স্মরন;[20]

The Raja calls Sirajuddaula a snakelet which is already so poisonous that it ought not to be allowed to grow into adulthood. It will be too terribly poisonous then. It is most advisable, the Raja stresses, that this wild youth is deprived of his kingdom with the help of the generous English:

> "এই কালে এত বিষ!- পুর্ণকলেবর
> হবে যবে এ ভুজঙ্গ, না জানি তখন
> হবে কিবা তিব্র বিষধর। . . .
> সহৃদয় ইংরেজের লইয়া আশ্রয়
> রাজ্যভ্রষ্ট করি এই দুরন্ত যুবায়।"[21]

However, after Raja Rajballabh has spoken, Nabinchandra introduces into his narrative a remarkably strong contrarian voice. This is a moment when Raja Krishnachandra asks his wife seated behind the *purdah* for her opinion. Her answer arouses our interest and curiosity. She knows, she says, of the truth of the terrifying picture of the Nawab they have drawn. But, the Rani exclaims, to conspire is not becoming of the ruler of Krishnanagar. How could the king be so deluded, how could they all countenance such an ignoble, cowardly plot, she laments aloud:

যেই কাল রঙ্গে সবে চিত্রিলে নবাবে,
জানি আমি এই চিত্র অতি ভয়ঙ্কর;[22]
. . . এ চক্রান্ত
কৃষ্ণনগরাধিপের উপযুক্ত নয়।
কেন মহারাজ এত হইলেন ভ্রান্ত ?
কাপুরষ-যোগ্য এই হিন মন্ত্রণায়
কেমনে দিলেন সায় একবাক্যে সব,
বুঝিতে না পারি আমি; না বুঝিনু হায়![23]

The Rani reminds the conspirators of the cowardice of Lakshman Sen and the sorrows it bequeathed:

লক্ষ্মণসেনের সেই কাপুরুষতায়
সহি এত ক্লেষ !. . .[24]

Moreover, she asks them to consider the likelihood of the Nawab's replacement, his general, turning out to be a greater tyrant:

সেনাপতি সিংহাসনে বসিবেন যবে,
তিনি যদি হন অধিক অত্যাচারি,[25]

After Aurangzeb, Mughal glory is on the wane, the fall of Delhi is imminent, French might has been humbled by Clive in the south, she points out. If they defect now to the English with the Nawab's general, the Rani cautions the plotters, Clive's triumph will be unassailable:

মোগল-গৌরব-রবি, আরঙ্গজিব সনে
অস্তমিত; নহে দূর দিল্লীর পতন।
শুনিয়াছি দাক্ষিনাত্যে ফরাশি-বিক্রম
হতবল, মহাবল ক্লাইবের করে।[26]
. . .
তাহাতে তোমরা যদি সহ সেনাপতি
বর তারে, তবে তাঁর প্রতাপ অমোঘ
হইবে অপ্রতিহত।[27]

Besides, the very need for the plot appears doubtful to her as the Marathas grow stronger in the south. Very soon, she says, the Maratha king will be the Lord of India and the country will be saved. India, the Rani infers, stands upon cross roads and great political convulsions hint their proximity. To plot now means to swim the ocean of the great unknown, she warns:

দাক্ষিনাত্যে যেইরূপ মহারাষ্ট্র পতি
হ'তেছে বিক্রমষালী, কিছু দিন আর,
মহারাষ্ট্র-পতি হবে ভারত-ভূপতি!
অচিরে হইবে ভারত-উদ্ধার।...
"বিষম বিকল্প স্থানে আছি দাড়াইয়া
আমরা, অদূরে রাজ-বিপ্লব দুর্ব্বার।
নাহি কাজ অদৃষ্টের সিন্ধু সাঁতারিয়া,[28]

Having made this little address, she attempts to dissuade the conspirators with a remarkable plea. The Yavan and the English are both foreign races, yet, she says, they are as apart as the heavens and the netherworld. The Muslims have dwelt in this country for more than five hundred years with the descendants of the Aryans. All these years have turned a mere acquaintance into a bond of affection rendering futile all conflicts of *jāti* and *dharma.* They are now like those little shrubs that grow at the foot of the great banyan and seem to become a part of it:

"জানি আমি যবনেরা ইংরাজের মত
ভিন্নজাতি; তবু ভেদ আকাশ পাতাল।
যবন ভারতবর্ষে আছে অবিরত
সার্দ্ধপঞ্চশত বর্ষ। এই দীর্ঘকাল
একত্রে বসতি হেতু, আর্য্যসুত সনে
হইয়াছে পরিনয় প্রণয় স্থাপিত;
নাহি বৃথা দ্বন্দ্ব জাতি-ধর্ম্মের কারনে।
অশত্থ-পাদপ-জাত উপবৃক্ষ মত,
হইয়াছে যবনেরা প্রায় পরিনত।"[29]

The English, on the other hand, are of recent acquaintance. Their traditions and laws are far too strange. Indians are not familiar with an atom worth of them. It is not known where they dwell beyond the oceans. In form, faith, beliefs and colour they are terrifyingly alien:

"অন্য তরে-ইংরাজেরা নব্য পরিচিত;
ইহাদের-রীতি নীতি আচার বিচার
অনুমাত্র নাহি জানি। না জানি নিশ্চিত
কোথায় বসতি, দূর সমুদ্রের পার।
আমাদের সঙ্গে দেখ ভাবিয়া অন্তরে
কিবা ধর্ম্মে, কিব বর্ণে, আকারে আচারে,
ভয়ানক অসাদৃশ্য। . . ."[30]

Is this a strange instance of a writer speaking from both sides of the emotional breach while also widening it?

The ambivalence of Nabinchandra's verse sounds all the more unusual when compared to Hemchandra's who had chosen to pare away all inflections from his tone. Published a decade before *Palaśīr Juddha*, Hemchandra's *Bīrbāhu Kābya* throughout kept itself from the kind of ambiguities that we observe in Nabinchandra's work. *Bīrbāhu Kābya* is set in Kannauj ruled by a fictional king—Birbahu. One day, when the great hero is engaging in some merriment in the woods with his women, a *yogini* appears before him and chides him. She laments that the Kshatriya is no more seen performing his charge in India. Hence, the Yavan's might waxes and Hindu women suffer dishonour. The *yogini* reminds Birbahu of the sacredness of Kannauj and his worthy descent. She tells Birbahu that it is not becoming of him to revel with women in the woods and fritter away his days:

আজি বুঝিলাম মর্ম্ম,
কেন ক্ষত্রিয়ের ধর্ম্ম,
ভারত ভিতরে আর দরশন হয় না।
কেন বা জবন-দল,

ধরে এত বা বল,
কেন হিন্দুমহিলার কুলমান রয় না॥
ভারতে কনোজ ধাম,
প্রসিদ্ধ পবিত্র নাম,
তুমি সেই কনোজের বংশধর হইয়া।
এই ভাবে অকারণে,
বৃথা কাল বনে বনে,
অপচয় করিতেছ রামাগনে লইয়া॥[31]

Soon after the incident Birbahu has a dream which stirs in him a terrible rage. Strange contrasting sights illumined the sky in the dream. In one vision a woman stood beneath a tree and demons walked past gazing at her. In another vision he sees hundreds of Hindu women being violated by a Muslim sovereign. Birbahu heard the twang of the mighty bow Gāṇḍīva driving away a hunting party far. Beside the predatory Muslim king stood a fairy wielding a sword in the right hand and the *Qur'ān* in the other. Surrounding her stood the descendants of Kshatriyas, their heads lowered. He saw sons of Yayāti fleeing incognito to distant lands and hiding. The envoys of the *mlechchhas* raged in their place and kept the Hindus from doing their duties:

বিচিত্র স্বপনে দেখে গগন ভিতরে।
বিপরিত নানা ছবি শুন্য আলো করে॥
এক ধারে নারি এক রহে তরতলে।
তাঁরে হেরি রাক্ষসেরা অধোমুখে চলে॥
অন্য পাশে একজন যবন ভুপতি।
শত হিন্দু নারি ধরে করয়ে দুর্গতি॥
এক পাশে আখণ্ডল সহ নিজগন।
গাণ্ডীব নিনাদে দূরে কে পলায়ন॥
আর পাশে ডানি হাতে তরবারি ধরি।
করান ধরিয়া বামে রহে এক পরী॥
তাহারে হেরিয়া যত ক্ষত্রিয়তনয়।
করপুটে পদতলে হেঁটমুখে রয়॥
এক ধারে যযাতির পুত্র কয় জন।

ছদ্মবেশে দূর দেশে রহে সংগোপন॥
স্থানান্তরে ম্লেচ্ছদূত করিয়া গৰ্জ্জন।
হিন্দুরে স কার-কাযে করে নিবারন॥[32]

Meanwhile, there were auguries of trouble. Sultan Bakhsh who ruled Kabul had a general named Ali Muhammad. Ali defeated and deposed the ruler of Delhi and seated himself upon his throne. He then set about pillaging Mathura, Kalpi and Kalinjhar. Having discharged this enterprise, he turned upon Kanyakubja:

সিন্ধুরাজ্য শেষ ভাগে কাবুলের দেশ।
তাহার ন্রপতি নাম সুলতান বকেশ॥
তাঁর সেনাপতি নাম আলি মহম্মদ।
খেদাইয়া দিল্লীরাজে নিল রাজপদ॥
লুটিল মথুরাপুরী কুল্পী কলিঞ্জর।
কান্যকুব্জ লুটিবারে আসে অতঃপর॥[33]

Birbahu fights with all his might and valor when attacked but is beaten and deprived of his kingdom. The palace that witnessed the Rājsuya *yajna* is now conquered by the Muslims. Birbahu vows to slay them all with his arrows:

যে ভবনে রাজসুয়-যজ্ঞ অধিঠান।
সেই পুরি আজি জয় কৈল মুসলমান॥
তবে রে যবন তোর নিকট মরন।
স্ববংশে আমার শরে হইবি নিধন॥[34]

His grief and wounds smarting him, the defeated Birbahu addresses the land of his birth. He seeks her forgiveness for not being able to reclaim her for the sovereignty of Hindus, for failing to adorn her with jewels. He wished to rebuild the palaces that lined the Ganga and Yamuna, to have the joyous drums of victory sounded. But the dreams now lay shattered:

কত দিন মনে মনে করিলাম পন॥
পুনশ্চ হিন্দুর রাজ্য স্থাপন করিব।
পুনর্ব্বার অলঙ্কারে তমারে তুষিব॥
পুনঃ নির্ম্মাইবা পুরী যত হৈল গত।
গঙ্গা যমুনার তীরে ছিল যত যত॥
বিজয়দুন্দুভি পুনঃ হরিষে বাজাব।[35]

The ignominy is compounded when Birbahu's virtuous wife, Hemlata, is imprisoned by the victorious Sultan who has designs on her. In the end, Birbahu invites the Sultan to face him in a duel. The Sultan accepts the challenge. On the appointed day, standing before his adversary in the arena, Birbahu publishes a vow to the world. He swears not to remove the warrior's garb, or to meet his wife and son, till the *mlechchha* is not driven of the land. Birbahu excoriates the Hindu rulers present calling them a disgrace upon the Kshatriya name:

যত দিন ম্লেচ্ছহীন না হইবে দেশ।
তত দিন না ছাড়িব সংগ্রামের বেশ॥
না ভেটিব হেমলতা না হেরিব সুতে।
ম্লেচ্ছ নাম যত দিন জাগিবে ভারতে॥
বলি রধিরাক্ত অসি ফিরায়ে শিরেতে।
হিন্দু নরপালগন কহেন ক্রোধেতে॥
ধিক্ ক্ষত্রিকুলে ধিক্ হিন্দুরাজগন।[36]

Birbahu defeats the Sultan and reclaims his kingdom.

The breach was indeed being deeply and firmly incised. Yet, like with Nabinchandra, we note instances of authors trying to be two voices at the same time, attempting, as though, to speak across it. This again happens in Prasanna Kumar Nag's *Rājputāngana Kābya* (রাজপুতাঙ্গনা কাব্য, 1882). Another effort in blank verse, this panegyric to Rajput gallantry is the tale of the fall of Chittor to Akbar's armies. At one point in the poem, in the thick of battle, a frenzied Rajput warrior calls Akbar a thieving Yavan and an abomination give to rapine. In his fury he also describes him as a fiend deserving hell:

> . . . চৌর্য্যবৃত্তি জঘন্য যবন . . . পাপিষ্ঠ তস্করাধাম, কোথা সে পিশাচ নরক রৌরব?[37]

A Muslim warrior, calling the Rajput the disgrace of Kshatriyas, asks him not to disdain Muslims as inferior. To discriminate on the basis of birth, he tells the Rajput, is the sign of the self-absorbed and an inferior intelligence. The Muslim also says that there is but one race of men displaying various humours, qualities and lineaments. He reminds the Rajput that to discriminate in war on the basis of birth or race is a mark of the feeble and the unmanly:

> হীনজাতি বলি কহ বৃথা গঞ্জ কেনে, রে নিবোধ ক্ষত্রকুল গ্লানি ?
> জন্মহেতু ভেদজ্ঞান কে করে সংসারে ? যে করে সে
> হিনবুদ্ধি আত্ম-অভিমানি। জাতি এক,
> বহু পদ-মান, গুন-মাত্রা-অনুগামি॥
> . . . রনে জাতি-চর্চা ভীরু নিবীর্যলক্ষন।[38]

Prasanna Kumar invests the character of Akbar too with lucent nobility. After Chittor has fallen he instructs his generals that the women are to be honoured. None of them are to be touched or asked anything, the Emperor directs. Akbar orders the royal women to be brought to his camp for an audience with him with the utmost of respect:

> ". . . সাবধান, বামাদেহ না পরশে কেহ,
> না শুধায় কেহ কিছু; সম্ভ্রমে যতনে
> আনহ শিবির দ্বারে অঙ্গনা এ সবে।"[39]

In fact, we observe that the bestowal of nobility upon Muslim characters by Hindu authors is not quite uncommon. When in a story by one Dhirendranath Pal the Hindu heroine is rendered destitute by fate she becomes an aristocratic Muslim lady's handmaid. Her mistress assures her that her faith will never be violated:

> তোমার ধর্ম্মের উপর হাত দেয় কাহার সাধ্য।[40]

However, the same author could revert to speaking in an unqualified monophony. Dhirendranath had his heroine courted by none other than the Mughal prince Khusrau. Khusrau strives for her affections in the guise of a Rajput soldier. When Pal's heroine discovers his identity, she spurns him. This because, marrying a Muslim will mean loss of caste and she will not be able to offer libations to her dead mother any more:

> আমি যে তোমাকে বিবাহ করিলে আমার মাতাকে আর জল গণ্ডুষ দিতে পারিব না . . .।[41]

In sheer defiance of the fairytale routine, the girl values a dead mother over a live prince.

We come across at least one extreme instance in which someone had to pretend that the last hundred odd years of Indian history had not happened at all. This was Bhudev Mukherjee who wrote the *Swapnalabdha Bhāratbarṣer Itihāsa* (স্বপ্নলব্ধ ভারতবর্ষের ইতিহাস, 1881). Incorporating Islam and Muslims into his national imagining, Bhudev re-imagined India's recent past. In this alternative history of India revealed in a dream, we witness the Marathas defeat the Afghans in the third battle of Panipat. Following this, the Mughal emperor Shah Alam voluntarily abdicates in favour of the young Peshwa Ramchandra who is then installed upon the throne of Delhi. During the coronation, the wizened Emperor delivers an address in which he acknowledges that India does, after all, belong to the Hindus. Only the Hindus are the true children of this country being born of her womb. But the Muslims are no strangers to her either. India has held them to her breast for ages and been a foster mother to them:

"ভারতভূমি যদিও হিন্দুজাতীয়দিগেরই যথার্থ মাতৃভুমি, যদিও হিন্দুরাই ইঁহার গর্ভে জন্মগ্রহন করিয়াছেন, তথাপি মুসলমানেরাও আর ইঁহার পর নহেন, ইনি উঁহাদ্গিকেও আপন বক্ষে ধারন করিয়া বহুকাল প্রতিপালন করিয়া আসিতেছেন। এতএব মুসলমানেরাও ইঁহার পালিত সন্তান।"[42]

Having said this the Emperor asks his audience if two children can be brothers even if one were to be of the womb and the other a foundling whom the mother had given her breast? Answering the question himself, Shah Ālam says indeed they can be, as per every scripture. As a result, a brotherly bond has been birthed between Hindus and Muslims, dwellers of India both. No dispute, says the Emperor, can undo this relation. Now he asks the assemblage if Indians will dispute like they always have, will they always fight their kin and brothers, bankrupt themselves and be fed upon by others? An instant murmur of "no, no" rises from the gathering:

এক মাতারই একটি গর্ভজাত ও অপরটি স্তন্যপালিত দুইটি সন্তানে কি ভ্রাতৃত্ব-সম্বন্ধ হয় না ? অবশ্যই হয়—সকলের শাস্ত্র মতেই হয়। এতএব ভারতবর্স-নিবাসি হিন্দু এবং মুসলমানদিগের মধ্যে পরস্পর ভ্রাতৃত্বসম্বন্ধ জন্মিয়াছে। বিবাদ করিলে কি সেই সম্বন্ধের উচ্ছেদ করা হয়। আর আমাদিগের মধ্যে কি পূর্ব্বের মত বিবাদ চলিবে ? আমারা কি চিরকালেই জ্ঞাতিবিরোধে আপনাদ্গিকে সর্ব্বস্বান্ত এবং অপরের উদরপূরন করিব ? (এই পর্য্যন্ত বলা হইলেই সভা হইতে "না-না"—"না না"—এই ধ্বনি উঠিল)।[43]

This was, thus, the backdrop against which we have a Bankimchandra penning his tales of Hindu valor. He, as we might have realised by now, aught neither be regarded misshapen nor free-standing. His writings very much belonged to an intellectual current and were a part of the multiple responses that issued from it. Furthermore, he was not the only one setting novels in the Mughal past. Just as it inspired the poets above, many novelists contemporary to Bankim had their imaginations enlivened by the age of the Mughals.

Bhudev Mukherjee, whose acquaintance we have already made, wrote the *Angurīya Binimai* (অঙ্গুরীয় বিনিময়), the story of an improbable romance between Shivaji and Roshanara Begum, in 1857.[44] Shashichandra Dutta published his *Upanyāsmālā* (উপন্যাসমালা), in 1877 turning the lives of Humayun, Akbar and Shahjahan into exciting yarns. Pratapchandra Ghosh wrote a two volume biographical novel, *Bangādhip Parājai* (বঙ্গধিপ পরাজয়)[45] on the life of Raja Pratapaditya. Even someone like Ramesh Chandra Dutta produced works such as *Mahārāṣtra Jibanprabhāt* (মহারাষ্ট্র জিবনপ্রভাত) and *Rājput Jiban-Sandhyā* (রাজপুত জিবন-সন্ধা) in 1878 and 1879. Bankim was responding to his times, as we all are prone to do. It is important to note that even a twenty-two year old Tagore had the plot of his first novel unfold in the Mughal days. This was *Bou Thākurānir Hāt* (বউ ঠাকুরানির হাট), published in 1883 and based, like the effort by Pratapchandra Ghosh, on the life of Raja Pratapaditya. However, Tagore chose not to eulogise the Raja, showing him as a doer of many dastardly deeds. Our writers, thus, were never too far from nuance and ambiguities when assessing a past they were obviously obsessed with. To cite an example, though R.C. Dutt's work was a hagiography of Rana Pratap, he made an occasional attempt to maintain a sense of balance. He presented the Hindus and Muslims as being equally admiring of Pratap's bravery. When the accounts of Pratap's doings reached Delhi,

> Be it Hindu or Muslim all hailed him, even those who had fought against him could not keep from lauding his bravery.
> কি হিন্দু, কি মুসলমান, সকলে জয় জয় রব করিতে লাগিলেন, যাহারা প্রতাপসিংহের সহিত যুদ্ধ করিতেছিলেন, তাহারাও শত্রুর বীরত্ব দেখিয়া সাধুবাদ না দিয়া ক্ষান্ত থাকিতে পারেন নাই![46]
>
> . . . Even the great Akbar marvelled at the tales of Pratap's bravery.
> . . . মহানুভব আকবর এই ক্ষত্রিয়ের বীরত্বকথা শুনিয়া চমৎকৃত হইলেন।[47]

Though this is an aspect sometimes ignored in scholarly assessments of Bankim's works, he was not immune to similar nuances either. Not even the much censured *Ānandamath* (আনন্দমঠ) is entirely bereft of them. A closer reading of the text suggests that besides being a manifesto of Hindu regeneration, *Ānandamath* was also intended as a critique of what Hinduism had come to be. There is a perceptible vacillation of the authorial voice and intentions in the text. At places, it is also permeated with a sense of irony. In the end, it appears as though both the English and the Muslims in the novel are there only to occasion Hinduism's cleansing of accretions, even the name 'Hindu' since it is of foreign provenance, as the ending suggests.

The novel is set against a grievous famine that struck Bengal in the year 1770. Not finding food in his village, Mahendra, who is fated to play an important role in the narrative, is leaving for the city with his wife Kalyani and infant daughter. Unkind providence separates him from his wife and child. He meets Bhabananda, the *santān*, as the ascetics inhabiting the abbey Anandamath are called, when he is searching for them. Bhabananda, in his conversation with Mahendra, appears to express Bankim's agenda for Hindus with his critique of Hindu cowardice:

> Bhabananda: Even a snake rears its hood if you step on its nape. Is not your patience eroded by anything? There are other countries—Magadh, Mithila, Kashi, Delhi, Kashmir—where else do you see such misery? Where else do starved humans feed on grass, thorns, the earth of termite hills? Does our Muslim king protect us? We have lost our *jāti*, *dharma*, honour, *kula* and families and are about to loose our lives. We Hindus cannot preserve our *Hinduāni* unless we drive off these opi[illegible]e addict *neḍes*.
>
> ভবা । . . . সাপের ঘারে পা দিলে সেও ফনা ধরিয়া উঠে। তোমার কি কিছুতেই ধৈর্য্য নষ্ট হয় না ? দেখ যত দেশ আছে,—মগধ, মিথিলা কাশি, দিল্লী, কাশ্মির, কোন দেশের এমন দুর্দ্দশা, কোন দেশের মানুস খেতে না পেয়ে ঘাস খায় ? কাঁটা খায় ? উইমাটি খায় ?...আমাদের মুসলমান রাজা রক্ষা করে কই ? ধর্ম্ম গেল, জাতি গেল, মান গেল, কুল গেল, এখন ত প্রান পর্য্যন্তও যায় । এ নেশাখোর নেড়েদের না

তাড়ালেই আর কি হিন্দুর হিন্দুয়ানী থাকে ?[48]

Bhabananda contrasts the Muslim depravities with the virtues of the English. Already there is an inkling of what is to come:

> Bhabananda: An Englishman does not take to his heels even when losing his life, Muslims scoot if they run into a sweat and look for *sharbat.* The English are tenacious, they finish what they take up, the Muslims are disorderly . . . finally, there is courage . . . a band of Muslims flees at the sight of a single canon ball and not one Englishman flees even if facing a band of canon balls.
> ভবা । ধর এক ইংরেজের প্রাণ গেলেও পলায় না, মুসলমান গা ঘামিলে পলায়—শরবত খুঁজিয়া বেড়ায়—ধর তার পর ইংরেজের জিদ আছে—যা ধরে, তা করে, মুসলমানের এলাকাড়ি . . . তার পর শেষ কথা সাহস . . . একটা গোলা দেখিলে মুসলমানের গোষ্ঠীশুদ্ধ পলায়—আর গোষ্ঠীশুদ্ধ গোলা দেখিলে ত একটা ইংরেজ পলায় না।[49]

Bankim's intentions, apparently nothing beyond a reinstallation of Hindu glory, seem to become clearer when the three images of the Mother are introduced to Mahendra in the abbey by Satyananda, the *brahmachārī*:

> Brahmachari: She tramples beneath her heels beasts such as the horse and the lion, she has established her august seat where the wild beasts dwell. She is the color of gold, the bearer of all prosperity. Bow to her.
> ব্রহ্ম। ইনি কুঞ্জর কেশরী প্রভৃতি বন্য পশুসকল পদতলে দলিত করিযা, বন্য পশুর আবাসস্থানে আপনার পদ্মাসন স্থাপিত করিয়াছিলেন । ইনি বালার্কবর্নাভা, সকল ঐশ্বর্য্যশালিনি। ইহাকে প্রনাম কর।[50]

> Brahmachari: Kali—dark and draped in darkness. She has lost all and hence is naked. The whole country today is a cremation ground, that is why she wears the garland of skulls. She is trampling upon Śiva beneath her feet—Oh mother!
> ব্রহ্ম। কালি—অন্ধকারসমাচ্ছন্না কালিমাময়ী। হৃতসর্ব্বস্বা, এই জন্য নগ্নিকা। আজি দেশে সর্ব্বত্রই শ্মশান—তাই মা কঙ্কাল মালিনী। আপনার শিব আপনার পদতলে

দলিতেছেন—হায় মা![51]

This is what mother will be. Ten arms extended towards the ten quarters, all bearing various weapons, the enemy vanquished at her feet, the lion at her feet devouring foes. . . .

"এই মা যা হইবেন। দশ ভুজ দশ দিকে প্রসারিত—তাহাতে নানা আয়ুধরূপে নানা শক্তি শোভিত, পদতলে শত্রু বিমর্দ্দিত, পদাশ্রিত বিরকেশরী শত্রুনিপীড়নে নিযুক্ত। দিগ্‌ভুজা।"[52]

The novel, however, soon changes tenor. Bankim inducts contrarian voices and begins a review of traditional Hinduism. Mahendra is introduced to a critique of Vaishnavism and non-violence:

Mahendra: I cannot understand, why are the *santāns* Vaishnav? The creed of a Vaishnav is *ahiṁsā*.

Satyananda: Of Chaitanyadev's Vaishnav. It is a feature of the unnatural Vaishnavism that emerged in emulation of atheist Budddhism. A true Vaishnav chastens the evil and redeems the earth . . . Chaitanya's Vishnu is all love, but God is not all love—he is infinite power too. Chaitanya's Vishnu is all love, the *santāns* Vishnu is all strength. We are all Vaishnavs, him and us. But we are both only half Vaishnavs. Do you understand?

মহেন্দ্র। ইহা বুঝিতে পারি না। সন্তানেরা বৈষ্ণব কেন? বৈষ্ণবের অহিংসাই পরম-ধর্ম্ম।

সত্য। সে চৈতন্যদেবের বৈষ্ণব। নাস্তিক বৌদ্ধধর্ম্মের অনুকরনে যে অপ্রাকৃত বৈষ্ণবতা উৎপন্ন হইয়াছিল, এ তাহারই লক্ষন। প্রকৃত বৈষ্ণবধর্ম্মের লক্ষণ দুষ্টের দমন, ধরিত্রীর উদ্ধার।. . . চৈতন্যদেবের বিষ্ণু প্রেমময়—কিন্তু ভগবান কেবল প্রেমময় নহেন—তিনি অনন্তশক্তিময়। চৈতন্যদেবের বিষ্ণু শুধু প্রেমময়—সন্তানের বিষ্ণু শুধু শক্তিময়। আমরা উভয়েই বৈষ্ণব—কিন্তু উভয়েই অর্দ্ধেক বৈষ্ণব। কথাটা বুঝিলে ?[53]

Caste too is critiqued during the initiation of a new recruit:

Satyananda: Now, caste. What caste are you? Mahendra is a Kāyastha I know. What caste is the other one.

The other man said, "I am born of Brahmans."

Satyananda: Good. But will you be able to renounce your castes?

All *santāns* are one caste. In this great task we make no distinction of Brahman and Shudra. What do you have to say?
Both: We too will not. We are all children of one mother.
সত্য। আর এক কথা—জাতি। তোমরা কি জাতি ? মহেন্দ্র কায়স্থ জানি। অপরটি কি জাতি ?
অপর ব্যক্তি বলিল, "আমি ব্রাহ্মণকুমার।"
সত্য। উত্তম। তোমরা জাতিত্যাগ করিতে পারিবে ? সকল সন্তান এক জাতিয়। এ মহাব্রতে ব্রাহ্মণ শুদ্র বিচার নাই। তোমরা কি বল ?
উভ। আমরা সে বিচার করিব না। আমরা সকলেই এক মায়ের সন্তান।[54]

Soon, we trace a sense of irony in Bankim's voice when he is describing the activities of the *santāns*. We start wondering if he really countenances their doings:

The *santāns* adorned the feet of Vishnu with *tulsi* and sandalwood paste and snatched guns and pistols from whoever had one. . . . Then they took to dispatching scouts to the villages. A scout will go to a village and ask of the Hindus, "Brothers, will you worship Vishnu?" Thus they will gather bands of twenty or twenty-five, take them to a Muslim village and torch it. When the Muslims will scamper to save their lives, the scouts will rob them of all and distribute the loot among these neo-devotees of Vishnu.
এদিকে সন্তানসম্প্রদায় নিত্য সচন্দন তুলসিদলে বিষ্ণুপাদপদ্ম পুজা করে, যার ঘরে বন্দুক পিস্তল আছে কারিয়া আনে।
. . . তার পর তাহারা গ্রামে গ্রামে চর পাঠাইতে লাগিল। চর গ্রামে গিয়া যেখানে হিন্দু দেখে বলে, ভাই বিষ্ণুপূজা করবি ? এই বলিয়া ২০।২৫ জন জড় করিয়া, মুসলমানের গ্রামে আসিয়া পড়িয়া মুসলমানের ঘরে আগুন দেয়। মুসলমানেরা প্রানরক্ষায় ব্যতিব্যস্ত হয়, সন্তানেরা তাহাদের সর্ব্বস্ব লুঠ করিয়া নূতন বিষ্ণুভক্তদিগকে বিতরন করে।[55]

A few pages after, when we come to the part where he describes the capture of a village by the *santāns*, we frankly wonder whose side he is really on. Not on the side of the *santāns*, we think, for the chaos and disorder they bring:

That night the chant of *hari* resounded across the land. The *santāns* roamed singing *Vande Mātaram* and *Jagdīś Hare*. Some robbed the weapons of enemy some of clothes. Some kicked the faces of the dead, others made some different mischief. Some rushed towards the villages, some to the towns. They accosted travellers on the way or barged into houses and said, "Say *'Vande Mātaram'* or you will be killed." A few robbed the sweetmeat shops, some entered the milkmen's houses, supped from their pots of milk, and said, "We are the cowherds of Braja, where are the milkmaids?" Great hubbub descended upon the villages and the towns that night. All said, "Muslims have been beaten, the country belongs to Hindus again. Let all chant *hari* in unison." In the villages the people gave chase to beat a Muslim whenever they spotted one. That night people grouped and forayed into the Muslim neighbourhoods and fired them. They robbed the occupants of all. Many Yavans were killed. Many Muslims shaved their beards, smeared earth on their bodies and took to telling beads. If confronted they will say, "I am a Hindu."

সেই রজনিতে হরিধ্বনিতে সে প্রদেশভুমি পরিপূর্না হইল। সন্তানেরা দলে দলে যেখানে সেখানে উচ্চৈঃস্বরে কেহ ‘‘বন্দে মাতরম’’ কেহ ‘‘জগদিশ হরে’’ বলিয়া গাইয়া বেড়াইতে লাগিল। কেহ শত্রূসেনার অস্ত্র, কেহ বস্ত্র অপহরন করিতে লাগিল। কেহ ম্রতদেহের মুখে পদাঘাত, কেহ অন্য প্রকার উপদ্রব করিতে লাগিল। কেহ গ্রামাভিমুখে, কেহ নগরাভিমুখে ধাবমান হইয়া, পথিক বা গ্রহস্থকে ধরিয়া বলে, ‘‘বল বন্দে মাতরম, নহিলে মারিয়া ফেলিব।’’ কেহ ময়রার দুকান লুঠিইয়া খায়, কেহ গোয়ালার বাড়ি গিয়া হাঁড়ি পাড়িয়া তাহাতে চুমুক মারে, কেহ বলে ‘‘আমরা ব্রজগোপ আসিয়াছি, গোপিনি কই?’’ সেই এক রাত্রের মধ্যে গ্রামে গ্রামে নগরে নগরে মহাকোলাহল পড়িয়া গেল। সকলে বলিল, ‘‘মুসলমান পরাভূত হইয়াছে, দেশ আবার হিন্দুর হইয়াছে। সকলে একবার মুক্তকন্ঠে হরি হরি বল।’’ গ্রাম্য লোকেরা মুসলমান দেখিলেই তাড়াইয়া মারিতে যায়। কেহ কেহ সেই রাত্রে দলবদ্ধ হইয়া মুসলমানদিগের পাড়ায় গিয়া তাহাদের ঘরে আগুন দিয়া সর্ব্বস্ব লুঠিয়া লইতে লাগিল। অনেক যবন নিহত হইল, অনেক মুসলমান দাড়ি ফেলিয়া গায় মৃতিকা মাখিয়া হরিনাম করিতে আরস্ক করিল, জিজ্ঞাসা করিলে বলিতে লাগিল, ‘‘মুই হেঁদু।[56]

We cease to have doubts when we arrive at the end of the novel. The authorial voice stops playing hide and seek behind the cloak of irony and comes out in the open speaking via the preceptor of the *santāns*. It has been suggested that this closure was interpolated to propitiate the English in whose employ Bankim was, but have not we noticed this critique developing already? Surely, all that we cited above, besides the hint of irony, cannot be interpolations. We quote the entire conversation between Satyananda and the preceptor following the final battle between the *santāns* and the English:

> "Do not despair," the physician said. "Deluded," he went on, "you won a war by amassing wealth through rapine. Sin never yields a propitious end. Hence, you will not be able to redeem the country. But what will ensue will be good. If the English does not become king the true faith cannot be restored. I will explain the matter to you as understood by great souls. Listen carefully. *Sanātanadharma* is not the worship of three hundred and thirty millions of gods. This is a debased worldly faith. Under its influence the genuine *sanātanadharma*—what the *mlechchhas* call *Hindudharma*—has gone extinct. True *Hindudharma* is a way of *Jñāna* and not *karma*. This *Jñāna* is of two kinds—of the external world and internal, of the mind. Internal knowledge is the dominant half of *sanātanadharma*. But internal knowledge cannot grow unless you acquire knowledge of the external world. Unless you understand the gross you cannot comprehend the subtle. External knowledge has to be disseminated for the retrieval of *sanātanadharma*. This knowledge does not exist in our country any more, nor is there any one to train us in it. We are not adept at teaching the masses. We must acquire this knowledge from other countries. The English is learned in external knowledge and is an excellent teacher of people. I must install him as the ruler. When the people of this country acquire English learning, they will be masters of matter and will also understand the mind. Then nothing will impede the spread of *sanātanadharma*. True faith will be reenergised of its own. Until that happens and the Hindu acquires knowledge and strength, the rule of the English will endure. The masses will be content and observe *dharma* unimpaired. Hence, O wise one, disarm yourself of the desire to fight the English and follow me."
>
> Satyananda said, "O great soul, if you wished to make the English king and if it is their rule which is propitious for the country at this juncture, why did you engage us in this bestial warfare?"

The sage replied, "Today, the English are traders and only interested in wealth. They do not desire to rule. But due to the *santān* revolt they will be forced to rule. They will not be able to earn wealth if they do not. The *santān* revolt was organised to anoint the English as the ruler. Come, you will understand all this once you realise knowledge."

Satyananda: "O great soul, I do not seek knowledge, I have no use for it. I will discharge the vow I have taken. Bless me that I never waver from devotion to my mother."

Sage: "The vow is discharged, good has been done to the mother, rule of the English is installed. Renounce war, let people till the soil, let the earth attain verdure, let prosperity grow."

Satyananda's eyes emitted sparks. He replied, "I will drench my mother in the blood of the foe and make her verdant."

Sage: "Where is the enemy? There is no enemy anymore. The English are a friendly power. Moreover, no one has the strength to earn a final victory over the English."

Satyananda: "Then I will give up my life here before the image of my mother."

Sage: "In ignorance? Come, you will acquire knowledge. There is a temple to the mother upon a peak in the Himalayas, I will show you her image there."

Saying this, the sage held Satyananda's hand. What resplendence! In the demure light, in the grave shrine of Vishnu, before the enormous four armed image, one immensely gifted man held the hand of another. Who held whom? *Jñāna* held *bhakti*, *dharma* held action, renunciation held the (established) order, good embraced peace. Satyananda is peace. The sage is good. Satyananda is the order, the sage is renunciation.

Renunciation led the order away.

চিকিৎসক বলিলেন, ‘‘সত্যানন্দ কাতর হইও না। তুমি বুদ্ধির ভ্রমক্রমে দস্যুবৃত্তির দ্বারা ধন সংগৃহ করিয়া রণজয় করিযাছ। পাপের কখন পবিত্র ফল হয় না। অতএব তোমরা দেশের উদ্ধার করিতে পারিবে না। আর যাহা হইবে, তাহা ভালই হইবে। ইংরেজ রাজা না! হইলে সনাতনধর্ম্মের পুনরুদ্ধারের সম্ভাবনা নাই। মহাপুরুষেরা যেরূপ বুঝিয়াছেন, এ কথা আমি তোমাকে সেইরূপ বুঝাই। মনোযোগ দিয়া শুন। তেত্রিশ কোটি দেবতার পূজা সনাতন ধর্ম্ম নহে, সে একটা লৌকিক অপকৃষ্ট ধর্ম্ম; তাহার প্রভাবে প্রকৃত সনাতনধম্ম—ম্লেচ্ছরা যাহাকে হিন্দুধর্ম্ম বলে—তাহা লোপ পাইয়াছে। প্রকৃত হিন্দুধর্ম্ম জ্ঞানাত্মক, কর্ম্মাত্মক নহে। সেই জ্ঞান দুই প্রকার, বহির্বিষয়ক ও অন্তর্বিষয়ক। অন্তর্বিষয়ক যে জ্ঞান, সে-ই সনাতনধর্ম্মের প্রধান ভাগ। কিন্তু

বহির্বিষয়ক জ্ঞান আগে না জন্মিলে অন্তর্বিষয়ক জ্ঞান জন্মিবার সম্ভাবনা নাই। স্থূল কি, তাহা না জানিলে, সূক্ষ্ম কি, তাহা জানা যায় না। এখন এদেশে অনেক দিন হইতে বহির্বিষয়ক জ্ঞান বিলুপ্ত হইয়া গিয়াছে—কাজেই প্রকৃত সনাতনধর্ম্মও লোপ পাইয়াছে। সনাতনধর্ম্মের পুনরুদ্ধার করিতে গেলে, আগে বহির্বিষয়ক জ্ঞানের প্রচার করা আবশ্যক। এখন প্রদেশ বহির্বিষয়ক জ্ঞান নাই—শিখায় এমন লোক নাই; আমরা লোকশিক্ষায় পটু নহি। এতএব ভিন্ন দেশ হইতে বহির্বিষয়ক জ্ঞান আনিতে হইবে। ইংরেজ বহির্বিষয়ক জ্ঞানে অতি সুপণ্ডিত, লোকশিক্ষায় বড় সুপটু। সুতরাং ইংরেজকে রাজা করিব। ইংরেজ শিক্ষায় এদেশিয় লোক বহিস্তত্ত্বে সুশিক্ষিত হইয়া অন্তস্তত্ত্ব বুঝিতে সক্ষম হইবে। তখন সনাতনধর্ম্মের প্রচারে আর বিঘ্ন থাকিবে না। তখন প্রকৃত ধর্ম্ম আপনা আপনি পুনরুস্কিপ্ত হইবে। যত দিন না তা হয়, যত দিন না হিন্দু আবার জ্ঞানবান গুনবান আর বলবান হয়, ততদিন ইংরেজরাজ্য অক্ষয় থাকিবে। ইংরেজরাজ্যে প্রজা সুখি হইবে—নিষ্কণ্টকে ধর্ম্মাচরন করিবে। এতএব হে বুদ্ধিমন্—ইংরেজের সঙ্গে যুদ্ধে নিরস্ত হইয়া আমার অনুসরন কর।"

সত্যানন্দ বলিলেন, "হে মহাত্মন! যদি ইংরেজকে রাজা করাই আপনার অভিপ্রায়, যদি এ সময়ে ইংরেজের রাজ্যই দেশের পক্ষে মঙ্গলকর, তবে আমাদ্দিগকে এই নৃশংস যুদ্ধকার্য্যে কোন নিযুক্ত করিয়াছিলেন?"

মহাপুরুষ বলিলেন, "ইংরেজ এক্ষনে বনিক—অর্থসংগ্রহেই মন, রাজ্যশাসনের ভার লইতে চাহে না। এই সন্তানবিদ্রোহের কারনে, তাহার রাজ্যশাসনের ভার লইতে বাধ্য হইবে; কেন না, রাজ্যশাসন ব্যতিত অর্থসংগ্রহ হইবে না। ইংরেজ রাজ্যে অভিষিক্ত হইবে বলিয়াই সন্তানবিদ্রোহ উপস্থিত হইয়াছে। এক্ষনে আইস—জ্ঞানলাভ করিয়া তুমি স্বয়ং সকল কথা বুঝিতে পারিবে।"

সত্যানন্দ। হে মহাত্মন! আমি জ্ঞানলাভের আকাঙ্ক্ষা রাখি না—জ্ঞানে আমার কাজ নাই—আমি যে ব্রতে ব্রতি হইয়াছি, ইহাই পালন করিব। আশির্ব্বাদ করুন আমার মাতৃভক্তি অচলা হউক। মহাপুরুষ। ব্রত সফল হইয়াছে—মার মঙ্গল সাধন করিয়াছ—ইংরেজরাজ্য স্থাপিত করিয়াছ। যুদ্ধবিগ্রহ পরিত্যাগ কর, লোকে কৃষিকার্য্যে নিযুক্ত হউক, পৃথিবী শস্যশালিনী হউন, লোকের শ্রীবৃদ্ধি হউক।

সত্যানন্দের চক্ষু হইতে অগ্নিস্ফুলিঙ্গ নির্গত হইল। তিনি বলিলেন, "শত্রুশোনিতে সিক্ত করিয়া মাতাকে শস্যশালিনি করিব।"

মহাপুরুষ। শত্রু কে ? শত্রু আর নাই। ইংরেজ মিত্ররাজা। আর ইংরেজের সঙ্গে যুদ্ধে শেষ জয়ী হয়, এমন শক্তি কাহারও নাই।

সত্যানন্দ। না থাকে, এইখানে এই মাতৃপ্রতিমাসম্মুখে দেহত্যাগ করিব।

মহাপুরুষ। অজ্ঞানে ? চল, জ্ঞানলাভ করিবে চল। হিমালয়শিখরে মাতৃমন্দির আছে, সেইখান হইতে মাতৃমুর্ত্তি দেখাইব।

এই বলিয়া মহাপুরুষ সত্যানন্দের হাত ধরিলেন। কি অপূর্ব্ব শোভা! সেই গম্ভির বিষ্ণুমন্দিরে প্রকাণ্ড চতুর্ভুজ মূর্ত্তির সম্মুখে, ক্ষীনালোকে সেই মহাপ্রতিভাপূর্ণ দুই পুরুষমূর্ত্তি শোভিত—একে অন্যের হাত ধরিয়াছেন। কে কাহাকে ধরিয়াছে ? জ্ঞান

আসিয়া ভক্তিকে ধরিয়াছে—ধর্ম্ম আসিয়া কর্ম্মকে ধরিয়াছে; বিসর্জ্জন আসিয়া প্রতিষ্ঠাকে ধরিয়াছে; কল্যাণী আসিয়া শান্তিকে ধরিয়াছে। এই সত্যানন্দ শান্তি। এই মহাপুরুষ কল্যাণী। সত্যানন্দ প্রতিষ্ঠা, মহাপুরুষ বিসর্জ্জন।
বিসর্জ্জন আসিয়া প্রতিষ্ঠাকে লইয়া গেল।[57]

Ironies are discernible in *Sītārām* (সীতারাম) too, another of Bankim's novels in which a Hindu hero battles Muslim tyranny. Early in the novel we see a character, Shri, urging Hindu solidarity when persuading Sitaram to save the life of a character who has been unfairly sentenced to death by the *qāzī* of the village:

> Shri: There is God, there is *dharma*, there is Narayan. None of this is untruth. If you save the poor and the afflicted no harm will come to you. If a Hindu does not help another who will?
> Sitaram thought for a long while and said, "You have spoken the truth. If a Hindu does not help another who will? I vow before you, I will do all within my power for Gangaram."
> শ্রী। দেখ, দেবতা আছেন, ধর্ম্ম আছেন, নারায়ন আছেন। কিছুই মিথ্যা নয়। তুমি দীন দুঃখিকে বাঁচাইলে তোমার কোন অমঙ্গল হইবে না। হিন্দুকে হিন্দু না রাখিলে কে রাখিবে ?
> সিতারাম অনেকক্ষন ভাবিল। পরে বলিল, "তুমি সত্যই বলিয়াছ, হিন্দুকে হিন্দু না রাখিলে কে রাখিবে ? আমি তোমার কাছে স্বীকার করিলাম, গঙ্গারামের জন্য আমি যথাসাধ্য করিব।"[58]

Sitaram agrees and does as urged. But when he founds a little principality later he calls it Mohammadpur and moto equal treatment to Hindus and Muslims:

> He recognised the sovereign in Delhi as his Emperor and dispatched *zamindāri* taxes to his treasury as was always done. In every manner he maintained accord with the Muslims, his new city he named Mohammadpur. When he treated the Hindus and Muslims the same, there was no reason for him to invite the displeasure of Muslims.
> . . . দিল্লীশ্বরকে সম্রাট স্বীকার করিয়া জমিদারীর খাজনা পূর্ব্বমত রাজকোষাগারে পৌঁছিয়া দিতে লাগিলেন, এবং সর্ব্বপ্রকারে মুসলমানের সঙ্গে সদ্ভাব রাখিতে লাগিলেন;

আর নূতন নগরীর নাম "মহম্মদপুর" রাখিয়া, হিন্দু ও মুসলমান প্রজার প্রতি তুল্য: ব্যবহার করিতে লাগিলেন, তখন মুসলমানের অপ্রীতিভাজন হইবার কোন কারণই রহিল না।[59]

In the end we see the Hindu hero being disintegrated by moral turpitude. His being Hindu does not keep Sitaram from some severe censure by the author:

> The Sitaram who had staked his all to found a Hindu empire, now neglected the work of the state for Shri. The Sitaram who had tried to protect Gangaram, for he had sought refuge in him, with his life, lusting after Shri the same Sitaram now abandoned Gangaram after wielding the King's sceptre. The one who indulged the people was now growing self-indulgent.
> . . . যে সীতারাম হিন্দুসাম্রাজ্য সংস্থাপন জন্য সর্ব্বস্ব পণ করিয়াছিলেন, সে সীতারাম রাজ্যপালন ত্যাগ করিয়া কেবল শ্রীকে খুঁজিয়া বেড়াইল। যে সীতারাম আপনার প্রান দিয়া শরণাগত বলিয়া গঙ্গারামের প্রান্রক্ষা করিতে গিয়াছিলেন—সেই সীতারাম রাজা হইয়া, রাজদণ্ডপ্রণেতা হইয়া, শ্রীর লোভে গঙ্গারামকে ছাড়িয়া দিল। যে লোকবৎসল ছিল, সে এখন আত্মবৎসল হইতেছে।[60]

What do we make of Bankimchandra? We do notice that scholars have conceded the complexities and ambiguities that the act of reading him entails. Amiya P. Sen, for example, locates Bankim between "unrelieved obscurantism on the one hand and a radical break with tradition on the other."[61] At another place he also calls it a "vacuous debate" to dispute whether he was a "revivalist" or "reformer" since "within the cultural framework of neo-Hinduism, revival always implied a degree of reform, and reform often appeared to be an attempt to revive the 'authentic' religious and cultural life of the Hindus."[62] The duality and, on occasions, multiplicity of voices in Bankim's texts have been taken heed of by the likes of Sudipta Kaviraj and Tanika Sarkar too. Kaviraj recognises that "as a serious artist, Bankimchandra created an artistic world of great internal variety."[63] Sarkar, on the other hand, observes that Bankim "is a difficult author to read with any absolute certainty since he seems to straddle very different positions with equal felicity at different times; and also because he seems to mock at convictions and resolutions that he himself had constructed."[64] Definitely, Bankim's description of the chaos unleashed by the *santāns* upon capturing a village as well as the closure of *Ānandamath* seem to underline Sarkar's observation. Bankim could indeed "straddle" worlds and ideas. He hastened to defend Hinduism in the columns of the *Statesman* when Reverend Hastie heaped infamies upon it in 1882. But he also, as pointed out by Tapan Raychaudhari, "did not give up tabooed food until 1885" and "remained a moderate drinker all his life."[65] One must not also forget that only a few years ago, in 1879, he had published *Sāmya* (সাম্য), a meditation on the state of the Indian peasantry replete with egalitarian ideas. "His self conscious return to Hinduism," Raychaudhari concludes, "was a matter of philosophical belief, rather than ritually correct conduct emphasised in the tradition."[66] Thus, he set about to discover a pure Hinduism "cleared of the accumulated rubbish of the centuries" equipped with "comparative philology, sociology, study of myths, Christian higher criticism and the methodology of 'scientific history'."[67] The effort shows in his attempt to retrieve the historical Krishna from what he saw to be a mesh of myths. What emerged from the attempt in *Kṛṣṇacharitra* (কৃষ্ণচরিত্র) was a very new, non-traditional Krishna. This Krishna was "sought to be created by a genuine historical argument, that is not poetic, which self-consciously follows a method quite unlike the unrigorous procedure of narration of the *Purānas*."[68] Kaviraj has identified even the nurturing nature invoked as mother in the song *Vande Mātaram* as something without precedent. This because, while Indian thought saw nature as "sustainer and therefore deserving worship" in earlier religion the bounties of nature were "not appealed to for avenging actions."[69] Bankim was layered and unusual. Hence, we also ought to engage with the layers that his texts conceal. Bankim has been faulted for his treatment of Muslims in his novels. Amiya P. Sen complains that the "major failing within the structure of Bankim Chandra's political thought" was his "obviously unfair and unkind treatment of the Indian Muslim."[70] He also argues that in *Ānandamath* "the Santans want only to destroy Muslim life and property, in *Sitārām* beef eating is taboo within the boundaries of Mohammadpur."[71] One can understand Sen's concerns for it does indeed appear upon a first reading that Bankim is making a ghoul out of the Muslim. But even his treatment of Muslim characters is replete with segueing shades and is often ambivalent. We saw above that it is genuinely doubtful at places in *Ānandamath* if he is countenancing the *santāns* actions. Sitaram, of course, loses his kingdom because of his depravities. Moreover, Muslims are not without nobility in his novels. One has the example of Ayesha in *Durgeśnandinī* (দুর্গেশনন্দিনী). Tanika Sarkar too has noted how in *Rājsingha* (রাজসিংহ) the stereotype of fanatical Aurangzeb is "defamiliarised, redeemed and humanised."[72] She regards this yet another example of Bankim's inability to "form and celebrate an agenda with sustained conviction even in his last, dogmatic, markedly authoritarian phase."[73] By now we have seen that Bankim was actually the part of a long literary tradition of coming to terms with the Muslim. This tradition cast forth multiple responses, as we have seen, all with their peculiar nuances and ambiguities. Bankim's ideas are but new eddies in this current. Like their predecessors, they too display different hues. Sometimes they are confident and on occasions not so much, they, instead, seem to critique themselves.

Bankim's endings seem to baffle and have roused much curiosity. The conclusion of *Ānandamath* apparently turns all that the novel said till then on its head. Amiya P. Sen has argued that "Bankim genuinely believed in what he said" "that Indians were, as yet, unprepared to accept the responsibilities of power."[74] Kaviraj sees Bankim's endings suggesting "a dream of these interrupted actions being begun elsewhere again."[75] Fortunately for us, others are rather more comprehensible than Kaviraj's dreamy vagueness. Sisir Kumar Das affirms that the "the beneficial aspect of British rule, brought up in the last chapter of the novel, is not an integral part of the narrative."[76] Raychaudhari, on the other hand, doubts that since "such sentiments are nowhere echoed in the serious essays" whether they are "to be taken at their face value or as devices to counterbalance the seditious undertone of the novels in question."[77] We, on our part, will avoid these speculations altogether. We will not see *Ānandamath*'s closure as some kind of sleight of hand or subterfuge and recognise even this closure as a part of the trend of the age, its shifting sand of ideas. The overt critique of the *santāns* effort made in the end of *Ānandamath* finds a tacit echo in *Sitārām* too. Bankim, like many of his contemporaries, was attempting to find what he thought to be the correct project for national regeneration and a critique of the projects adopted by his principal characters was a part of this effort. So also was finding out how this project should engage with the Muslim. We will see similar critiques later in our narrative, being made by the popular Girish Chandra Ghosh (1844–1912) and the relatively unknown Pramathnath Sarkar.

The cultural and emotional chasm revealed itself as a constant process. The responses that the same evoked were heterogeneous and also in a state of constant flux. Some, as we saw above, remained firmly on one side of it. Some others attempted to straddle it and speak from both sides of it. What both responses do, with the anxiety palpable in them, is to affirm the presence of the faultline for us.

Tagore, whose writings have never been studied in the context, is a fine example of someone trying to come to grips with the rupture with multiple responses over the years. Tagore penned his share of poetic encomiums to Hindu and Sikh nobility and gallantry exhibited in defiance of warlike Muslim rulers. In the bleak stanzas of *Bandi Bīr* (বন্দি বীর)[78] Tagore recounted the capture and stoic death of the brave Banda Bahadur. The poem *Prārthanātīta Dān* (প্রার্থনাতীত দান) again extolled the Sikh attitude of serene courage before agony and tyranny. In the poem, a band of Sikhs is beaten and imprisoned by the Pathans. One of the Sikhs is the young Taru Singh. The Pathan Nawab who is to decide his fate offers to spare his life if he crops and hands him his hair. He, after all, can bear no anger for someone so brave. Taru Singh thanks him for the show of ruth and says that he will get more than what he has asked for. He will hand him his head along with the hair:

> . . .
> নবাব কহিল, 'মহাবির তুমি,
> তোমারে না করি ক্রোধ—
> বেনীটি কাটিয়া দিয়ে যাও মোরে
> এই শুধু অনুরোধ।'
> তরূসিং কহে, 'করূনা তোমার
> হৃদয়ে রহিল গাথা—
> যা চেয়েছ তার বেশি দিব,
> বেনির সঙ্গে মাথা।'[79]

Tagore cast Guru Govind Singh in the poems *Guru Gobind* (গুরু গোবিন্দ)[80] and *Śeṣ Śikkhā* (শেষ শিক্ষা).[81] In the former we see Govind Singh living out his days in the wilderness and awaiting the time when he will be ready to follow his calling. In *Śeṣ Śikkhā* we have the Guru raising a Pathan boy whom he had orphaned in a sudden fit of wrath. The boy's father was a horse merchant and the Guru had lobbed off his head when he once questioned his uprightness while dealing with him.[82] The boy grows to be a youth greatly devoted to the Guru, caring for him like a son and shadowing him always. Govind Singh on his part sees in him a son come to replace the ones he had lost in war. The youth's presence scattered the emptiness in the Guru's heart:

বালক যুবক হল গোবিন্দের হাতে
দেখিতে দেখিতে। ছায়া-হেন ফিরে সাথে,
পুত্র-হেন করে তার সেবা। . . .
যুদ্ধে হয়েছে গত
শিখগুরু গোবিন্দের পুত্র ছিল যত—
আজি তার প্রৌঢ়কালে পাঠানতনয়
জুড়িয়া বসিল আসি শূন্য সে হৃদয় গুরুজির।[83]

One day, the Guru owns his deed before the youth. The time has come, Govind Singh says, for him to avenge his father and be a worthy son. The Guru asks the Pathan to unsheathe his sword and sate his father's spirit with the blood of his murderer. The young Pathan casts away the sword and flings himself upon the Guru's feet. "Do not play with Satan thus," the youth beseeches the Guru. "I have forgotten that my father's blood was spilt, I have known you as my father, master and friend," he says, "let my heart remain hued with this love, let it pall all thoughts of vengeance." Having said this, the young Pathan seeks the Guru's blessings and runs away from his presence:

. . .
আজ আসিয়াছে দিন,
রে পাঠান, পিতার সুপুত্র হও যদি
খোলো তরবার—পিত্রঘাতকের বধি
উষ্ণ রক্ত-উপহারে করিবে তর্পণ
তৃষাতুর প্রেতাত্মার।'
ফেলি অস্ত্রখান তখনি চরনে তার পড়িল পাঠান।
কহিল, 'হে গুরুদেব, লয়ে শয়তানে
কোরো না এমনতরো খেলা। ধর্ম জানে
ভুলেছিনু পিতৃরক্তপাত; একাধারে
'পিতা গুরু বন্ধু বলে জেনেছি তোমারে
এতদিন। ছেয়ে থাক মনে সেই স্নেহ,
ঢাকা পড়ে হিংসা যাক মরে। প্রভু দেহো)
পদধূলি।' এত বলি বনের বাহিরে

ঊর্দ্ধশ্বাসে ছুটে গেল, না চাহিল ফিরে,
না থামিল একবার. . .।[84]

But the Guru, apparently, was adamant upon expiating. Another day, he calls the Pathan for a game of chess. As the day wore on, he repeatedly beat the Pathan. Of a sudden, after beating him yet another time, Govind Singh flings the pieces upon his opponent and roars with laughter. Jeering the youth the Guru says that one who is so unmanly as to play with his father's murderer is bound to be defeated always. In an instant, like a flash of lightning, the youth pulls his dagger out of the scabbard and plants it in the Guru's breast. The sage dies smiling and blessing his assailant. As life ebbs out of him, Govind Singh addresses the Pathan as his son, glad that he has learnt not to let a wrong go unpunished. This was the *Śeṣ śikkhā*, the last lesson the Guru wanted to impart:

একদিন আরম্ভিল শতরঞ্চ খেলা
গোবিন্দ পাঠান-সাথে। শেষ হল বেলা
না জানিত কেহ। হার মানি বারে বারে
মাতিছে মামুদ।
. . .
কখন হঠাৎ
চতুরঙ্গ বল ছুঁড়ি করিল আঘাত
মামুদের শিরে গুরু; কহে অট্টহাস,
'পিতৃঘাতকের সাথে খেলা করে আসি
এমন যে কাপুরুষ, যয় হবে তার!'
তখনি বিদ্যুৎ হেন ছুরি খরধার
খাপ হতে খুলি লয়ে গোবিন্দের বুকে
পাঠান বিঁন্ধিয়া দিল। গুরু হাসিমুখে
কহিলেন, এতদিনে হল তোর বোধ
কি করিয়া অন্যায়ের লয় প্রতিশোধ।
শেষ শিক্ষা দিয়ে গেনু—আজি শেষবার
আশীর্বাদ করি তোরে হে পুত্র আমার।'[85]

The poignancy of this story notwithstanding, it is not obvious what message Tagore wanted to convey through it, except that the Guru did not discriminate on the basis of religion. As understood by us, the poet's dominant intention is to emphasise the Guru's humanity and universal love, while unwittingly he also provides us a glimpse of his varicolored etching of the Muslim.

Horikhelā (হোরিখেলা)[86] is a paean to the valour of Rajput women. The queen of Bhunag invites the Pathan chieftain Kesar Khan who is besieging her fort to play Holi with her. On the day of the festival, the queen and a hundred Rajput warriors dressed as women revel with their foes. When the Pathans are completely abandoned the Rajputs throw off women's vestures and slaughter them all.

Tagore, however, did not dehumanise the Muslim as many of his predecessors. We have already seen how Govind Singh and a Pathan boy come to form filial ties. Further, one calls to the mind the character of Aurangzeb as presented in the poem *Mānī* (মানী). The Aurangzeb that Tagore limns here is altogether spite free. In the poem, we have the armies of the Emperor pursuing Yashwant, the Rajput ruler of Achalgarh. When Aurangzeb is told of his capture he marvels that a Rajput free as the lightning in the sky and the mirage in the desert has been seized. The Emperor is not at all ungenerous in praising his adversary:

> . . .
> শুনিয়া কহে আরঙজেব,
>   কি কথা শুনি অদ্ভুত।
> এতদিনে কি পড়িল ধরা
>   অশনিভরা বিদ্যুৎ?
> পাহাড়ি লয়ে কয়েক শত
> পাহাড়ে বনে ফিরিতে রত
> মরুভুমির মরিচি-মতোশ
>   স্বাধিন ছিল রাজপুত।[87]

The defeated hero is brought to the court where he is asked to salute the Emperor. But he is still defiant and refuses. The proud Rajput shrugs and says that he bows his head only at the feet of his elders. The Emperor is so impressed that he seats his captured foe by his side. "O brave, in all India which country do you desire?" Aurangzeb asks him. "It is Achalgarh, the best in the land, which I prefer to the entire world," the Rajput retorts. The court jeers him silently, but the Emperor replies restoring Yashwant his kingdom, "Stay *achal* (immobile) in Achalgarh." A forgiving and bounteous Aurangzeb reinstates the Raja on his throne for he so admires his sturdy rebelliousness:

. . .
কহিল সবে বজ্রনাদে
'সেলাম করো বাদশাজাদে'—
হেলিয়া যশোবন্ত-কাঁধে
        কহিলা ধিরে নরনাথ,
'গুরুজনের চরন ছাড়া
        করি নে কারে প্রনিপাত।'

. . .
বাদশা ধরি সুরতানেরে
বসায়ে দিল নিজপাশ—
কহিলা, 'বির, ভারত মাঝে
        কি দেশ—'পরে তব আশ?'
কহিলা রাজা, 'অচলগড়
দেশের সেরা জগৎ-পর।'
সভার মাঝে পরস্পর
        নিরবে উঠে পরিহাস।
বাদশা কহে, অচল হয়ে
        অচলগড়ে করো বাস।[88]

Further, as the short story *Durāśā* (দুরাশা) shows, Tagore could and did present the Muslim as a nuanced character and not a mere caricature enslaved to passions. Written in the form of a monologue, Tagore makes the reader confidant to his protagonist in this story, a Muslim woman of noble birth who had been in love with a Brahman sepoy. By the time the narration ends, the reader is complicit in pathos with her. Tagore does not flinch from indicting the Brahman in her voice. As a young girl, the woman was rejected and insulted by her object of adoration. Tagore has her bitterly realise in the end that it was no idealism but a mere slavery to a habit that had made him do so:

> যে ব্রাহ্মণ্য আমার কিশোর হৃদয় হরন করিয়া লইয়াছিল আমি কি জানিতাম, তাহা অভ্যাস তাহা সংস্কার মাত্র।[89]

And, of course, there is the instance of Tagore's compassionate depiction of an Afghan in the story *Kābuliwālā* (কাবুলিআলা).

A similar nuance and evolution is discernible in the political essays of Tagore. Following the founding of the Congress and the incipient beginnings of political agitation, it was being obvious to him that Muslims were rather lukewarm towards the organisation. In the articles that he wrote over the 1890s we have Tagore ascribing the absence of Muslim enthusiasm to the machinations of the government. In the essay *Ingrāj O Bhāratbāsī* (ইংরাজ ও ভারতবাসী) he dwelt at some length upon the Englishman's relationship with India. The trenchant essay brings out the strangeness of this tie and indicts it. Throughout its length Tagore accents the uniqueness of the English in the line of India's rulers. The Englishman's rule differed in being a purely businesslike effort bearing no trace of affection for the ruled. The English, contended Tagore, attempt to do good without empathising, protect without loving and dispense justice without respecting. The poet compared this state of things to planting copious seeds in earth without bothering to water it. The Englishman made himself essential to India but did not care to endear himself to the land:

ইহারা দয়া করে না, উপকার করে; স্নেহ করে না, রক্ষা করে; শ্রদ্ধা করে না, অথচ ন্যায়াচরনের চেস্টা করে; ভুমিতে জল সেচন করে না, অথচ রাশি রাশি বিজ বপন করিতে কার্পণ্য নাই।[90]

. . . ইংরাজ নিজেকে আমাদের পক্ষে আবশ্যক করিয়া তুলিয়াছে, কিন্তু প্রিয় করিয়া তোলা আবশ্যক বোধ করে নাই।[91]

Those who came before were different, as he saw it. Though the Muslim rulers of the past were often tyrants, they did form a genuine association of the heart with the land and the people they ruled. The ruler and the ruled made an exchange of and inspired each other's philosophy, poetry and the arts. Thus, writes Tagore, the Muslim could harass but not insult. The self respect of the masses was not mortified:

মুসলমান রাজা অত্যাচির ছিল, কিন্তু তাহাদের সহিত আমাদের অনেক বিষয়ে সাম্য ছিল। আমাদের দর্শন কাব্য, আমাদের কলা বিদ্যা, আমাদের বুদ্ধিবৃতিতে রাজায়-প্রজায় আদান প্রদান ছিল। সুতরাং মুসলমান আমাদিগকে পিড়ন করিতে পারিত, কিন্তু অসম্মান করা তাহার সাধ্য ছিল না।[92]

Tagore observed that the ruler being bereft of love for his subjects is agitating a fear and a sense of foreboding among them. One attestation of this was the way people discussed the worsening of the Hindu-Muslim discord. The poet found the impression being passed around in private that the disharmony grows acuter because the government makes no attempt of dispelling it. The ruler's politics allows no quarters for affection and they furnish the relations of the two communities with the seeds of jealousy. Allowing for the likelihood that it may not be deliberate, Tagore contrasts this attitude with the precedent of Akbar. The *natural* (italics mine) enmity of the two communities was waxing because, unlike Akbar, the English had made no attempt to cohere the country with an ideal of love:

> তাহাদের রাজনীতির মধ্যে প্রেমনীতির স্থান নাই। ভারতবর্ষের দুই সম্প্রদায়ের মধ্যে তাহারা প্রেমের অপেক্ষা ঈর্ষা বেশি করিয়া বপন করিয়াছে। ইচ্ছাপূর্বক করিয়াছে এমন নাও হইতে পারে; কিন্তু আকবর যে-একটি প্রেমের আদর্শে খণ্ড-ভারতবর্ষকে এক করিবার চেষ্টা করিয়াছিলেন, ইংরাজের পলিসির মধ্যে সেই আদর্শটি নাই বলিয়াই এই দুই জাতির স্বাভাবিক বিরোধ হ্রাস না হইয়া উতরোতর বৃদ্ধি পাইবার উপক্রম দেখা যাইতেছে।[93]

Tagore returned to regarding the government attitude and its impress upon the ties of Hindus and Muslims in the essay *Subichārer Adhikār* (সুবিচারের অধিকার). He begins the essay referring to a recent jailing of thirteen Hindus in the Satara district by the local English magistrate. As he reports the affair, the magistrate had forbidden music on the occasion of some local Hindu festival. The stricken Hindus attempted to both follow the government writ and appease their deity. They carried out the worship aided by a single instrument. Though no Muslims took exception, the government did and thirteen leading Hindus of the town were jailed. We find Tagore contemplating the incident as being the manifestation of a certain government anxiety. As he understood, the government wanted to keep the Hindus and Muslims from advancing down the path of unity under the leadership of the Congress. Thus, the rulers appeased the Muslims to pulverise the Hindu ego with their help. The government sought to keep the Muslims satisfied and the Hindus stupefied:

> পাছে কনগ্রেস প্রভ্রতির চেস্টায় হিন্দুমুসলমানগন ক্রমশ ঐক্যপথে অগ্রসর হয় এইজন্য তাঁহারা উভয় সম্প্রদায়ের ধর্মবিদ্বেস জাগাইয়া রাখিতে চান, এবং মুসলমানের দ্বারা হিন্দুর দর্প চুর্ন করিয়া মুসলমানকে সন্তুষ্ট ও হিন্দুকে অভিভুত করিতে ইচ্ছা করেন।[94]

Hereon, the poet's tone keeps growing progressively more resentful of the government's handling of the two communities. If the Hindus and Muslims occasioned to have a dispute, writes Tagore, the former will be privy to most of the rulers' censure and the latter their indulgence. This further inflamed jealousies amid the two while imbedding the seeds of a lasting dispute:

> . . . দমনটা অধিকাংশ হিন্দুর উপর দিয়াই চলিতেছে এবং প্রশ্রয়টা অধিকাংশ মুসলমানেরাই লাভ করিতেছেন . . . উভয় সম্প্রদায়ের মধ্যে ঈর্ষানল আরো অধিক করিয়া জম্বলিয়া উঠিতেছে . . . এবং চিরবিরোধের বিজ বপন করা হইতেছে।[95]

The poet also wonders if the government is rather afraid of the Muslim for its sceptre to hit the Hindu harder:

> . . . এমন সন্দেহ হয় যে, ইংরাজ মুসলমানকে মনে মনে কিছু ভয় করিয়া থাকেন। এইজন্য রাজদণ্ডটা মুসলমানের গা ঘেঁষিয়া ঠিক হিন্দুর মাথার উপরে কিছু জোরের সহিত পড়িতেছে।[96]

The Hindu had taken to agitation, joining the Congress, expressing dissent in England and writing essays in the *Amritabājār* (অমৃতবাজার). The Muslim, on the other hand, had assumed an aspect of humble devotion towards the government, obstructing the Congress' way. Because of these reasons a malady had afflicted the English mind. Further, as observed by Tagore, more than the Congress, a Hindu effort like cow protection had stirred the government. Hindus had failed to combine from the beginnings of history, not even for their own defence. But now they careered to unity for protecting the humble cow. Thus, when the effort brought forth tensions with the Muslims the English were quick to feel greater empathy for them:

> আমরা কনগ্রেসে যোগ দিয়াছি, বিলাতে আন্দোলন করিতেছি, অমৃতবাজারে প্রবন্ধ লিখিতেছি . . . অপর পক্ষে, মুসলমানগন রাজভক্তিভরে অবনতপ্রায় হইয়া কনগ্রসের উদ্ক্ষ্যেপথে বাধাস্বরূপ হইয়া দাঁরাইছেন। এই সকল কারনে ইংরাজের মনে একটা বিকার উপস্থিত হইয়াছে . . .।
>
> কেবল ইহাই নহে। কনগ্রেস অপেক্ষা গোরক্ষনী সভাটাতে ইংরাজের মনে অধিক আন্দোলন উপস্থিত করিয়াছিল। তাঁহারা জানেন, ইতিহাসের প্রারস্ককাল হইতে যে হিন্দুজাতি আত্মরক্ষার জন্য একত্র হইতে পারে নাই, চাই-কি গো রক্ষার জন্য সে জাতি একত্র হইতেও পারে। অতএব, সেই সুত্রে যখন হিন্দু-মুসলমানের বিরোধ

আরম্ভ হইল তখন স্বভাবতই মুসলমানের প্রতি ইংরাজের দরদ বাড়িয়া গিয়াছিল।[97]

Tagore, apparently, continued to hold the English responsible for inciting the differences haunting the Hindus and Muslims till pretty late. In the essay *Swadeśī Samāj* (স্বদেশী সমাজ) written in 1904 the poet presented the narrative of pre-colonial India as one of continued synthesis. When Muslims clashed with India, wrote Tagore, her society was threatened in some measure. But Hindu society's response was to arrive at a synthesis with the aftermath of this clash. Thus, the societies represented by Hinduism and Islam came to be bridged and their boundaries blurred. This was evident in various movements like Nānakpanth, Kabīrpanth, and Vaishnavism:

ইহার পরে এই ভারতবর্ষেই মুসলমানের সংঘাত আসিয়া উপস্থিত হইল। এই সংঘাত সমাজকে যে কিছুমাত্র আক্রমন করে নাই, তাহা বলিতে পারি না। তখন হিন্দুসমাজে এই পরসংঘাতের সহিত সামঞ্জস্যসাধনের প্রক্রিয়া সর্বত্রই আরম্ভ হইয়াছিল। হিন্দু ও মুসলমান সমাজের মাঝখানে এমন একটি সংযোগস্থল সৃষ্ট হইতেছিল যেখানে উভয় সমাজের সিমারেখা মিলিয়া আসিতেছিল; নানকপন্থী কবীরপন্থী ও নিম্নশ্রেনীর বেষ্ণব সমাজ ইহার দৃষ্টান্তস্থল।[98]

However, we discover his ideas to have undergone a paradigm shift after 1905. Now he seems to be very acutely aware that what is being manifest in politics is a social and cultural inheritance. In the midst of the anti-partition agitation, he wrote that the very fact that the Muslim can be turned against the Hindu is suggestive of a primal sin that pervades the relations of the two communities. The two had shared the same earth for centuries and yet had not developed the ties, enjoined by humanism and religion, which normal neighbours are expected to:

হিন্দু-মুসলমানের সম্বন্ধ লইয়া আমাদের দেশের একটা পাপ আছে . . . প্রতিবেশীর সঙ্গে প্রতিবেশীর যে সম্বন্ধ মনুস্যোচিত, ধর্মবিহিত, তাহা আমাদের মধ্যে হয় নাই।[99]

The cultural rupture, as he saw, had come to haunt the political edifice that was being raised.

The rupture bares itself in its entire enormity in the plays of Girish Chandra Ghosh. Ghosh was a prolific writer of historical plays which were also successfully staged. Ghosh's play *Satnām* (সযনাম) was performed in the Classic Theatre of Calcutta in 1904. Set against the reign of Aurangzeb, in what appears to be the north-west of the country, the play relates the Satnāmis' uprising against the Mughals. Early in the play, Ghosh's is a singular tone in its eschewal of all ambiguity. *Satnām* depicts the armies of Aurangzeb retreating from Kabul, ravaging the country on the way. The troops loot, rape and inflict untold suffering. In the chaos, the preceptor of a principal character, Ranendra, is killed by the soldiers. When Ranendra discovers the blood drenched corpse of his *mahant,* he swears that now his life's vow is vengeance and his only *dharma* the slaughter of Yavans. Ranendra pledges to touch the *śāstras* and practice *yoga* again only when the entire race of Yavans has been effaced:

> আজ হতে জিঘাংসা আমার জীবনের ব্রত, যবন হত্যা আমার ধর্ম্মানুষ্ঠান। . . . জবনকুল নির্ম্মূল করিতে পারি, তবে আবার শাস্ত্রধ্যয়ন করবো, তবে আবার যোগক্রিয়া করবো।[100]

Later, when exhorting Hindus to combat Yavans, he berates the forgiving nature of his people. "You forgive out of fear," Ranendra hectors, "you forgive fearing defeat at the hands of the Yavan. What cowardice! You all collectively desire to enter the fire but do not have the courage to face the Yavan":

> . . . তোমার মার্জ্জনা ভয়েঃ—যবনের নিকট পরাস্ত হবে, এই ভয়ে মার্জ্জনা। দেখ কি ভিরুতা! সকলে ঐক্য হয়ে অগ্নিকুণ্ডে পড়তে চাচ্ছো, কিন্তু যবন সম্মুখিন হতে সাহসী হচ্ছেনা।[101]

Satnām could have continued and ended on this register,

but it does not. When the play is very nearing its end, Ranendra engages in a lengthy dialogue with another character investing Ghosh's intent with subtlety:

> Ranendra: I cannot delay more. You are a Hindu maiden, why do you want to embrace the Mohammedan faith? Do you not know that the Vedas contain the *Qur'ān*? The *Qur'ān* has nothing which is not in the Vedas. The Vedas are ancient, the Mohammedan faith is new. Why do you renounce the ancient word and put faith in the *Qur'ān*?
> Gul: Sir, if you answer a question of mine I will know if the Hindu faith is eternal or the Mohammedan creed is eternal. I will know if the Vedas contain the *Qur'ān* or the *Qur'ān* includes the Vedas.
> Ranendra: Yes, ask.
> Gul: Do the Vedas allow for a *Musalmāni* to be made a Hindu?
> Ranendra: Yes, definitely.
> Gul: Tell me if it is written. What I observe in practice is that food is not rendered impure if cats and dogs enter a (Hindu) kitchen, but all of it must be thrown away if a Muslim does. I see Hindus bestowing love on insignificant animals but they regard a Muslim' touch defiling. What the Vedas enjoin, why is it not manifest in practice? The Muslims are called cruel, *vidharmi*. Why are Muslims cruel? To spread their faith, to benefit humankind. A Muslim believes with all his heart that by embracing his faith a man is saved. This is why he unsheathes his sword and says, "Accept the *Qur'ān* or die." The desire is that even if one in a hundred accepts Islam, even out of fear, may he attain paradise. Muslims are cruel wishing paradise for humans. In this great task Muslims have shed rivers of blood and attempted to do good to people. And what does Hindus' Vedanta say? Keep other races away, renounce your own society, live in a cave in the mountains and work for your own salvation. I cannot imagine a greater selfishness. Then why do you call the Hindu *dharma* eternal?
> Ranendra: You are a goddess, an extraordinary woman, you have spoken right. But know that this is not the essence of Hindu *dharma*. This form of the Hindu faith has been propagated by the dwellers of darkness, the knave, the cunning and those greedy for wealth. They are not true Brahmans. They are called Brahmans because they are born of Brahmans. But see, great souls like

Chaitanya and Nanak have converted even the Yavan to the *sanātana dharma*. The invocation to Ganga composed by the Muslim Daraf Khan is recited by Brahmans after they have bathed. Too much religion has done India ill. The Satnāmis have taken up arms to remove this superstition.

রণেন্দ্র। আমি অধিক বিলম্ব করতে পারবো না। তুমি হিন্দু কুমারি;- কি নিমিত্ত মহম্মদিয় ধর্ম্ম গ্রহন করিতে চাও ? তুমি কি জান না, কোরাণ বেদের অন্তর্গত ? কোরাণ এমন কিছুই নাই, যাহা বেদে নাই। বেদ পুরাতন, মহম্মদিয় ধর্ম্ম আধুনিক। পুরাতন আপ্তবাক্য পরিত্যাগ করে কোরাণে তোমার কেন শ্রদ্ধা ?

গুল। মহাশয়, আমার একটি কথার উত্তর দিলে আমি বুঝতে পারবো যে হিন্দুধর্ম্ম সনাতন কি মহম্মদীয় ধর্ম্ম সনাতন ধর্ম্ম। কোরাণ বেদের অন্তর্গত কি বেদ কোরাণের অন্তর্গত আমার উপলব্ধি হবে।

রণেন্দ্র। কি বল।

গুল। বেদে কি এমন বিধি আছে, যে মুসলমানীকে হিন্দু করা যায় ?

রণেন্দ্র। অবশ্য আছে।

গুল। লিপিবদ্ধ থাকলে থাকতে পারে। কিন্তু কার্য্যে তো দেখি, রন্ধনগৃহে কুক্কুর, বিড়াল প্রবেশ করলে ভোজ্যবস্তু নষ্ট হয় না, কিন্তু মুসলমান প্রবেশে সে সকল আহার্য্য দ্রব্য পরিত্যাগ করতে হয়। দেখতে পাই সামান্য পশুকে হিন্দু আদর করে, কিন্তু মুসলমান স্পর্শে হিন্দু আপনাকে অপবিত্র জ্ঞান করে। যদি বেদে বিধি থাকে, তবে কার্যে সে পরিচয় কই ? কিন্তু মুসলমানকে নির্দ্দয় বলেন, বিধর্ম্মি বলেন। মুসলমানের নির্দ্দয়তার কারন কি ? ধর্ম্ম প্রচার—মানবের হিত। মুসলমান কায়মনোবাক্যে জানে, যে মোহম্মদীয় ধর্ম্ম গ্রহনে মনুষ্যে পরমার্থ লাভ হয়। সেই নিমিত্ত অসি মোচন করে বলে যে, কোরান গ্রহন কর নয় মরো। উদ্দেশ্য এই, শত ব্যক্তির মধ্যে ভয় হোক্, যা'তে হোক্—একজনকেও যদি মুসলমান-ধর্ম্মে দিক্ষিত করা যায়, তা হ'লে সে স্বর্গে যাবে। মানবের স্বর্গ কামনায় মুসলমানের নিষ্ঠুরতা। এই মহাকার্য্যে মুসলমান নদির স্রোতের ন্যায় শোনতপ্রবাহ দানে মানবের হিত সাধনের চেষ্টা করেছে। কিন্তু হিন্দুর বেদান্তে কি বলে ? অপর জাতি দূরে থাক, নিজ সমাজ পরিত্যাগ করে, পর্ব্বত গুহায় বাস করো,—আপন মুক্তি সাধন করো। স্বার্থপরতা! - এর অধিক স্বার্থপরতা আমার কল্পনায় আসে না! তবে হিন্দুধর্ম্ম সনাতন ধর্ম্ম কেন বলেন ?

রণেন্দ্র। তুমি দেবী, তুমি আসাধারন রমনী, তুমি যথার্থই বলেছ। কিন্তু জেনো হিন্দুধর্ম্মের মর্ম্ম তা নয়। ধূর্ত্ত শঠ, নিশাচর, কপট, অর্থলোভী ব্যক্তিরা হিন্দুধর্ম্মের এই রূপ ধর্ম্ম প্রচার করেছে। তারা প্রকৃত ব্রাহ্মন নয়। ব্রাহ্মনের ঔরসে জন্ম, এই নিমিত্ত ব্রাহ্মন বলে। কিন্তু দেখ, চৈতন্য নানক প্রভৃতি মহাপুরুষ আবির্ভাব হয়ে যবনকেও সনাতন ধর্ম্ম প্রদান করেছেন। মুসলমান দবাফ খাঁ রচিত গঙ্গাস্তোত্র, স্নানান্তে বেদজ্ঞ ব্রাহ্মনে পাঠ করে। ধর্ম্মবিপ্লবেই ভারতের দুগতি হয়েছে। সৎনামীর সেই কুসংস্কার দূর করবার জন্য অস্ত্রধারন।[102]

The breach, apparently, was the deposit of a remarkable welter of sentiments. Often, while this welter took shape in the works of an author, as both Bankim and Ghosh substantiate, what was developed was also a critique of the society that was addressed. This is consummately brought to our notice by an obscure work by an obscure author. The play *Rānā Pratāp* (রানা প্রতাপ) by Pramathnath Sarkar was published in 1905, the very year in which Bengal was cleaved into two. Though we do not know if *Rānā Pratāp* was ever performed, Sarkar's effrot reveals the diversity with which the Hindu gaze took stock of the Muslim. When exhorting his soldiers, the besieged Pratap calls the Muslims wicked Yavans who have descended from the heights of Hindukush and Bactria. They intended to plant their empire in India. Hence, as long as he held on to his life, it was the duty of the Kshatriya, descended of the Sun and born of braves, not to let them dwell in Chittor as India's defender:

> ". . . সুদুর উতরকুরু, সুদুর বাহ্লিকতথা হতে আসি যদি দুর্ম্মতি যবন স্থাপিতে বাসনা করে সাম্রাজ্য ভারতে; তবে সুর্য্যকুলোদ্ভব—বিরকুলোদ্ভব ভারতের রক্ষয়িতা ক্ষত্রিয় হইয়া চিতোরে যবনে দিব থাকিতে জিবন?"[103]

Meanwhile, Mansingh, the Mughal general, soliloquies in his camp. A country carved up into many little kingdoms never progresses, says he. Even Lord Krishna desired to see the land of Bharata united under a single sovereign. Now, finally, in Akbar there is someone capable of discharging that role, so he is helping him conquer all of India:

> "শত শত ক্ষুদ্র রাজে বিভক্ত যে দেশ, উন্নতি কখনো তার নহে সম্ভাবিত, শ্রিকৃষ্ণে হয়েছিল বাসনা হৃদয়ে একজন সম্রাটের দেখিতে অধিন ভারতভুমিরে . . . যোগ্যপত্র মাত্র দেখি আকবরে। ভাবি তাই সমুচিত ভারতবিজয়ে হইতে সহায় তার . . .।"[104]

Prince Salim, on the other hand, nurtures very different sentiments. He peps up his soldiers saying that the *Qur'ān* directs the slaughter of the idol worshippers. Moreover, the

Hindu is not human at all, only an animal in human guise:

> "প্রতিমা পুজক বধে কোরানে আছে উপদেশ . . .[105]
> হিন্দু তো মানুস নহে, নরপশু জানিও তাহারে . . . ।"[106]

The author is not very generous when constructing the character of Akbar either. The reason that the Emperor reveals during a soliloquy for being kind to the Hindus is rather less than admirable. "I have won over the sovereigns of India with kindness, have made no distinction between the Hindu and the Muslim and now my conduct is bearing fruit," says the Emperor. "Now the Hindu fights his own kind and sends his women for my pleasure," Akbar glees telling the audience why he chose to be genial to his subjects:

> "করেছি রাজন্যগনে মোর বশিভুত উদারতা দেখাইয়া; হিন্দু মুসলমানে না রেখেছি ভেদ কিছু; ধরেছে সুফল এ আচরন মম; হিন্দুর বিরুদ্ধে করে যুদ্ধ হিন্দুগনে অনুকুল মম; পাঠায় রমনিগন আনন্দ বাসরে তোষিতে আমার চিত . . . ।"[107]

However, more than the confession that Akbar is made to make, it is the end of the play that excites our curiosity. After his defeat and many years of wandering, when Rana Pratap is lying on his death bed, a disembodied voice calls out to him from the heavens. The Rana is told that one day a foreign people of Aryan descent will arrive in India from across the seven seas. They will seize the sceptre of the land from Yavans with leonine valour. The king is assured that he may die in peace for in their refuge Chittor will be eternally tranquil and safe:

> "আর্য্যবংশোদ্ভব এক বিদেশিয় জাতি সপ্তসিন্ধু হয় পার আসিবে ভারতে; প্রকাশি উতরকালে কেশরিবিক্রম, যবন-রাজের কর হইতে গ্রহন করিবে শাসনদন্ড; মিবারে সে জাতি করিবে আশ্রয়দানে চির নিরাপদ।"[108]

The preternatural allusion is clearly to the future arrival of the English and establishment of their rule in India. The end of the play reminds us of the closure of Bankimchandra's *Ānandamath.* One might recall how Bankim ends the novel with the preceptor of the *santāns* instructing them to give up the fight against the English. Sarkar appears to be assigning to the English the same mission and destiny as his illustrious predecessor in the world of letters. Unlike Girindramohini and Kaliprasanna, Sarkar felt no need to sing songs to the Muslim. As a Hindu, he saw his people realising a distinct political destiny bequeathed to them by their foreign masters. It does not appear like this playwright assigned a place to the Muslim in this unfolding future. Thus, in 1905, as Bengal was being sundered, the preferred political destinies too had riven. As we will see in the next chapter, the Muslim intelligentsia had also chosen a distinct future for their people while the anti-partition agitation raged and the heavens addressed Rana Pratap.

References

1. Baridbaran Ghosh, ed., *Samakālīn Sāhitye Bangabhanga* (সমকালিন সাহিত্যে বঙ্গভঙ্গ). Calcutta, 2005, p. 55.
2. Ibid., p. 31.
3. Shantikumar Dasgupta and Haribandhu Mukhi, eds., *Rangalāl Rachanābalī* (রঙ্গলাল রচনাবলী). Calcutta: Duttachaudhari and Sons, 1974, p. 138.
4. Ibid., p. 142.
5. Ibid., p. 143.
6. Ibid., p. 152.
7. Ibid.
8. *Rangalāl Rachanābalī*, p. 216.
9. Ibid., p. 218.
10. Ibid.
11. *Hemchandrer Granthābalī* (হেমচন্দ্রের গ্রন্থাবলী). Calcutta: Basumati Sahitya Mandir, p. 14.

12. *Nabīnchandrer Granthābalī* (নবীনচন্দ্রের গ্রন্থাবলী). Calcutta, 1904, p. 424.
13. Ibid., p. 412.
14. Ibid., p. 418.
15. Ibid., p. 419.
16. Ibid., pp.419–20.
17. Ibid., p. 420.
18. Ibid., p. 423.
19. Ibid., p. 424.
20. Ibid., p. 425.
21. Ibid., p. 426.
22. Ibid., p. 432.
23. Ibid., p. 433.
24. Ibid.
25. Ibid.
26. Ibid., pp.423–24.
27. Ibid., p. 424.
28. Ibid., p. 435.
29. Ibid., p. 436.
30. Ibid., p. 437.
31. Sajanikanta Sen, ed., *Hemchandra-Granthābalī* (হেমচন্দ্র-গ্রন্থাবলী), first edn. Calcutta: Bangiya Sahitya Parishad, 1953, vol I, p. 20.
32. Ibid., p. 21.
33. Ibid., p. 22.
34. Ibid., p. 28.
35. Ibid., p. 43.
36. Ibid., p. 72.
37. *Rājputāngana Kābya* (রাজপুতাঙ্গনা কাব্য). Calcutta: Kuntalin Press, 1882, p. 119.
38. Ibid., pp.119–20.
39. Ibid., p. 156.
40. "Diljān Bāndi" (দীলজান বাঁদি) in *Aitihāsik Galpa* (ঐতিহাসিক গল্প). Calcutta, 1884, p. 67.
41. Ibid., p. 76.
42. Pramathnath Bishi, ed., *Bhūdev-Rachanāsambhār* (ভূদেব-রচনাসম্ভার). Calcutta: Mitra O Ghosh, 1968, p. 345.
43. Ibid., p. 346.

44. The complete text of this work can be found in Kanchan Basu, ed., *Duṣprāpya Sāhitya Saṅgraha*, Dwitīya Khanda (দুষ্প্রাপ্য সাহিত্য সংগ্রহ [দ্বিতীয় খণ্ড]), sec. edn. Calcutta: Reflect Publications, 1992, pp.436–85.
45. The first volume was published in 1869 and the second in 1884.
46. Romesh Chandra Dutt, *Rājput Jiban-Sandhyā* (রাজপুত জিবন-সন্ধ্যা), sixth edn. Calcutta: Elm Press, 1878, p. 134.
47. Ibid.
48. *Bankim Rachanābali* (বঙ্কিম রচনাবলি), eighth edn. Calcutta: Sahitya Sansad, 1979, vol. I, p. 675.
49. Ibid.
50. Ibid., p. 677.
51. Ibid.
52. Ibid.
53. Ibid., p. 698.
54. Ibid., p. 699.
55. Ibid., p. 705.
56. Ibid., p. 724.
57. Ibid., p. 735.
58. Ibid., p. 824.
59. Ibid., p. 835.
60. Ibid., p. 876.
61. *Hindu Revivalism in Bengal. 1872–1905.* New Delhi: OUP, 1993, p. 84.
62. *Bankim Chandra Chattopadhyay. An Intellectual Biography.* New Delhi: OUP, 2008, p. 4.
63. *The Unhappy Consciousness. Bankimchandra Chattopadhyay and the Formation of Nationalist Discourse in India,* third edn. New Delhi: OUP, 1998, p. 2.
64. See "Imagining a Hindu Nation: Hindu and Muslim in Bankimchandra's Later Writings," in *Economic and Political Weekly,* vol. 29, no. 39 (Sept 24, 1994), p. 2553.
65. *Europe Reconsidered. Perceptions of the West in Nineteenth Century Bengal,* sec. edn. Delhi: OUP, 1989, p. 123.
66. Ibid.
67. Ibid., p. 148.
68. See *The Unhappy Consciousness,* p. 73.

69. Ibid., p. 140.
70. See *Hindu Revivalism in Bengal*, p. 124.
71. Ibid., p. 125.
72. See *Imagining a Hindu Nation,* p. 2559.
73. Ibid.
74. See *Hindu Revivalism in Bengal*, p. 61.
75. See *The Unhappy Consciousness,* p. 26.
76. *The Artist in Chains. The Life of Bankim Chandra Chatterjee.* New Delhi: New Statesman Publishing Company, 1984, p. 147.
77. See *Europe Reconsidered,* p. 167.
78. Written in 1899 and included in the compilation *Kathā* (কথা). See *Rabindra Rachanābalī* (রবীন্দ্র রচনাবলী). Calcutta: Vishvabharati, 1976, vol. VII, pp. 55–59.
79. Written in 1899, in ibid., p. 62.
80. Written in 1888, in ibid, pp. 63–68.
81. Written in 1899, in ibid., pp. 68–73.
82. Ibid., p. 68.
83. Ibid., p. 72.
84. Ibid., pp.72–73.
85. Written in 1899, in ibid., pp. 75–83.
86. Written in 1899, in ibid., p. 59.
87. Ibid., p. 61.
88. *Rabindra Rachanābalī* (রবিন্দ্র রচনাবলী). Calcutta: Vishvabharati, 1978, vol. XXI, p. 203.
89. Written in 1893 and included in the compilation *Rājā Prajā* (রাজা প্রজা). See *Rabindra Rachanābalī* (রবিন্দ্র রচনাবলী). Calcutta: Vishvabharati, 1986, vol. X, p. 381.
90. Ibid., p. 382.
91. Ibid., p. 388.
92. Ibid., p. 392.
93. Written in 1894, in ibid., p. 419.
94. Ibid.
95. Ibid., p. 420.
96. Ibid., p. 421.
97. Included in the collection *Ātmaśakti* (আত্মশক্তি). See *Rabindra Rachanābalī* (রবিন্দ্র রচনাবলী). Calcutta: Vishvabharati, 1975, vol. III, p.

547.

98. *Byādhi O Pratikār* (ব্যাধি ও প্রতিকার). Written in 1907 and included in the collection *Samūha* (সমূহ), in *Rabīndra Rachanābalī,* p. 628.
99. Dr Debipada Bhattacharya, ed., *Giriś Rachanābalī* (গিরিশ রচনাবলী). Calcutta: Sahitya Sansad, 1974, vol. IV, p. 304.
100. Ibid., p. 313.
101. Ibid., p. 347.
102. *Rānā Pratāp* (রানা প্রতাপ). Calcutta: S.K. Lahiri and Co. Publishers and Booksellers, 1905, p. 61.
103. Ibid., p. 70.
104. Ibid., p. 92.
105. Ibid., p. 93.
106. Ibid., p. 65.
107. Ibid., p. 126.
108. Ibid.

4

Becoming Muslims 1857–1905

SINCE THE MEDIEVAL TIMES we have observed a streak of ambivalence towards the Bengali language among those denizens of Bengal who were endeavouring to be Muslim. In the first chapter we saw some writing in it with apologies and some others with defiance. In both cases the authors displayed an incertitude towards the language they were expressing themselves in. We again witnessed this in the second chapter following the progressive and heavy Sanskritisation of the Bengali language. The masses of the Muslims in Bengal quite obviously did not care for or understand this language. This was very well demonstrated to us by the likes of Mālé Mohammad and Mohammad Danesh. As about the elite, the *ashrāf*, among the Muslims of Bengal, they had always looked westwards and spoken Urdu and Persian. A typical representative of the class was Nawab Abdul Latif whose Mohammedan Literary Society transacted all its business in Persian. Being Bengali and being Hindu seemed synonymous. It seemed as though Bengali is destined to be the language exclusively of the Bengali-Hindu.

However, a chain of developments beginning in the early decades of the nineteenth century ensured the resolution of the Bengali-Muslim's cultural quandary. They culminated in him finding himself being both Bengali and Muslim with equal firmness. The *ātrap*, the peasantry and the various service classes that made up the overwhelming majority of the Muslims of Bengal, were privy to the teachings of certain proselytizing movements which sought to make them more surely and self-consciously Muslim. These were the *Tarīqah-i-Mohammadiya* (the path of Mohammad) and *Farāizi*-movements. *Tarīqah-i-Mohammadiya* belonged to the Waliullah school of Delhi, and was, in all intents and purposes, an extension of the *jihād* launched in northern India by Shah Syed Ahmad (1786–1831) of Rai Bareli. It was organised and propagated in Bengal by two Patna Caliphs—Maulana Inayat Ali (1794–1858) and Wilayat Ali (1791–1835). The concerns of the *Farāizi* movement, however, were more local. It derived its name from the Arabic for fundamentals (*farāiz*). This because, Haji Sharī'atullah, its founder, lay emphasis upon the performance of the fundamentals of Islam—*kalimah, namāz, rozah, zakāt,* and *hajj.* Sharī'atullah also forbade the Muslim peasantry from paying the cesses levied upon them by their Hindu zamindars for the celebration of the Hindu festivals. In theological terms a radical feature of the movement was the suspension of the Friday prayers and 'Īd in British India which was regarded *Dār-ul-harb* (land of war). However, unlike Syed Ahmad, Sharī'atullah was no supporter of a *jihād.* Both were movements of a kind which sought to purge Islam in Bengal of all they regarded "spurious accretion."[1]

A similar movement, but less well organised, was that of Titu Mir (1782–1831). A disciple of Syed Ahmad, he led for a brief duration a peasant uprising in the eastern countryside of Bengal. Titu's followers had an especially strong presence in the districts of 24 Parganas, Nadia, and Faridpur. Titu, like the *Farāizis,* stressed the observance of the fundamentals of Islam and also things like the assumption of proper Arabic names, growing of beards, performance of the *qurbānī,* construction of mosques, etc. Titu died fighting the British in 1831.

These movements, thus, oriented the broad masses of

the Muslims of Bengal towards the Islam of the Book. Interestingly, as half the century trundled by, this factor became the key to the Bengali-Muslim's search for his own distinctive Bengali idiom. This search was also linked to the dissolution of the social-exclusivity of the *ashrāf*. The *ashrāf*, according to Rafiuddin Ahmed, were bent on a total exclusion of Bengali and the introduction of Urdu as the mother tongue of the Muslims of Bengal. Partly out of their "pathological dislike for Bengali" and partly because of the "linguistic and cultural gulf separating them from the main body of the Bengali-Muslims was created a chasm inconsistent with their new political aspirations. Since the *ashrāf* would disdain to learn Bengali, the Bengali speaking Muslims had to be induced to learn Urdu."[2] But they were in no position to enforce their will. While the Bengal peasantry was being oriented towards scriptural Islam, a section of it, it appears, had also attained a measure of economic prosperity. Tazeen M. Murshid notices a "process of differentiation" that had its inception in the Bengal peasantry in the middle of the nineteenth century. As a result, he says,

> Substantial *raiats* came to enjoy superior rights, particularly in the western districts of Bengal. Certain areas like Dinajpur, which had a high rate of produce per head gave rise to a class of rich peasants who successfully prevented the *zamindar* from siphoning off all the surplus. In every village there were substantial cultivators. The hypothesis may be advanced that since the majority of the East Bengal peasantry was Muslim, at least a section of those rich peasants would also be Muslim and constitute the strata from which a Muslim middle class could emerge.[3]

Apparently, as they prospered, the rich peasants claimed a superior social status. The result was a proliferation of *ashrāf* in the countryside. In the 1872 census the number of claimants to *ashrāf* status was a mere 266, 378 (23,189 Sheikhs, 9,858 Syeds, 2,205 Mughals) out of a total Muslim population of a little over 17,609,135. By 1901 out of a total Muslim population of slightly above 21.5 million the number of Sheikhs alone was 19,527,221![4] This new *ashrāf* needed Bengali, both for temporal and spiritual reasons. They spoke and wrote no Arabic or Persian and could access the scriptures of their faith only in translation. They also needed to compete with the Bengali Hindu for jobs and access to educational institutions. True, the highly Sanskritised Bengali taught in the *pāthshālās* was resented, but the times demanded prudence. Signing as an 'East Bengal Mohammadan,' an anonymous letter writer to the editor of the *Moslem Chronicle* lamented the fact that the scheme of instruction in the *pāthshālās* is framed with a "too exclusive a reference to the requirements of the Hindu students" and has placed the Muslim students at a "great disadvantage."[5] But, as Rafiuddin Ahmed points out, the learning of Urdu offered little immediate benefit, even to those who were most vociferous in its support. Thus, we see that when Urdu classes were introduced in the Mymensingh Zillah School in 1872–73, only an "insignificant fraction"[6] of the Muslim boys ever showed any interest in learning the language. Presumably, to compete with the Bengali-Hindu for jobs knowledge of Bengali could not be done without.

As a result, from the middle of the nineteenth century onwards, several initiatives were taken to resolve the tension between being Bengali and being Muslim. The first concerted effort for claiming Bengali for the Bengali-Muslim was made in 1860 when the Bangiya Sahitya Bishayini Mussalman Samiti was founded in Calcutta at the initiative of the Dhanbali *zamindar,* Nawab Syed Ali Chaudhary. We also come across a body called Muhammedan Society for Vernacular Literature being founded in Mymensingh in 1900, headed by the local *zamindar* Ali Chaudhary Saheb.[7] Calcutta Mohammedan Union was established in 1903. Its objectives, besides the promotion of education in Muslim society, were the translation of Persian and Arabic works on history, geography, science and religion into Bengali.[8] The

Union accepted the Bengali language as the means of both secular and religious instruction. In 1904, we see the Islam Mission Samiti being founded in the Rajshahi district. Its highest priority was the propagation of Islam and it pledged to send "preachers and missionaries to dark corners of the country where the rays of Islam had not penetrated."[9] But it also committed itself to the publication of booklets on religion and the translation of books on Islam in Bengali. Propagation of Islam, thus, was a major reason why an interest was taken in disseminating Bengali literacy among Bengali-Muslims. By the end of the nineteenth century the Bengali-Muslim intelligentsia had accepted this as a practical necessity. Almost a decade and a half before the Islam Mission Society was founded, Mohammad Riazuddin Ahmed had started the journal *Islām Prachārak* (ইসলাম প্রচারক) in 1891. In his very first editorial he seemed somewhat resentful of the neglect of Arabic and Persian in Bengal, but he also conceded the inevitability of the position Bengali had acquired among the Bengali-Muslims:

> In the present times, our sacred faith's soothing refulgence has been dimmed by the Muslims of Bengal. The sole reason behind this is the lack of religious preachers and religious books in our society. "Lack of religious books" must mean their lack in the Bengali language; otherwise, so many religious works exist in Arabic, Persian and Urdu that one will not equal their numbers even by piling the religious texts of all other nations of the world. Their existence notwithstanding, raised on the Bengali language, how many in the country of Bengal can understand the worth of these great works? On the one hand, the contrary currents of the age have made the cultivation of Arabic and Persian gradually go extinct of the country, on the other, the cultivation of the Bengali language among Muslims is growing by the day. In such a situation, the Muslims must be mindful of the currents of time and act accordingly.
>
> বৰ্ত্তমান সময়ে নানা কারনে আমাদের পবিত্র ধৰ্ম্মের বিমল জ্যোতিঃ বঙ্গদেশীয় মুসলমানদিগের দ্বারা হীনপ্রভঃ হইয়া পড়িতেছে। আমাদের সমাজে ধৰ্ম্মপ্রচারক ও

> ধর্ম্মগ্রন্থের অভাবেই ইহার একমাত্র কারন। 'ধর্ম্মগ্রন্থের অভাব' বলিতে—বাঙ্গালা ভাষায় ধর্ম্মগ্রন্থের অভাব বলিতে হইবে; নচেৎ আরবী, পারসী, উর্দ্দূ ভাষায় আমাদের ধর্ম্মেগ্রন্থ এত অধিক পরিমাণে বিদ্যমান আছে যে, পৃথিবীর অন্য সমুদয় জাতির ধর্ম্মে-গ্রন্থ একত্র করিলেও আমাদের ধর্ম্মেগ্রন্থসমুহের সমান হইবে না। থাকিলে কি হইবে, বঙ্গভাষাপরিপলাবিত বাঙ্গালা দেশে কয়জন লোক ঐ সকল মহাগ্রন্থের মর্ম্ম বুঝিতে সক্ষম। একেত' কালের বিপরীত স্রোতে এ দেশ হইতে আরবী, পারসী ভাষার চর্চ্চা ক্রমশঃ বিলুপ্ত হইতেছে, পক্ষান্তরে মুসলমানদিগের মধ্যে বাঙ্গালা ভাষার অনুশীলন দিন দিনই বাড়িয়া উঠিতেছে; এরূপ অবস্থায় মুসলমানদ্গিকেও সময়ের স্রোতের প্রতি লক্ষ্য রাখিয়া কার্য্য করা উচিত।[10]

As the new century arrived, the grudging acceptance of the local tongue had been replaced by an uninhibited enthusiasm for it. However, it had to be shaped as a distinct cultural artefact and made suitable for Muslims. *Nabanūr* (নবনূর) was started in 1903 and was edited by Syed Emdad Ali. In his first editorial he exhorted all Muslim writers to serve the cause of Bengali and also lend it a distinct Muslim character:

> Today we call upon every Muslim servant of the Bengali language to help in our sacred mission. Lending the Bengali language a distinct form and garnering strength for Muslim Bengali literature is an unavoidable duty for every Bengali-Muslim, as we believe. This will corporeally enhance the Bengali language, besides, as priceless jewels from ancient Arabic and Persian literature find way in Bengali literature in translation they will grace and illumine the breast of Bengali literature like a necklace of pearls.
>
> আজ আমরা বঙ্গ ভাষার প্রত্যেক মুসলমান সেবককে সাদরে আমাদের এই পুন্যব্রতে সাহায্যার্থে আহ্বান করিতেছি। বঙ্গভাষাকে একটা নূতন মূর্ত্তি প্রদান করিয়া মুসলমান বাঙ্গালা সাহিত্যের শক্তি সঞ্চয় করা প্রত্যেক বঙ্গীয় মুসলমানেরই অবশ্য কর্ত্তব্য-কর্ম্ম বলিয়া আমাদের বিশ্বাস। ইহাতে বঙ্গভাষারও অঙ্গবৃদ্ধি হইবে এবং আরবী-পারসী প্রভৃতি প্রাচীন সাহিত্য হইতে কত অমূল্য রত্ন ভাষান্তরিত হইয়া বঙ্গসাহিত্যের বক্ষে মনিমালার ন্যায় দীপ্তি বিকাশ করিবে।[11]

We seem to be at a point of imbrications wherein the two

halves of the Bengali-Muslim identity, religious and lingual, reinforced each other. This makes the depiction of Hindus in the writings of Bengali-Muslim authors all of greater interest. Their acceptance of Bengali, after all, was also linked to a heightened awareness of Islam.

The *Musalmāni Bānglā* that we saw emerging in the previous century quietly attained oblivion.[12] It did not quite cease to exist but became a medium of the lowbrow publications. The new Bengali-Muslim writer wrote a prose no less Sanskritised than his Hindu counterpart. An apt example is Mohammad Dad Ali. Dad Ali's volume of poetry *Bhāngāprān* (ভাঙ্গাপ্রান) was first published in 1888. The sixth edition of *Bhāngāprān* acquired by this writer carried opinions of notables on Dad Ali's poetic effort. They all emphasised one aspect, how "chaste," meaning how Sanskritised, Dad Ali's Bengali is. Advaita Prasad De, Sub-Judge at Mymensingh, expressed his gladness "that a Mahomedan gentleman wrote in chaste Bengali such good poetry."[13] Gopalchandra Lahiri, Principal, Pabna Institution, said that "In him are combined both Hindu and Mahomedan ideas and feelings, derived from close familiarity with both literatures."[14] M. Ataur Rahman, an English lecturer at Government College, Rajshahi, however, expressed the following reservation:

> I am afraid the average Mussulman reader will find many words unfamiliar to him, but the author has taken care to explain such words in the footnote, which will therefore be found very useful. The same care has been taken to explain the words of Arabic or Persian origin for the benefit of non-Muslim readers.[15]

Indeed, Dad Ali's poetry was saturated with Sanskritic imagery and allusions. The first of the poems in the volume, an invocation of the blessings of *Allāh*, was entitled *Īśwar Stotra* (ঈশ্বর স্তোত্র). Dad Ali bestowed on the Deity Sanskritic appellations such as *anādi* and *ananta*. We realise what had warranted the reservations of Mr Ataur Rahman when the invocation calls the glories of *Allāh* beyond the comprehension of even Purahar and Abjayoni. A footnote at the bottom of the page edified the reader on Purahar and Abjayoni—the gods Śiva and Brahma. Leave alone the Muslims, even Hindus must have found the reference hard to get:

অনাদি অনন্ত প্রভো! বিশ্বের আধার তুমি
ব্রহ্মাণ্ডের রচয়িতা তুমিই ব্রহ্মাণ্ড স্বামী
আমি অতি মূঢ়মতি
না জানি ভকতি স্তুতি
কিরূপ স্তুতিতে তুষ্টি হইবে তোমার
সকরনে শিক্ষা দাও করুনা-আধার।[16]
. . .
তোমার অনন্ত শক্তি বুঝে সক্তি আছে কার
পুরহর, পুরন্দর, অব্জযোনি মানে হার
মানব কি ছার তায়
তোমার মহিমা গায়
কি যে তুমি—তাহা নিজেই বিদিত
কি সাধ্য তোমায় বুঝিবে নর-চিত।[17]

The next ode, addressed to the Prophet, made almost a Hindu *avatār* out of him. Dad Ali showed the Prophet being sent down upon earth by *Allāh* to redeem humanity of sins:

কি নৈবেদ্য দিয়া দেব! সেবিবে তোমায় দাস
তুমিই ভরসাস্থল মিটাইতে অভিলাস
স্বপনেতে উরে উরে
জনম সার্থক কর
কোকনদ দুটি পদ রদ ও রসনে
ওষ্ঠাধর পরশিয়া সফলি জীবনে।
নিখিল ব্রহ্মাণ্ডপতি সৃজিত মানবকুল

ভবনদে পাপস্রোতে ভাসিয়া না পায় কুল
পাপিগনে উদ্ধারিতে
প্রেরিলেন এ মরতে
তোমায় আরবদেশে মক্কানামা স্থানে
কোরেশ বংশেতে যাহা শ্রষ্ঠ গুন মানে।[18]

Dad Ali's Bengali was nothing exceptional or out of the ordinary as far Bengali-Muslim writing was concerned. He was the part of a trend which had been running its course for almost three decades already. Mir Mosarraf Hosain, the first among Bengali-Muslim novelists, published his *Ratnabati* (রত্নবতি) in 1861.[19] All the characters of *Ratnabati* are Hindus. The world of the novel is one of enchantment in which spells are cast and characters transmogrify. At no point in the narrative does the voice of the author intervene autonomously, he is always complicit with his characters. Thus, more than being a case of a Muslim depicting Hindus, *Ratnabati* seems to be an instance of a Muslim trying to impersonate a Hindu author. This point of beginning was one of a complete accession to a Sanskritic hegemony as far as the literature of the Bengali-Muslims is concerned.

Ratnabati was written in a plodding prose typical of the times heavily drawing upon the Sanskrit lexicon. Throughout his career, this continued to be the defining feature of Hosain's prose. In fact, when he published the verse work *Gorāi Brij Athabā Gauri Setu* (গোরাই ব্রিজ অথবা গৌরি সেতু) in 1873, the journal *Bangadarśan* (বঙ্গদর্শন) commended him generously for his language. The anonymous review said:

> The book is in verse. It is not such bad verse. This writer has published other Bengali books. Many Hindus cannot write the chaste Bengali of his works.
> This is a laudable instance. Bengal is a country of both Hindus and Muslims, not Hindus alone. But Hindus and Muslims are apart at the moment, bereft of affection. For the true betterment of Bengal it is necessary that Hindu-Muslim unity is born. Till the

day the upper class Muslims will be proud of being foreign and of Bengali not being their language, will refuse to write and learn Bengali and cultivate only Urdu and Persian, this unity will not be born. This because, at the root of national unity lies the unity of language. That is why, Mir Mosarraf Hosain's fondness for the Bengali language is very pleasing for the Bengalis. We hope that other well educated Muslims too will follow his example.

গ্রন্থখানি পদ্য। পদ্য মন্দ নহে। এই গ্রন্থকার আরো বাঙ্গালা গ্রন্থ প্রকাশ করিয়াছেন। তাঁহার রচনার ন্যায় বিশুদ্ধ বাঙ্গালা অনেক হিন্দুতে লিখিতে পারে না। ইহার দ্রষ্টান্ত আদরণীয়। বাঙ্গালা হিন্দু-মুসলমানের দেশ—একা হিন্দুর দেশ নহে। কিন্তু হিন্দু-মুসলমান এক্ষনে পৃথক—পরস্পরের সহিত সহৃদয়তাশূন্য। বাঙ্গালার প্রকৃত উন্নতির জন্য নিতান্ত প্রয়োজনীয় যে হিন্দু-মুসলমানের ঐক্য জন্মে। যতদিন উচ্চ শ্রেণীর মুসলমানদিগের মধ্যে এমত গর্ব থাকিবে যে, তাঁহারা ভিন্ন দেশীয়, বাঙ্গালা তাঁহাদের ভাষা নহে, তাঁহারা বাঙ্গালা লিখিবেন না বা বাঙ্গালা শিখিবেন না, কেবল উর্দু ফারসীর চালনা করিবেন, ততদি সে ঐক্য জন্মিবে না। কেননা জাতীয় ঐক্যের মূল ভাষার একতা। অতএব মীর মশাররফ হুসেন সাহেবের বাঙ্গালা ভাষনুরাগিতা বাঙ্গালীর পক্ষে বড় প্রীতিকর। ভরসা করি, অন্যান্য সুশিক্ষিত মুসলমান তাঁহার দৃষ্টান্তের অনুবর্তি হবেন।[20]

Again, in 1874, when Hosain started the journal *Ājijān Nehār* (আজিজান নেহার), the *Grāmbārtā Prakāśikā* (গ্রামবার্ত্তা প্রকাশিকা) commented on its language:

The language is very pleasing. Does not appear to have been written by a Muslim. In fact, we advise several Hindu writers to sacrifice their felicity before it.

ভাষা অতি মনোরম। মুসলমান লিখিত বলিয়া মনে হয় না; এমন কি অনেক হিন্দু লেখকের লিপিচাতুর্য্যকে ইহার নিকট বলিদান দিতে পরামর্শ দি।[21]

The praise was not unwarranted. Hosain was an ardent protagonist of the Bengali language's cause among his co-religionists and never ceased to urge them to remember their claim over it. In 1899 he wrote in *Hitakārī* (হিতকারী):

The country language or the mother tongue of the Muslims

dwelling in Bengal is Bengali. Those with no faith in their mother tongue are not human. The mother tongue has complete claim over special household rituals. Gaining great learning in other languages neglecting the mother tongue earns one no influence. Nor does one receive affection from family, kin and the one closest to one's heart—one's wife. The inconveniences too are manifold. From household tasks to the official affairs the Bengal dwelling Muslim needs Bengali.
বঙ্গবাষী মুসলমানদের দেশভাষা বা মাতৃভাষা "বাঙ্গালা"। মাতৃভাষায় যাহার আস্থা নাই, সে মানুষ নহে। বিশেষ সাংসারিক কাজকর্ম্মে মাতৃভাষারই সম্পুর্ণ অধিকার। মাতৃভাষায় অবহেলা করিয়া অন্য ২ ভাষায় বিরাট পণ্ডিত হইলেও তাহার প্রতিপত্তি নাই। পরিবার, আত্মি. স্বজন, অমন কি প্রানের প্রান যে স্ত্রী, তাহার নিকটেও আদর নাই। অসুবিধাও বিস্তর। ইস্তক ঘরকন্নার কার্য্য নাগাদ রাজসংশ্রবী যাবতীয় কার্য্যে বঙ্গবাষী মুসলমানদের বাঙ্গালা ভাষার প্রয়োজন।[22]

Besides the cause of Bengali, Hosain was enthusiastic about Hindu-Muslim amity and was sufficiently impartial with his characterisation in the beginning. He did not flinch from depicting a particularly bestial Muslim landlord in the play *Zamindār Darpan* (জমিদার দর্পন, 1872). In an essay entitled *Go-Jiban* (গো-জিবন) published in 1888 he went as far as to suggest that for the sake of cordiality with Hindus-Muslims ought to refrain from eating beef. The well meaning Hosain, however, had his very Muslimness questioned for making this rather radical suggestion. Before being published as a pamphlet, *Go-Jiban* had been serialised in the journal *Ahmadī* (আহমদী). *Ākhbāre Eslāmiā* (আখবারে এসলামিয়া), a rival publication, responded immediately and published a mordant critique:

Anyone who is a Muslim will never willingly have himself counted a *kāfir* by casting aspersions, making hateful remarks and ridiculing what the *śāstras* declare to be *halāl*. Hence, he (Hosain) is not a Muslim.
যিনি মুসলমান হইবেন তিনি কখনই আপন শাস্ত্রনুমোদিত হালাল বস্তুর প্রতি ব্যঙ্গ জনক উক্তিতে ঘৃণা ও উপহাস বাক্য প্রয়োগ দ্বারা জানিয়া শুনিয়া কাফের শ্রেণীতে গন্য হইবেন না। এতএব তিনি মুসলমান নহেন।[23]

We find Hosain at his polemical best in *Go-Jiban.* Here was someone advocating truce with all the eloquence at his disposal. Hosain began the essay arguing for his right to think free:

> At several places in India, a movement is being waged about cow-slaughter. Meetings and associations are congregating and torrents of speeches are being let loose. Heart felt articles are being published in the English and Bengali newspapers. In places, Hindus and Muslims are finding means to protect cows together, combining their minds and efforts. Protests are being made in some English newspapers. In a time like this, I regarded it improper to keep silent.
>
> I am a Muslim, a great enemy of cows. I can digest cow flesh . . . but, guided by reason, how do I hide what I see to be just and reasonable? What do I do, the world might be unfree but the mind is not.
>
> *Halāl* and *harām* are two words in currency among us Muslims. *Halāl* is acceptable and *harām* is not. It has to be accepted that beef is *halāl*, it can be consumed.
>
> ভারতে অনেক স্থানে গোবধ লইয়া বিশেষ আন্দোলন হইতেছে। সভা সমিতি বসিতেছে, বক্তৃতার স্রোত বহিতেছে, ইংরেজি বাঙ্গালা সংবাদ পত্রিকায় হৃদয়গ্রাহী প্রবন্ধসকল প্রকাশ হইতেছে, কোন কোন স্থানে হিন্দু মুসলমান একত্রে, একপ্রানে, একযোগে গোবংশ রক্ষার উপায় উদভাবন করিতেছেন। কোন কোন ইংরেজি পত্রিকায় আবার প্রতিবাদ চলিতেছে। এ সময় আর নিরব থাকা উচিত মনে করিলাম না।
>
> আমি মোসলমান—গোজাতির পরম শত্রু। আমি গো-মাংস হজম করিতে পারি . . . কিন্তু ন্যায় চক্ষে যাহা দেখিতেছি যুক্তি ও কারনে যাহা পাইতেছি, তাহা কোথায় ঢাকিব?. . . কি করি জগত পরাধিন কিন্তু মন স্বাধিন।
>
> আমাদের মধ্যে "হালাল" ও "হারাম" দুইটি কথা আছে। হালাল গ্রহনীয়, হারাম পরিতাজ্য। এ কথাও স্বীকার্য্য যে—গোমাংস হালাল, খাইতে বাধা নাই।[24]

But it is nowhere written in the scriptures that cow bones must be bitten into, that cow flesh must swallowed, or else one will have to rot in hell.

> কিন্তু শাস্ত্রে একথা লিখা নাই যে গোহাড় কামড়াতেই হইবে, গোমাংস গলাধ করিতেই

হইবে, না করিলে নরকে পচিতে হইবে।[25]

Consumption of cow-flesh was thus not essential to being a Muslim. Hosain then went on to elaborate the usefulness of the animal almost in the same vein as a devout Hindu:

> Milk is the best edible in Bengal. Not just in illness, but till life departs from the body we need milk. If the source of this milk is eaten up nothing can save us.
> In this country no other animal is used for tilling the soil. Hence, bulls are needed for the work. If we kill them, carve them up, stick knives into their throats and consume them, what hope is there of some other food?
> গোরসই বংগের উপাদেয় খাদ্য। শুধু অসুস্থ শরীরে, এমন কি প্রানসঞ্চার হইতে বিয়োগ পর্য্যন্ত দুগ্ধের প্রয়োজন; সেই দুগ্ধের মুল গোধনকে উদরসাৎ করিয়া ফেলিলে কি রক্ষা আছে!
> এদেশে অন্য কোন পশুর দ্বারা ভুমি কর্ষনের প্রচলিত নাই। কাজেই বলদের দরকার . . . এহেন গোরত্মকে মারিয়া, কাটিয়া, গলায় ছুরি বসাইয়া উদরসাৎ করিলে অন্য খাদ্যের আশা আর থাকে কোথা ?[26]॥
>
> There are other meats and fish, eat as much as you please. But do not be cruel to a useful animal.
> And something else, Hindus and Muslims are the dominant races of Bengal. The two share such intimate ties that though different in faith, they are one in mind and *karma*—in affairs of the world I must indeed call them brothers. In peril, in joy and sorrow and in prosperity they have no way but to help each other. Those who are so close, companions forever, what do we gain by hurting them?
> Religion is not hurt if we give up beef nor are the affairs of the household disrupted. Nor is the way to our advancement sown with thorns. Life too, I suspect, is not endangered. In such a situation, why cannot we give up violence on the cow?
> Brothers! If we shared Bengal with Christians and not Hindus and if pigs were slaughtered in all their households, on all joyous occasions, in weddings, funerals, on streets, fields and *bāzārs*, what would have been our condition?
> নানাবিধ মাংস আছে, মৎস্য আছে, যত ইচ্ছা তত খাও, কিন্তু উপকারি পশুর প্রতি

নির্দ্দয় ব্যেভার করিও না।

আর একটি কথা। এই বঙ্গরাজ্যে হিন্দু-মুসলমান উভয় জাতিই প্রধান। পরস্পর এমন ঘনিষ্ট সম্বন্ধ যে ধর্ম্মে ভিন্ন, কিন্তু মর্ম্মে এবং কর্ম্মে এক—সংসার কার্য্যে ভাই না বলিয়া আর থাকিতে পারি না। আপদে বিপদে, সুখে দুঃখে, সম্পদে পরস্পরের সাহায্য ভিন্ন উদ্ধার নাই। সুখ নাই, শেষ নাই, রক্ষার উপায় নাই। এমন ঘনিষ্ট সম্বন্ধ যাহাদের সঙ্গে, এমন চিরসঙ্গি যাহারা, তাহাদের মনে ব্যথা দিয়া লাভ কি ? ধর্ম্মে আঘাত লাগে না, গোমাংস পরিত্যাগ করিলে ঘরকন্নারও ব্যাঘাত জন্মে না। উন্নতির পথেও কাঁটা পড়ে না। প্রানের হানিও বোধহয়—হয় না। এ অবস্থায় গো হিংসা পরিত্যাগ করিলে হানি কি ?

ভাইরে! এই বঙ্গরাজ্যে হিন্দুর সহিত বাস না হইয়া যদি খৃস্টানের সহিত বসবাস হইত আর তাহাদের প্রতি ঘরে ঘরে—আমোদে, আহ্লাদে, বিবাহে, শ্রাদ্ধে, পথে ঘাটে, মাঠে, বাজারে—প্রকাশ্য স্থানে শুকর বধ হইত, তাহা হইল আমাদের দশা কি ঘটিত ?[27]

Having tried to introduce his co-religionists to the revulsion felt by Hindus at the sight of slaughtered cows, Hosain tried to convince them that religion must be understood in its context. He rejected that it was necessary to sacrifice cows to discharge one's religious duty as a Muslim:

> The common folk know that faith and one's Muslimness cannot be preserved if a cow is not sacrificed on Eid-ul-Azha. This is entirely untrue.
> সাধারনে জানে যে 'ইদজ্জহায়' গরু কোরবানি না করিলে ধর্ম্ম বজায় থাকে না, মোসলমানিত্ব রক্ষা পায় না—এটি সম্পূর্ণ ভুল।[28]

> . . . In Arabia till date they sacrifice more of sheep, camels too are sacrificed. But no one sacrifices cows.
> আরবদেশে আজ পর্য্যন্ত দোম্বাই অধিক পরিমানে বলি হয়, উটও বলি হইয়া থাকে। আরবে কেহই গরু কোরবানি করে না।[29]

It is the time and place that ensures what is mentioned in the scriptures and is regarded sacred. Knowing this, one must make the necessary compromises:

Who ever thought that the Muslim faith will explode upon all of India? Who ever thought that Muslims will dwell with Hindus in every neighbourhood, town and village? . . . If this was known there would have been conventions and arrangements, descriptions to the effect of welfare of cows . . . the scriptures (*śāstras*) do not mention the cow specially, nor other animals. They mention only sheep and camels which are useless in India, they are worthless and insignificant in Bengal. From this we can easily infer that it is necessity that warrants allusions (in the scriptures) and sacredness.
কে ভাবিয়াছিল মোসলমান ধর্ম্ম সমস্ত ভারতে বিস্ফোরিত হইয়া পরিবে? কে ভাবিয়াছিল যে মোসলমান জাতি ভারতের নগরে নগরে গ্রামে গ্রামে পাড়ায় পাড়ায় হিন্দুর সহিতে একত্রে বাস করিবে ? . . . তাহা হইলে বিধি হইত, ব্যবস্থা হইত, গোজাতির উপকার বিসয় বর্নিত হইত। . . . শাস্ত্রে যেমন গোজাতির বিষয় বিশেষ রূপে কোন কথা লিখা নাই, অন্যান্য পশু সম্বন্ধেও লিখা নাই; আছে কেবল উঁট আর দোম্বার কথা যাহা ভারতের নিষ্প্রয়োজন, যাহা বঙ্গের অপুচ্ছ ও তুচ্ছ। ইহাতেও উপলহিইতেছে, সহজ জ্ঞানে ইহাতেই তো বুঝা যাইতেছে, প্রয়োজনানুসারে বর্ননা, আবশ্যকতানুসারেই পবিত্রতা।[30]

. . . Just because the scriptures do not mention the benefits of cows should we not accept their usefulness?
কেবল শাস্ত্রে গোজাতির কোন প্রকার উপকারের কথা লিখা নাই বলিয়া তাহার উপকারিতার বিষয় স্বিকার করিব না ?[31]

Besides, Hosain wondered, if the Muslims regard the cow so essential to their diet, why is it that they keep the butcher, the killer of cows, at an arm's length:

The butcher (*qasāi*) is base and loathsome, we do not regard him a member of the community of humans. Since he is a killer of cows, he suffers all the insults and punishment. But no one ever said anything to the eaters of cows.
কসাই নীচ, অতি জঘন্য, কসাইকে মনুষ্য দলের মধ্যে পরিগনিত করেন নাই। গো-জিবন হত্যা করে বলিয়া এত অপমান, এত শাস্তি আজ পর্য্যন্ত ভোগ করিতে হইতেছে। কিন্তু গোখাদককে কেহ কিছু বলেন নাই।[32]

Now, Hosain tried to enthuse the Hindus of his district to pick up cudgels to defend the cow. He found evidence of Muslims in other provinces uniting to protect the cow. Even if this was imagination, he managed to sound earnest in suggesting a Hindu-Muslim rapprochement in the task:

> In other provinces Hindus and Muslims are finding several ways of protecting cows in unison. Hindu brothers of Tangail! Will you be entirely silent on the matter?
> অন্যান্য প্রদেশে হিন্দু মোসলমান একত্র হইয়া গোধন রক্ষার জন্য কত কি উপায় করিতেছেন। টাঙ্গাইল মহকুমার হিন্দু ভ্রাতাগন! এ বিষয়ে কি একেবারেই নীরব থাকিবেন ?[33]

> How sad that when Muslims, following their scriptures, are raising their voice on cow-slaughter, the Hindu brothers of Tangail are silent. Brothers! Know that in India, unless Hindu and Muslims do something united, the task can never be carried out.
> তবে নিতান্তই দুঃখের বিষয় যে, মোসলমান তাহার শাস্ত্র বজায় রাখিয়া গোবধ জন্য চিৎকার করিতেছে, টাঙ্গাইল হিন্দু ভ্রাতাগন নীরব! ভ্রাতাগন! জানিবেন ভারতে হিন্দু মোসলমান একত্র হইয়া একযোগে কোন কার্য্য না করিলে কখনই তাহা সিদ্ধ হইবে না।[34]

Finally, Hosain tried to establish that beef is not just inessential but is actually inimical to the Bengali constitution. Hence its consumption by the Bengali-Muslim is sheer amentia:

> We must fill our stomachs knowing its capacity of digestion. We are denizens of Bengal. What is our natural nourishment?
> পাকস্থলির পেষনশক্তির শক্তি বুঝিয়াই উদর পূর্ন করা উচিত। আমরা বঙ্গবাসি। আমাদের সাধারন খাদ্য কি ?[35]
> If we see a bowl of beef every evening, what does the heart say? What do the eyes wish to see? What does the hand wish to pick up and put in the mouth? The food you consume every day—rice, *dāl*, vegetables, milk and fish—is satiating and to our taste. Tell me, have you ever felt revulsion, or you will ever?

প্রতি সন্ধ্যা গোমাংস ব্যেনজন পুর্ন বাটি সম্মুখে দেখিলে মনে কি বলে ? চক্ষু কি দেখিতে ইচ্ছা করে ? না হাতে তুলিয়া মুখে দিতে ইচ্ছা হয় ? প্রতিদিন যে খাদ্য খাইতেছেন, যথা ভাত, ডাইল, তরকারি, দুধ, মৎস্য ইত্যাদি। ইহা তৃপ্তিকর এবং রুচিকর।...বলুন তো কোনদিন কি ঘৃনা হইয়াছে ? না হইবে?[36]

This was obviously designed by God himself. It was He who wished that the Bengali-Muslim feed on nourishments other than beef. Hosain also warned his audience that beef hazarded one's health. He suggested that they corroborate his warning by visiting a *hakīm*:

> The One who provides us nourishment and protects us, has created all we feed on, I refuse to believe that there can be the smallest of the small error in His judgement.
> যিনি আহারদাতা, যিনি আমাদের রক্ষাকর্তা, যিনি খাদ্যখাদ্যের সৃষ্টিকর্তা, তাঁহার বিবেচনায় ভুলভ্রান্তির অতি ক্ষুদ্র অংশের ক্ষুদ্র অংশও যে আছে, আমি একথা বিশ্বাস করি না।[37]

> Had it been our duty to ingest cow-flesh, then He would not have enriched the fields of Bengal with so many delicious fruits, vegetables and grains. Nor would there have been so many fish in our rivers. The Compassionate God has bounteously provided what is needed in a country. Living in Bengal ought we emulate the European diet?
> গোমাংস খাওয়াই যদি আমাদের কর্তব্য হইত, তবে এত সুস্বাদু ফলমুল শস্যাদি দ্বারা বঙ্গক্ষেত্র পরিপুরিত করিতেন না। নদি জলেও এত মৎস্য জন্মিত না। যে দেশে যাহা প্রয়োজন, সে দেশের জন্য করুনাময় ভগবান তাহা অপর্য্যাপ্তরুপে দান করিয়াছেন। বঙ্গে থাকিয়া কি ইউরোপীনের খাদ্যের অনুকরন করা উচিৎ ?

> . . . ask a *hakīm* about the benefits or otherwise of cow-flesh and note the replies. What causes worms in the intestines? Which meat is most responsible for arthritis?
> কোন হাকিমকে জিজ্ঞাসা করিয়া দেখিবেন, গোমাংসের গুনাগুন বিষয় জিজ্ঞাসা করিয়া দেখিবেন তিনি কি বলেন। মলাধারে হারগাঁথা কৃমি কোন মাংসে জন্মিয়া থাকে ? বাতরোগের জন্ম কোন মাংসে বেশি হয় ?[38]

A few years before publishing *Go-Jiban*, Hosain had begun the monumental *Biṣād-Sindhu* (বিষাদ-সিন্ধু),[39] a three volume work which narrated the tale of the martyrdom of Hasan and Husain. Hosain, as it appears, had begun the effort at addressing both Bengali Hindus and Muslims already. *Go-Jiban* was only a continuation of his project of crafting a common language in which to talk to both. He had begun the work, he wrote introducing it to his readers, because he wanted the Bengali reader to know of the tragedy behind Moharram. With obviously Hindus in mind he apologised for the stray use of words of Persian and Arabic provenance. Interestingly, he called them *jātia* (national) words:

> What caused this event and what lay at the root of this terrible battle, many might be aware of these profound facts. I have taken the summary of the original event from Persian and Arabic texts and composed *Biṣād Sindhu*. Creating a mirror translation of ancient poetry, emulating the felicity of the ancient poets, while maintaining the sanctity of the sacred texts, is a desire akin to that of a dwarf seeking to grab the moon. But to make the main event of Moharram beloved of, and easily comprehensible to, Bengali readers is my intention. To avoid sin as per scriptures and bound by firm societal fetters, I have had to use some 'national' (*jātia*) words in *Biṣād Sindhu*. If the learned see some wrong in this, I seek their generous forgiveness.
> এই ঘটনার মুল কি এবং কি কারনে সেই ভয়ানক যুদ্ধ সংঘটিত হইয়াছিল, ইহার নিগূঢ় তত্ব বোধ হয় অনেকেই অবগত আছেন। পারস্য ও আরব্যগ্রন্থ হইতে মুল ঘটনার সারাংশ লইয়া "বিষাদ-ষিন্ধু" বিরচিত হইল। প্রাচিন কাব্য গ্রন্থের অবিকল অনুবাদ করিয়া, প্রাচিন কবিগনের রচনা কৌশল এবং শাস্ত্রের মর্যাদা রক্ষার আকাঙ্খা বামনের বিধু ধারনের আকাঙ্খা বলিতে হইবে। তবে মহরমে মুল ঘটনাটি বঙ্গভাষাপ্রিয়, প্রিয় পাঠক-পাঠিকাগনের সহজে হৃদয়ঙ্গম করিয়া দেওয়াই আমার একমাত্র মুখ্য উস্কেশ্য। শাস্ত্রানুসারে পাপভয়ে ও সমাজের দৃঢ় বন্ধনে বাধ্য হইয়া "বিষাদ-ষিন্ধু" মধ্যে কতকগুলি জাতিয় শব্দ ব্যভার করিতে হইবে। বিজ্ঞমণ্ডলী ইহাতে যদি কোন প্রকার দোষ বিবেচনা করেন, সদয়ভাবে মার্জনা করিবেন।[40]

Hosain, of course, tried to compensate for his use of *jātia* words by trying to explain them to his Hindu audience. For example, when he used the word *qāsid* (messenger) he immediately provided a rather drawn out explanation:

> Readers! Though a *qāsid* is a carrier of messages, do not assume that he is like the Bengali mailman or courier. A bearer of royal correspondence, civilised and wise—a good Muslim—such is meant by a *qāsid* by the writer. A *qāsid*'s attire cannot be beyond civilisation. Calm, grave, truthful, of sweet speech and pleasing in appearance, without these qualities one cannot grace the position of a *qāsid.* There is but little difference between a *dūta* and *qasid,* though the *qāsid* is not as honourable as a *dūta.*
>
> পাঠক! কাসেদ যদিও বার্তাবহ, কিন্তু বঙ্গদেশীয় ডাকহরকরা কি পত্রবাহক মনে করিবেন না। রাজপত্রবাহক অথচ সভ্য ও বিচক্ষন—মহামতি মুসলমান—লেখক ইহাকেই 'কাসেদ' বলিয়া নির্দেশ করিয়া গিয়াছেন। কাসেদের পরিচ্ছদ সভ্যতাবর্জিত নহে। সুধির, সুগম্ভির, সত্যবাদী, মিষ্টভাষী ও সুশ্রী না হইলে কাসেদ-পদে কেহ বরিত হইতে পারিত না। তবে 'দূতে' ও 'কাসেদে' অতি সামান্য প্রভেদমাত্র; 'কাসেদ' দুতের সমতূল্য মান্য নহে।[41]

At one point when two characters are to be married, he takes the pains to explain Muslim wedding rites and customs:

> Here I have something to tell my Hindu readers. I must explain our wedding rites in brief, or else the wedding at hand will strain comprehension. Among us, till the marriage is not solemnised, no man or woman from the groom's side sees the bride.
>
> If the groom is of age, he must utter a few words in Arabic at the direction of the priests (*purohit*) irrespective of the country. As rejoinders to these, a representative appointed by the parents of the groom must say a few words. The fundamental of the marriage is a proposal and an acceptance. Two witnesses are needed to testify that the bride has consented to the union. Besides this, our weddings do not involve any other religious rite, ritual, or chanting of sacred words. The rites that are held as per worldly custom, or those that are held by some believing that they are warranted by religion, are not countenanced by the scriptures.

এই স্থানে হিন্দুপাঠকগনের নিকট কিছু বলিবার আছে। আমাদের বিবাহ প্রথা একটু সংক্ষেপে বুঝাইয়া না দিলে এ উপস্থিত বিবাহ বিষয় বুঝিতে একটু আয়াস আবশ্যক হইবে। আমাদের বিবাহ না হওয়া না পর্য্যন্ত পাত্রপক্ষীয় কোন পুরুষ কি স্ত্রি পাত্রীকে দেখিবার প্রথা নাই।

পাত্র পূর্ণবয়স্ক হইলে পুরোহিতের উপদেশকৃমে যে দেশে হউক না কয়েকটি কথা আরবিয় ভাষায় উচ্চারন করিতে হয়। পাত্রপক্ষীয় অভিভাবকগনের মনোনিত প্রতিনিধিকে পাত্রের সেই কথাগুলির প্রত্যুত্তরস্বরূপ কয়েকটি কথা বলিতে হয়। বিবাহের মুল কথাই এই যে, প্রস্তাব আর স্বীকার (ইজার কবুল)। পাত্রি যে বিবাহে সম্মত হইয়াছেন, তাহার প্রমানস্বরূপ দুইটি সাক্ষীর প্রয়োজন। তদ্ভিন্ন আমাদের বিবাহে অন্য কোন প্রকার ধর্ম্মার্চনা, কি মন্ত্রপাঠ, কি অন্য কোন প্রকার ক্রিয়া কিছুই নাই। তবে লৌকিক প্রথানুসারে ধর্মভাবে শিথিলযত্ন ব্যক্তিগন, কি কেহ আমাদের ধর্মের অঙ্গ মনে করিয়া যে কিছু অনুষ্ঠান করেন তাহা শাস্ত্র সম্মত নহে।[42]

Jātia usages, however, are the exception rather than the rule in *Biṣād-Sindhu.* Throughout the length of the text, we find Hosain's language to be predominantly Sanskritic. The mosque, for example, is almost always called an *upāsanā-mandir* (উপাসনা-মন্দির).[43]

Biṣād-Sindhu also has a kind and noble polytheist in Azar. We take this to be another manifestation of Hosain's effort to engage his Hindu readership, or to find one, for that matter. Azar is introduced in the story when a soldier, Simar, who has severed the head of Husain from his body and is carrying it to Yazid to be rewarded, stops in his house for food and rest:

> Simar: . . . Severing the head from the body, I am carrying it to the king, he will reward me. The reward is a lakh of rupees. You are an idolater, I accepted your hospitality only upon seeing that there are images of gods and goddesses in your house. Had you been a disciple of Mohammad, I would have never come to your house. Not even your kindness and generosity would have made me relent, nor would I have accepted your food.
>
> সীমার—. . . দেহ হইতে মস্তক ভিন্ন করিয়া মহারাজের নিকট লইয়া যাইতেছি, পুরস্কার পাইব। লক্ষ টাকা পুরস্কার। তুমি পৌত্তলিক, তোমার গৃহে নানা দেবদেবির

মূর্তি আছে দেখিয়াই আতিথ্য গ্রহন করিয়াছি। মোহম্মদের শিষ্য হইলে কখনও তোমার গৃহে আসিতাম না। তোমার আদর অভ্যর্থনাতেও ভূলিতাম না, তোমার আহার গৃহন করিতাম না।[44]

In the night, when Simar slept, Azar and his wife and sons sit surrounding Husain's head. They decide to do all to keep Husain's remains from dishonour. Muslim or polytheist, says Azar, all are the creation of one God:

> The tragedy which is making birds and beasts weep, is lacerating the breast of all nature with sorrow—the sight of Husain's severed head—whose heart will not ache before it? Be it a worshipper of gods and goddesses or an enemy of Islam, all will sorrow if told of such an ineffable tragedy. Thus, father and sons all wept together mourning Husain.
>
> Azar said, "Every man is made of the same matter and is a creation of God. The differences of *jāti* and dharma are all whims (*līlā*) of the creator. Mutual jealousies or loathing because of this is a sign of imbecility. Just because the faith is different, will not a man feel pain in another's pain? Whatever be the faith, who will not join in this sacred task? Will not he feel the same hurt? Whatever be the religion, who will refuse the task of preserving sanctity? The great Mohammad is holy, Husain is holy, his head is holy, such sacrilege of something so sacred?
>
> সীমারের নিদ্রার ভাব জানিয়া, আজর স্ত্রীপুত্রসহ হোসেনের মস্তক ঘিরিয়া বসিলেন এবং আদ্যন্ত সমুদয় ঘটনা বলিলেন।
>
> যে ঘটনায় পশুপক্ষীর চক্ষের জল ঝরিতেছে, প্রকৃতির অন্তর ফাটিয়া যাইতেছে, সেই দেহ বিচ্ছিন্ন হোসেন মস্তক দেখিয়া কাহার হৃদয়ে না আঘাত লাগে ? দেব-দেবির উপাসক হউন, এসলাম ধর্মবিদ্বেষীই হউন, এ নিদারুন দুঃখের কথা শুনিলে কে না ব্যথিত হয়েন ? পিতাপুত্র সকলে একত্র হইয়া হোসেন-শোকে কাঁদিতে লাগিলেন।
>
> আজর বলিলেন, ''মনুষ্যমাত্রেই এক উপকরনে গঠিত এবং এক ঈশ্বরের সৃষ্ট। জাতিভেদ, ধর্মভেদ, সেও শর্বশক্তিমান ভগবানের লীলা। ইহাতে পরস্পর হিংসা দ্বেষ, ঘৃনা কেবল মূঢ়তার লক্ষন!. . . ধর্মের বিভেদ বলিয়া, মানুষের বিয়োগে মানুষ মানুষ মনোবেদনায় বেদনা বোধ করিবে না ? যন্ত্রনা অনুভব করিবে না ? যে ধর্মই কেন হোক না, পবিত্রতা রক্ষা করিতে, তৎকার্য্যে যোগ দিতে কে নিবারন করিবে ? মহাপুরুষ মোহম্মদ পবিত্র, হাসান পবিত্র, হোসেনের মস্তক পবিত্র, সেই পবিত্র

মস্তকের এত অবমাননা?[45]

Mosarraf published the essay *Sat-Prasanga* (সৎ-প্রসঙ্গ) in 1898 radically contesting the notion that there were any cogent causes behind Hindu-Muslim conflicts. The essay was an exercise in some brash rhetoric. At the very start of it he asked:

'Hindu–Muslim disputes'—disputes on what? For what? Even if one possessed the strength to contemplate without bias, without leaving one's seat for ten nights and ten days, it will be difficult tracing the root of this dispute.'
"হিন্দু-মুসলমানে বিবাদ"—কি লইয়া বিবাদ ? কিসের জন্য বিবাদ ? নিরপেক্ষচিত্তে যদি দশ রাত্রি, দশদিন একাসনে বসিয়া চিন্তা করিবার শক্তি জন্মে, তথাপি বিবাদের মুল কারন খুঁজিয়া পাওয়া দুঃসাধ্য![46]

Hosain apparently found it hard to believe that the two, being equally fettered, had some occasion to dispute. After all, Hindus and Muslims both suffered the same political subjugation:

Hindus and Muslims both are beggars at the feet of the British lion! Both are obedient (to it) with reverence and bowed heads. Both are entitled to the same joys equally.
হিন্দু মুসলমান উভয়ে ব্রিটীশ সিঙ্গের পদপ্রসাদে ভিখারি! উভয়েই নতশিলে—ভক্তি সহকারে আজ্ঞাকারি। উভয়েই সমপ্রকারে সুখ সম্ভোগের অধিকারী।[47]

Politically, thus, there was no cause for quarrel. Nevertheless, the quarrels, Hosain recognised, emerged from matters of belief and culture. But he earnestly hoped that such pugnacity could be banished from the hearts:

So this is the dispute! I loathe the side of the banana leaf you regard pure. The moment I venture close to your divan something happens to the water in your *hukkah*. . . . At my prayer time, the dulcet, collective, sacred call of *azān* pours poison down your ears. At your prayer time, the sound of conches, bells and cymbals, calls

of Bholanath and Sitaram pierce my ears with darts making me deaf.
... If the Satan lying beneath the minds of both is banished by the grace of God, there will be again affection and simplicity.
এই তো বিবাদ ! তুমি কলাপাতার যেদিকে পরিশুদ্ধ মনে করি আমি সে দিক ঘৃনা করি। আমি তোমার তক্তপোষের নিকট যেই গিয়াছি অমনি তোমার হুকার জল কি যেন হইয়াছে! . . . আমার ঈশ্বরোপাসনাকালীন সুমধুর ঈশ্বরের নাম সম্বলিত উপাসনা আহ্বান সূচক পবিত্র "আজান" ধ্বনি তোমার কর্নকুহরে বিষ ঢালিয়া দিল। তোমার উপাসনা সময়ের শঙ্খ, ঘন্টা কাসির বাদ্য, হরহর বোম ভোলানাথ শব্দ জয় সিতারাম বোল আমার কর্নে মহাশালকা বিদ্ধ করিয়া বধির করিয়া তুলিল।
. . . উভয়ের মনোভাবান্তরস্থ দুস্মতি শয়তান পরস্পরের মনোমন্দির হইতে ঈশ্বরানুগ্রহে দুরভুত হইলেই আবার প্রেম, আবার প্রনয়, আবার সরলতা . . . ।[48]

As though to expedite the purging of belligerence from his co-religionists' hearts, he reminded them how closely twined their lives were with the Hindus:

To print one invitation letter one has to seek refuge with a Hindu. . . . Among the staff of the Muslim *zamindārs* most are Hindus.
. . . একখানি নিমন্ত্রন পত্র ছাপাইতে হইলে অন্ততঃ একজন হিন্দুর আশ্রয় বরন করিতেই হইবে . . . মুসলমান জমিদারদিগের কাযকারকগনের মধ্যে প্রায় সকলেই হিন্দু।[49]

... In many law courts there are no Muslim lawyers or pleaders. In the western province (UP?), during the last Moharram, in the capitals of many Rajas, in cities and villages, the Hindus participated with the Muslims in the T'azia procession with all their hearts.
. . . আবার অনেক বিচার আদালতে মুসলমান উকিল, মোক্তার একেবারেই নাই। . . . গত মহরম পর্বোপলক্ষে পশ্চিম প্রদেশে অনেক রাজ রাজড়ার রাজধানীতে, নগরে, গ্রামে, হিন্দুগন মুসলমানের সহিত একত্রে এক যোগে তাজিয়াদারী মরচিয়া খানির মজলিসে মনখুলিয়া যোগ দিয়াছেন।[50]

Hosain also pointed out to his co-religionists that a Hindu had redeemed the honour of Nawab Sirajuddaula. Hosain lavishly praised Akshay Kumar Dutta who had recently published a biography of the Nawab and had attempted to display that Siraj was not the debauch he was made out to be:

> He has freed brave Sirajuddaula of calumny. Has pointed out to our eyes the Nawab's honesty and sagacity with firm, imperishable evidence.
> . . . মহাবীর নবাব সিরাজুদ্দৌলাকে, বিঘোর কলঙ্ক হইতে মুক্ত করিয়াছেন, চক্ষে অঙ্গুলি দিয়া নবাবের সততা, সদবুদ্ধিমত্তা এবং বিচক্ষনতার বিষয় সুদৃঢ় অক্ষয় প্রমান দ্বারা দেখাইয়া দিয়াছেন . . .।[51]
> Glory to you Akshaybabu! Glory to your love of the land!
> ধন্য অক্ষয়বাবু! ধন্য আপনার স্বদেশানুরাগ।[52]

However, it appears that Hosain was a more complex character than his writings suggest. Like the Hindu wordsmiths we made acquaintance of in the previous chapter, Hosain too could inhabit and express contradictory emotional states. A year before writing *Sat-Prasanga,* he had written the poem *Bartamān Musalmān Samājer Ekkhāni Chitra* (বর্তমান মুসলমান সমাজের একখানি চিত্র).[53] It was an attempt at presenting a vignette of the then state of Muslims. Hosain's bitter verse censured the Muslims for not realizing Hindu chicanery which had done the community so much damage. Hosain found Muslims being perpetually harried by Hindus. The grasping Hindu had taken all from the Muslim, but he was oblivious to what was being done to him. The Hindus had acquired wealth, the poem complained, by taking up service under Muslims and bringing about their ruination:

> চিরকাল হিন্দুগন
> করিতেছে নির্যাতন
> তবু জ্ঞান হল নারে হায়।
> নিতেছে সকল টেনে,
> তবু তারে নাহি চিনে,
> চক্ষে ধাঁধা এমনি লাগায়॥[54]

. . .

দেখ যত হিন্দু ঘর
কিসে হল ধনেশ্বর,
খোঁজ দেখি কারন ইহার।
প্রতি মুসলমান ঘরে,
চাকুরির সাজ পরে,
সর্বনাশ করিল সবার॥[55]

The Hindu continued to be a scheming, malevolent being in the novel *Gāzī Miān Bastāni* (গাজী মিঞার বস্তানি). Hosain published this work in the same year as *Sat-Prasanga,* in1898. At a point in the novel we have a Hindu character making the following remark to another:

> "Brother! The *neḍes* are a mote in my eye. If I had the power, I would have driven all Muslims from Bengal."
> "ভায়া! নেড়ে জাত আমার চক্ষের শূল। আমার ক্ষমতা থাকলে বাঙ্গালা দেশ থেকে সব মুসলমানগুলোকে তাড়িয়ে দিতাম।"[56]

A Muslim character, on the other hand, casts aspersions on Hindu gods:

> Hari used to steal butter to sate the fire in his belly. . . . He used to rob women of their clothes and then sit upon a tree branch. . . . Is this Hindus' Hari? The Hari who used to play hide and seek in the woods with the wife of his maternal uncle Ayan Ghosh.
> . . . হরি তো পেটের জঙ্গলায় মাখন চুরি করিয়া খাইত।...সে হরি যে স্ত্রিলোকের কাপড় চুরি করিয়া গাছের এক আগডালে বসিয়া থাকিত।...একি সেই হিন্দুর হরি ? যে হরি আপন মাতুল আয়ান ঘোষের স্ত্রিকে লইয়া জঙ্গলে জঙ্গলে লুকোচুরি খেলিয়া বেড়াইত . . .।[57]

We also see a Muslim in the novel bemoaning the softness of his people and the cleverness of the Hindu:

> The Muslims are a soft party. They possess no strength, no

certitude. They are bent by the slightest wound. The Hindu is clever in the matter. Is very competent in getting work done by hook or crook and making some profit.

"... মুসলমান জাতিই হচ্ছে নরম দেল। শক্তি নাই ধারনা করবার বল নাই। সামান্য আঘাতেই নওয়াইয়া পড়ে।... এ বিষয়ে চতুর বলি হিন্দু। কার্য উদ্ধারে ভারি মজবুত। ভারি পাকা।... যেন-তেন প্রকারেন কার্য্য উদ্ধার করে কিছু লাভ করবেই করবে।[58]

It is likely that the beginnings of political agitation were bringing about a shift in the attitudes of the emerging Muslim litterateurs. One example of the changing sentiments is the essay *Bangiya Musalmān* (বঙ্গিয় মুসলমান) by Nausher Ali Khan Usufji. Usufji begins by trying to establish the local provenance of Bengali-Muslims:

Categories such as Sheikh, Syed, Mughal, and Pathan among Muslims only indicate a diversity of descent and not religious or social superiority. However, being aware of the truth I must own that in Bengal it is hard to find any among the aforesaid types who are not of mixed descent.

মুসলমানদের মধ্যে শেখ, সৈয়দ, মোগল ও পাঠান এই শ্রেনি বিভাগ কেবল তাহাদের বংশানুক্রমিক বিভিন্নতা সুচক, ধর্ম্ম কি সমাজ সম্বন্ধিয় কোন প্রাধান্য প্রকাশক নহে। কিন্তু আমাকে সত্যের অনুরোধে বলিতে হইতেছে যে বঙ্গে প্রকৃত অর্থাৎ অমিশ্র বংশিয় উক্ত কয়েক শ্রেনির পাওয়া সুকঠিন।[59]

Muslims in Bengal had been left listless by the extinction of the Muslim ruling houses:

The moment the sun of Muslim glory set... the same very moment Muslim life in Bengal lost all consciousness of life.

যে মুহর্তে মুস্লেম গৌরব-রবি অস্তমিত হইল ... সেই মুহর্ত হইতে বঙ্গীয় মুসলমানদের জীবন জীবন চেতনা হারাইল ...।[60]

They now quite visibly lagged behind the Hindus, but this was because they were not used to servitude, the Hindus were:

> Five hundred years' servitude had habituated the Hindus to learning another's tongue, during the days of Muslim sovereignty they used to cultivate Arabic and Persian. Hence, at the start of English rule, being used to learning foreign tongues, Hindus began replacing Persian with English. . . .
> ৫০০ শত বসরের পরাধিনতায় হিন্দুজাতিকে পরকীয় ভাষা শিক্ষা করিতে অভ্যস্ত করিয়া ছিল, মুসলমান রাজত্বের সময়ে হিন্দুগন আরবি পারসি শিক্ষা করিত, অতএব ইংরেজ-শাসনের প্রারম্ভে হিন্দুগন পরকিয় ভাষা শিক্ষা করিতে অভ্যস্ত থাকায় পারষীর পরিবর্ত্তে ইংরেজি বুলিগ্রহন আরম্ভকরিলেন . . .।[61]

> Any attempt at betterment of Muslims was impeded by Hindu exclusivity and xenophobia. Muslim students objected to the text-books in government schools and colleges because the Bengali authors designate the Muslims day and night *mlechchha, yavan, neḍe, turuk, muslā* in their works. . . .
> মুসলমানদিগকে বাঙ্গালি গ্রন্থকারগন তো দিবা নিশি ম্লেচ্ছ, যবন, নেড়ে, তরুক, মোসলা প্রভৃতি নামে তাহাদের স্বস্বগ্রন্থে অভিহিত করিয়া থাকেন . . .।[62]

> The English writers cause the Muslims great pain by bestowing infamy upon the age of Muslim rule. . . .
> ইংরেজ গ্রন্থকারগন মুসলমান রাজত্বকে কু-রঞ্জিত করিয়া মুসলমানদের মনে দারুন ব্যেথা জন্মায় . . .।[63]

Moreover, the Muslims are politically ineffective because of disunity. There was also an insidious enmity between Hindus and Muslims. Hence, Usufji feared the Hindu quest for political representation and found it natural that the Muslims were suspicious of their intentions:

> Presently brotherly sentiments between Muslims have been rendered too feeble. . . .
> বর্তমান সময়ে মুসলমানদের মধ্যে ভ্রাতৃবন্ধন বড়ই শিথিল হইয়া পড়িয়াছে . . .। [64]

> The way Hindus and Muslims view each other cannot be termed one of fellow feeling.

হিন্দু ও মুসলমান পরস্পর পরস্পরকে যে চক্ষে দেখেন, তাহাকে সম্মিলনের ভাব বলিতে ইচ্ছা হয় না . . .।[65]

. . . if the Hindus, after capturing the district and local boards, choose to pass measures inimical to the Muslim diet and Muslim interests
. . . হিন্দুগন যদি মিউনিসিপালিটী ডিষ্ট্রিক ও লোকাল বোর্ডে কর্ত্তত্ব পাইয়া মুসলমানদের স্বার্থের, মুসলমানদের আহার্য দ্রব্যের বিরুদ্ধে বাইল করিতে (উপবিধি) করিতে প্রস্তুত হন।[66]

Why should not the Muslims doubt their earnestness?
তাহাদের সরলতায় মুসলমানগন কেন না সন্দেহ করিবে ?[67]

Sheikh Usman Ali was one among the contemporary Muslim authors who actively engaged himself in appraising and commenting upon the social and political scene. In an essay written in 1897, *Congress O Musalmān Jāti* (কংগ্রেস ও মুসলমান জাতি), Ali noted the very lukewarm response of Muslims towards the Indian National Congress. He, however, felt that it was not because of any innate ill-will on the part of the community. Muslims were otiose and they were not aware what the organisation was about:

প্রকৃত কথা এই যে অধিকাংশ মুসলমান কংগ্রেস কি জানেন না। আলস্যই ইহার প্রধান কারন। আমরা চিরদিন আলস্যই কাটালাম।[68]

He advised the Muslims to get rid of their sloth and join the Congress.

Despite advising political concord, Usman Ali could not circumvent the social and cultural reality. He published *Debalā* (দেবলা), a long narrative poem of eight cantos, in 1901. *Debalā*'s subject was the romance of prince Khizr, son of Allauddin Khilji, and the fictional princess of Gujarat, Debala Rani. Debala is noble and somewhat resembles Dhirendranath Pal's heroine. When Khizr despairs, she consoles him saying that certain social conventions cannot be escaped. Trying to do so can only bring ignominy:

> . . . কেন বৃথা কর রোষ সমাজের প্রতি।
> লংঘিতে সমাজ বিধি হয় অধোগতি॥[69]

As with the Hindu authors, this seems to be an instance when a Muslim writer is both widening the social and cultural rupture and trying to speak across it.

Mohammad-Kazem-al-Qureishi (better known as Kaikobad) was a towering figure among the Bengali-Muslim writers of the times. Kaikobad published *Aśru-Mālā* (অশ্রু-মালা), a much appreciated collection of poems, in 1895. In the preface to the second edition of the volume the publisher called him worthy of a special place among the very first Bengali-Muslim writers who accepted the Bengali language as their mother tongue and tirelessly served and nurtured it all their lives:

> যে সকল মুসলমান লেখক সৰ্ব্ব প্রথম বাংলা ভাষাকে মাতৃ ভাষা রুপে বরন করিয়া তাহার পরিচর্য্যায় আজিবন অক্লান্ত ভাবে খাটিয়াছেন, কবি কায়কোবাদ সাহেব তাহাদের আগে . . . স্থান পাইবার উপযুক্ত।[70]

Kaikobad himself claimed no special credit for serving the Bengali language. He termed his effort an elegy and dedicated it to some long lost love of his. As a result, some intensely lachrymose verses such as *Prem Sangit* (প্রেম সঙ্গিত),[71] *Prem Pratimā* (প্রেম প্রতিমা)[72] and *Pranair Pratham Chumban* (প্রনয়ের প্রথম চুম্বন)[73] found place in *Aśru-Mālā*. However, six poems in the collection were compiled under a head called *Jātia* (জাতীয়) or "national." Here we find the poet taking a radical departure from romantic sorrow. Now we have Kaikobad beating out very different verses and loudly bemoaning the lost glories of the Muslims of India. One of the poems in the section, *Moslem Śmaśān Purātan Dillī* (মোসলেম শ্মশান পুরাতন

দিল্লী), is a threnody to the past splendour of Old Delhi. The once imperial capital appeared to Kaikobad a cremation ground, *Śmaśān*, of all that the Muslims of India had lost, hence the title. Old Delhi was where the spiritual wealth of the Muslims was incinerated, it was the site where the standard of Muslim glory was deluged away (by time?). Kaikobad saw the old mansions crumbling and overgrown with shrubs and creepers. Wild trees now rose ripping through their walls. The sights tormented the poet's spirit so much that he felt like giving up his life:

> অই স্থানে মোসলেমের অপার্থিব ধন
> ভস্মিভুত চিরতরে ভিষন অনলে!
> অই স্থানে ইশ্লামের গৌরব কেতন
> ভাষীয়া গিয়াছে হায় প্লাবনের জলে![74]
> হর্ম্ম্যগুলি একে একে গিয়াছে ভাঙ্গিয়া,
> চারি দিকে কত ক্ষুদ্র ঝোপ, কত গুল্ম লতা
> উঠিয়াছে বন্য বৃক্ষ প্রাচির ভেদিয়া,[75] . . .
> সে দৃশ্য দেখিলে প্রানে কি গভীর ক্লেশ
> ইচ্ছা হয় এ পরান দেই লুটাইয়া![76]

The intensity of the pain notwithstanding, Kaikobad overcame the death wish to continue on his creative career. Kaikobad resorted to the cremation ground metaphor again in 1904 when he published his grand epic poem *Mahā-śmaśān* (মহাশ্মশান). This imposing, more than a thousand page, exertion by the poet was a paean to the crushing defeat inflicted by the Afghan arms upon the Marathas in 1761. Kaikobad, however, did not seek to glorify his Muslim protagonists by presenting the Hindus as timid and faint hearted. The first edition of his work carried the following lengthy preamble:

> I have attacked no community in this poem of mine. The Hindus attack the Muslims unprovoked (in their writings), earn accolades

by ushering them on stage as peons and *chaprāsīs*, coolies and labourers and douse the resentment in their hearts by calling them sweet names such as *bhuru chāchā* and *neḍe māmā*. I have not treated the Hindus similarly. My co-religionists might call me bad for not picturing the Hindus in mean colours. But I cannot violate the truth. However, I am a Muslim and whether I have sympathies and a leaning of the heart for the Muslims, those who are capable of analysing poetry and entering a poet's heart will know, the rest will not.

What do the Muslims gain if the Hindus are shown as unmanly, drenched in the colours of cowardice? Does Muslim gallantry lie in slaying cowards? A fox can be killed by even women, but it takes brave men to hunt lions. That is why I have not observed parsimony in depicting the bravery of the Hindus. I have only enhanced the bravery of the victorious Muslims by truthfully rendering the terrifying gallantry of the Hindus. The Muslim is a brave man, so is the Hindu, the warm blood of the two brave races has committed their glory and bravery to the eternal annals of history. The tales of their gallant deeds will testify to their courage as long the earth endures and history lasts. This redounds to the glory of both the races. But Hindus are the conquered and vanquished while the Muslims are the victors and anointed with the glory of victory.

আমার এই কাব্যে আমি কোন সম্প্রদায়ের লোককেই আক্রমন করি নাই; হিন্দুলেখকগন যেমন মুসলমানদ্গিকে অযথা আক্রমন করিয়া, তাহাদ্গিকে পিয়ন চাপরাশী কুলি মজুররুপে রঙ্গমঞ্চে আনয়ন করিয়া বাহবা লাইয়াছেন ভুরু চাচা, নেড়ে মামা ইত্যাদি মধুর সম্ভাষনে আপ্যায়িত করিয়া মনের ক্ষোভ মিটাইয়াছেন, আমি হিন্দুদিগের প্রতি তেমন ব্যেবহার করি নাই... হিন্দুদ্গিকে হিনবর্ণে চিত্রিত করি নাই বলিয়া আমার স্বজাতিয় ভ্রাতৃগন আমাকে মন্দ বলিতে পারেন। কিন্তু সত্যের অপবাদ করিবার অধিকার ত আমার নাই। তবে আমি মুসলমান, মুসলমানদিগের প্রতি আমার সহানুভুতি ও হৃদয়ের টান আছে কি না, তাহা যিনি কাব্য বিশ্লেষন করিয়া কবি হৃদয়ে প্রবেশ করিতে সক্ষম তিনিই বুঝিতে পারিবেন, অন্যের পক্ষে দুরাশা।

বিশেষতঃ হিন্দুদ্গিকে কাপুরুষ সাজাইয়া, ভিরুতার বর্নে রঞ্জিত করিয়া মুসলমানদিগের কি লাভ ? কাপুরুষ বধে মুসলমানদিগের কি বিরত্ব? শৃগাল বধকরিতে রমনীরাও পারে, সিংহ বধ করিতে বিরেরই দরকার; তাই হিন্দুদিগের বিরত্ব প্রদর্শন করিতে আমি কৃপণতা করি নাই। আমি তাহাদিগের সেই ভিষন বিরত্ব যথাযথ ভাবে চিত্রিত করিয়া বিজয়ী মুসলমান বীর পুরুষদিগের বীরত্বের মাত্রা আরও অধিক বৃদ্ধি

করিয়াছি। মুসলমানগন বীর পুরুষ, হিন্দুগনও বীর পুরুষ, এই দুই বীর জাতি হৃদয়ের উষ্ণ শোনিতে আপনাদিগের জাতিয় গৌরব ও ভীষন বীরত্ব কালের অক্ষয় পটে লিখিয়া গিয়াছেন; যত দিন পৃথিবী থাকিবে, ইতিহাস থাকিবে, ইহাদিগের বিরত্ব ও জাতীয় গৌরবের কথা ততদিন, তাহার সাক্ষ্য প্রদান করিবে। ইহা উভয় জাতির পক্ষে গৌরবের কথা, তবে হিন্দুগন বিজিত ও বিধ্বস্ত, মুসলমানগন জয়দৃপ্ত ও বিজয় গৌরবে সম্মানিত।[77]

The introduction to the second edition elaborated why he had chosen to write the epic:

For long, I have nurtured a desire in my heart to compose a war epic on the courage and gallantry of the Indian Muslims after reading which the Bengal Muslims will be able to claim with pride that once the Indian Muslims were peerlessly brave . . . that is why, as relics of their past glory, whatever deeds and memories I have found, I have limned with the brush of my poetry and held before the eyes of my readers and tried amply to awake faint memories of their past glory.

আমি বহু দিন যাবত মনে মনে এই আশাটি পোষন করিতে ছিলাম যে ভারতিয় মুসলমানদের শৌর্য্য বীর্য্য সঙ্কলিত এমন একটি যুদ্ধ কাব্য লিখিয়া যাইব, যাহা পাঠ করিয়া বঙ্গিয় মুসলমানগন স্পর্দ্ধা করিয়া বলিতে পারেন যে এক সময়ে ভারতীয় মুসলমানগনও অদ্বিতীয় মহাবীর ছিলেন...তাই তাহাদের অতীত গৌরব নিদর্শন স্বরুপ যেখানে যে কীর্ত্তিটুকু যেখানে যে স্মৃতিটুকু পাইয়াছি, তাহাই কবি-তুলিকায় অঙ্কিত করিয়া পাঠকদের চক্ষের সামনে উপস্থিত করিয়াছি, এবং তাহাদের সেই অতিত গৌরবের ক্ষীন স্মৃতিটুকু জাগাইয়া দিতে বহু চেষ্টা করিয়াছি।[78]

Despite the above expostulation, Kaikobad unwittingly points to us that the terrain of thought we are out to explore is full of surprises, revealing a brook now, a glad^ then. Kaikobad had apparently imbibed so much of the Sanskritic imagery that we also see him imagining Islam as a mother goddess. His Islam is evoked as a demon slaying Hindu goddess holding the *Qur'ān* in one hand and dispatching *kāfirs* with another:

পাপ তাপ হারিনী কাফের মর্দিনী
  শত্রু সংহারিনী
  ভীমা!
কোরান ধারিনী অধর্ম নাশিনী
  অতুল গৌরবময়ী
  বামা![79]

Thus, Kaikobad too was no different from his Hindu and Muslim peers of the age in his emotional complexity. His voice never lost inflections as he went about telling this tale of Muslim triumph, nor did he flinch from introducing counterpoints to his thesis. There is evidence in *Mahāśmaśān* that Kaikobad tried sufficiently to view the course of events through the eyes of his Hindu protagonists. For example, on the eve of the battle he has Peshwa Sadashiv compose and dispatch a letter to the Mughal Emperor Shah Shuja. "I can bear this pain no more," he wrote. "The cup brims over, there is no more room in it, do what you must now. A terrible storm will blow over this battlefield moments later, then there will be no time left to say or to listen. India's fate will be incinerated forever in that conflagration, the sun of India's glory will set forever. We two races of Hindus and Muslims are the beloved sons of India. Blinded by petty selfishness we shed each other's blood, we erode our strength day by day. Because of the error of our deeds, soon our mother will be fettered, her glorious crown will fall at the feet of Ahmed. If we are to lose this battle, if the Maharashtra sun slides into darkness forever, what does the Indian Muslim gain, the throne of India? The foreign Ahmed will rob India for all his life. The crown of India will grace Ahmed's head. Why do you degrade yourself nurturing delusions and false hopes? We must be bound in truce with the Indian Muslims, living as brothers, we must rule the country together. We have no quarrel with Ahmed Shah, let him return to his country":

সদাশিব ক্ষিপ্র হস্তে লিখিতে লাগিলা
সেষ পত্র অতি ত্রস্তে সুজার নিকটে,
"পারিনে-পারিনে আর সহিতে যন্ত্রনা,
পরিপূর্ন পাত্র এবে, বিন্দুমাত্র স্থান
নাহি আর; যা কর্ত্তব্য করিবে এখনি।
কিছুক্ষন পরে আজি যে ভিষন ঝড়
উঠিবে এ রণক্ষেত্রে, হায় সে সময়ে
কহিবার শুনিবার ক্ষণমাত্র আর
রহিবে না অবসর, জনমের মত
সে অনলে অভাগিনি ভারতের ভাগ্য
যাইবে জস্বলিয়া, হায় যাইবে ডুবিয়া
ভারত-গৌরব-সূর্য্য অতল সাগরে।
আমরা উভয়জাতি হিন্দু মুসলমান
ভারতের প্রিয়পুত্র, তুচ্ছস্বার্থ তরে
অন্ধ হয়ে, না বুঝিয়া বৃথা রক্তপাতে
দিন দিন ধ্বংসিতেছি শক্তি আপনার
আমাদের কার্য্যে-দোষে অচিরে জননী
হইবে শৃঙ্খল্যাবদ্ধ, মহিমা-মণ্ডিত
মাথার মুকুট তার পড়িবে খসিয়া
আমাদের পদতলে জনমের মত।
মানিলাম তর্কস্বলে এ মহাসমরে
আমাদেরি পরাজয়, মহারাষ্ট্র রবি
যদিও ডুবিয়া যায় চির অন্ধকারে,
ভারতিয় মোসলেমের কি লাভ তাহাতে ?
বিদেশী আমেদ সাহা, চরণে তাহার
লুন্ঠিবে ভারতবর্ষ জনমের তরে।
ভারতিয় মুসলমান পাইবে কি কভু
ভারতের সিংহাসন ? ভারত-মুকুট
শোভিবে নিশ্চয় সেই আমাদের শিরে।
না বুঝে দুরাশা ছলে কেন অধঃপাতে
যাইতেছ? ভারতিয় মোসলেমের সনে
সন্ধি সূত্রে থাকি বন্ধ, ভাই ভাই মত
এক যোগে এই ভারত করিব শাসন।

আমেদ সাহার সনে বাদ বিসম্বাদ
নাহি আমাদের, তিনি স্বদেশে আপন
যান চলি এই ইচ্ছা আমাদের মনে।"[80]

There were other Muslim authors who were inspired by the theme of war. Syed Abdul Hosain published the *Sirājuddaulā Upanyās* (সিরাজউদ্দৌলা উপন্যাস) in 1905 seeking to redeem the character of the last Nawab of Bengal. The battle which unseated the last Nawab also inspired Abdul Hamid Khan Usufjai, the editor of *Ahmadī*, the journal which had originally published Hosain's *Go-Jiban*. His collection of verse, *Udāsi* (উদাসি), published in 1900, contained the poem *Nabhosthal* (নভস্থল). Usufjai evoked the memories of Plassey in the poem and indicted the Hindu and the Muslim in equal measure for the foolishness which put them in chains:

দেখাইবে পলাশির রন সজ্জা চাতুরির
দেখাইবে সে মোসলেমের রবি অস্ত হায়!!
হীন্দু মোসলেমে মিলে নিজ বেড়ি নিজে নিলে
নিজে দিলে কি শৃংখল তুলিয়া গলায়!![81]

Usufjai definitely sought regeneration for the Muslim but not by presenting the Hindu as malformed and malevolent.

Mojammel Haq, plucked at almost the same notes as Ususfjai. For him too the redemption of the Muslim did not involve tarring the Hindu. He wrote the poems of his collection *Jātiya Foārā* (জাতিয় ফোয়ারা) in the last decade of the nineteenth century and the early years of the twentieth. He advised his fellow Muslims to be firm in faith and action and strive for the ascent of the community:

স্বধর্ম পালিয়া স্বকাজে থাকিয়া
জাতিয় উন্নতি সাধে[82]

But Haq could be scathing on his community too. He did

not quail from asking his co-religionists as to how living under the same regime as the Hindus they could be so far behind them:

হিন্দু ভ্রাতৃগন আনন্দে কেমন
সহ ধনমান সংসার জীবণ
স্বদেশে বীদেশে করিছে খেপণ
হেরে বিমোহিত মণ।
এ দেখেও কি হে সুপথে আসিতে
যায় না—মজে না চিত . . .।[83]

In their apparent catholicity towards the Hindu, the likes of Usufjai and Haq seem to have been cultivated by a trend that had been at work for about four decades. They were individuals in whom the Bengali and Muslim halves of their identities appear to have attained a firm overlap. The Bengali-Muslim's consciousness now spanned the two halves of his identity more confidently. The Bengali language had been laid claim upon, the likes of Kaikobad had also fostered pride in the past of Indian Islam and its conquests. Now was the time to improve the temporal fortunes of the community. As half of the first decade of the twentieth century wore out, we see the journal *Islām Prachārak* (ইসলাম প্রচারক) frequently voicing this concern.

Islām Prachārak published the first part of the essay *Unnatir Upāy Ki?* (উন্নতির উপায় কি?) in 1902–3, its Chaitra-Baishakh issue. The writer, one Sheikh Fazlul Karim, raged against the state the Muslims had fallen into:

> We have received the name "fallen Muslims" for some days. The poet's verse, the speaker's garrulity, the pomposity of the writer's pen pushing, and the assessment of the general state of the society, have made this a settled notion. But the issue is how long will the name "fallen" endure? How will our path to advancement be eased.
> ''পতিত মুসলমান'' নামটা আমরা অনেক দিন হইতেই পাইয়াছি। কবির কাব্যে,

বক্তার গলাবাজিতে, লেখকের মসী-লেপনের আড়ম্বরে এবং সমাজের সাধারন অবস্থা পর্য্যালোচনা করিতে করিতে ধারনাটাও জমিয়া গিয়াছে। কিন্তু কথা হইতেছে,—এ "পতিত" নামটা আর কতদিন থাকিবে ?—এখন কেমন করিয়া আমাদের উন্নতির পথ প্রশস্ত হইবে,—তাই।[84]

The article suggested a somewhat bellicose religiosity as the solution to the galling issue:

> The warm blood of religion must be run through our society, a part of our lives must be expended for the world (*duniā*). . . . Today there is no one to administer medicine to our disease weakened society, the servants of our society are not getting medication these days.
>
> . . . আমাদের সমাজের শরীরে ধর্ম্মের উষ্ণ রক্ত স্রোত বহাইতে হইবে; "দুনিয়ার" জন্যও আমাদের জিবনের এক অংশ ক্ষয় করিতে হইবে।
>
> . . . আজ আমাদের রোগ-ক্লিষ্ট সমাজের ঔষধ খাওয়াইবার কেহই নাই; আজ আমাদের সমাজ সেবকগন পথ্য পাইতেছেন না।[85]

Islām Prachārak's next number published the remainder of the article which continued to dwell on the issue. The author observed some distressing realities all around:

> . . . The Hindu is supreme everywhere, the Muslim is slave in all places. We cannot blame the Hindu too much for this. We do not depend on our strength and valour. We have lost our national life and national unity but aspire to equality of honour.
>
> . . . হিন্দু, সকল স্থানেই প্রধান মুসলমান সকল স্থানেই গোলাম। এজন্য আমরা হিন্দুকে বেশী দোষ দিতে পারি না। কারন নিজের বল-বির্য্যের উপর আমাদের আত্মা নির্ভরতা নাই। আমরা জাতীয় জীবন ও জাতীয় একতা হারা; অথচ সমান সম্মান পাইবার অভিলাষী।[86]

Having made this discovery the author went on to make some social and political observations. He also acknowledged the senselessness of what he saw:

Why does the Hindu loath us today? Not just because of the equality, affability and freedom of English rule but because of the vacuousness of our nationalism. But if the Hindus understand that Muslims are their close kin and neighbours, that they have had their salt for a long time, only then will they (Hindus) cease to be perfidious towards their country. Realising the fundamental necessity of Muslim strength to India's advancement, they will invite us of their own. It is to be deplored that even among the *Congresswālās* there are some who abhor the Muslims and think much of themselves for it. I do not know when the curtain will descend upon this horrid drama of Hindu-Muslim national differences.

Today there are no (worthy) people in Muslim society. As ragged beggars they look to the Hindu to make the government heed the stories of their sorrow and penury. To what extent the result has been as expected, we all know.

. . . In these evil times, tethered by the same chain, Hindu-Muslim controversies are doubtless idiocy and a betrayal of the salt.

আজ হিন্দু, আমাদিগকে কেন ঘৃণা করে ? কেবল ইংরেজ রাজত্বের সাম্য মৈত্রী স্বাধীনতার দোহাই বলে নয়,—আমাদের জাতীয়তার অন্তঃসার শুন্যতার জন্য। কিন্তু হিন্দু যদি বুঝিতে পারে, মুসলমান তাহাদের নিকট আত্মীয় এবং প্রতিবাসী; অনেক দিন তাহারা মুসলমানের নিমক খাইয়াছে; তবেই তাহাদের স্বদেশ দ্রোহিতা ঘুচিবে। ভারতের উন্নতির মূলে মুসলমান শক্তির আবশ্যকতা বুঝিয়া আপনা হইতেই আমাদিগকে ডাকিয়া লইবে। বড় পরিতাপের বিষয়, কংগ্রেস ওয়ালাদের মধ্যেও অনেকে মুসলমানকে ঘৃণা করিয়া, আপনাদিগকে বাহাদুর মনে করে। জানি না, হিন্দু মুসলমানের জাতিগত পার্থকের এই ঘৃণিত নাটকের কতদিনে যবনিকা পতন হইবে।

আজ মুসলমান সমাজে লোক নাই। আজ দীনহীন ফকিরের বেশে হিন্দুর মুখ চাহিয়া, তাহারা নিজেদের দুঃখ দারিদ্রের কথা গবর্ণমেণ্টের কর্ণগোচর করিতেছে। ইহার ফল কতদূর আশানুরূপ হইতেছে, তাহা সকলেই জানিতে পারিতেছেন।

. . . এই দুর্দ্দিনে, একই শৃঙ্খলে শৃঙ্খলিত হইয়া হিন্দুর মুসলমান বিদ্বেষ নিতান্তই মূঢ়তা ও নিমখারামি পরিচারক, সন্দেহ নাই।[87]

The quest for *unnati*, or advancement, ended with this call to unity:

We are no more fallen Muslims. We are no more penniless *faqīrs*.

> Like the rest, we are an unfearing, progressive, industrious race. God's blessing has graced our crown after a long time.
> . . . Brother Muslims! Come, assemble beneath the national standard of the crescent—let us unite around this centre today, let us all be initiated into the same vow, let us all have our initiation with the same *mantra.* Think of it, every district of this huge Bengal country together forms the enormous Muslim society. Just as by agitating our limbs we fulfil our needs, similarly, unless we, the limbs of our society, agitate and awake, there is no advancement.
> আমরা আর সেই পতিত মুসলমান নহি। আমরা আর সে দীন হীন ফকির নহি। আমরাও অন্যের মত বিক্রান্ত উন্নত কর্ম্মবীর জাতি। দেবতার আশীর্ব্বাদ অনেক দিন পরে মস্তকে পড়িয়াছে।
> . . . ভাই মুসলমান! আইস, অর্দ্ধচন্দ্রাঙ্কিত জাতীয় পতাকার তলে আইস—আজ একই কেন্দ্রে আমরা একত্রিত হই; আজ একই মন্ত্রে আমরা দীক্ষিত হই। ভাবিয়া দেখ, আমাদের প্রত্যেক জেলা লইয়া এই বিশাল বঙ্গ দেশের বিরাট মুসলমান সমাজ গঠিত। আমাদের হাত পা নড়িলে যেমন সমস্ত শরীর আলোড়িত ও অভাব পূর্ণ হয়, তেমনি আমাদের সমাজের অঙ্গ প্রত্যঙ্গ—আমরা না নাড়িলে, আমরা না জাগিলে, আমাদের উন্নতি নাই।[88]

It its Magh (January–February), 1905 issue *Islām Prachārak* tried to delve into the Hindu loathing for Muslims. An article entitled "Sottoi Ki Musalmān Ghrinār Pātra?" (সত্যই কি মুসলমান ঘৃণার পাত্র ?) by Usman Ali brought the following to the notice of the readers:

> . . . All Hindus turn up their noses with ghastly hatred and disregard hearing the mere name "Muslim."
> . . . হিন্দু মাত্রেই সাধারণতঃ মুসলমানের নাম শ্রবন করিবা মাত্র উৎকট ঘৃনা ও অবজ্ঞায় নাসিকা কুঞ্চিত করিয়া থাকেন।[89]

But Muslims obviously deserved better. Usman Ali attempted to convince Hindus of this by rather aggressively suggesting that it is actually the Muslims who are closer to "true" Hinduism. Ali referred to an article, *Baidik Juger āchār Byebhār* (বৈদিক জুগের আচার ব্যেবহার), recently published in some journal called *Bangabhāṣā* (বঙ্গভাষা) wherein a contrast had been drawn between contemporary and Vedic Hinduism. The author of the article, said Ali, had established by studying the Vedas and *śāstras* that the ancient Aryans observed no caste differences. Further, they ate all that could be digested, cows, buffaloes, pigs and fowl. The article also, Ali claimed, pointed out the Hindus' great fall from grace as they had deviated from monotheism and taken to superstitious idolatry. The author of this article had also proved the absence of the *upavita* (sacred thread) in the Vedic age:

> অতঃপর আচার ব্যেবহারের কথা। বঙ্গভাযা দ্বিতীয় ভাগ আষাঢ় শ্রাবন সংখ্যায় "বৈদিক জুগের আচার ব্যেবহার" শীর্ষক অতি গবেষনা পুর্ণ একটি সুন্দর প্রবন্ধ প্রকাশিত হইয়াছে; তাহাতে লেখক বেদাদি বহু শাস্ত্র গ্রন্থ হইতে প্রমান করিয়াছেন যে, পুরাকালে আর্যদের মধ্যে জাতিভেদ ছিল না, গো মহিষ মেষ বরাহ কুকুট প্রভৃতি কোন হজমি বস্তুই অনাদেয় ছিল না . . . সেই বৈদিক জুগের সহিত বর্তমান জুগের তুলনা করিয়া লেখক দেখাইছেন যে হিন্দুদিগের মহা পতন হইয়াছে, পবিত্র একেশ্বরবাদের স্থানে কু-সংস্কার পুর্ণ পৌত্তলিকতা স্থান পাইয়াছে . . . তিনি আরও প্রমান করিয়াছেন যে, বেদিক জুগে উপবিত ছিল না . . .।[90]

Ali reminded the Hindus that they buried their dead in the days of yore. He asked his brother Hindus if they still commit their dead to the earth. The Hindus had given up on this ancient way, but the Muslims still buried their dead as decreed by their scriptures:

> তোমাদের মধ্যে প্রাচিনকালে মৃতদেহের সমাধি হইত। . . . ভাই হিন্দু। তুমি এখন কি মৃতদেহ প্রোথিত কর ? নিশ্চই কর না। কিন্তু আমরা আমাদের শাস্ত্র মতে মৃতদেহ যথারিতি সমাহিত করিয়া থাকি।[91]

The Muslims were thus closer to Vedic Hinduism than the present day Hindus. They observed no caste and were monotheists. And, of course, the Muslims buried their dead. Ali drew his article to a close sounding quite cocky:

... If the aforementioned practices existed only in the Vedic age, and since we act in accordance with them, you concede that we are like those of the Vedic age.

. . . উল্লিখিত বিষয়গুলি যদি কেবল বৈদিক যুগেই আচরিত হইত, তবে আমরা তৎসমুদয় আচরন করি বলিয়া আমরা নিতান্তই বৈদিক যুগের লোক স্বীকারই করিতেছ।[92]

Ali urged the Hindus to contemplate and realise that the Muslims are in no manner inferior, nor do they deserve hate and disregard:

. . . এখন বিবেচনা করিয়া দেখ, মুসলমান কোন মতেই, বা কোন বিষয়েই হীন বা অবজ্ঞার পাত্র নহে।[93]

However, by the end of 1905, the tone of the journal had changed dramatically. We witness no more platitudes in its pages. The anti-partition agitation had caught on and the writers of *Islām Prachārak* spared only the severest censure for Hindus and advised caution to their co-religionists. The Paush issue of the journal carried the article *Banga-Bibhāg O Swadeśi Āndolan* (বঙ্গ-বিভাগ ও স্বদেশি আন্দোলন) authored by someone who called himself Ebne Mauza:

The cunning of the Hindus has hassled us on many occasions and deprived us of our wealth and lives. When the terrible conflagration of the sepoy mutiny engulfed all India in 1857, behind it all too were the clever Hindus. . . . In the end, the Muslims' fate was undone, the glory of the Mughals was extinguished for ever.

হিন্দুগনের চতুরতায় আমরা অনেক সময়েই বিড়ম্বিত হইয়াছি ও ধনে প্রানে মারা পড়িয়াছি। এই ১৮৫৭ খৃঃ অব্দে সিপাহি বিদ্রোহের ভিষন অগ্নি সমগ্র ভারত সত্ব প্রজ্জস্বলিত হইয়া উঠিয়াছিল, উহার মুলেও ছিলেন সুচতুর হিন্দুগন। . . . কিন্তু কার্য্যকালে মুসলমানেরই কপাল পুড়ি—মোগলের—গৌরব চিরদিনের জন্য অস্তমিত হইল।[94]

The Muslims could not trust Hindu politics anymore

because of their experience with representative institutions:

> The affection that existed between Hindus and Muslims in the countryside earlier is now no more. The chief cause behind this is the English educated babus' generosity and devotion to duty!! The loathsome depiction of Muslims in theatre has had dreadful consequences. Hate between communities is growing by the day, Hindu writers, editors, and orators are fanning it.
>
> Have our Hindu brothers made a fair use of the right to self rule granted to us by the generous British government? Witnessing the transactions of the Districts Boards, Local Boards, Union Committee and Municipality we sigh in disappointment. Did the government extend self rule to the masses of this country so that the Hindus could realise their selfish ends? Hindu "generosity" has kept even a single Muslim from being Municipal Commissioner, it has ensured that the no proper roads have been laid in the Muslim neighbourhoods, but what beautiful streets there are where the babus dwell!
>
> পূর্ব্বে পল্লিগ্রামের হিন্দু-মুসলমানের মধ্যে যে সদ্ভাব ছিল, এখন আর তাহা নাই। এহার প্রধান কারন উচ্চ ইংরাজি শিক্ষিত বাবু গনের কর্ত্তব্য নিষ্ঠা ও উদারতা!! থিয়েটার সমুহে মুসলমান চিত্র অতি ঘৃণিত ভাবে প্রদর্শিত হওয়াতে, উহার ফল আরও ভয়ঙ্কর হইয়াছে। দিন দিনই এই সাম্প্রদায়িক বিদ্বেষ বাড়িতেছে, হিন্দু লেখক, সম্পাদক ও বক্তাগন তাহাতে আরও বাতাস দিতেছেন।
>
> এই যে উদারনীতি ব্রিটীশ গবর্নমেণ্ট আমাদ্গিকে স্বায়ত্ত-শাসনের অধিকার প্রদান করিয়াছিলেন, হিন্দু ভ্রাতৃগন কি তাহার সদ্বব্যেবহার করিয়াছিলেন ? ডিষ্ট্রেক্ট বোর্ড, লোকাল বোর্ড, ইউনিয়ন কমিটি ও মিউনিসিপ্যালিটীর কার্য্যকলাপ দর্শনে আমাদ্গিকে একেবারে নিরাশার দীর্ঘ নিশ্বাস পরিত্যাগ করিতে হয়। গবর্নমেণ্ট কি কেবল হিন্দুদিগের স্বার্থ সাধন জন্যাই স্বায়ত্ত শাসনের ক্ষমতা এ দেশবাসিকে দিয়াছিলেন ? হিন্দু উদারতায় কখনও এক জন মুসলমান মিউনিসিপ্যাল কমিশনর হইতে পারেন নাই; হিন্দু উদারতায় মুসলমান পল্লিতে উপযুক্ত রাস্তা ঘাট কখনই নির্ম্মিত হয় নাই—কিন্তু বাবুদিগের বাস পল্লিতে কেমন সুন্দর রাস্তার বন্দোবস্ত![95]

Hence, the agitation was to be shunned and complete faith invested in the government:

> If the Hindus had genuinely treated us well, had displayed us

sympathy, then in simple faith we would have regarded the Hindus our well-wishers. But now our eyes are opened, we know the extent of their Muslim-love. We will no more be swindled by them and invite trouble for ourselves. We will do nothing unpleasant to the government. Our devotion towards the British government is unshakeable. Though the foreign policy of the English is somewhat against our national interests, but their India policy is wholly in our favour—this we must acknowledge in an uninhibited tone.

হিন্দুগন যদি বাস্তবিক আমাদের প্রতি সদ্বব্যেবহার করিতেন—আমাদের প্রতি সহানুভুতি প্রদর্শন করিতেন, তাহা হইলে আমরা সরল বিশ্বাসের বশবর্ত্তী হইয়া হিন্দুদ্গিকে আমাদের হিতকাঙ্ক্ষিই মনে করিতাম; কিন্তু এক্ষনে আমাদের চক্ষু ফুটিয়াছে—আমরা তাহাদের মুসলমান-প্রিতির পরিমান বেশ বুঝিতে পারিতেছি। আমরা আর তাহাদের ধোকায় পড়িয়া আপনাদের বিপদ ডাকিয়া আনিব না। আমরা গবর্নমেণ্টের অপ্রীতিকর কোনও কার্য্যই করিব না। ব্রিটিশ গবর্নমেণ্টের প্রতি আমাদের ভক্তি অচলা। যদিও ইংরেজের পররাষ্ট্রণীতি কতকটা আমাদের জাতিয় স্বার্থের প্রতিকুল, কিন্তু ভারতের স্বরাষ্ট্রনীতি আমাদের সম্পূর্ণ অনুকুল—একথা আমরা মুক্তকন্ঠে বলিতে বাধ্য।[96]

All the above pieces by various authors point towards a deepening distrust between the Hindus and the Muslims. The unfolding course of events was driving the Muslims to one singular emotional, psychological conviction—"we must place our trust in the British and be loyal to them while simultaneously being aware of the anti-Muslim machinations of the Hindus." As we reach the end of our story and recall the songs of Girindramohini and Kaliprasanna, we realise that their notes were to be deadened soon. Contrary to what Girindramohini had expected, no unbreakable fraternal bonds were emerging to bind the Hindu and the Muslim. Kaliprasanna's *Musalmāni Bānglā* too had clearly failed to charm the Muslims. The minstrelsy of Girindramohini and Kaliprasanna had been futile after all. They had sung their songs too late.

References

1. Rafiuddin Ahmed, *The Bengal Muslims. 1871–1906. A Quest for Identity*, sec. edn. New Delhi: OUP, 1988, p. 58.
2. Ibid., p. 124.
3. *The Sacred and the Secular: Bengal Muslim Discourses, 1871–1977*. Calcutta: OUP, 1995, p. 50.
4. See *The Bengal Muslims*, p. 115.
5. Issue dated 18 April 1895. Nehru Memorial Museum and Library.
6. *The Bengal Muslims*, p. 128.
7. *The Moslem Chronicle*, 1 March 1900.
8. Dhurjati Prasad De, *Bengal Muslims in Search of Social Identity, 1905–47*. Dhaka: The University Press Limited, 1998, p. 50.
9. Ibid., pp. 50–52.
10. See Dr Qazi Abdul Mannan, *Ādhunik Bānglā Sāhitye Muslim Sādhanā* (আধুনিক বাংলা সাহিত্যে মুসলিম সাধনা). Dhaka: Student Ways, 1969, p. 240.
11. Ibid., p. 346.
12. In the cryptic words of Suniti Kumar Chatterji, the educated Muslims did not "take kindly" to the language any more. *The Origin and Development of the Bengali Language*, p. 212.
13. *Bhāngāprān* (ভাঙ্গাপ্রান), published by Mohammad Yusuf Ali, printed by Shri Baikunthanath Sircar, Dhaka, 1927, p. ii.
14. Ibid.
15. Ibid., p. iv.
16. Ibid., p. 1.
17. Ibid., p. 3.
18. Ibid., p. 10.
19. See *Duṣprāpya Sāhitya Sangraha*, Dwitīya Khanda, pp. 486–504.
20. See Anisujjaman, *Muslim-Mānas O Bāngla Sāhitya (1757–1918)*, p. 197.
21. See *Ādhunik Bānglā Sāhitye Muslim Sādhanā*, p. 214.
22. Ibid., 327.
23. See *Ādhunik Bānglā Sāhitye Muslim Sādhanā*, p. 218.
24. Dr Bishnu Dey and Kamalendu Dhar, eds., *Mīr Mośarraf Hosain Rachanāsaṅgraha* (মীর মশাররফ হোসেন রচনাসংগ্রহ). Calcutta: Kamal Sahitya Bhavan, 1978, p. 361.
25. Ibid., p. 362.
26. Ibid., p. 363.
27. Ibid, p. 364.
28. Ibid., p. 365.
29. Ibid., p. 367.
30. Ibid., p. 368.

31. Ibid., p. 369.
32. Ibid., p. 370.
33. Ibid.
34. Ibid., p. 372.
35. Ibid.
36. Ibid., p. 373.
37. Ibid.
38. Ibid., p. 374.
    The Bangladeshi novelist Humayun Ahmad too alludes to a certain prejudice against beef in his memoirs. Recounting his childhood in Sylhet in the 1960s, he tells us that a visiting son-in-law was never served beef. The reason being that beef was not regarded "respectable" meat. Serving a son-in-law beef was tantamount to insulting him. The right menu for him were fish heads and mutton: খাবার সময় জানাইয়ের পাতে তুলে দেয়া হবে মাছের মাথা...ক্ষেত্রবিশেষ খাষির মাংস। গরুর মাংস কখনো না। গরুর মাংস জাতের মাংস না। জামাইয়ের পাতে গরুর মাংস দেয়া জামাইকে অপমান করার মত অপরাধ।
    See *Kichu Śaiśab* (কিছু শৈশব), Anyaprokash, Dhaka, 2007, p.77.
    We should not be surprised if Hosain's *Go-Jiban* was actually the expression and rationalisation of a cultural prejudice against beef eating that already existed among sections of the Bengali-Muslim society.
39. It was a three volume work published over seven years. The first volume *Mohurram* (মহরম) was published in 1885, the second *Uddhār* (উদ্ধার) in 1887 and the third *Ezid-Badh* (এজিদ-বধ) in 1891.
40. *Bīṣād-Śindhu* (বিষাদ-ষিন্ধু), Mir Mosarraf Hosain. New Delhi: IMH Press Pvt. Limited, 1999, p. iv.
41. Ibid., p. 9.
42. Ibid., p. 14.
43. For example, see p. 57.
44. Ibid., p. 142.
45. Ibid., p. 143.
46. Dr Qazi Abdul Mannan, ed., *Mośorraf Rachanā-Sambhār* (মশাররফ রচনা-সম্ভার), vol. 2. Dhaka: Bangla Academy, 1980, p. 564.
47. Ibid., p. 365.
48. Ibid., p. 366.
49. Ibid., p. 367.
50. Ibid., p. 368.
51. Ibid., p. 369.
52. Ibid., p. 370.
53. Published 1897.
54. Dr Qazi Abdul Mannan, ed., *Mośorraf Rachanā-Sambhār* (মশাররফ রচনা-সম্ভার). Dhaka: Bangla Academy, 1984 , vol. 3, p.383.
55. Ibid., p. 384.

56. Ibid., p.104. *Neḍe* literally means "shaven headed." It was a commonly used pejorative for Muslims by Bengali-Hindus.
57. Ibid., pp. 169–70.
58. Ibid., pp. 200–201.
59. Nausher Ali Khan Usufji, *Bangiya Musalmān,* (বঙ্গিয় মুসলমান, নওসের আলি খাঁ ইউসফজী). Calcutta: Hindu Press, 1890, p. 4.
60. Ibid., p. 28.
61. Ibid., p. 31.
62. Ibid., pp. 34–35.
63. Ibid., p. 35.
64. Ibid., p. 56.
65. Ibid., p. 59.
66. Ibid.
67. Ibid., p. 60.
68. See *Ādhunik Bānglā Kābye Hindu-Musalmān Samparka, 1857–1920,* p. 305.
69. Ibid., p. 308.
70. *Aśru-Mālā* (অশ্রু-মালা), published by Abdul Khayer Saifuddin Ahmed, sec. edn., Dhaka, 1914.
71. Ibid., p. 63.
72. Ibid., p. 67.
73. Ibid., p. 93.
74. Ibid., p. 150.
75. Ibid., p. 152.
76. Ibid., p. 153.
77. Kaikobad, *Mahāśmaśān Kābya Arthāt Pānipater Tritīya Juddha O Mahārāṣṭrīyadiger Patan* (মহাশ্মশান কাব্য অর্থাত পানিপতের তৃতীয় যুদ্ধ ও মহারাষ্ট্রীয়দিগের পতন), published by Abdul Khayer Saifuddin Ahmed, sec. edn. Dhaka: 1917, Introduction, pp. viii–ix.
78. Ibid., p. xiii.
79. See Muniruzzaman Mohammad, *Ādhunik Bānglā Kābye Hindu-Musalmān Samparka, 1857–1920,* p. 340.
80. *Mahāśmaśān,* pp. 702–3.
81. *Ādhunik Bānglā Kābye Hindu-Musalmān Samparka,* p.372.
82. Ibid., p. 367.
83. Ibid., p. 368.
84. *Islām Prachārak,* Chaitra-Baishakh, 1309–10 (Bengali year) (ইসলাম প্রচারক চৈত্র, বৈশাখ, ১৩০৯-১০). Dhaka University Library, p. 143.

    Chaitra is the last month on the Bengali calendar. It corresponds to the period from mid-March to mid-April. Baisakh is the first month of the year and extends from mid-April to mid-May. The Bengali years 1309 and 1310 will be the Gregorian years 1902–3 and 1903–4.

85. Ibid., p. 146.
86. *Islām Prachārak,* Jaishtha-Ashadh, 1310 (ইসলাম প্রচারক, জৈষ্ঠ, আষাঢ়, ১৩১০), p. 214 (Jaistha extends from mid-May to mid-June, Ashadh from mid-June to mid-July.)
87. Ibid., p. 215.
88. Ibid., p. 219.
89. *Islām Prachārak,* Magh, 1311 (Bengali) (ইসলাম প্রচারক, মাঘ, ১৩১১), p.315. (The Bengali year 1311 will be the Gregorian years 1904–5. The month of Magh extends from mid-January to mid-February.)
90. Ibid., p. 397.
91. Ibid., p. 399.
92. Ibid., p. 400.
93. Ibid.
94. *Islām Prachārak,* Paush, 1312 (Bengali) (ইসলাম প্রচারক, পৌষ, ১৩১২), pp.361–62. (The month of Paush extends from mid-December to mid-January. The Bengali year 1312 will correspond to the Gregorian years 1905–6.)
95. Ibid., p. 363.
96. Ibid., p. 368.

5

Conclusion

OUR TALE HAS MEANDERED its course through the long centuries gathering leaves of verse and prose. As we arrive at the destination we had set ourselves, the year 1905, it is time to look back upon the path travelled and take stock. In what manner has our material, involving mainly verse and some prose, enhanced our understanding of what we had set about to investigate? How indeed 'Hindus' and 'Muslims' were present at their own becoming and what variety of interventions and developing discourses set this process of transformation into motion? We are dealing with conscious subjects here and their conscious, diverse articulations. They were led to their religious affiliations by the presence of a new thought system and praxis called Islam which acted as a marker of new identities that came in the making.

We have made use of a variety of texts by many different authors in our discussion, both of the pre-colonial and colonial times. It bears emphasis that their manifold expressions of "Hinduness" and "Muslimness" ought not to be reduced to a "monologic whole." Each of the texts we studied represents the "field of vision" of a specific author and, hence, "each makes sense at the level of a specific consciousness."[1] We must not, thus, ignore the fundamental plurality of the "unmerged consciousnesses" that they articulate. The process of spiritual transformation we have been studying is neither single track nor does it produce the singularity of one end-goal. Rather, the process brings forth a plurality of end-goals. These end-goals, in turn, result in the creation of multiple *subjectivities* which call themselves, or may be labeled, 'Hindus' and 'Muslims.' In this sense, we suggest, no two Muslims or Hindus are the same, just as two leaves, even if of the same tree, are never exactly alike. However, what is common through this process on either side of the divide is that each of our authors is trying to arrive at what in his *subjective* view is a singular goal, a conscious identification of oneself as 'Hindu' or 'Muslim.' He attempts this at one level by articulating what *he* thinks amounts to being 'Hindu' or 'Muslim,' at another by engaging with the "other" in the vicinity by casting him in the stories he tells. The result is, of course, multiple articulations and negotiations with the "other."

For the medieval poets who aspired at "Muslimness" it involved expressing oneself in a properly "Islamic" language, preferably Arabic, if not, then Persian. Nevertheless, because of their geographical location, these languages were not viable options for them, either because of their own lack of proficiency in them or because they were incomprehensible to the audience they were addressing. Thus, the very act of composing poetry necessitated coming to terms with an "otherness" of language and culture for these versifiers. They had no option but to write in Bengali, in their eyes the language of *Hinduāni.* As a result, it appears to us, they are further spurred into striving towards their preferred subjectivities and they identify themselves as "Muslims" with even greater vigour. The strain of this effort is borne out in the variety of ways they justify writing in Bengali. Shah Mohammad Saghir declared that the truth of the word does not depend on the language, Syed Sultan, on the other hand, blamed it on destiny. Ill fate, as he said, has bred Bengalis in Bengal. He had no option but to address them in the only language they understood. The very choice of language, thus, became an act of casting an "other" for these poets, something that, in their minds, diverted them from the subjectivities of their choice. Hence, there were others far more apologetic than Saghir and Sultan. In the seventeenth century Sheikh Mutalib timidly hoped that the believers (*momin*) will pray for him and deliver him of the sin he has incurred by rendering the *Musalmāni śāstra* in Bengali. Once past the hurdle of justifying the choice of language, these poets explicitly asserted their subjectivities. They found various ways of doing it, in the spatial location of their stories, for example. So often, they unfolded in the deserts of Arabia or Persia. Syed Sultan, so very upset that his compatriots, despite being nominally Muslim, take such delight in the tales of Rama and Krishna, moved his story to Arabia after beginning it under the Indian skies. Along the way he had the Vedas discarded by *Allāh*, the Hindu deities who had received them too were derided for their inefficiency for they could not keep their human wards from sin. Sultan, thus, readied the world for Islam and the arrival of the Prophet. When the Prophet finally does arrive he has to fight a round with *Hinduāni* before he can establish the true creed. This is a typical case of a medieval poet arriving at his preferred subjectivity in his own unique manner. Sultan does impart to his audience what *he* thinks is Islam, but it is a creed which, in our eyes, is heavily tinged with the local cultural reality. It incorporates the local deities and cosmogony. Even if they are invalidated in the end, they still remain integral to Sultan's idea of history and unfolding time. The "other" is cast in a role in which he finally stands defeated, one way or another. However, the inevitable defeat notwithstanding, coming to terms with the "other" was essential to Sultan to anchor his own self. It is the same that we see Sheikh S'adi doing in the eighteenth century in the *Gadā-Mālikā Sambād* (গদা-মালিকা সম্বাদ). He too arrived at and imparted his preferred subjectivity, but it incorporated his version of the local theogony. Both Sultan and S'adi are distinct notes in a unique polyphony internal to a distinct cultural cosmos, the great many articulations of a local Islam. Thus, "conversion" to or "adoption" of Islam in the context of Bengal becomes the dialogue between a subjective ideal multifariously sought and interpreted by our poets and its interaction with the local cultural reality and "otherness." The very internal logic of this process enjoined that it will result in a multiplicity of ends and they formed a set of complex, parallel realities as devises for our protagonists to anchor their selves till colonialism arrived on the scene in the eighteenth century.

The dilemmas of the non-Muslim poet who chose to identify himself as 'Hindu' were different. Unlike his 'Muslim' contemporaries, he did not need to justify the language in which he was versifying, nor did he need to incorporate into his view of history a starkly different cosmogony. The non-Muslim poet, as we feel after studying his efforts, found himself dealing with a chafing encroachment upon his emotional landscape. This was a very starkly different "other" whose deity refused incorporation into his prolific pantheon. This emotional and spiritual encroachment, it appears to us, he saw arriving in alliance with the temporal authority, a state which often projected the hard power of a different faith. Hence, this poet inveighed against the *qāzī*, "the most visible representatives of royal authority vis-à-vis non-Muslims"[2] who so often is seen vowing to put down *Hinduāni*, his way of life. The non-Muslim is relatively more secure in his subjectivity compared to his compatriots striving towards "Muslimness." The non-Muslim's subjectivity, after all, is not a confession derived from a Book and a Prophet, but a world view and a way of existence. Hence, unlike in case of the "Muslim" poet, he does not have to impart this world view to his audience. He frets, instead, to keep it from being corrupted. His concern is the danger posed to his cultural world by the temporal authority. Probably that is why the *qāzī* makes so frequent an appearance in his tales as he was the immediate, local agency of this threat. This is where the defensive stance of the non-Muslim poet's subjectivity fundamentally differs from that of the 'Muslim's.' The 'Muslim' had to deal with the abstract, for example, assigning a location to Indic deities in his view of Islamic history. The non-Muslim dealt with the real and the immediate perceived as a cultural threat. It is because of this distinction, we suggest, that we see greater depiction and representation of violence by deities and saints in the poems by the non-Muslims that we studied. The *qāzīs* who desecrated altars and forbid the *kīrtan,* for example, meet a dreadful end in each one of them. Whenever he needed to, the non-Muslim poet also summoned the help of his deities, Manasa, Sitala or Annapurna to conquer and convert the "other." But, as he went about this task, a contrarian note sometimes suffused his verses. We recall the Muslim who tried to keep the *qāzī* from desecrating the altar of Manasa with the plea that all are created by the same God as well as the passionate appeals of Bhabananda to Jahangir to realise the oneness of God. Even Chaitanya, who harangued *qāzīs* and Muslim troopers, appears eventually to be intending at truce, however violent the path to it. The non-Muslim too thus arrived at a plurality of 'Hinduness.'

As we move into the second half of the eighteenth century, the non-Muslim poets appear to have continued in the same vein as earlier. We recall the *Manasā Mangal* (মনসা মঙ্গল) by Vishnu Pala in which Manasa chastens and earns the submission of Hasan and Husain. However, we observe a striking difference in the verses wrought by the Muslim poets. In the earlier centuries, as we argued above, they had dealt with the abstract, the contest of ideas and sentiments in the realm of the spirit. The "other" they had dealt with was an alien language and history and they employed not violence but linguistic tropes to resolve the tensions that emerged in their tales. Now we see them pitching their poems on a different register. In the Satyapir and Manikpir stories we read in the third chapter, the miracle working *pīrs* make unabashed used of force to earn the submission of the unbeliever. In fact, they even use deceit to work their way out of difficult situations. More strikingly, these characters appear to be motivated by an altogether new concern, the *public projection* of the preferred subjectivity of their authors. We saw how Satyapir beat Hanuman and earned his homage and then demanded that he tell Rama to direct the denizens of Ayodhya to worship him. Satyapir also coerced submission out of the arrogant householder Manik, the *kāfir* who could not stand the sight of a *faqīr*, with a combination of deceit and miracle. The king or the private householder, no one is spared. Off course, to ensure that he is paid homage in public, Satyapir had to conquer individuals in the realm of the private too. We also witnessed Manikpir humbling the pride of Ganga, exact her cooperation in his plan of raising a mosque at Triveni and then besting the Emperor in Delhi. Along the way, they do display themselves as Hindu deities whenever needed, but they also emphasise that the deity is not them, *they* are the deity. Paying homage to Manikpir, thus, was the same as offering worship to Rama or Krishna. The "other's" cosmos is, as a result, completely subverted from within.

While Satyapir and Manikpir were setting out on their adventures, Europeans were disembarking on the shores of Bengal. We took note of how their presence spurred the development of the Bengali language. The Europeans produced the first printed texts and a Bengali type. Later, the college of Fort William commissioned the production of the first prose works in Bengali. Unbeknownst to them, the Europeans also seem to have introduced the Bengalis to something else. This was a consciousness of linear, temporal passage of time as "history." The past now seems to have been alleviated from vague remembrance and tradition, for the emergent Bengali-Hindu intelligentsia it appears to have become a set of sovereign facts with implications for the present. That is why, perhaps, by the middle of the nineteenth century we have a venture like the *Bibidhārtha-Sangraha*

(বিবিধার্থ-সঙ্গহ). The *Bibidhārtha*, as we saw, attempted a positivist reconstruction of the past as a set of events and facts, but this reconstruction also had an ideological charge, it was to remind Hindus of what they had lost. The struggles that had transpired till now in the fantasy world of the *kāvyas* were now transferred to the passage of history. Now no deities battled unjust *qāzīs,* but heroic Hindus and Sikhs fought marauding Muslim invaders. The past had begun to become an ideological formulation.

It is this idea of the past as an ideological formulation that is inherited by the Bengali-Hindu litterateurs in the second half of the nineteenth century. Because of the context in which this occurs it carried a greater emotional charge than in the previous decades. This past was now integral to the varied imaginings of Indian nationhood that were being proffered. Thus, the authors we made acquaintance of in the fourth chapter appear to be engaged in resolving a double problematic, arriving at their *own kind* of Hinduism while also preparing a template for Indian nationhood. Often, the two quests appear to have merged in their minds. The geographical enormity and human diversity of India meant that an Indian nationhood could be located not in language or ethnicity but only in a purportedly collectively lived imagined past. Many of our protagonists concluded that this collectively lived past is 'Hinduism' and its resistance of the Muslim invader. Thus, fragments of local histories, be it the doomed bravery of Banda Bahadur or the reckless courage of Rana Pratap, came to be collated into a 'national' history. Also, absolutely central to preparing this template was finding a location for the Muslim within the new imaginaire, or deciding if at all to include him and grant him a location. This problematic drew rich and complex responses from our protagonists. Except Hemchandra, in whose story the evil of the Muslim is never alleviated, no author quite completely banished the Muslim from the imagined nation. As we saw, what made the Chittor created by Rangalal all the more glorious was that it was altogether undefiled by the touch of the Muslim. Later, he even went as far as to call the Hindu and the Muslim as incompatible as butter and fire. However, even this Rangalal had to have a line of Pathans sired by a Hindu character. For Rangalal, the options were twofold when coming to terms with the Muslim—either complete banishment from the nation and the past he was imagining for it, or a grudgingly granted location in this imagining. This accession appears to have been contingent upon complete subordination. After all, Bapparao begot his Pathan sons from the princesses of lands he had conquered and subdued. Nabinchandra too made Muslims the shrubs at the foot of the great banyan tree that is the Indian nation. Bhudev, on the other hand, made them the adopted sons of mother India, while also affirming that the land is indeed more truly of the Hindus. Bankim, thus, when he chose to be a novelist, launched his boat upon these very currents of thought. Naturally, he drifted along with the rest adding his voice to the polyphony they made. We noticed how perilous it is to assign to *Ānandamath* (আনন্দমঠ) an internal homogeneity it does not possess. Bankim, as it seemed to us, was being quite wry and ironic while describing the doings of the Santans. It also does not appear like he is on their side all the time. The hero of *Sītārām* (সীতারাম), of course, chose to call his principality Mohammadpur and he lost it not because of the Muslims but his own depravities. Tagore too joined in and, as the decades rolled, developed his ideas. He began by blaming the British for the rift between the Hindus and Muslims but, in the end, concluded that it is a history of mutual exclusion that is to be blamed. Even the pugnacious Girishchandra closed his play *Satnām* (সৎনাম) with a dialogue between a Hindu and a Muslim character through which he formulated his own subjectivity—his understanding of what Hinduism had come to be and what it ought to be. A great variety of political destinies could be derived from these formulations. One was of course, as Bankim and Pramathnath suggested, that Hindus put faith in the English and realise the destiny that their presence bequeathed upon them.

The Muslim wordsmiths joined in a little late but were no less prolific when they did. In the second half of the nineteenth century they finally completely exorcised the trepidation they often felt while expressing themselves in Bengali. A most nettlesome cultural quandary finally began to be resolved. Interestingly, as we pointed out, the process commenced as the Muslim masses of Bengal gained greater exposure to the fundamentals of scriptural Islam. Continued adherence and exposure to the scriptures demanded that they be translated in the native language of the faithful. At the beginning of the fourth chapter we saw societies being formed with this object. The Bengali-Muslim's attitude towards the Bengali language, thus, began by being purely utilitarian, thence he moved on to aesthetic and ideological concerns. However, what is unique about the Bengali-Muslim author is that in his case the aesthetic and ideological are never apart. A Bengali-Hindu author never had to bother about the ideological implication of a choice of word, but a Bengali-Muslim writer's choice of lexicon always carried an ideological and political charge. As we saw, one of the Muslim admirers of Dad Ali's poetry suspected if his verses will be comprehensible to Muslims. Dad Ali's language, after all, lavishly drew upon Sanskrit. That is why we see *Bangadarśan* (বঙ্গদর্শন) expending eloquence in praising Mosarraf Hosain because his language was so very Sanskritic. It also seems that for Hosain himself maintaining the purity of Bengali meant not tempering with its predominantly Sanskritic lexicon. That is probably why he took the trouble to apologise to his readers for using a few Arabic and Persian words in the introduction to *Biṣād Sindhu* (বিষাদ-সিন্ধু). In the aesthetics of their language Ali and Hosain are an inverse of Mālé Mohammad and Mohammad Danesh. We recall how at the turn of the nineteenth century "popular Bengali" (*chalita Bāngālā*) for Mālé Mohammad had meant seeding Bengali with Arabic and Persian words. Aesthetically, thus, the late nineteenth century Bengali-Muslim writer was an involution, he was more akin to the medieval Muslim poet whose language was indistinguishable from his non-Muslim counterparts.

However, the late nineteenth century Bengali-Muslim writer's affinity with the medieval Muslim poet is purely limited to the preferred aesthetics of language. In other matters he was a very different individual. Unlike his medieval brother, he did not have to wage struggles in the realm of the spirit. These struggles were now quelled, as the nineteenth century Bengali-Muslim was now assuredly Muslim and expressed himself confidently in Bengali without needing to apologise to his co-religionists. The struggle that faced the Bengali-Muslim writer, instead, was the ferment of political nationhood felt all around. This ferment pullulated with ideas and responses. Thus, when the Bengali-Muslim chose to write in a language as Sanskritised as his Hindu counterpart, he immediately drew comments. His choice carried significant implications for this ferment. *Bangadarśan*, when reviewing *Gorāi Brij Athabā Gauri Setu* (গোরাই ব্রিজ অথবা গৌরি সেতু), advised all well educated Muslims to follow Hosain's example. As the review said, only a unity of language could foster national unity. As they went about their creative quests, the Muslim writers too, like their Hindu coevals, unleashed a rich and complex mêlée of voices and ideas. Hosain, we saw, wrote a passionate denunciation of cow-slaughter. He also cast a noble polytheist in his *Biṣād-Sindhu.* In *Sat-Prasanga* (সৎ-প্রসঙ্গ) he tried to deny altogether that there is occasion for dispute between Hindus and Muslims. Both, after all, suffered the same political subjugation. Besides, the lives of Muslims were too entwined with that of Hindus'. However, it is apparent to us that, just like the Hindu litterateurs, the Muslim writer too could simultaneously inhabit multiple levels of consciousness. Hosain's poem *Bartamān Musalmān Samājer Ekkhāni Chitra* (বর্তমান মুসলমান সমাজের একখানি চিত্র) and novel *Gāzī Miān Bastāni* (গাজী মিঞার বস্তানি) spoke scathingly of Hindu chicanery and duplicity. Hosain's contemporary, Usufji meditated on the political intentions of the Hindus and found them less than earnest. Sheikh Usman Ali, on the other hand, advised his co-religionists to join the Congress. However, his characters accepted the cultural faultline without demurring. In *Debalā* (দেবলা), Debala Rani reminded her suitor Khizr that trying to circumvent societal conventions can only bring ignominy. Culturally Kaikobad too was an ardent separatist, lamenting the lost glories of Muslim history. Interestingly he too was engaged in a project similar to the Bengali-Hindu intellectuals—collating far off local histories to form a "national" history for Indian Muslims. That is why he wrote *Mahāśmaśān* (মহাশ্মশান) to remind Muslims of Bengal and rest of India how indomitably brave they once were. However, he seems not to have noticed that, by delighting in the Maratha defeat in the third battle of Panipat, *Mahāśmaśān* actually ended up celebrating the bravery of the Afghan Muslim. Emotionally, like most other literary works we surveyed, *Mahāśmaśān* too lacked internal homogeneity. Kaikobad, as we saw, had the Peshwa Sadashiv Rao dispatch a passionate letter to the Emperor in Delhi pointing out the senselessness of the impending battle and need for Hindus and Muslims of India to unite. Of course, Kaikobad imagined Islam as a mother-goddess too. The likes of Abdul Hamid Khan Usufjai and Mojammel Haq represented another shade in the ideological and political spectrum. They chided Muslims for lagging behind the Hindus and passionately desired temporal regeneration for their community. They, however, do not appear to have linked this project to cultural and political separatism. Initially the concerns of the journal *Islām Prachārak* (ইসলাম প্রচারক) were similar. The gentlemen contributing to its pages debated the best possible means of restoring the temporal fortunes of their co-religionists. Even when they found the solution in a greater, more passionate adherence to Islam they still reached out to Hindus. Politically they were for unity. To earn the affection of Hindus, one writer went to the extent of demonstrating that it is the Muslims who far more resemble the Vedic Aryans in their manners and ways than contemporary Hindus. However, the anti-partition agitation seems to have abruptly put these efforts to an end. Ignoring the political serenades sung to them, they chose a separate political destiny. The cultural faultline had sabotaged the foundations of Indian nationhood.

References

1. See Mikhail Bakhtin, "Dostoevsky's Polyphonic Novel and its Treatment in Critical Literature," in *Problems of Dostoevosky's Poetics*, ed. Carlyl Emerson, Manchester University Press, 1984, p. 21.
2. *The Rise of Islam and the Bengal Frontier*, p. 101.

Bibliography

Primary Sources

Journals and Newspapers

Bibidhārtha-Sangraha (বিবিধার্থ-সঙ্গহ). Calcutta: Asiatic Society Library.

Islām Prachārak (ইসলাম প্রচারক). Dhaka: Dhaka University Library.

The Moslem Chronicle. New Delhi: Nehru Memorial Museum and Library.

Others

Abdul-Karim, *Corpus of the Arabic and Persian Inscriptions of Bengal.* Asiatic Society of Bangladesh, 1992.

Abdul-Mannan, Dr Qazi, ed., *Mośārraf Rachanā-Sambhār* (মশাররফ রচনা-সম্ভার). Dhaka: Bangla Academy, vol. 2, 1980.

—, ed., *Mośārraf Rachanā-Sambhār* (মশাররফ রচনা-সম্ভার). Dhaka: Bangla Academy, vol. 3,1984.

Ahmed, Humayun, *Kichu Śaiśab* (কিছু শৈশব). Dhaka: Anyaprokash, 2007.

Bandyopadhyay, Brajendranath, and Sajanikanta Das, eds., *Bhāratchandra-Granthābalī* (ভারতচন্দ্র-গ্রন্থাবলী), third edn. Calcutta: Bangiya Sahitya Parishad, 1962.

Bandyopadhyay, Debnath, ed., *Lor Chandrāni O Sati Moina* (লোর চন্দ্রানি ও সতি মইনা), fourth edn. Calcutta: Sahitya Sansad, 2006.

—, ed., *Padmābati, Jāisī O Alāol* (পদ্মাবতী, জায়সী ও আলাওল). Calcutta: West Bengal State Book Board, 1985.

Bandyopadhyay, Hem Chandra, *Hemchandrer Granthābalī*

(হেমচন্দ্রের গ্রন্থাবলী). Calcutta: Basumati Sahitya Mandir.

Basu, Ram Ram, *Rājā Prātāpāditya Charitra* (রাজা প্রতাপাদিত্য চরিত্র). Calcutta: Ranjan Publishing House, 1942.

Basu, Satyendranath, ed., *Śri Chaitanya Bhāgbat, Śrīla Brindābandas. Thākūr Birachita* (শ্রিচৈতণ্যভাগবত, শ্রিল বৃন্দাবন দাস ঠাকুর বিরচিত). Calcutta: Deb Sahitya Kutir, 2001.

Bhattacharya, Dr Ashutosh, ed., *Bāiś Kabīr Manasā-Mangal bā Bāisā* (বাইশ কবির মনসা-মঙ্গল বা বাইসা). Calcutta University, 1962.

Bhattacharya, Dr Debipada, ed., *Girīś Rachanābalī* (গিরিশ রচনাবলী). Calcutta: Sahitya Sansad, vol. IV, 1974.

Bhattcharya, Satyanarayan, ed., *Kabi Kṛṣṇarām Dāser Granthābalī* (কবি কৃষ্ণরাম দাসের গ্রন্থাবলী). University of Calcutta, 1958.

Bishi, Pramathnath, ed., *Bhudev-Rachanāsambhār* (ভুদেব-রচনাসম্ভার). Calcutta: Mitra O Ghosh, 1968.

Bose, Satyendranath, ed., *Śrīla Brindābandās Thākur Birachita Śri Chaitanya Bhāgbat* (শ্রীল বৃন্দাবনদাসঠাকুর বিরচিত শ্রীচৈতন্যভাগবত). Calcutta: Deb Sahitya Kutir, 2001.

Chattopadhyay, Bankim Chandra, *Bankim Rachanābalī* (বঙ্কিম রচনাবলি), eighth edn. Calcutta: Sahitya Sansad, vol. I, 1979.

Chattopadhyay, Bhaktimadhab, ed., *Rāmāi Panditer Śūnya Pūrān* (রামাই পণ্ডিতের শূন্য পূরান). Calcutta: Firma KLM Limited, 1977.

Dad Ali, *Bhāngāprān* (ভাঙ্গাপ্রান), sixth edn. Dhaka: Published by Mohammad Usuf Ali, 1927.

Dasgupta, Jayanta Kumar, ed., *Kabi Bijaygupter Padmapurān* (কবি বিজয়গুপ্তের পদ্মাপুরান). Calcutta University, 1962.

Dasgupta, Shantikumar, and Haribandhu Mukhti, eds., *Rangalāl Rachanābali* (রঙ্গলাল রচনাবলী). Calcutta: Duttachaudhari and Sons, 1974.

Dey, Dr Bishnu, and Kamalendu Dhar, eds., *Mīr Mośārraf Hosain Rachanāsangraha* (মীর মশাররফ হোসেন রচনাসংগ্রহ). Calcutta: Kamal Sahitya Bhavan, 1978.

Dutt, Romesh Chandra, *Rājput Jīban-Sandhyā* (রাজপুত জিবন-

সন্ধ্যা), sixth edn. Calcutta: Elm Press, 1878.

Enamul Haq, Dr Mohammad, ed., *Śāh Mohammad Saghir Birachita Usuf-Jolekhā* (শাহ মুহম্মদ সগীর বিরচিত ইউসুফ-জোলেখা), sec. edn. Dhaka: Moula Brothers, 1998.

Ghosh, Baridbaran, ed., *Samakālīn Sāhitye Bangabhanga* (সমকালিন সাহিত্যে বঙ্গভঙ্গ). Calcutta: Punashcha, 2005.

Hosain, Mir Mosarraf, *Bīṣād Śīndhu* (বিষাদ-সিন্ধু). New Delhi: IMH Press Pvt. Limited, 1999.

Kaikobad, *Aśru-Mālā* (অশ্রু-মালা), sec. edn., published by Abdul Khayer Saifuddin Ahmed, Dhaka, 1914.

—, *Mahāśmaśān Kābya Arthāt Pānipater Tritīya Juddha O Mahārāṣṭrīyadiger Patan* (মহাশ্মশান কাব্য অর্থাত পানিপতের তৃতীয় যুদ্ধ ও মহারাষ্ট্রীয়দিগের পতন), sec. edn. Dhaka: published by Abdul Khayer Saifuddin Ahmed, 1917.

Majumdar, Bimanbehari, ed., *Gaurī-Mangal* (গৌরী-মঙ্গল), Asiatic Society, 1971.

Mandal, Panchanan, comp., *Punthi-Parichai* (পুঁথি-পরিচয়), Visvabharati, 1958.

—, comp., *Punthi-Parichai* (পুঁথি-পরিচয়), Visvabharati, 1980.

Maulik, Kshitishchandra, ed., *Prāchīn Purbabanga Gītikā* (প্রাচীন পুর্ববঙ্গ গীতীকা). Calcutta: Firma K.L. Mukhopadhyay, vol. 1, 1970.

—, ed., *Prāchīn Purbabanga Gītikā* (প্রাচীন পুর্ববঙ্গ গীতীকা). Calcutta: Firma K.L. Mukhopadhyay, vol. 2,1971.

—, ed., *Prāchīn Purbabanga Gītikā* (প্রাচীন পুর্ববঙ্গ গীতীকা). Calcutta: Firma K.L. Mukhopadhyay, vol. 3, 1971.

Mukhopadhyay, Dilip, ed., *Śrī Śrī Chaitanya Charitāmrita, Śrīla Kṛṣṇadās Kabīrāj Goswami Birachita* (শ্রী শ্রী চৈতন্য চরিতামৃত, শ্রীল কৃষ্ণদাস কবিরাজ গোস্বামী বিরচিত). Calcutta: Benimadhab Seal's Library, 2006.

Nag, Prasanna Kumar, *Rājputāṅganā Kābya* (রাজপুতাঙ্গনা কাব্য). Calcutta: Kuntalin Press, 1882.

Pal, Dhirendranath, "Dīljān Bāndi" (দীলজান বাঁদি), in *Aitihāsik Galpa* (ঐতিহাসিক গল্প). Calcutta, 1884.

Sarkar, Pramathnath, *Rānā Pratāp* (রানা প্রতাপ). Calcutta: S.K. Lahiri & Co. Publishers and Booksellers, 1905.

Sen, Kaliprasanna, ed., *Śrī Rājmālā, Tripur Rājanyabarger Itibritta, Tritīa Lahar, Pandit Prabar Swargia Gaṅgādhar Siddhāntabāgīś Birachita* (শ্রীরাজমালা, ত্রিপুর-রাজন্যবর্গের ইতিবৃত্ত, তৃতীয় লহর, পণ্ডিত প্রবর স্বর্গিয় গঙ্গাধর সিদ্ধান্তবাগীশ বিরচিত), (১৩৪১ ত্রিপুরাব্দ). Agartala State Press, 1931.

Sen, Nabinchandra, *Nabīnchandrer Granthābalī* (নবীনচন্দ্রের গ্রন্থাবলী). Calcutta, 1904.

Sen, Sajanikanta, ed., *Hemchandra Granthābalī* (হেমচন্দ্র গ্রন্থাবলী). Calcutta: Bangiya Sahitya Parishad, vol. I, 1953.

Sen, Dr Sukumar, ed., *Chandimangal* (চণ্ডিমঙ্গল). New Delhi: Sahitya Akademi, 1986.

—, ed., *Viṣnu Pāla's Manasā Mangal* (বিষ্ণু পালের মনসামঙ্গল). Calcutta: Asiatic Society, 1968, work no. 289, issue no. 1587.

Sharif, Ahmad, ed., *Muhammad Khān Birachita Satya-Kali-Bibād-Sambād bā Jug-Sambād* (মুহম্মদ খান বিরচিত সত্য-কলি-বিবাদ-সংবাদ বা যুগ-সংবাদ). Dhaka: Department of Bengali, University of Dhaka, 1959.

—, ed., *Madhyajugen Kābya-Sangraha* (মধ্যযুগের কাব্য-সংগ্রহ). Dhaka: Bangla Academy, 1962.

—, ed., *Rasul Bijay* (রসুল বিজয়), published by the University of Dhaka, 1964.

—, ed., *Saiyad Sultān Birachita Nabibangśa,* Pratham Khanda (সৈয়দ সুলতান বিরচিত নবিবংশ [প্রথম খণ্ড]). Dhaka: Bangla Academy, 1978.

—, ed., *Saiyad Sultān Birachita Nabibangśa,* Dwitīya Khanda (সৈয়দ সুলতান বিরচিত নবিবংশ [দ্বিতীয় খণ্ড]). Dhaka: Bangla Academy, 1978.

—, ed., *Soāl Sāhitya* (সওয়াল সাহিত্য). Dhaka: Bangla Academy, 1976.

Tagore, Rabindranath, *Rabindra Rachanābalī* (রবিন্দ্র রচনাবলী). Calcutta: Vishvabharati, 1975, vol. III.

—, *Rabindra Rachanābalī* (রবিন্দ্র রচনাবলী). Calcutta: Vishva-bharati, 1976, vol. VII.

—, *Rabindra Rachanābalī* (রবিন্দ্র রচনাবলী). Calcutta: Vishva-bharati, 1986, vol. X.

—, *Rabindra Rachanābalī* (রবিন্দ্র রচনাবলী). Calcutta: Vishva-bharati, 1978, vol. XXI.

Usufji, Nausher Ali Khan, *Bangiya Musalmān* (বঙ্গিয় মুসলমান, নওসের আলি খাঁ ইউসফজী). Calcutta: Hindu Press, 1890.

SECONDARY SOURCES

Books

Abdul-Mannan, Dr Qazi, *Ādhunik Bānglā Sāhitye Muslim Sādhanā* (আধুনিক বাংলা সাহিত্যে মুসলিম সাধনা). Dhaka: Student Ways, 1969.

Ahmed, Rafiuddin, *The Bengal Muslims, 1871–1906. A Quest for Identity*, sec. edn. New Delhi: OUP, 1988.

Anisujjaman, *Muslim-Mānas O Bāngla Sāhitya (1757–1918)* [মুসলিম-মানস ও বাংলা সাহিত্য (১৭৫৭-১৯১৮)]. Calcutta, 1971.

—, *Swarūper Sandhāne* (স্বরূপের সন্ধানে). Dhaka: Jatiya Sahitya Prakashani, 1976.

Bakhtin, Mikhail, "Dostoevsky's Polyphonic Novel and its Treatment in Critical Literature," in *Problems of Dostoevsky's Poetics*, ed. Carlyl Emerson, Manchester University Press, 1984.

Basu, Kanchan, *Dusprāpya Sāhitya Sangraha*, Dwitīya Khanda (দুস্প্রাপ্য সাহিত্য সংগ্রহ [দ্বিতীয় খণ্ড]), sec. edn. Calcutta: Reflect Publications, 1992.

Bhattacharya, Dr Ashutosh, *Bānglā Mangalkābyer Itihās* (বাংলা মঙ্গলকাব্যের ইতিহাস), fourth edn. Calcutta: A. Mukherjee & Company Pvt. Limited, 1964.

Chakrabarty, Dipesh, *Provincializing Europe. Postcolonial Thought and Historical Difference.* Princeton University Press, 2000.

Chakravarty, Kunal, *Religious Processes. The Purānas and the Making of a Regional Tradition.* New Delhi: OUP, 2001

Chatterji, Suniti Kumar, *The Origin and Development of the Bengali Language*, third edn. New Delhi: Rupa & Co., 2002.

Clark, T.W., "Encounter and Growth in Bengali Literature. A Survey of Medieval Bengali Literature," in Edward C. Dimock, Jr., ed., *Bengal. Literature and History*, Asian Studies Center. Michigan State University, 1967.

—, ed., "Encounter and Growth in Bengali Literature. A Survey of Modern Bengali Literature," in Edward C. Dimock, Jr., ed., *Bengal. Literature and History*, Asian Studies Center, Michigan State University, 1967.

Das, Sisir Kumar, *The Artist in Chains. The Life of Bankim Chandra Chatterjee.* New Delhi: New Statesman Publishing Company, 1984.

De, Dhurjati Prasad, *Bengal Muslims in Search of Social Identity, 1905–47.* Dhaka: The University Press Limited, 1998.

De, Sushil Kumar, *Bengali Literature in the Nineteenth Century (1757–1857).* Calcutta: Firma K.L. Mukhopadhyay, 1962.

Eaton, Richard M., *The Rise of Islam and the Bengal Frontier, 1204–1760.* University of California Press, 1993.

Ghosh, J.C., *Bengali Literature.* London: OUP, 1948.

Heidegger, Martin, *Being and Time.* New York: Harper Perennial Modern Thought, 2008.

Husain, Dilwar, *Bāngla Upanyāse Mughal Itihāser Byabahār, 1857–1916* (বাংলা উপন্যাসে মুঘল ইতিহাসের ব্যেবহার, ১৮৫৭-১৯১৬), Dhaka: Bangla Academy, 1984.

Joshi, Shashi, and Bhagwan Josh, *Struggle for Hegemony in India, Culture Community and Power, 1920–47,* 3 vols., vol. III: *1941–47.* New Delhi: Sage Publications, 1994. (vol. I: *1920–34;* vol. II: *1934–41.*)

Kaviraj, Sudipto, "The Two Histories of Literary Cultures in Bengal," in Sheldon I. Pollock, ed., *Literary Cultures in History. Reconstructions from South Asia.* New Delhi: OUP, 2003.

—, *The Unhappy Consciousness. Bankimchandra Chattopadhyay and the Formation of Nationalist Discourse in India*, third edn. New Delhi: OUP, 1998.

Laing, R.D., *The Divided Self*, Penguin Modern Classics, 2010.

Morgan, Charles, and James R. Averill, "True Feelings, the Self, and Authenticity," in Monica Greco and Paul Steiner, eds., *Emotions. A Social Science Reader*. Routledge: New York, 2008.

Munirujjaman, Mohammad, *Ādhunik Bānglā Kābye Hindu–Muslimān Samparka, 1857–1920* (আধুনিক বাংলা কাব্যে হিন্দু-মুসলমান সম্পর্ক, ১৮৫৭-১৯২০). Dhaka: Bangla Academy, 1970.

Murshid, Tazeen M., *The Sacred and the Secular. Bengal Muslim Discourses, 1871–1977*. Calcutta: OUP, 1995.

Musa, Mansur, ed., *Mohammad Enāmul Haq Rachanābalī* (মুহম্মদ এনামুল হক রচনাবলী), first edn. Dhaka: Bangla Academy, 1991, vol. I.

Ray, Niharranjan, *History of the Bengali People from the Earliest Times to the Fall of the Sena Dynasty*, trans. John W. Hood. New Delhi: Orient Blackswan, 2013.

Raychaudhari, Tapan, *Europe Reconsidered. Perceptions of the West in Nineteenth Century Bengal*, sec. edn. New Delhi: OUP, 1989.

Rolland, Romain et al., *International Library of Music for Home and Studio*. New York: The University Society, Inc., Educational Publishers, vol. II, 1961.

Roy, Asim, *The Islamic Syncretistic Tradition in Bengal*, Princeton University Press, 1983.

Sarkar, Sir Jadunath, ed., *The History of Bengal. Muslim Period, 1200–1757*, repr. Delhi: B.R. Publishing Corporation, 2003.

Sen, Amiya P., *Bankim Chandra Chattopadhyay. An Intellectual Biography*. New Delhi: OUP, 2008.

—, *Hindu Revivalism in Bengal, 1872–1905*. New Delhi: OUP, 1993.

Sen, Dineshchandra, *Bangabhāṣā O Sāhitya. Ingrāj Prabhāber Pūrba Parjanta* (বঙ্গভাষা ও সাহিত্য, ইংরাজ প্রভাবের পুর্ব্ব পর্যন্ত), eighth edn. Calcutta: Dasgupta and Company Limited, 1949.

Sen, Dr Sukumar, *History of Bengali Literature.* New Delhi: Sahitya Akademi, 1960.

Sen, Kshiti Mohan, *Hinduism*, Penguin Books, 2005.

Sharif, Ahmed, *Madhyajugen Sāhitye Samāj O Sanskritir Rūp* (মধ্য যুগের সাহিত্যে সমাজ ও সংস্কৃতির রূপ). Dhaka: Muktadhara, 1977.

Stewart, Tony K., "Alternate Structure of Authority. Satya Pīr on the Frontiers of Bengal," in David Gilmartin and Bruce B. Lawrence, eds., *Beyond Turk and Hindu. Rethinking Religious Identities in Islamicate South Asia.* University Press of Florida, 2000.

—, "In Search of Equivalence: Conceiving the Hindu–Muslim Encounter through Translation Theory," in Richard M. Eaton, ed., *India's Islamic Traditions, 711–1750.* New Delhi: OUP, 2003.

Talbot, Cynthia, "Inscribing the Other, Inscribing the Self: Hindu–Muslim Identities in Pre-Colonial India," in Richard M. Eaton, ed., *India's Islamic Traditions, 711–1750.* New Delhi: OUP, 2003.

Thapar, Romila, "Imagined Religious Communities? Ancient History and the Modern Search for a Hindu Identity," in *Cultural Pasts. Essays in Early Indian History.* New Delhi: OUP, 2000.

Thompson, E.P., *The Making of the English Working Class, Vintage.* New York, 1966.

Zbavitel, Dusan, *Bengali Literature,* Otto Harrassowitz, 1976.

Articles

Clark, T.W., "Evolution of Hinduism in Medieval Bengali Literature: Śiva, Caṇḍi, Manasā," *Bulletin of the School of Oriental and African Studies, University of London,* vol. 17, no. 3, 1955, pp. 503–18.

Connel, Joseph T., "The Word 'Hindu' in Gaudiya Vaishnava Texts," *Journal of the American Oriental Society*, vol. 93, no. 3 (July–Sept 1973), pp. 340–44.

Freitag, Sandria B., "Sacred Symbols as Mobilising Ideology: The North Indian Search for a 'Hindu' Community," *Comparative Studies in Society and History* 22(4), pp. 597–625.

Sarkar, Tanika, "Imagining a Hindu Nation: Hindu and Muslim in Bankimchandra's Later Writings," *Economic and Political Weekly*, vol. 29, no. 39 (Sept 24, 1994), pp. 2553–61.

Index